THE S. MARK TAPER FOUNDATION

IMPRINT IN JEWISH STUDIES

BY THIS ENDOWMENT

THE S. MARK TAPER FOUNDATION SUPPORTS

THE APPRECIATION AND UNDERSTANDING

OF THE RICHNESS AND DIVERSITY OF

JEWISH LIFE AND CULTURE

The publisher gratefully acknowledges the generous support of the Jewish Studies Endowment Fund of the University of California Press Foundation, which was established by a major gift from the S. Mark Taper Foundation.

# Purity, Body, and Self in Early Rabbinic Literature

# Purity, Body, and Self in Early Rabbinic Literature

―――

Mira Balberg

UNIVERSITY OF CALIFORNIA PRESS
*Berkeley   Los Angeles   London*

University of California Press, one of the most distinguished university presses in the United States, enriches lives around the world by advancing scholarship in the humanities, social sciences, and natural sciences. Its activities are supported by the UC Press Foundation and by philanthropic contributions from individuals and institutions. For more information, visit www.ucpress.edu.

University of California Press
Berkeley and Los Angeles, California

University of California Press, Ltd.
London, England

© 2014 by The Regents of the University of California

Library of Congress Cataloging-in-Publication Data

Balberg, Mira, 1978–.
 Purity, body, and self in early rabbinic literature / Mira Balberg.
  p. cm.
 Includes bibliographical references and index.
 ISBN 978-0-520-28063-2 (cloth : alk. paper)
 1. Purity, Ritual—Judaism. 2. Rabbinical literature—History and criticism. I. Title.
 BM702.B277  2014
 296.7—dc23

                                                                2013031180

Manufactured in the United States of America

23  22  21  20  19  18  17  16  15  14

10  9  8  7  6  5  4  3  2  1

In keeping with a commitment to support environmentally responsible and sustainable printing practices, UC Press has printed this book on Natures Natural, a fiber that contains 30% post-consumer waste and meets the minimum requirements of ANSI/NISO Z39.48–1992 (R 1997) (*Permanence of Paper*).

CONTENTS

*Acknowledgments*   *vii*

    Introduction   *1*
1. From Sources of Impurity to Circles of Impurity   *17*
2. Subjecting the Body   *48*
3. Objects That Matter   *74*
4. On Corpses and Persons   *96*
5. The Duality of Gentile Bodies   *122*
6. The Pure Self   *148*

    Epilogue: Recomposing Purity and Meaning   *180*

*Notes*   *185*
*Bibliography*   *237*
*Subject Index*   *253*
*Source Index*   *257*

ACKNOWLEDGMENTS

This book owes its existence to the mentorship, guidance, and advice of many teachers, colleagues, and friends. The study presented here is based on my doctoral dissertation, which was written at Stanford University under the tutelage of my *doktormutter*, Charlotte Fonrobert. Charlotte's advising, which was as kind and nurturing as it was rigorous and uncompromising, allowed me to trace the intellectual conversations in which I wish to participate, and helped me develop a scholarly voice that I can call my own. My dissertation committee members, Shahzad Bashir, Maud Gleason, and Steven Weitzman, have all been pillars of support, encouraging when necessary and cautioning when necessary, and offering invaluable insights at key moments.

For many years, the Hebrew University in Jerusalem was my home. It was there that I first got acquainted with the rich and fascinating world of rabbinic literature, made my first steps in the critical inquiry of Mishnah, Midrash, and Talmud, and acquired priceless textual and philological tools. I am indebted to all my teachers at the Hebrew University, and most of all to the two mentors who have been especially instrumental in shaping my interests and skills, and who continued to offer guidance and support even after I crossed the ocean: Robert Brody, who provided a role model not only of scholarly integrity and scrupulousness but also of magnanimity of spirit, and Joshua Levinson, who opened the gates of the cultural study of rabbinic literature for me and continuously broadened my horizons.

I am extremely fortunate to have become part of the Religious Studies department at Northwestern University, one of the loveliest, most vibrant, and warmest intellectual communities I have ever encountered. It is a wonderfully nourishing environment for scholars in the beginning of their careers, in no small measure thanks to the fine leadership of our department chair, Kenneth Seeskin. I am especially grateful to my colleagues, who are at this point also my dear friends, who offered thoughtful feedback and insights on parts of this book in the course of its making: Brannon Ingram, Sarah Jacoby, Michelle Molina, and Barry Wimpfheimer.

Several brilliant scholars significantly contributed to this book, helping me identify points of weakness, hone points of strength, enrich my readings and analyses, and draw connections I would not have been able to draw otherwise. Much of the research in the infrastructure of this book was conducted in dialogue with Vered Noam and Yair Furstenberg, whose vast knowledge of purity in ancient Judaism was an invaluable resource for me. Ishay Rosen-Zvi's scrupulous reading of the manuscript and his remarkably astute comments and criticisms showed me the path for transforming this project from an experiment into a book. Ellen Muehlberger and Catherine Chin both offered new and fresh angles through which to consider my sources and ideas, and helped me contextualize the Mishnah more broadly in the world of Graeco-Roman late antiquity. Katelyn Mesler was a perceptive conversation partner, and particularly aided me in conquering the French parts of the bibliography. Elizabeth Shanks Alexander suggested thoughtful observations and sound advice during the book's revision process. Finally, Yair Lipshitz and Moulie Vidas are exciting, inspiring, and unfailing friends, incisive critics and fervent supporters, who both add color, spark, and joy to my life and to my scholarship.

Eric Schmidt of the University of California Press gave this book the best home I could hope for, and gave it highly attentive, thoughtful, and supportive care throughout the process. I am deeply thankful to him and to all the UC Press team for bringing this book to life.

Tim DeBold has been my partner, companion, and most beloved friend from the time in which this book was merely a random collection of confused thoughts. He was the first reader of every page of this book, and the voice of reason and sensibility at numerous points during its making. I am grateful to him for that, and for his even temper, exquisite humor, razor-sharp mind, and endless kindness, which make every day of my life worth living.

Finally, I wish to thank my parents, Ephrat and Isaac Balberg, who have given me the blood of my life, and whose enduring love sees me through in every path I choose to take. May I be worthy of all they have given me.

# Introduction

"From the day the Temple was destroyed there has been no impurity and no purity," medieval and modern Jewish authors often proclaim,[1] identifying the Roman demolition and burning of the Jerusalem Temple in the year 70 C.E. as a point of no return, after which the complex array of biblical laws pertaining to ritual purity and impurity became almost entirely inapplicable. According to this prevalent view, to write a book on the ways in which the rabbis of Roman Palestine in the second and third centuries C.E. reinterpreted, reshaped, and reconstructed the biblical concepts of purity and impurity is to be immersed in obsoleteness. It is to engage with an arcane body of legal themes that are not only without consequence for our time, but were, so it is often believed, even without consequence for the rabbis' own time.

Those who are inclined to dismiss all concerns with practices of ritual purity and impurity as a thing of the distant past, or perhaps, for some, of the unknown messianic future,[2] might want to stop and consider the following question, posted on the Israeli orthodox website *Kippa* on April 25, 2010:

> I am a *hozer bi-teshuva* (recently became religious and observant), and most of my coworkers are entirely secular, who are in the habit of eating nonkosher food even in our workplace. I try to refrain from touching objects that we all share, yet several questions have come up recently:
>
> 1. If someone who sat in my working environment has been eating nonkosher food, should I take any measures in case they dropped some bits of their food in my vicinity?
> 2. If a person ate nonkosher food and then touched certain objects (folder, fax machine, keyboard), should I refrain from touching these objects?

And if such contact took place, does the impurity of the food pass on to the objects? . . .

3. If I happened to touch such an object, how should I go about purifying myself from this impurity?³

The anonymous inquirer's questions are, to be sure, guided by a number of misconceptions in terms of codified Jewish law. Nonkosher food does not convey impurity of any sort, certainly not to those who happen to touch it by mistake and most certainly not to objects that came into contact with it. But it is exactly these misconceptions and the lack of commensurability between the inquirer's presuppositions and the governing paradigms in Jewish law that reveal the enduring relevance and power of the concepts and rhetoric of ritual purity and impurity. The person who posed this question did not know what, exactly, constitutes a source of impurity and how impurity is contracted, but he had a strong sense that the difference between his religious self and his nonobservant coworkers must be somehow expressed through palpable "impurity." Moreover, he had a strong sense that interaction with them, in one way or another, endangers him, and specifically endangers him through the material environment that he reluctantly shares with those different from him. These notions, which dominate almost every cultural system of purity and impurity (even though they are completely misguided in the context of contemporary Jewish law), speak to the force of ideas of purity and impurity in one's self-making as a pious subject, and to the way these concepts give concrete form to the desire to conduct oneself and one's body by separation from others and by constant reflection on oneself and one's surroundings.

Purity and impurity, then, as potent and dominant themes in Judaism's religious vocabulary, did not become obsolete even when some or all of the practices pertaining to them were no longer performed. Rather, they live on as powerful conceptual and hermeneutic tools through which ideas about self and other can be manifested, through which one's body and environment can be scrutinized and defined, and through which one constitutes and forms oneself as a subject. This book explores the early rabbis' comprehensive attempt to recompose and interpret the biblical code of purity and impurity, and examines how this enterprise of recomposition constructed a new and powerful discourse that is deeply engaged with and informed by concerns with body, self, lived environment, and religious subjectivity.

In this book I trace and analyze the ways in which the early rabbis, in their remaking of the biblical laws of purity and impurity, negotiate and develop a unique notion of a bodily self. I argue that the rabbis construct the drama of contracting, conveying, and managing impurity as a manifestation of the relations between oneself and one's human and nonhuman surroundings, and that they create a new array of physical and mental purity-related practices that both assume and generate a particular kind of subject. This book, then, seeks to introduce rabbinic legal discourse into the landscape of ancient and late ancient modes of reflection on, engagement with, and shaping of the self, and to explore the rabbis' textual reconstruction of biblical purity and impurity as a site in which inherited scriptural traditions are remolded in the cultural and intellectual climate of the Graeco-Roman Mediterranean of the high empire.

At the center of this study stands the Mishnah, the earliest comprehensive rabbinic legal codex known to us. More specifically, this study focuses mainly on one of the six divisions, or "orders," that comprise the Mishnah, the division dedicated to the topic of purity and impurity, which is known as *Seder Tohorot* (the Order of Purities). The final compilation of the Mishnah can be dated with relative confidence to the first quarter of the third century C.E., and is commonly associated with the name of Rabbi Yehuda the Patriarch (who died around 220 C.E.) and his circle. However, the Mishnah consists of hundreds of legal and interpretive traditions, generated and transmitted by different named and unnamed rabbis over a time period that spans between a few dozen years and a few hundred years. While the most dominant sages of the Mishnah, to whom the greatest amount of material in this work is attributed, seem to have been active primarily in the course of the second century C.E., a substantial amount of foundational legal teachings in the Mishnah apparently dates back to the first century C.E., and the Mishnah even contains traditions, albeit few and far between, from sages who presumably lived as early as the mid-second century B.C.E. The diverse and multilayered nature of the Mishnah and the fact that it constitutes a repository of traditions created over a rather long period of time compel us to consider this rich and complex work both in terms of its organic continuity with earlier Jewish legal and interpretive works, and in terms of its active transformation and change of concepts, practices, and legal modes of thought inherited from the rabbis' predecessors.

The foundation of the Mishnah, and the point of departure of its makers, is the patrimony they received from previous generations: first and foremost, the laws of the Pentateuch, but also various traditions, regulations, and customs that emerged during the time known as the Second Temple period (538 B.C.E.–70 C.E.). Ideas and rules of purity and impurity were undoubtedly among the most dominant components of the legal and cultural traditions the rabbis inherited. In the biblical Priestly Code, the laws of purity play a key role in the cult of the Tabernacle and in the organization of the camp of Israel, and the rhetoric of impurity and purification is also highly prevalent in the books of the Prophets. It is especially in the literature of the Second Temple period, however, that purity and impurity emerge as a central concern and as a source of ongoing preoccupation.[4] This preoccupation is manifested not only in the presumed scrupulous observance of ritual purity laws at the time (at least in some circles),[5] which led later rabbis to describe this period longingly as "the time in which purity burst out in Israel,"[6] but also in the fact that the language of impurity and the metaphors it engenders colored the social and religious discourse of this period in a remarkable way. In the literature of the turn of the first century C.E., the theme of purity recurs as one of the pivots of the consistent effort to distinguish "us" from "them": non-Jews from Jews,[7] Sadducees from Pharisees,[8] followers of Jesus from the ones renouncing him,[9] and sons of light from sons of darkness.[10]

The rabbis who created the Mishnah were heirs to the notions and practices of purity and impurity that their predecessors developed, as well as to the emphasis on scrupulousness in observance of purity as a way of differentiating insiders from outsiders and of expressing utmost piety. The twelve tractates that comprise the Order of Purities, and likewise other mishnaic tractates and textual units that discuss matters of purity and impurity, present an ambitious and comprehensive attempt further to develop, systematize, arrange, scrutinize, and augment this biblical and postbiblical inheritance, and to weave out of numerous legal details a rich picture of everyday activities, encounters, and practices that are defined and governed by observance of ritual purity. In essence, the Mishnah's vast purity and impurity corpus can be seen as a direct continuation of frames of thought and of hermeneutic and legislative endeavors that preceded it,[11] and as an edifice whose foundations are firmly grounded in the Second Temple period. However, the construction of this impressive mishnaic edifice cannot be understood merely in terms of the preservation and systematization of past teachings and customs. Rather, it is the result of a creative encounter between the formative biblical purity texts and the established interpretive traditions that accompanied them, on the one hand, and the ideas, perceptions, convictions, and concerns of the mishnaic rabbis, who were denizens (however reticent) of the cultural and intellectual world of the Graeco-Roman Mediterranean of the Antonine period, on the other hand. This creative encounter gave birth to striking conceptual innovations that profoundly transformed the biblical notions of purity and impurity, and that introduced new focal points around which the rabbinic purity discourse was constructed, thereby giving the observance of purity laws in their rabbinic setting new and vibrant meanings.

As I will show throughout the book, while the rabbis adhere to the basic schemes of purity and impurity put forth in the Priestly Code, and do not add any new sources of impurity to the biblical system, they suggest an array of unprecedented principles regarding the contraction, conveyance, and management of impurity, as well as sets of practices that derive from these principles. The purpose of this study is to trace the new principles that the rabbis introduced to the biblical system of purity and impurity, and to reconstruct and explain the conceptual framework that brought them about. I will argue that a central dimension of the rabbinic reconstruction of the purity system is unparalleled attention to questions of subjectivity, and more specifically, to the ways in which persons relate to themselves, to their bodies, and to their material surroundings. Whereas in the Bible and in Second Temple literature the dominant focal points of the discourse on purity and impurity are the sancta and the Temple,[12] and by extension the camp, the city, and the community insofar as those bear a sanctity of their own,[13] the Mishnah's Order of Purities introduces the *self*, the individual subject of the law, as a new focal point.[14] This is not to say that the Temple or the community are of no interest to the rabbis, but it is to say that the discourse on these topics in the context of purity and impurity is reoriented toward the self, the agent whose body (as well as property, which, as I will argue, functions in the Mishnah as part of one's extended body) goes through the vicissitudes of purity and impurity.

The rabbinic shift of focus from the Temple to the self seems, on the face of it, to lend itself readily to the prevalent view that the Mishnah is in essence a response to the destruction of the Temple in 70 C.E. and, later on, to the demolition and resettlement of Jerusalem and its region following the Bar Kokhva revolt in 132–135 C.E. Various scholars hold the view that the Mishnah and the rabbinic enterprise more broadly were devised in an attempt to provide viable substitutes to the destroyed Temple, and thereby to allow Jewish life to persist in a new, durable configuration under the new circumstances.[15] Within this paradigm, it seems almost warranted to assume that the emergence of the self as a critical focal point of the rabbinic discourse of purity and impurity is a facet of the rabbinic effort to replace Temple-based forms of piety with Temple-less forms of piety. My analysis in this study, however, does not subscribe to this paradigm, and does not examine the rabbinic discourse of purity and impurity through the lens of the destruction of the Temple, for the simple reason that there are no real grounds for identifying a break between perceptions and practices of purity that prevailed during the time of the Temple and perceptions and practices of purity that prevailed after its destruction. As I will argue in the first chapter, it is evident that purity was pursued beyond the Temple and beyond Jerusalem even while the Temple was still functioning, and it is also quite evident that purity-related practices were still prevalent in Palestine for decades after the destruction of the Temple (with the obvious exception of elements that could only take place in the Temple, such as purificatory sacrifices). In addition, some of the central legal innovations that stand at the core of the rabbinic transformation of the biblical impurity system clearly date back to the first century C.E. or even earlier. The Mishnah's discourse of purity and impurity should be understood, I contend, not as a "response" to specific historical crises, but as the result of a very gradual evolvement and change of social, intellectual, and ideological concerns and interests that converged in the encounter between the rabbis, the traditions they interpreted, and the greater cultural context in which this interpretation was taking place.

With this view of the mishnaic discourse of purity and impurity as a site in which biblical institutions are transformed and reshaped and cultural modes of engagement with notions of body and self are negotiated, this book engages in conversation with three central fields of interest: purity in ancient Judaism, the body in rabbinic culture, and the self in antiquity. However, since the topic of this book is the reinterpretation and reinvention of an inherited ritual language in a changing world, it invites to this conversation a wide variety of scholars, students, and interested readers who are fascinated by the relations between tradition and innovation in religious communities.

## PURITY IN ANCIENT JUDAISM

The constitutive corpus for the discourse of ritual purity and impurity in ancient Judaism is chapters 11–15 in the book of Leviticus and chapter 19 in the book of Numbers. These chapters, which discuss a number of creatures, substances, and bodily conditions that are considered sources of impurity and are thus proscribed in different ways, have elicited ongoing interest among traditional and modern scholars alike. Whereas scholars of the Hebrew Bible or the ancient Near East are mainly interested in deciphering the biblical purity laws in terms of their meaning or origin, scholars of postbiblical Judaism are concerned with the question of how the biblical purity system was applied and interpreted in different social and religious contexts. The working assumption that guides studies of the latter interest, which includes this book, is that in postbiblical ancient Judaism the biblical purity system itself is not negotiable, and its particular details are a given; the question is what, if anything, is *done* with this system. While the topic of purity in postbiblical Judaism has received some scholarly attention over the past century, the last two decades can be described as a time of an unprecedented boom of interest in this topic.[16] Within this fairly recent abundance of studies, one can identify two central modes of engagement with the topic, which I will define here as sociohistorical and textual-conceptual.

Studies conducted with a sociohistorical orientation are concerned with questions of actual observance of purity laws in ancient Jewish societies, namely, how many people observed these laws, which laws exactly were observed, how they were observed by different groups, what were the different levels of observance during different periods, and so forth.[17] Many of these studies focus mainly on the two centuries before the destruction of the Jerusalem Temple, a period from which there is relatively abundant evidence, and use rabbinic sources primarily to reconstruct a historical account of the prerabbinic period. This tendency not only is a result of the relative paucity of archeological and nonrabbinic textual evidence from the time after the destruction of the Temple, but also often stems from the prevalent assumption that after the destruction of the Temple the observance of ritual purity was, on the whole, irrelevant and unattainable (except for little "pockets" of observance, like the laws of menstrual purity or the laws of corpse impurity that pertain to priests).[18] Guided by this assumption, Jacob Neusner dedicated the twenty-two volumes of his *History of the Mishnaic Laws of Purities* to arguing that, after the destruction of the Temple, purity turned from an everyday concern, centered on eating practices, to an abstract notion with no bearing on everyday life that the rabbis utilized to develop their inquiry of reality.[19] More recent scholarship, however, which relies both on careful textual analysis and on archeological evidence,[20] persuasively shows that while some purity laws could obviously not be observed in the absence of a Temple (mainly laws that require sacrifices as part of the purification process), various purity-related practices, most notably practices pertaining to the preparation and consumption of food, were maintained throughout the mishnaic period, although they had apparently been in rapid decline as of the second half of the second century C.E.[21]

In contrast to sociohistorical studies, the main purpose of textual-conceptual studies is to examine how notions of purity and impurity are interpreted in different ancient Jewish texts. The purpose of such studies is not to uncover what different Jewish groups did, but how these groups perceived different aspects of the concepts of purity and impurity: which cosmic powers they stood for, what their moral and theological undertones were, what social and communal ideologies they served, and so forth. The main characteristic of existing textual-conceptual studies of this sort is their clear comparative orientation and diachronic organization, since their central undertaking is to examine several different corpora against one another and to point to similarities and differences between the ideas of purity and impurity in these corpora. Whereas earlier textual-conceptual studies attempted to encompass the treatment of purity and impurity in given texts as one indivisible whole,[22] more recent works have focused on specific aspects of purity or impurity, and thus were able to present a much more detailed, nuanced, and scholarly sound picture.[23]

While I fully acknowledge the tremendous value of studies of both approaches and am greatly indebted, in almost every page of this book, to the many penetrating questions they raise and cogent insights they provide, this book falls under neither the sociohistorical nor the textual-conceptual category. Instead, it suggests a break from these two common modes of engaging with purity in ancient Judaism. While I subscribe to the view that purity and impurity were, at least to a certain extent, matters of practical and not just theoretical concern for the mishnaic rabbis, I do not wish to utilize the mishnaic texts for historical reconstruction of actual practices, but rather to explore the *discourse* of impurity that the rabbis construct in the Mishnah, a compilation that uniquely and famously merges together depictions of the (real or imagined) past, practical prescriptions for the present, utopian ideas, and interpretive imagination.[24] The Mishnah presents its rulings and guidelines in matters of purity and impurity as one whole, complete, and comprehensive system, offering no hint of distinction between laws that in certainty could not have been followed at the rabbis' time and laws that were an inextricable part of the rabbis' world. Rather, the Mishnah incorporates all its rulings into a timeless framework, as an everlasting key component of one's lived experience and of one's self-governance as a subject of the law. My interest lies in this timeless framework that the rabbis construct, which consists of both concrete and applicable everyday practices and hypothetical or idealized ways of conduct, and in the subject that this framework, with its multiple discursive and practical components, creates.

With this interest in the discursive and ideational aspects of purity and impurity, my perspective is closer to the textual-conceptual orientation in the study of purity in ancient Judaism. However, I differ from the majority of studies directed by this orientation in that my approach is distinctly synchronic and not diachronic. This book is concerned with the Mishnah as an independent cultural creation, which, while consisting of various sources, also stands as a unified text. I am not examining the Mishnah from an external point of reference, but rather from within its own concepts, concerns, and modes of discourse. Clearly, as I mentioned, the ingenuity of the rabbis and the uniqueness of their ideas can only be appreciated vis-à-vis the traditions they inherited, but my main purpose is not to examine how the rabbis differ from what preceded them, but to analyze what the rabbis did with the materials they inherited to construct something new and inimitable. This approach allows me to examine aspects of rabbinic purity laws that have not drawn scholarly attention in the past, since they could not be construed as part of the common ground of ancient Judaism.

## THE BODY IN RABBINIC CULTURE

In many ways, the cultural orientation in the study of rabbinic literature and the interest in the representation and construction of the body in this literature are so closely intertwined that "the body in rabbinic culture" is somewhat redundant. Pioneered and deeply influenced by Daniel Boyarin's *Carnal Israel: Reading Sex in Talmudic Culture*, corporeal-cultural studies of rabbinic literature are guided by the premise that reading texts is reading culture. Often utilizing Foucault's notion of *discourse* as a complex and diverse array of statements, rhetorical structures, beliefs, and courses of actions, students of rabbinic literature as culture attempt to read rabbinic texts in their greater social context without simplistically seeing them as historical sources, and examine the very production of rabbinic texts as a form of cultural practice. The centrality of practice in the cultural approach to rabbinic literature emphatically brings the body to the fore as the main locus of practice, not simply as an interesting topic to be examined, but as a site through which identities are performed and cultural concerns are negotiated.[25]

In my view of rabbinic texts as cultural products, in my vested interest in the ways the rabbis integrate biblical concepts and institutions with ideas and practices from the intellectual and religious cultures that surround them, and in my approach to rabbinic literature through the methodological lens of discourse analysis, I am inspired by and beholden to the many studies that apply cultural-critical tools and frames of thought to suggest new and provocative ways to engage with rabbinic literature.[26] Needless to say, my focus on purity and impurity, as discursive sites in which dramas of interpretation and innovation take place in the body itself, makes this book a very "corporeal" study and puts it in dialogue with other studies of rabbinic literature that have put the body at their center. There are, however, several little-discussed aspects of embodiment and corporeality that this book particularly emphasizes, and through which I hope to bring rabbinic texts into broader contemporary conversations that prolifically challenge our view of the body as a self-contained and well-defined unit and our way of approaching human materiality more broadly.[27]

First, the very concept of impurity, which stands at the center of this book, and the modes of operation of impurity as the rabbis conceived them bring to the fore phenomena such as decomposition and contagion, which compel us to think of the body as an entity whose boundaries and constituent elements are not stable, but are rather constantly mutating. The rabbinic impurity discourse, which habitually parses the body into parts and fragments, does not put forth any coherent notion of *the* body as a single self-explanatory unit, but rather depicts a complex web of organs, limbs, and visceral components, a web in which different bodies are connected and then separated, and in which bodies are continually being remolded and redefined. Thus, rather than positing the question of what can be done to and with the body as a biosocial given, this book engages time and again with the question of *what* the body *is:* where does it begin and end, what does it consist of, and what makes a body into a person.

Second, the prominent place of inanimate objects in the rabbinic discourse of purity and impurity provokes us to think of them not simply as external additions to the human habitat, but also, as I argue in detail in the third chapter, as extensions of the human body. Through my heightened attention to the relations of the human body, as a material entity among material entities, with its nonhuman environment, I hope to introduce inanimate objects as a new point of interest in the study of rabbinic culture, and in the study of late antiquity more broadly.

Finally, one of my main goals in this book is to tie together the study of the body with the study of self and subjectivity. While several studies have discussed the body as a site for the construction of specific identities—ethnic, religious, sexual, and so forth[28]—the question of whether and how one's body is identical to or different from one's self has received little scholarly attention in rabbinic studies. The themes of purity and impurity, however, raise questions that pertain to the ways in which one's body is understood and negotiated as both identical to and disparate from the legal subject that governs this body and interprets it.

Throughout this book, I explore the rabbinic treatment of questions such as "What parts of my body are really 'me'"? "In what sense is a dead body still a person?" and "What makes a human body different from other organic and nonorganic entities?" Of course, as I show in the fifth and sixth chapters, a sense of self can never be extricated from an array of political, social, and sexual identities, but I propose to examine these identities as part of a larger matrix of relations between one and one's body, relations that are established through various practices, both corporeal and mental.

## THE SELF IN ANTIQUITY

The concept of self, as well as other related or overlapping terms such as *I*, *subject*, and *person*, is extremely elusive, and these words have different sets of meanings in different cultural and scholarly contexts.[29] In this book I use the term *self* in a very broad sense, to refer to a human entity that is seen as capable of *reflecting* on its own actions, thoughts, biography, and so forth.[30] While the terms *subject* and *person* are oftentimes used interchangeably with the term *self*, for the sake of consistency I use *subject* either as the opposite of object (that is, to denote agency) or specifically when discussing a subject of someone or something, and I use *person* to denote a human being as opposed to other creatures, material artifacts, or organic matter. While all three terms will inevitably overlap from time to time, my main interest is in the category of *self* as a way of conceptualizing one's understanding of one's own (and others') being.

Whereas modern philosophers and psychologists dedicate endless efforts to proposing exacting and exhaustive definitions of the self,[31] several scholars of antiquity have attempted to determine whether this term is applicable to ancient contexts, and if so, in what ways. To be clear, none of the scholars who questioned the validity of the category of self in respect to antiquity denied that the inhabitants of the ancient world had thoughts, feelings, ideas, and biographies that were unique to them, as well as an ability to reflect on what they did, what they thought, and what they wanted. What some scholars did deny, however, is that the ancients centered their concept of self on the irreplaceable and one-of-a-kind individual with which the self has been identified since Rousseau.[32] Nevertheless, the important observation that notions of self in antiquity are not identical to notions of self in modern times does not mean that ancient writers were not concerned with the fundamental questions "What am I?" and "What should I be?"; these we can define as the critical questions that pertain to the self. Such concerns were brought to the foreground in the last few decades in numerous fascinating and wide-ranging studies, which were dedicated to deciphering the varieties of concepts of self and subjectivity in ancient and late ancient literature—Greek, Roman, and early Christian.[33]

While one important aspect of the study of self and subjectivity is deciphering different philosophical-psychological concepts of self, that is, approaching the self as *something one thinks about,* a different perspective on the self in antiquity pertains to the question of self-formation, or to the self as *something one develops and cultivates.* This perspective was introduced by Pierre Hadot and, more rigorously and influentially, by Michel Foucault. Hadot made the argument that in the ancient world philosophy was "a way of life," which meant living in a certain way and striving to become a certain kind of person, rather than merely contemplating abstract ideas.[34] Accordingly, those committed to a philosophical way of life were constantly engaged in active attempts to cultivate certain character traits and dispositions within themselves through various mental and physical practices.[35] Following in the footsteps of Hadot, and integrating Hadot's ideas into his own larger framework of an archeology of knowledge, Michel Foucault developed the idea that in the ancient world persons had to *become* subjects by taking on certain modes of living and certain activities; in other words, the self was something one had to make.[36] In his works on self-formation, and particularly in *The Care of the Self,* Foucault tied together body, self, and practice, suggesting that to attain a personal ideal of what one ought to be is essentially to shape, control, and reflect on the body through a set of fixed practices, which he called "techniques of the self."[37] While Foucault's reconstruction of ancient ideas and practices of the self was harshly criticized as lacking and inaccurate,[38] his notion of techniques of the self has remained extremely influential. Moreover, Foucault's broader understanding of the self as a discursive construct, as something that is formed through certain social practices and changes along with them, allowed the self to take a much more central place in the study of ancient literatures and cultures. Following Foucault, the variety of ancient concepts of self was no longer conceived as the arcane interest of philosophers, but as a gateway for engaging with essential questions of identity, body, class, gender, and so on.[39]

Guided by ongoing attention both to conceptual aspects of self and subjectivity and to questions of self-formation and self-cultivation, I attempt in this book to introduce rabbinic sources—and emphatically, rabbinic *legal* sources—into the vibrant conversation about the self in antiquity and late antiquity.[40] The critical contribution of rabbinic legal discourse to this conversation lies not only in the centrality and heft of rabbinic legal compilations within the corpus of early Judaism, but also in the unique nature of rabbinic law as an intriguing site for the examination of practices of self-formation. Rabbinic legislation, or *halakhah,* can be viewed as a radical attempt to construct a self whose every single quotidian activity, from sneezing to shoe-lacing, is shaped and reflected upon through the prism of commitment to the law, and thus as shaping a mode of living that entails incessant self-scrutiny and striving for self-perfection. Through my discussions on the relations between halakhic practice and the constitution of self, and by pointing out ways in which mishnaic themes resonate with ideas on self-formation that can be found in Greek and Roman literature, I hope to show the enormous potential that the study of *halakhah* has for the exploration of the self in antiquity.[41]

This book does not purport to present a systematic and exhaustive picture of the self in the Mishnah, but rather, much more modestly, to show how the mishnaic discourse of purity and impurity constructs and develops certain ideas about the self and certain techniques of the self. These ideas and techniques pertain to the ways in which one governs one's body, one's possessions (which are an extended part of the body, as I suggest), and one's behavior, as well as to the ways in which one conducts oneself vis-à-vis the law and its rabbinic self-proclaimed representatives. It is important to emphasize, however, that I am in no way suggesting that the Mishnah's discourse of purity and impurity was meant by the rabbis as a manual of self-formation and self-reflection in disguise, or even that the rabbis consciously asked themselves, when developing the laws of purity and impurity, "What is a person?" and "What kind of person should one be?" Rather, I hold that the rabbis' corpus of purity and impurity is in essence a technical legal corpus meant to provide a comprehensive picture of a central aspect of Jewish ritual life, but that this corpus both is *guided* by unspoken, and perhaps unconscious, assumptions about personhood and subjectivity, and *creates* certain dispositions and attitudes toward the self through its authoritative rhetoric. It is the underlying assumptions about selfhood underneath the surface of the Mishnah, on the one hand, and the idealized self on its horizon, on the other hand, that I wish to uncover in this study.

## READING THE MISHNAH

Among the various rabbinic compilations, the Mishnah stands out as highly unified in its style and structured in its form, in such a way that the composition as it we have it before us reads as a distinct textual unity.[42] However, while it is quite evident that the Mishnah was shaped by a conscientious and dominant redactor or several redactors, and thus can be discussed as a textual whole, it is nonetheless clear that the Mishnah was created and compiled in a lengthy process, and that different people took part in its making at various points in time. The collective nature of this work and the absence of any narrating voice from the text do not allow us to speak of an author in the ordinary sense of the word in respect to the Mishnah. Therefore, while I am very aware of the awkwardness of attributing agency to a literary work, I oftentimes use phrases such as "the Mishnah says" or "the Mishnah explains," since such phrases best reflect the manner in which the mishnaic text is introduced to its reader: without an identifiable narrating voice and without a programmatic introduction, as a creation of everyone and of no one at the same time.

The Mishnah's standing as a cohesive textual unit does not obfuscate the fact that it consists of multiple layers, traditions, and sources. The Mishnah comprises different tractates, each one of them presumably a unit unto itself, with its own complex history of formation and redaction; different passages in the Mishnah are likely to have been shaped at different periods, by different people, and to have been compiled at different stages; and even within the same passage, different statements or narratives may derive from different sources. Although I am fully cognizant of the enormous complexity of the Mishnah as a text, in this book I am not concerned with investigating the formation or redaction of the mishnaic text, nor am I attempting to ascribe different mishnaic traditions to different periods. First, I am very skeptical regarding our ability to recover the different stages of the development of the text, an enterprise that is usually undertaken by identifying the particular sage or sages whose statements are included in a passage as the key to dating the passage to a particular period. Even if we take the attributions of statements as reliable, and even if we exclude the possibility that the words of a sage from one period were integrated into a passage from another period, the overwhelming majority of passages I examine in this book are anonymous. Second, and more importantly, I do not think that the question of when a specific tradition emerged is of particular importance when trying to identify certain mindsets in the Mishnah as a cohesive redacted work. The very fact that a specific tradition was introduced sometime during the period in which the Mishnah was formed and that the redactors considered this tradition to be worth preserving is an indication that the view expressed in this tradition was part of the thought-world of the rabbis who formed the Mishnah. It was not necessarily something to which they all subscribed, nor was it necessarily the only view on the matter, but it is constitutive of the mishnaic discourse *as such,* which is where my interest lies.

One of the main challenges with which every reader of the Mishnah is faced is the fact that it is entangled in a web of textual and interpretive relations with other rabbinic compilations. The Halakhic Midrashim, which are contemporaneous with or slightly later than the Mishnah, not only present numerous textual parallels with the Mishnah but also provide important scriptural reasonings for its rulings.[43] The Palestinian and Babylonian Talmuds, which were compiled between two hundred and four hundred years after the Mishnah, are the most immediate tools that we have when trying to interpret the mishnaic sources and to understand the way they resonate in the larger frameworks of rabbinic law and thought. However, while an examination of the topic of purity and impurity across rabbinic literature is certainly a worthwhile endeavor, since my main purpose in this study is to present a rich and coherent thematic picture of purity and impurity in the Mishnah, I choose to engage midrashic and talmudic materials only when they significantly promote our understanding of specific mishnaic passages.

Somewhat different is my approach to the Tosefta, an early rabbinic compilation that is structured in correlation with the order of the Mishnah, uses the same rhetorical forms and style, and presents an array of materials relevant to the Mishnah—alternative traditions, additional rulings, parallel texts, interpretive clauses, and so forth.[44] A lively discussion has been taking place in recent scholarship on the question of whether the Tosefta is later than the Mishnah and should be seen as an early commentary on it,[45] or earlier than the Mishnah and should be seen as its main source.[46] (There is also a recent third suggestion, according to which the two are free renditions of the same essential text.)[47] Personally I tend to adopt Shamma Friedman's view of the Tosefta as a compilation of various materials *relevant* to the Mishnah: some of these materials are the sources of the Mishnah, some of them are later interpretations, and so on, but the compilation as a whole is later.[48] Either way, it is my conviction that the Tosefta is complementary to the Mishnah and cannot be viewed as its own independent text. This is not to say that the redactors of the Tosefta did not have an agenda of their own, which may have been different from that of the redactors of the Mishnah, but it is to say that the Tosefta was meant to be studied alongside the Mishnah, whether the Mishnah as we know it or an earlier version of it. Therefore, whenever I find traditions in the Tosefta that are particularly illuminating vis-à-vis themes I identify in the Mishnah, I use them to broaden our scope and to suggest different angles from which to understand the mishnaic text. Thus, while the focus of this book is the Mishnah, I use the Tosefta as an important source for presenting a richer and more complete picture of the mishnaic traditions.

Naturally, the lion's share of rabbinic traditions on purity and impurity can be found in the twelve tractates that compose the Order of Purities, which is dedicated exclusively to this topic. However, important textual units that are germane to purity and impurity can also be found in other mishnaic tractates such as *Hagigah, Eduyot*, and more. The particular themes with which I am concerned in this study are not concentrated in a limited number of textual units, but are dispersed and arise in very different contexts and in very different textual settings. In order to present a picture that is as broad and rich as possible, I chose to discuss a large number of individual passages as units unto themselves. While I always make a point of presenting the general context of the passages in question and not isolating them from their original textual settings, I am aware that by picking and choosing relevant texts I am emphasizing some aspects of some texts over others, and am certainly not doing justice to the corpus as a whole. However, I see no other way of analytically engaging with such a large corpus in a meaningful way, which is what this book sets out to achieve.

The book consists of six chapters, in each of which I explore a different facet of the mishnaic purity and impurity discourse from the perspective of the relations between body and self. While each of the chapters is concerned with different themes and texts, the book's argument builds from chapter to chapter, since the argument presented in each chapter serves as a point of departure for the subsequent chapter.

The first chapter sets the stage for the chapters that follow by overviewing some of the central innovations that the rabbis introduced into the biblical system of impurity, innovations that effectively turn impurity from a concern restricted to those who function as sources of impurity or to those in their immediate vicinity to a concern pertaining to anyone and everyone at any given time. Through this transformation in the scope and impact of impurity, the rabbis of the Mishnah portray the entire lived world as infused with impurity, and depict one's daily interactions with people and things as governed by constant attention to impurity. Thus, I argue, the rabbis posit the engagement with impurity—avoiding it, managing it, purifying oneself from it, and so on—as a critical component in one's formation as a committed rabbinic Jewish subject.

The second chapter explores the most dominant and paradigmatic actor in the realm of purity and impurity, the human body. I attempt to decipher how the rabbis perceived of the body as a material entity and how they imagined its physical function in the contraction and transmission of impurity, and focus on their construction of the body as a fluid and modular entity whose boundaries are in constant flux. I then turn to show that the rabbis divide the body into different areas, in such a way that areas that are less consequential to the subject and that one does not strongly identify with oneself are not susceptible to impurity. Thereby, the rabbis create a unique paradigm of a bodily self in which the body is identical to the self only insofar as the body is invested with subjectivity.

The third chapter moves from the human body to inanimate objects, which, as I argue, were conceived by the rabbis as extensions of the human body and as entities in which, like in the body, one must invest subjectivity in order to introduce them into the realm of impurity. The susceptibility to impurity of inanimate objects, whether artifacts or foodstuffs, is largely determined by the consciousness of their owners, since one must *care* about the object in question and must actively identify it as one's own to allow it to be rendered impure. The mishnaic subject thus not only responds to the world of impurity but also, through the force of deliberation, thought, and intention, constructs the world of impurity, in such a way that the ability of objects to contract impurity serves in the Mishnah as a marker of these objects' consequentiality for human beings.

The fourth chapter focuses on the rabbinic reconstruction of corpse impurity. At the center of this chapter stands the unprecedented rabbinic ruling that fragments of corpses must be either significant enough in size or of a form that is distinctly and recognizably human in order fully to convey impurity. I argue that the rabbis construct the ability of corpse fragments to convey impurity as dependent upon their ability to invoke the mental picture of a whole human being, and I further argue that for the rabbis the point of reference against which all corpse fragments are assessed and measured is distinctly and paradoxically a *living* body. Thereby, I argue, the rabbis create a system in which the corpse loses its power to convey impurity the more it resembles lifeless and formless organic matter, that is, the more it becomes something one cannot identify with oneself.

The fifth chapter turns to discuss the role and function of non-Jews in the mishnaic system of impurity. In the mishnaic setting, the purity status of non-Jews is strangely dual: while they are considered to be entirely insusceptible to the ritual impurities to which Jews are susceptible, they are also considered to convey the same impurity as persons with abnormal genital discharges, regardless of their physical condition. Attempting to disentangle this perplexing duality, I suggest how these two seemingly contradictory notions came to be, and how they are utilized by the rabbis to construct a discourse not only about Gentiles, but also and especially about the subjectivity of Jews. Whereas the inability of Gentiles to contract impurity is presented in the Mishnah as a result of a lack of legal subjectivity, their perpetual impurity is strongly identified with effeminacy and loss of bodily control. Thus the rabbis define Gentiles through their lacking or deficient subjectivity and, by way of contrast, also construct an ideal rabbinic Jewish subject.

Finally, the sixth chapter examines the pursuit of ritual purity as a means and an end in the rabbinic ethics of the self. I show that the Mishnah's idealized subjects are distinguished, first and foremost, by their mental disposition toward purity, that is, by their ability to be attentive to impurity at all times. This attentiveness manifests itself in constant reflection on one's actions and encounters, in regular physical self-scrutiny, and, perhaps most importantly, in unrelenting reflection on one's own mental dedication to purity. I argue that through the recurring theme of self-examination the rabbis construct one's relation to the law as entailing a certain relation to *oneself*. They shape the mishnaic intended subject as possessed of both self-control and self-knowledge, thus turning the everyday engagement with purity and impurity into an arena in which one's meritorious qualities are both exhibited and cultivated, and turning the quest for purity into a quest for self-perfection as a subject of the law.

# 1

# From Sources of Impurity to Circles of Impurity

The collections of laws in Leviticus 11–15 and Numbers 19, according to which certain creatures, substances, and bodily phenomena constitute sources of ritual impurity, have been daunting to traditional exegetes and modern scholars alike for centuries. The biblical text's silence as to the principles that govern the rendition of particular things as impure (if any such principles exist), as well as the lack of apparent explanation of the very concept of impurity and its import, posed a significant challenge for interpreters who sought to incorporate the laws of impurity into whatever they perceived to be the general theological or ethical arc of the Hebrew Bible. While some asserted, like William Robertson Smith, that "rules like this have nothing in common with the spirit of the Hebrew religion,"[1] many others, from the author of *The Letter of Aristeas* in the second century B.C.E. to the French-Bulgarian psychoanalyst Julia Kristeva in the late twentieth century, strove to uncover the hidden meanings of the biblical ritual purity code. The main purpose of such readers throughout the generations has been to determine why it is that some particular substances and conditions, rather than others, are identified as sources of impurity, and their premise has been that deciphering the logic according to which certain things are classified as impure is the key to decrypting the biblical concept of impurity at large. Whether they offered symbolic readings of the social imperatives entailed in the purity laws,[2] pragmatic explanations of the laws as promoting public health or economic interests, conjectures on the demonological background of the notion of impurity, or reconstructions of the ancient Israelite cosmology,[3] exegetes and scholars generally shared the view that understanding ritual purity means finding a paradigm or set of paradigms to account for the specific *sources* of ritual impurity.

In light of this overarching tendency to interpret biblical impurity laws by asking what it is that makes certain things impure, it is perhaps quite surprising to find that in the entire vast corpus of classical rabbinic literature, arguably the corpus most committed to close and scrupulous readings of biblical law in the ancient world, no attempt whatsoever is made to explain why particular substances and conditions are considered to be sources of impurity and others are not, and no suggestions are raised as to the underlying logic—religious, moral, practical, or otherwise—that governs the biblical classification system. In general, the rabbis seem reluctant to ascribe any intelligible meaning to the peculiarities of the biblical impurity code, and in several passages they identify certain aspects of the impurity laws as ordinances that are so bizarre and unfathomable that they are particularly vulnerable to mocking attacks from insiders and outsiders alike.[4] To the extent that they reflect on the nature and purpose of purity laws at all, the rabbis' prominent approach is to explain the biblical laws of impurity as cultivating obedience for obedience's sake,[5] rather than as laws charged with profound meaning that await an inspired exegete to lift the veil off of their obscure surface.

While this could lead one to believe that ritual impurity was a topic of no interest or importance for the rabbis, and that their engagement with it was limited merely to acknowledging its place within the biblical legal system, nothing could be further from the truth. As I venture to show throughout this book, at least as far as the early rabbis (the *tannaim*) are concerned, impurity was a central and critical category, which fundamentally shaped and informed the rabbis' notions of interactions with one's fellow humans, with one's physical environment, and with oneself. Not only were the rabbis highly invested in the laws of ritual purity, they also dedicated tremendous intellectual efforts to developing these laws in multiple directions and, more importantly, to making them meaningful and powerful in the cultural world of their own intended audience. Yet the rabbis' intricate and elaborate discussions of ritual impurity were not in any way geared toward the question of *why* some particular substances and conditions and not others constitute sources of impurity. For them, the few sources of impurity mentioned in the Hebrew Bible were a nonnegotiable given, a mundane fact of halakhic life like the number of days in a week. Rather, the questions with which the rabbis were most concerned, and which constitute, so to speak, the beating heart of their impurity discourse, are two: first, how a state of impurity can be correctly diagnosed; and second and more prominently, how impurity, once it originates in the biblically determined sources of impurity, is *transmitted* further.

The vested interest of the rabbis in the transmission of impurity, that is, in the "travel" of impurity from the source to other objects or persons, led them to offer a lens very different from the biblical one when viewing and depicting the lived world in terms of impurity. Whereas the biblical texts zoom in on the sources of impurity themselves and at most on whatever is in their immediate proximity, the rabbis zoom out and include in their frame a whole array of people and things affected by the biblically determined sources of impurity. Thus, as we approach the rabbinic discourse of impurity and seek to understand its shaping forces and its cultural implications, we too must first adjust our lenses accordingly to include not only the sources of impurity but also the expanding circles that surround them. The purpose of this chapter is to offer such a preliminary adjustment of lenses, which will allow us to grasp the picture of impurity that the rabbis put forth in its fuller scope, and will help set the stage for the rabbinic dramas of engagement with impurity that will be discussed in the chapters to follow.

The point of departure of this chapter is an outline of the biblical impurity system, which is proposed partially in order to make the readers familiar with some key terms and concepts that will recur throughout the book, but also and more importantly in order to serve as the backdrop against which the radically innovative aspects of the rabbinic impurity discourse can be understood in all their magnitude. After outlining the biblical scheme of the workings of impurity, I suggest a brief overview of the central ways in which this biblical scheme was developed and approached in the postbiblical period, by pointing to some of the shared themes and principles, as well as divergences, between rabbinic purity legislation and the purity texts from Qumran. The purpose of this general overview is to help us assess in which ways the Mishnah's legal discourse of purity and impurity is commensurate and correspondent with trends and views that preceded its creators, and in which ways the Mishnah's purity discourse presents a conceptual shift from those trends and a unique reconstruction of notions and practices of purity and impurity. Focusing on the principles and perspectives that are distinctive to the rabbinic purity discourse, I show that the rabbis significantly expanded the realm of impurity, not by adding new sources of impurity but rather by devising new and far-reaching modes and processes of transmission of impurity to secondary and tertiary contractors. Thereby, I argue, the rabbis turned the contraction of impurity from a noticeable event to an *ongoing reality*.

I then continue to discuss the implications of this substantial expansion of the realm of impurity for the Mishnah's construction of impurity as a factor in one's daily lived experience. Through an examination of various scattered passages in which the rabbis comment on the places and situations in which one might encounter impurity, and on the modes of behavior and action one should undertake in response to potential or actual encounters with impurity, I piece together an account of the ways in which the rabbis conceived impurity to be operating in the lived world and to be defining one's everyday experiences. I argue that the rabbis of the Mishnah create a picture of a world perfuse with impurity, in which almost every quotidian activity or interaction entails a possibility of knowingly or unknowingly contracting impurity, and thus make the engagement with impurity a critical, constant, and determinant component of the everyday life of the mishnaic subject. Grasping the pervasiveness of impurity in the rabbinic picture of the everyday, and thereby the extent to which the mishnaic subject's life consists of a series of actual or potential encounters with impurity, we may begin to see why and how, in the rabbinic discourse, engagement with impurity becomes a defining component of one's sense of self.

## BIBLICAL FOUNDATIONS AND RABBINIC INNOVATIONS

### The Biblical Impurity System: An Outline

Impurity is a complex and multifaceted concept in the Hebrew Bible, and the appellation *tame*, "impure" or "unclean," is used in the Bible in a variety of contexts and with different underlying meanings.[6] In contrast, in the Mishnah the term *impure* is used in a rather restricted fashion, referring almost exclusively to the sources of ritual impurity denoted in the Priestly Code of the Pentateuch, and specifically in chapters 11–15 of the book of Leviticus and in chapter 19 of the book of Numbers.[7] In what follows I will suggest a brief outline of the biblical system of ritual impurity as it is presented in these particular Priestly texts, since this is the only dimension of biblical impurity that the rabbis systematically develop.[8]

Generally speaking, in the Priestly Code impurity is depicted as a phenomenon that stems from several natural sources. These sources are not very many in number, and include the following:

I. *Dead creatures.* This category includes animal carcasses,[9] dead creeping or crawling creatures such as rodents or insects,[10] and human corpses.[11]

II. *Impure substances.* The only bodily substance that is explicitly mentioned as impure in and of itself is semen, which renders both women and men who come into contact with it impure.[12] In addition, it is mentioned that the ashes of the red cow, which are used for purification from corpse impurity, are a source of impurity.[13]

III. *Men and women who are in a physical state that renders them impure.* This category includes women after childbirth,[14] men and women with scale disease,[15] men with abnormal genital discharges,[16] and women with genital bleeding, whether normal (that is, menstrual) or abnormal.[17] Such men and women remain in a state of impurity either until a designated number of days has passed (in the case of a parturient and a menstruating woman) or until their pathological physical condition has changed and an additional period of seven days has passed (in the case of persons with abnormal discharges and scale diseases). After the specified time has passed, these persons complete their purification process through various rites, which most commonly include washing in water and bringing sacrifices to the

sanctuary (in the case of persons with scale disease, the purification rite is more elaborate).
IV. *Afflicted objects.* Garments and houses that are considered to be afflicted with a particular form of mildew *(tzara'at)* are seen as comparable to human beings afflicted with scale disease.[18]

If we leave the questions of what, exactly, "impurity" is and what renders these particular things "impure" aside, one practical facet of impurity is made abundantly clear in the biblical text: all these sources of impurity have an *effect on their surroundings*. These sources of impurity transform the ritual status of persons and objects that touch them, and sometimes also of spaces into which they enter or in which they reside, in such a way that these objects, persons, and spaces themselves become impure. It is thus important to distinguish between the aforementioned sources of impurity and the animals that are listed as forbidden for consumption,[19] which are also referred to as "impure": unlike the former, the latter are not said to have any effect on the one who eats them or touches them (while they are still alive). Eating a rabbit, for instance, is a breach of a divine decree, and therefore a transgression, but it does not bring about ritual impurity; in contrast, carrying an animal carcass is by no means a transgression, but it does render one ritually impure.

The Priestly Code presents different sets of effects in respect to each of the impurity sources mentioned above:

I. *Dead Creatures:*
   - Animal carcasses render anyone who touches them or carries them impure for one day, as well as his or her garments. Purification is attained by washing in water.
   - Dead creeping or crawling insects render anyone who touches them impure for one day, as well as any object, food, or liquid into or onto which they fall. Purification (which is possible for persons and objects but not for foods and liquids) is attained by washing in water.
   - Human corpses render anyone and anything that touches them impure for *seven* days, as well as anyone and anything that shares the same confined space with them. Purification is attained by a multiphased ritual that includes washing in water and sprinkling with a mixture of water and the ashes of a red cow.

II. *Impure substances:*
   - Semen renders persons and objects that have physical contact with it (including both men and women after intercourse) impure for one day, and purification is attained by washing in water.
   - Persons who collect and handle the ashes of the red cow and the water into which it is mixed are impure for one day, as are their garments, and their purification is attained by washing in water.

III. *Men and women who are in a physical state that renders them impure:*
- Men and women with abnormal genital discharges and menstruating women render anything they sit, lie, or ride on impure, as well as anyone they touch, anything that touches them, and anyone that touches what they sat, rode, or lied on. All of those are made impure for one day and are purified by washing in water. Menstruating women also render men who have intercourse with them impure, and impurity contracted through this form of contact persists for seven days.
- The effects of parturient women and of persons with scale disease on their surroundings are not explicitly mentioned in the Priestly text. However, it is mentioned that parturient women are barred from the sanctuary and from the sancta, and that a person with scale disease is removed from the camp of Israel altogether.[20] This indicates that persons in these bodily conditions were taken to have some sort of deleterious effect on their surroundings.[21]

IV. *Afflicted objects.*
Anyone who enters a house afflicted with mildew is rendered impure for one day, as are the objects in this house. The effect of afflicted garments on those who come into contact with them is not mentioned.

As a rule, in the biblical scheme impurity can only be contracted from one of the sources mentioned above. That is to say, a person or object can only become impure as a result of *direct* contact with one of the sources of impurity, but not as a result of contact with one who has touched one of the sources. For example, if Jill is menstruating and Jack touches her, Jack becomes impure; but Jack has no effect on whoever touches him. However, there are three notable exceptions to this rule: (1) objects on which a person with genital discharge sat, lied, or rode convey impurity in the same manner as this person himself or herself;[22] (2) a man who had intercourse with a menstruating woman renders the litter he lies on impure;[23] (3) persons or objects that had contact with a corpse convey impurity to whatever and whomever they touch.[24] These exceptional three function as primary sources of impurity even though they contracted their impurity from another source. The power to convey impurity to others is manifested in the duration of the time of impurity: whereas whatever has the ability to convey impurity to others is impure for at least seven days, whatever contracted impurity but has no power to convey it further is impure for one day only. The question why specific sources of impurity convey impurity in some ways and others in other ways need not concern us here. What I would like to stress, however, is that ritual impurity is conceived and described in the Hebrew Bible as *a conduit through which one thing transforms another.*

This basic view of impurity as the deleterious effect of one of the sources mentioned above on a thing or a person that had contact with it remained at the foundation of the ritual system of purity and impurity as this system continued to develop in the Persian, Hellenistic, and Roman periods. Nevertheless, as extant rulings and accounts regarding purity from the postbiblical period clearly show, the Priestly purity code underwent considerable development and broadening by different interpretive communities during the first centuries before and after the turn of the common era, in the course of which early Jewish legislators not only sought to make this code more comprehensive and cohesive, but also put forth new notions regarding the ways in which impurity is transmitted and regarding its impact on its surroundings.[25] Since this study ventures to examine how the rabbis transformed the notions of purity and impurity, and attempts to retrace the principles and views behind the Mishnah's unique approach to this halakhic area, it is called for at this point to consider, albeit briefly, in which ways the Mishnah corresponds with earlier postbiblical modes of discourse on purity and impurity, and in which ways it presents something new and inimitable.

### Approaches to the Biblical Purity Code in the Qumran Scrolls and in Rabbinic Traditions

Up until the discovery and publication of the Qumran Scrolls throughout the second half of the twentieth century, scholars were for the most part in the dark when attempting to identify and reconstruct the principles of purity and impurity, and the practices that these principles generated, that were at play among the Jewish societies of the Second Temple period. Aside from occasional references to matters of purity and impurity in apocryphal books, in the writings of Josephus and Philo, and in the New Testament, the main source through which scholars tried to reconstruct the "purity world" of this period was the rabbinic corpus, the earliest components of which were compiled over a century after the destruction of the Temple in 70 C.E.[26] Since it is highly debatable to what extent practices and ideas described or referenced in rabbinic texts can be projected onto earlier periods, it is quite difficult to determine with certainty which of the elements of the rabbinic purity legislation are unique to the circles of the rabbis (or the protorabbis), and which of these elements reflect more widely accepted views and modes of conduct regarding purity and impurity that prevailed in different Jewish circles in the Second Temple period. However, the vast body of writings found in Qumran, in which the topic of purity and impurity is remarkably prevalent, allowed scholars over the last several decades to reconstruct a much fuller picture of the perceptions and practices of purity and impurity in early Jewish communities around the turn of the Common Era. Thanks to the extensive and thorough work done to recover and explain the purity legislation of the Qumran Scrolls, we are in a much better position to examine the rabbinic interpretive and legislative approaches to purity against the cultural and hermeneutic background in which these approaches emerged.

In what follows, I consider, very generally and very briefly, the central correspondences and divergences between the purity discourse in the Mishnah and the purity discourse in Qumran.[27] My purpose, to be sure, is not to compare the details of specific purity laws as they are presented in Qumranic or rabbinic writings: such systematic comparison is well beyond the scope and interest of this study, and can be found in several different studies dedicated mainly or exclusively to this purpose.[28] Rather, my purpose is to point out how the topic of purity and impurity is *approached* in these two corpora and through what perspectives it is being considered: what kind of interpretive and legislative moves vis-à-vis the biblical purity code are at play in these corpora; what, if anything, is added by them to the biblical scheme; and most importantly, what the focal points on which the discourse of purity and impurity is centered are. As I will argue, while Qumranic and rabbinic texts often display similar or even identical legislative moves, the lens through which the world of impurity is presented and discussed in these two corpora is fundamentally different.

The most notable similarity between the purity legislation in Qumran and in rabbinic literature lies in the interpretive method that clearly forms the infrastructure of both corpora, a method that Jacob Milgrom aptly titled "homogenization," that is, a systematic attempt to deduce the workings of one source of impurity from the workings of another source of impurity.[29] To take a simple example, the Priestly text never mentions explicitly in which way a woman who experiences a genital discharge is to purify herself after this discharge is over; it does mention, however, regarding other cases of bodily impurity, that the person in question must wash in water in order to be purified. Guided by a working assumption of overall congruity within the biblical system, both rabbinic texts and Qumranic texts take for granted that the prescribed form of purification for all sources of impurity, without exception, is immersion in water.[30] Similarly, both rabbinic and Qumranic texts indicate that the impurity of a person with scale disease, whose mode of transmission of impurity is not specified in the Priestly Code, is transmitted in the same ways as the impurity of persons with genital discharges.[31] It is difficult to determine whether these "homogenizing" readings are rooted in a common interpretive tradition or emerged independently in both corpora as a result of the application of a similar method, but such readings certainly stand out as part of the shared discourse of impurity in early Judaism.[32]

To be sure, the process of homogenization is not always applied to the same biblical texts and does not always yield identical results across the two corpora, and there are multiple differences in various details between Qumran laws and rabbinic laws. For example, whereas the rabbis establish congruity between the impurity of a person with scale disease and a corpse, and thus determine that an afflicted person renders the house into which he or she enters impure in the same way that a corpse renders the space in which it is housed impure, no such ruling regarding a person with scale disease can be found in Qumran.³³ On the other end, several Qumranic texts enhance the impurity of a man who has had a seminal emission and make it both longer and transferrable, like the impurity brought about by other genital discharges, whereas the rabbis regard this form of impurity as very minor and essentially without impact on its surroundings.³⁴ To take one last example, several Qumranic texts seem to suggest, at least according to some scholars, that the mixture of purifying water *(mei hattat)*, which according to the Priestly Code is used only in the case of corpse impurity, is to be used for other impurities as well, an idea that has no trace in rabbinic literature.³⁵ These few examples suffice to illustrate, I believe, that the enterprise of systematizing the biblical laws of purity and impurity so as to fill lacunae and to establish greater coherence among these laws was a common enterprise in early Judaism, even if it was applied by different interpretive communities in different ways and in different cases.

Neither the Qumranic nor the rabbinic purity legislation modifies or alters the Priestly list of impurity sources in any significant way, and both essentially remain bound by the biblical scheme that includes only dead creatures, persons with genital discharges or scale disease, certain impure substances, and afflicted houses or garments as sources of impurity. The one source of impurity that both of these corpora do effectively add to the list of sources of impurity is outsiders, which in the rabbinic corpus pertains to non-Jews,³⁶ and in the corpus of Qumran apparently includes both non-Jews and persons who are not members of the community.³⁷ This addition to the biblical list of sources of impurity in both corpora speaks to the prevalence of the notion of outsiders as contaminating in the Second Temple period,³⁸ and reflects the shared cultural heritage of both the creators of the Qumranic texts and the early rabbis. However, it should be noted that the rabbis, as I will discuss at length in the fifth chapter, make a point of distinguishing the impurity of Gentiles, which they consider to be only statutory, from the biblical forms of impurity and introduce the impurity of Gentiles through analogy to one of the existing forms of ritual purity (namely, the impurity of genital discharges).³⁹ In other words, the rabbis are careful to indicate that Gentiles can be considered sources of ritual impurity only insofar as they are subsumed under one of the established Priestly categories of impurity. In contrast, the use of the terms *pure* and *impure* in Qumranic texts is much more liberal than it is in rabbinic texts, and the Qumranic authors (much like other authors in the Second Temple period) are not hesitant to use the language of purity and impurity even when referring to matters beyond the Priestly Code of ritual impurity. The frequent use of themes of purity and impurity in discussions of sin and moral atrocity in Qumran led several scholars to the conclusion that in Qumran sin was considered a source of physical-ritual impurity, and that unlike in rabbinic literature, moral and ritual impurity were not distinguished from each other by Qumranic authors.⁴⁰ Here I tend to agree with Martha Himmelfarb,[41] who showed that the conflation of impurity and sin in Qumranic texts is mainly evocative and rhetorical, and should not be taken as a testament to a view that each sinner is also impure and each impure person is also a sinner.[42] Accordingly, I do not take sin or immorality to be a source of ritual impurity in and of itself in the legislation of Qumran, and do not see a significant discrepancy between Qumranic and rabbinic texts as far as the *sources* of impurity are concerned.[43]

The main discrepancy between the Qumranic purity legislation and the rabbinic purity legislation, which led various scholars to characterize the Qumranic system as much more stringent and harsh than the rabbinic system,[44] has to do not with the sources of impurity themselves but mainly with the question of what *qualifies* as one of these sources of impurity and what does not. In general, rabbinic legislation tends to impose various restrictions and limitations on what can "count" as a source of impurity and what can contract impurity, whereas the Qumranic approach is on the whole much more inclusive and does not engage in the subcategorizing and classifying of potential sources in the same way that the rabbis do. To take a few notable examples: the rabbis distinguish between different kinds of genital bleeding and determine that some sorts of blood constitute sources of impurity and some do not, whereas no such distinction is traceable in Qumranic texts;[45] the rabbis distinguish between objects and materials that can contract impurity and objects and materials that cannot, determining among other things that stones and objects that are connected to the ground are not susceptible to impurity, whereas the Qumranic legislation mentions both stone objects and houses as requiring purification;[46] the rabbis do not consider a dead fetus to be a source of impurity as long as it is in its mother's womb, whereas in Qumran a dead fetus is regarded like any other corpse;[47] and many other similar examples can be found. As Vered Noam noted, the difference between the Qumranic approach and the rabbinic approach should not be understood in terms of stringency and leniency, but rather in terms of more straightforward and inclusive readings of the biblical texts as opposed to more restrictive and scrutinizing readings of these texts.[48] To a great extent, my analysis in this book is concerned exactly with those restrictive readings introduced by the rabbis, and with the principles that guided them when excluding certain elements from the impurity system and including others. These restrictive principles have evidently not been at play in the work of earlier interpreters.

While the rabbinic purity legislation is often viewed as more "lenient" than the Qumranic legislation in terms of what constitutes a source of impurity, the rabbinic system is far more "stringent" as far as modes of *transmission* of impurity are concerned. That is to say, while in the rabbinic system fewer objects or persons can potentially function as sources of impurity, whatever does function as a source of impurity is much more potent in its impact on its environment than it is in the

Qumranic system. As I will show in what follows, the Mishnah introduces new and unprecedented principles regarding the ways in which impurity is conveyed from the source to other people and things, ultimately suggesting that impurity can be contracted not only through direct contact with a source of impurity but also through various modes of *indirect* contact with a source of impurity. These new modes of transmission of impurity speak to the more general perspective of the rabbis on the presence and impact of impurity, which focuses not only on the source but also and perhaps especially on those who knowingly or unknowingly contract its impurity. It is in this perspective, I will propose, that the mishnaic purity discourse most radically diverges from the Qumranic discourse, and for that matter also from the biblical discourse.

## *The Extreme Transferability of Impurity in the Mishnah*

The biblical impurity system essentially consists of two kinds of participants: primary sources of impurity, in which impurity is either an intrinsic quality or a result of a certain bodily condition, and secondary sources of impurity, which contracted impurity from primary sources. Since the sources of impurity in the Priestly Code are quite limited in number, and their effect normally extends only to whatever has direct contact with them, in the picture that emerges from the Priestly Code impurity generally transpires as a *noticeable event*. Of course, some events that bring about impurity are an inseparable and even recurring part of life (birth, death, menstruation, seminal emission), whereas others are more rare and crisis-like (scale disease, abnormal genital discharges); but all these events are discernible and traceable to a particular point in time. Whoever is impure, whether on account of experiencing the bodily conditions mentioned above or on account of having direct contact with a source of impurity, is presumably *aware* of whatever brought about this impurity and is capable of saying at what point, more or less, this impurity transpired. As common and natural as impurity may be in the world of the Hebrew Bible, it is restricted to very specific factors and to those in their immediate vicinity.[49] Generally speaking, the basic view of the transpiration of impurity as a noticeable event, which impacts only the impure persons themselves and those in direct contact with them, is also dominant in the writings of Qumran. The Qumranic purity legislation focuses mainly on the ways in which impure persons and persons undergoing purification should take measures to distance themselves actively from the community, from sacred areas, from communal food, and so forth,[50] and on their obligation to profess gratitude and humility when eventually purified.[51]

The picture in the mishnaic discourse is notably different. While the Mishnah dedicates considerable attention to questions of the diagnosis of impurity and to processes of purification, it does not introduce the concern with impurity as restricted only to the sources of impurity themselves or to those who come into direct contact with them, but rather presents it as the daily and ongoing concern of *everyone,* even of persons who are not currently impure or known to have had contact with a source of impurity. In other words, impurity in the Mishnah is approached not only as a noticeable event, but also, and perhaps much more prominently, as *an ongoing reality.*

This approach to impurity, which marks the mishnaic discourse of purity and impurity as significantly different from what preceded it, is deeply connected to several conceptual developments introduced in the Mishnah, which greatly increased the transferability of impurity, and thereby made it a much more pervasive and all-encompassing reality. While some of these conceptual developments can be traced back, in a nascent form, to the Second Temple period, the cumulative effect of all these developments taken together is a substantial expansion of the realm of impurity and the transformation of impurity into an ever-present factor in the rabbinic construction of everyday life. In what follows, I will examine three central manifestations of the increased transferability of impurity in rabbinic legislation: the graded system of impurity, principles of duplication of impurity, and expansion of biblical modes of transmission of impurity.

*The Graded System of Impurity.* As I mentioned, in the Priestly Code the only participants in the impurity system, apart from the primary sources of impurity, are those who have direct contact with these primary sources. In contrast, in the mishnaic system even persons and objects several times removed from the source can be affected in terms of impurity. For the rabbis, impurity does not end with whatever had direct contact with the source. Rather, even an item that did not touch the source directly but only touched something that touched the source (or even only something that touched something that touched the source) is affected by the source's impurity, albeit in an attenuated manner. In order to understand this admittedly complex principle, which has no parallel in other codes of impurity,[52] it is necessary to delve for a moment into the rabbinic understanding of the concept of impurity or, more accurately, into the rabbinic understanding of *what is being transmitted* from one entity to another in the course of the contraction of impurity.

The effect of impurity is depicted in the Mishnah in a highly physical or even mechanical manner, as if by a transmission of substance from one entity (human or nonhuman) to another entity through contact. The verb that is most commonly coupled with the word *tum'a* (impurity) in the Mishnah is *qbl* (to receive), the same verb used to describe, for instance, the pouring of liquid from one receptacle to the other, as if to suggest that the impure substance A transmits something to B.[53] This "something" that is being transmitted is, in effect, the *ability to make other things impure:* in the Mishnah, to say that A makes B impure is to say that A gives B the capacity to affect C. Accordingly, the rabbis distinguish between making something ritually impure *(letamē)* and making something ritually disqualified *(lifsol)*: to make something impure is to invest it with the ability to make others impure; to make something disqualified is only to prohibit this thing from being used for sacred purposes.⁵⁴ For instance, an *impure* barrel of wine will make whatever touches it and whoever drinks from it impure, whereas a *disqualified* barrel of wine cannot be used in the sacral realm (that is, it cannot be given to the priests) but does not make others impure.

In the biblical impurity system, the chain of impurity almost always ends with B, the thing that contracted impurity directly from the source. The common paradigm is that when the source of impurity A (for example, a menstruating woman) touches another person or object B (for example, her husband), then B becomes impure in an attenuated manner, that is, only for one day. There is no indication that B can convey impurity to anything else, and it is actually hard to think what repercussions such doubly attenuated impurity would have for whatever touched B.⁵⁵ In contrast, in the Mishnah the chain of impurity does not end with B, which had direct contact with the source, but continues to move further in a graduated manner in such a way that even an item that is five times removed from the source is affected by its impurity in a minor form. Thus, if A is the primary source of impurity, B touched A, C touched B, D touched C, E touched D, and F touched E, F is still affected by A in terms of impurity. Let us illustrate this with a hypothetical example:

1. Jill (A) is menstruating; when she touches Jack (B), Jack becomes impure in the once-removed degree (in rabbinic terms, Jack is "first" of impurity, whereas Jill, the primary source, is a "father" of impurity).
2. Jack (B) touches Josh (C); Josh is now impure in the twice-removed degree (in rabbinic terms, he is "second" of impurity).
3. Josh (C) touches a heave-offering of oil (D); the oil becomes impure in the thrice-removed degree (it is "third of impurity").
4. The oil (D) is poured on a meal-offering designated for the Temple (E); the meal-offering becomes "fourth of impurity."
5. A piece of the meal-offering (E) falls into a container with purifying water (F); the water is now "fifth of impurity."

As this example illustrates, once the item in question is twice-removed from the source or more, its impact on other items becomes increasingly limited, and is restricted to sacred articles that are particularly vulnerable to impurity: a "second" of impurity can only affect heave-offerings *(terumah)*, holy articles *(qodesh)*, and purifying water *(mei hattat)*; a "third" of impurity can only affect holy articles and purifying water; and a "fourth" of impurity can only affect purifying water.⁵⁶ Nevertheless, this graded system indicates that for the rabbis of the Mishnah, the "contagious" effect of impurity is not limited to direct contact with the source, but is seen as continuing to travel well beyond it.

The extension of the effect of impurity beyond immediate contact with the source incorporates a whole new array of participants into the rabbinic impurity system. The realm of impurity is no longer confined to the sources of impurity and to objects and persons in their immediate vicinity, but consists of a number of concentric circles. At the center stands the primary source of impurity ("the father" in rabbinic terminology); at the circle that surrounds it stand persons and objects that had direct contact with the source ("first of impurity"); at the next circle stand those that had contact with those who had contact with the source of impurity ("second of impurity"), and so forth. The farther the circle from the center, the less likely the contraction of impurity is to be perceived as a noticeable event by a person in that circle: for instance, while a person would presumably be aware that he touched a menstruating woman, a priest is hardly likely to be aware that the person who brought him a heave-offering touched a menstruating woman, and thus that the heave-offering too is impure.

Whereas the graded system of impurity is guided by the view that an object or person can be affected by the source of impurity in an attenuated manner even without having direct contact with it, other principles of transmission of impurity in the rabbinic system put forth the notion that indirect contact with a source of impurity can sometimes generate the *same* degree of impurity as direct contact. The Mishnah enhances the transferability of impurity to include forms of indirect contact in two ways: first, by suggesting that in some instances impurity can be "duplicated" in such a way that even something twice-removed from the source contracts impurity as if it touched the source itself; and second, by notably expanding the biblical modes of conveyance of impurity. Whereas the second development cannot be traced in Qumranic writings and seems to be uniquely rabbinic, the first development apparently has its roots in the shared purity discourse of the Second Temple period, and its echoes can be found in Qumranic legislation. I therefore address the notion of "duplication" of impurity first, and then turn to the expansion of biblical categories of contact.

*Duplication of Impurity.* (1) *Liquids.* A central principle in the rabbinic system of purity and impurity is that liquids have the power to duplicate impurity ad infinitum. That is to say, if impure liquids have contact with any object, they make this object impure as if it had direct contact with the source that initially made the liquids impure. To illustrate this simply, if Jill (A) touches Jack (B) while Jack's hands are wet, and Jack then touches a loaf of bread (C) with his wet hands, the loaf of bread (C) becomes impure as if Jill (A) herself touched this loaf of bread. This unique quality of liquids is presented in several rabbinic passages with the cryptic idiom "those that made you impure did not make me impure, but you made me impure" *(metam'ekha lo tim'uni ve-ata timetani).*[57] In this idiom, the

*— cheese = Kosher but also (activators*
*— no contact with impure liquid (impurity)*

object that contracted impurity (in the example suggested above, the loaf) is depicted as complaining to the mediating liquid about the absurdity of the situation: while the source of impurity A (in this case, Jill), which made the liquid (the moisture on Jack's hands) impure, could not have made C (the loaf) impure on its own, the liquid that contracted impurity from A and transmitted it to C affected C as if C had contact with A itself.[58]

The same principle, as Joseph Baumgarten showed,[59] is traceable also in the Qumranic legislation: the Temple Scroll points out that any moist stains of wine or oil in the house of the dead must be scraped off, and the reason for this is evidently that these stains can convey corpse impurity to whoever touches them even after the house itself had been purified.[60] The "duplicating" force of liquids to convey impurity is probably also at play in the ruling that newly admitted members to the community are prohibited from touching communal liquids for two whole years (whereas they are allowed to touch communal food after only one year).[61] Both rabbinic and Qumranic texts, then, point to what seems to have been an established view in early Judaism,[62] according to which liquids serve as transmitters that create a connection between two things that otherwise cannot affect each other in terms of impurity.[63]

(ii) *Food.* Another new mode of transmission of impurity that we find in the Mishnah, in which impurity is "duplicated" in such a way that a person can be affected by a source of impurity without having direct contact with it, is the consumption of impure food (to be clear, not nonkosher food but rather kosher food that had contact with a source of impurity). The rabbinic principle is that one who consumes impure foods or drinks becomes as impure as the food or drink she consumed: for example, if a loaf of bread was touched by a menstruating woman, the person who then eats this bread becomes impure as if *she* touched the menstruating woman.[64]

The very notion that impure food—that is, food that itself contracted impurity from another substance—can convey impurity to the one who eats it is completely unprecedented in the Priestly Code. There are, however, several indications that this notion was already accepted in certain Jewish circles during the Second Temple period. Most famously, Jesus' dispute with the Pharisees on the washing of hands in Mark 7:1–23 seems to suggest that the Pharisees were concerned with the possibility that if they touched their food with impure hands they would render it impure and thus render themselves impure, as we can infer from Jesus' response, "There is nothing outside a person which by going into him can defile him."[65] In addition, while we do not find any explicit statements in Qumranic literature regarding the result of the consumption of impure foods, we do find warnings that impure persons must be careful not to engage with produce or communal food,[66] and that one must not eat any food touched by an impure person.[67] Such warnings do indicate, although not conclusively, that the view that impure foods are capable of conveying impurity to those who consume them was not limited to rabbinic or protorabbinic circles.

As the notions of the duplication of impurity through food and through liquids show, the expansion of biblical modes of transmission of impurity to include also indirect forms of contact evidently had its roots in the shared purity discourse of the Second Temple period. However, in the rabbinic legislation this nascent idea significantly developed and became much more dominant within the system as a whole. The increased prominence of the notion of the duplication of impurity in the Mishnah is especially illustrated through the rabbinic rulings regarding one form of duplication of impurity that cannot be traced outside the Mishnah, duplication that takes effect specifically when inanimate objects come into contact with corpse impurity.

(iii) *Inanimate objects and corpse impurity.* According to biblical law, every object or person that touches a corpse or shares a space with one becomes impure for seven days and can convey impurity further to whatever touches this object or person, which will in turn be impure for one day. For example, if a corpse is placed on a bed, the bed on which it lies will be impure for seven days, and if Jill then touches this bed, Jill will be impure for one day. The rabbis, however, rule that inanimate objects that touch a corpse *become like the corpse itself,* and whatever touches *them* will become impure for seven days and make whatever touches this object or person impure for one day.[68] In the rabbinic scheme, then, the bed on which the corpse lies becomes like the corpse itself: if Jill touches the bed, she will become impure for seven days, and if Jill touches Jack, he will become impure for one day (whereas in the biblical scheme Jack would not be affected at all). Furthermore, the rabbis rule that if an inanimate object touches something that has had contact with a corpse—that is, something which is impure for seven days—the inanimate object itself becomes impure for seven days, making whatever touches it impure for one day. To return to our example, if Jill touched the bed on which a corpse was placed, Jill becomes impure for seven days; if Jill then touches a cup, the cup becomes impure for seven days, like Jill; and if Jack then touches the cup, he becomes impure for one day. This means that even something or someone three times removed from a corpse can contract the same degree of impurity as something or someone that touched it directly.[69]

These three principles of duplication of impurity, whether they originated in the rabbinic system or were inherited from earlier interpretive traditions, amount to a significant expansion of the realm and repercussions of impurity. If impurity can be contracted not only directly from the source but also, in certain settings, from something that had contact with the source, then the presence of impurity in the world becomes much more pervasive and, at the same time, can much more easily escape one's consciousness: while one is likely to know if one touched an impure person, one is much less likely to know if one touched something that was touched by an impure person. This pervasiveness of impurity and its enhanced transferability in the mishnaic impurity system thus lead to a new perspective on impurity, at the center of which stand not the primary sources of impurity, but those who are likely to contract it.

The enhanced transferability of impurity in the Mishnah is manifested not only through the mechanisms of the duplication of impurity, some of which may date back to earlier traditions, but also in the construction of new modes of contraction of impurity that notably expand the Priestly paradigms of impurity transmission. These new modes of transmission, which to the best of my knowledge have no precedent in biblical or postbiblical literature, substantially increase the possibility of an inadvertent and unaware contraction of impurity, thus further increasing the pervasiveness of impurity in everyday encounters and experiences.

*The Expansion of Biblical Modes of Impurity Transmission.* (i) *Expansion of the biblical "tent."* According to the Priestly Code, the human corpse is the only source of impurity that conveys impurity not only to whomever touches or carries it, but also to everyone and everything that shares the same "tent" with it.[70] While the biblical verse seems to indicate that corpse impurity is conveyed only when one shares a specific confined space with the dead, the rabbis develop and expand the category of "tent" to include every kind of shared overhang (*ahel,* from the noun *ohel,* "tent") with the dead. According to the Mishnah, everything and everyone that is (1) situated under the same roof as a corpse, (2) situated under a corpse so that the corpse overshadows it, or (3) situated above a corpse so that it overshadows the corpse is deemed impure.[71] In this way, the rabbinic perception of overhang, which turns the biblical tent into a wholly abstract category, actually turns almost every kind of copresence with the dead into a form of physical contact. For instance, a person who stands under the shadow of a tree that also shadows a graveyard is rendered impure, even though she herself is completely outside the graveyard. The result of this rabbinic innovation is that corpse impurity becomes wildly more present in the world of the everyday: corpse impurity is no longer only the concern of the immediate relatives of the dead or those who share the same habitation with it, but is also the concern of the passersby who happen to stumble upon a dead body on the side of the road (which was not uncommon in the ancient world) or to pass next to a grave, even without touching it.[72]

(ii) *"Shift" impurity.* Apart from the case of corpse impurity, in which impurity is also conveyed through shared space, there is only one way in which impurity can be conveyed in the biblical scheme, namely, through direct physical contact.[73] The rabbis, however, introduce a new mode of impurity contraction that does not involve direct contact, which they call "shift" *(heset).* The category of shift pertains to any setting in which the source of impurity causes something else to move from its place, even without direct contact.⁷⁴ The quintessential example of this is a case in which a man with genital discharge is placed on one side of a scale and foods and liquids are placed on the other side of the scale: if the man's weight tips the scale and causes the foods and liquids to move, they are rendered impure.⁷⁵ As several passages in tractate *Zavim* powerfully portray, the meaning of this form of contraction is that almost every daily activity in which a pure person and an impure person both partake, even without touching each other, can cause the pure person to contract impurity. To take just two examples:

> If a man with genital discharge and a pure man sat together in a boat or a raft, or rode an animal together, even though their clothes do not touch—[the clothes of the pure person] are impure on account of treading (*teme'in midras*, that is, impure as if the impure person physically trod on them).
> If they both sat on a beam, on a bench, on a railing of a bed, or on a pole while those are wobbly, if they climbed a tree that is unsteady . . . [the pure one's clothes] are impure. (M. Zavim 3.1)

> R. Yehoshua says: If a menstruating woman sat with a pure woman in the same bed—the cap at the top of [the pure woman's] head is impure on account of treading.
> If she sat in a boat, the items at the top of the mast are impure on account of treading. (M. Zavim 4.1)

As these passages make clear, the notion of impurity contraction through shift makes the very physical presence of impure persons so powerful that the repercussions of indirect contact with them are identical to the repercussions of direct contact. In other words, the concept of shift-impurity inscribes everyday activities and interactions with a heightened potential of impurity: one need not only be careful whom one touches, but even with whom one sits, works, plays, rides, and so forth.

(iii) *Bodily fluids*. While the biblical text makes it clear that persons with genital discharges are impure as such, and that mere contact with the external surface of their bodies suffices to convey impurity, it also implies that the most immediate source of impurity in these cases is the genital discharge itself. The rule that whatever the person with genital discharge sits, lies, or rides on is as impure as the person herself strongly suggests that the genital emissions were seen as the actual cause of impurity.⁷⁶ The rabbis make this point explicit, determining that menstrual blood and abnormal genital emissions convey the same kind of impurity as the persons who emitted them, but they also maintain that the innocuous bodily fluids of impure persons, namely, their urine and saliva, convey the exact kind of impurity as the impure persons themselves.⁷⁷ This idea is not entirely without biblical precedent, since the Priestly Code does mention that if a person with genital discharge spits on another person, the other person becomes impure.⁷⁸ But whereas the Priestly text seems to envision spitting as a form of direct contact with the impure person, the Mishnah maintains that even if one encounters the bodily fluids of an impure person in the street, and the impure person him- or herself is nowhere in sight, contact with these fluids conveys impurity. Unlike menstrual blood and genital discharges, saliva and urine are commonly found in the public domain. Since it is impossible to trace the original "owner" of these fluids and to discern whether he or she was pure or impure, the marketplace and the street are viewed in the Mishnah as potentially laden with impurity, as we will see in greater detail below.

The extreme transferability of impurity in the Mishnah, which is expressed in the graded system of impurity, in the principles of "duplication," and in the expansion of biblical modes of transmission, generates a radically new perspective on purity and impurity and their place in everyday life. This perspective, which is almost completely absent both from the Priestly Code and from the writings of Qumran, is that of the "innocent passerby," that is, of a person whose body or possessions might contract impurity as a result of various daily interactions and encounters without his or her even being aware of it. The emergence of this new perspective in the discourse of purity and impurity, at the center of which stands not the unusual or noteworthy situation of the source of impurity but the person going about his or her most quotidian activities, constructs the mishnaic discourse of purity and impurity as fundamentally different from what preceded it.

In view of the various principles presented above, it becomes clear that in the Mishnah, unlike in the Priestly Code or in Qumran, the contraction of impurity is construed as a *default*. The effect of impurity in its rabbinic construction is so far-reaching, and the inadvertent contraction of impurity so probable, that the management of impurity becomes an ongoing daily task for anyone who wishes to remain pure. The concern with impurity, as I will now turn to show, thus profoundly shapes the very experience of everyday life in the mishnaic discourse.

## MAPPING THE EVERYDAY AS A REALM OF IMPURITY

Above I presented a number of prerabbinic and rabbinic principles that significantly increase the transferability of impurity, thus transforming the biblical picture in which impurity is confined in its scope and limited in its repercussions to a picture in which impurity is ubiquitous and widely effective. In what follows, I will demonstrate the extent to which this new picture of impurity shapes the mishnaic depiction of everyday encounters and activities, in such a way that impurity is constructed as an all-pervasive presence and a perpetual concern. As I will suggest, it is against this picture of impurity as ever-present and as a defining component of one's daily life that we can begin to understand how the way in which one manages one's body and one's possessions in terms of impurity became, for the rabbis, a critical site for reflections on and construction of one's relations with the material world and with oneself.

Before proceeding, however, I wish to make clear that by referring to a "concern" regarding impurity, I am not implying in any way that the rabbis or their contemporaries were *afraid* of impurity. Practically speaking, there is no danger in impurity: if one contracts it, one simply performs the ritual instructions for purification, which for the most part include no more than a quick visit to an immersion-pool. In general, I believe that the category of fear is entirely inappropriate for explaining ancient purity systems. As Robert Parker astutely put it, impurity "is not a product of the ill-focused terror that permanently invests the savage mind, because that terror is an invention of nineteenth-century anthropology."[79] Nevertheless, I find it self-evident that the contraction of impurity was seen by the rabbis as disadvantageous and undesirable, and that the effect of impurity was seen as a detrimental one, although by no means as acutely dangerous. It is difficult to know what, if any, the practical repercussions of a status of impurity in the tannaitic period were; but whether or not a ritual status of impurity actually meant exclusion from certain activities or places, it is clear that the concept of impurity served for the rabbis as a marker of harmful and unwanted effect. Concern with impurity is not tantamount to panic about impurity; rather, it is simply a state of being constantly conscious of the prospect of contracting impurity and of trying to avoid it to the best of one's ability, while still considering it to be, at times, unavoidable. This is essentially the state of mind depicted in the Mishnah.

### Doubtful Impurity: The Certainty of Uncertainty

The extreme transferability of impurity as it was construed in the rabbinic system inscribes the entire lived world with the potential presence of impurity. In the rabbis' view, every random object that was found on a street corner could have been touched by an impure person, thus becoming impure and thus acquiring the ability to further transmit impurity to anyone and anything that touches it. Every person one comes across—unless specifically known to be scrupulous in the observance of purity—could be a source of impurity that would make whatever she touches impure. For the rabbis, then, to interact with the human and material world was to risk the chance of contracting impurity.[80] Nowhere is the overall perception of the human and material environment as impure by default more explicit than in tractate *Tohorot* of the Mishnah, which sets guidelines for those who attempt to maintain a reasonable level of purity (presumably, mainly in order to have their meals in a state of ritual purity) within an overall impure world.[81] The tractate is concerned with various subtopics that pertain to this general theme, and its main portion addresses the topic of doubtful impurity *(safeq tum'a)*, that is, determining the ritual status of someone or something that could have been in contact with a source of impurity, but cannot be said to have had such contact with certainty.

As a rule, the determination of ritual status—that is, the discernment of something or someone as pure or impure—is performed through a tracing of the history of the object or person in question.[82] Simply put, it is necessary to determine with what this person or object had contact since the last time the person or object was known to be pure, as well as to determine whether the things or persons with which the person or object had contact were themselves pure or impure. The assumption in tractate *Tohorot,* however, is that most of the time tracing this history in full is impossible. Let us suppose that Jill was walking in the street and happened to stumble over a rug that someone had left there. According to the mishnaic scheme of transferability, if the rug was impure (for instance, if it was made impure by a corpse or was trodden on by a menstruating woman) and Jill had direct physical contact with it, Jill also becomes impure. But how can it be known if the rug was impure? To answer this question one would have to trace every single person who happened to touch the rug since it was made, which is of course impossible. In other cases, it can be known for sure whether the object or person in question is pure or impure, but it cannot be said with certainty whether contact indeed took place or not. For instance, the Mishnah mentions a case in which a person came across two dead creatures, a dead creeping-crawling creature (for example, a lizard), which is a source of impurity, and a dead frog, which is not impure. This person knows for sure that he touched one of them, but does not know which one he touched, and thus does not know whether he contracted impurity or not.[83]

Through the many examples that the Mishnah provides for such cases of doubt, it portrays the world as pervaded with impurity. To paraphrase Murphy's Law, the underlying mishnaic assumption is that everything that can become impure *will* become impure. For example, the mishnaic rule is that if one lost an article and found it the next day, this article is automatically rendered impure: the night that it spent away from its rightful owner is presumed to have entailed contact with a source of impurity.[84] Other passages in the tractate state even more pronouncedly that objects that have been left unattended, even for a short duration of time, can be assumed to have been touched by people in a state of impurity, and thus to have contracted impurity from them. For example:

> If a potter left his pottery-bowls and went down to drink—the inner ones are pure, and the outer ones are impure.[85]

> If one leaves artisans inside his home, the house is impure, the words of R. Meir. And the Sages say: [It is impure] up to the place where [the artisans] can reach with their hands and touch.[86]

In the first passage, the Mishnah describes a scene in which a potter, whose merchandise is lined up in rows against a wall, leaves his merchandise for a short time to get a drink. The rule here is that the outer pottery articles, that is, the ones farthest away from the wall and closest to the road, must have been touched (advertently or inadvertently) by passersby, and have thus become impure.[87] Two assumptions guide this ruling: first, that whatever is left unattended will be touched by someone; and second, that this someone is likely to be impure. Similarly, in the second passage R. Meir and the Sages are in dispute regarding a case in which one leaves artisans unattended in one's home. Whereas R. Meir believes that the artisans will touch everything in the house, and thus every item in the house is to be rendered impure after they leave,[88] the Sages maintain that they will only touch what is in their immediate vicinity. Here too, however, both R. Meir and the Sages share the premise that whatever is left unattended is touched, and whatever is touched becomes impure.

In addition, the assumption in the Mishnah is that every person one comes across, unless publicly known to be stringent in the observance of purity, is potentially impure, and thus contact with this person makes one impure by default. Guided by this assumption, the Mishnah describes the following scene:

> If one sat in the public domain, and another person came and trod on his garments, or [the other person] spat and he touched the spittle, on account of [him touching] this spittle they burn the heave-offering, and in regard to his garments, they follow the majority.[89]

In this scene, Jack (who is presumably pure) is sitting in the public domain when Josh, a man whom Jack probably does not know, comes and treads on Jack's cloak or spits in Jack's vicinity. If Josh happens to be a person with genital discharge or scale disease or a Gentile, then every garment on which he treads and everything that touches his saliva immediately becomes impure. While it cannot be known whether Josh is any of these things, the default option is that he was indeed impure and had transmitted this impurity further to Jack. The consequence is that if Jack had contact with Josh's spittle, Jack will be rendered impure in such a way that he will disqualify a heave-offering if he touches it, and it will have to be incinerated. As for Jack's garments, here the Mishnah is more lenient and suggests that, instead of automatically rendering the garments impure, it will be considered whether most of the people in this specific place are usually pure or impure. The Mishnah thus creates a picture of daily human interactions, even of the most random and mundane kind, as inherently defined by the risk of contracting impurity.

An especially pronounced example for this view of the lived world as pervaded with impurity can be found in the following passage of the Mishnah:

> If there is one mentally inept woman *(shotah)* in a town, or a Gentile woman, or a Kuthian[90] woman—all the spittles in this town are impure.[91]

As I have mentioned, the saliva of an impure person is itself a source of impurity. The most commonly encountered impure person in the mishnaic system is a menstruating woman (since unlike other forms of impurity that depend on abnormal bodily states, menstruation occurs on a regular basis), and the overall assumption is that Jewish menstruating women are aware of their status and are careful not to convey their impurity to others. Accordingly, they will be careful not to spit in public or at least to conceal their spittle, lest other people touch it and contract impurity.[92] However, if in a certain town there is a woman who is not mentally capable of being careful in such a way or a woman who is otherwise considered to be constantly impure and not to be careful about it,[93] any spittle found in this town potentially belongs to this woman and is thus potentially impure. Needless to say, in the ancient world spitting in the public domain was an ordinary thing,[94] and the streets of the town were always replete with spittle. This passage paints a forceful picture of a world in which it is not only a direct encounter with people or objects that harbors the risk of impurity, but even merely walking in the street exposes one to impurity. This is closely related, as Charlotte Fonrobert observed, to the place of fluids, and particularly bodily fluids, in the rabbinic system of impurity.[95] The very fact that saliva and urine, two substances that are commonly found in the public domain, have the same power to make something or someone impure that their original "owner" has marks the marketplace and the street as potentially laden with impurity, and defines one's very interaction with space—even if this space does not entail actual people or objects—as noxious in terms of impurity.

## Maintaining Purity within a World of Impurity

As I hope to have illustrated through the examples above, impurity in the Mishnah is depicted as an ineluctable reality. Not only does impurity potentially lurk everywhere, but it is also highly difficult to discern whether one actually contracted it or not, and thus one is prone to be almost always in a state of doubtful impurity. The mishnaic premise that "everything that can become impure will become impure" makes the task of maintaining oneself and one's possessions in a state of purity throughout one's daily interactions and activities seem almost impossible. Nevertheless, maintaining oneself and one's possessions in a state of purity is unquestionably assumed to be the task of the mishnaic subject. That is to say, while the rabbis of the Mishnah create a world in which impurity is the default, they also direct their text to an idealized agent (real or imagined) who operates in this world with the purpose of avoiding impurity to the best of his abilities.[96] To be sure, the Mishnah makes abundantly clear that a state of ritual purity can by no means be a perpetual one, but is rather always a temporary and transient state. By the mere fact of being in a physical body and of engaging with the material world, one contracts impurity, purifies oneself, and before long contracts impurity again, in an unending cyclical process. But it is nonetheless the mishnaic subject's responsibility to take measures to purify oneself after having contracted impurity, and to try to maintain this state of purity for a certain duration of time, at least for the purpose of engaging in particular activities, which in the Mishnah have mostly to do with the preparation and consumption of food.

Here a short digression is in order so as to contest a common view according to which, in the setting of the Mishnah, impurity is completely inconsequential throughout one's everyday life, since the only time in which impurity has any repercussions is when one is approaching the sanctuary or handling holy articles.[97] According to this view all the intricate considerations of impurity and doubtful impurity throughout daily interactions and spaces that we have seen pertain only to priests, or at most to pilgrims in the vicinity of the Temple. This, however, is not commensurate with the rhetoric of the Mishnah nor with the scenarios it discusses, which assume an overarching commitment to purity in nonconsecrated times, in nonconsecrated places, and in regard to nonconsecrated objects. While the Mishnah acknowledges that not everyone is or can be committed to this high standard of purity, it does posit an idealized subject who is strongly defined by his commitment to this standard.[98]

The view that impurity is only consequential in the vicinity of the Temple and the sancta is a long-standing one in the Jewish tradition,[99] and was most famously and influentially articulated by Moses Maimonides, who contended that "all that is written in the Torah and in the traditions [*divrei qabala,* that is, in rabbinic literature] regarding the laws of impurities and purities does not concern anything except for the Temple and its holy articles and heave-offerings and tithes."[100] The roots of this prevalent view are in the fact that according to the Hebrew Bible, the only realm in which impurity is *proscribed* is that of the sanctuary and the sancta.[101] However, there is no reason to assume, even in the biblical context, that if impurity is explicitly prohibited only in the context of the sanctuary and the holies, it is overlooked everywhere else.[102] The expectation that those who have become impure will purify themselves as soon as they can is made abundantly clear in various Priestly passages, without any suggestion that such purification is necessary only for the priests or only for those approaching the sanctuary.[103] Furthermore, it is stressed that anyone who does not take measures to purify himself or herself in due time commits a transgression,[104] regardless of whether he or she approached the sanctuary or not. The Priestly rhetoric leaves little room for doubt that constant striving toward ritual purity was expected of all the Israelites at all times, needing no further justification other than the all-encompassing requirement to be holy.[105]

While we have no way of knowing whether, to what extent, and by whom, if at all, ritual purity was observed in biblical times, it is quite evident that in the Second Temple period ritual purity was observed in everyday life, beyond the precinct of the Temple, and by nonpriests. While the ubiquity of the observance of ritual purity is debatable, the literary and archeological evidence from this period strongly suggest that such observance was not restricted to festival times or to the Temple area.[106] In an article that has become a classic, Gedalyahu Alon showed that in Second Temple literature we find persistent views according to which daily practices of religious significance must be conducted in a state of ritual purity.[107] This includes not only activities such as prayer and reading of the Torah,[108] but also, and most notably, the consumption of nonconsecrated foodstuffs *(hullin)*. Whereas in the Hebrew Bible the only restriction on the consumption of food in a state of impurity pertains to priests who eat holy foods,[109] a large number of Second Temple sources point to a lay custom of eating ordinary food in a state of ritual purity. The literary evidence for this practice brought forth by Alon is strongly supported by the Qumran Scrolls, which are unequivocal that the members of the community eat all daily meals in a state of ritual purity.[110] Moreover, as Jacob Milgrom showed, it seems that in the Qumranic legislation an impure person is prohibited from eating *anything at all* during his or her first day in a state of impurity (that is, before performing a preliminary rite of purification).[111] Thus, in the writings of Qumran "purity" in its most basic sense is purity that allows one to consume ordinary food.

As more recent scholarship has shown, the literary evidence for the custom of eating ordinary food in a state of purity is corroborated by archeological findings, and especially by the large number of stone vessels from the Second Temple and mishnaic periods found in various areas in Palestine. Since stone vessels were considered to be "impurity-proof," this was the material of choice for making utensils that were to be used in settings in which purity had to be maintained. It is not surprising that many remains of stone vessels were found in the vicinity of the Temple Mount in Jerusalem, but such vessels were also found in abundance in other parts of the country, especially in the Galilee.[112]

The Mishnah seems, in this respect, to be in keeping with evidence from the Second Temple period, and it does not suggest in any way that the pursuit of purity is restricted to the priests or to those about to approach the Temple.[113] As we have seen and will continue to see throughout this book, in the Mishnah considerations of purity guide one through the most quotidian aspects of life.[114] It is hardly clear why the rabbis would bother to elaborate on the ways in which household furniture such as commodes and beds contract impurity,[115] or on the ways in which fish, which cannot be brought to the Temple or given to the priests as a heave-offering, contract impurity,[116] if impurity is only of consequence for priests or in the vicinity of the Temple during festival times. By and large the assumption in the Mishnah, as it is in Second Temple literature, is that people strive (or should strive) to maintain themselves and their possessions in a state of purity at all times, to the limited extent that this is possible. Furthermore, in most of the legal discussions of the Mishnah the rabbis operate with the premise that nonconsecrated food is ideally handled, prepared, and consumed in a state of ritual purity.[117] Indeed, unless specified otherwise, the appellation "pure" in the Mishnah refers to the level of purity required to consume nonconsecrated food.[118]

Given that ritual purity is assumed to be a desirable and even expected goal of the mishnaic subject, the question arises of whether and how maintaining a state of ritual purity is even tenable in the conditions I described above, namely, in a world in which the transferability of impurity is so great and its incidence so ubiquitous that every person and every object is assumed to be impure unless distinctly known otherwise. Is purity not a lost cause to begin with? How can the Mishnah pose an unspoken expectation that its subjects should strive to be ritually pure, at least for the purpose of certain activities, and at the same time assert that they are inescapably surrounded by impurity and are prone to contracting it, knowingly or unknowingly, at any given point?

On the face of it, one could dismiss this question by saying that the Mishnah does not concern itself with tenability. It describes a world in which impurity is ever present, because this is the result of systematically applying the rabbinic developments in the concept and scheme of impurity unto the lived environment, and it maintains a view in which one strives to be pure because impurity is by definition an undesirable condition and purity a desirable one. Whether or not it is actually feasible for one to be ritually pure for more than a few seconds or minutes at best in the impure world that surrounds him—this, one could argue, was of little interest to the rabbis, who were invested in the production of principles and not in the trifles of practice.[119] However, a closer look at the Mishnah's way of approaching cases of doubtful impurity of the type described, that is, cases in which the guiding premise is that everything and everyone is impure by default, reveals that the rabbis were in fact highly concerned with the tenability of ritual purity. As we see in a series of rulings regarding doubtful impurity in tractate *Tohorot* (3.5–4.13), the rabbis make a concentrated and conscious effort to neutralize some of the most common settings in which one can contract impurity, and thereby to make the contraction of impurity somewhat more controllable and the pursuit of purity more feasible. As I will argue, had the rabbis not been actively invested in their subjects' ability to maintain a state of ritual purity, there would be absolutely no reason for them to put forth such peculiar rulings.

Here I will focus on the two most conspicuous rulings in this series, which introduce extremely lenient and completely counterintuitive principles for the determination of purity status in cases in which one cannot know for a fact whether impurity was contracted or not. Both of these rulings essentially present the notion that whenever impurity is *most likely* to have been contracted, it will be determined that impurity was *not* contracted.

The first ruling pertains to cases in which a person is suspected to have contracted impurity, but this person is not capable of accounting for him- or herself.

For example, a small child or a mentally inept person is found next to a dead rodent. If they touched it, they have become impure; but it cannot be determined with certainty that they are indeed impure, because they cannot provide a reliable answer to the question "did you touch it?" This principle also pertains to animals that are suspected to have wandered into an impure area (for example, a graveyard) and are carrying articles, thus making the articles they were carrying impure (animals in and of themselves, it should be noted, are not susceptible to impurity).[120] Such cases are referred to in the Mishnah as cases involving "one who has no mind to be asked" *(ein bo da'at lishael)*. We could assume that in cases of doubt of this sort, the rabbis would rule that the person or articles would be considered impure. After all, is it not *especially* mentally inept people and animals who are prone to touching things that mentally capable people will be careful not to touch, and to wander into places that mentally capable persons will be careful not to go? But the Mishnah, surprisingly, rules exactly the opposite: in any case of doubt in which one cannot account for oneself, the persons or articles in question are rendered *pure*. In contrast, in an identical case of doubt involving a mentally capable person, the default ruling is impurity. For example, if an adult capable person says that he is not sure whether he touched a dead rodent or not, he will be determined to be *impure*, even though he is far less likely to have touched the rodent than a child is:

> A deaf person, a mentally inept person *(shoteh)*, and a minor who were found in an entry way in which there is impurity, are held to be pure; and all mentally capable persons *(kol ha-piqeah)* are held to be impure.
>
> Whoever has no mind to be asked, his doubt is pure (that is, will be considered pure in a case of doubt).[121]

This ruling is highly counterintuitive, but it is this very counterintuitivity that indicates how invested the rabbis were in making purity a tenable goal. If persons and animals who cannot be responsible for avoiding impurity and who cannot be held accountable for their state of impurity were considered to be perpetually impure, as would have been the predictable ruling based on the premises we have examined throughout this chapter, then one's ability to maintain oneself and one's immediate environment in a state of purity would be significantly compromised. Through this overarching ruling the Mishnah does not dismiss the possibility that those who cannot give account of their actions have in fact encountered a source of impurity, but it allows one to *ignore* the ever-present potential of impurity that children and animals harbor, thus making the pursuit of purity more feasible.

The second mishnaic principle I will mention here pertains to cases of doubtful impurity in public as opposed to private domains. According to this principle, in a case of doubt regarding the contraction of impurity in a public domain, the ruling will be that the person or object in question is *pure,* whereas in a case of doubt regarding the contraction of impurity in a private domain, the ruling will be that the person or object in question is impure.[122] For example, if one is not sure whether one touched a dead rodent or not while walking in the town square, he will be declared pure; but if he is not sure whether he touched a rodent or not in his own home, he will be declared impure. Similarly, if one sat on a bench that was situated in someone's backyard, and it cannot be known whether this bench was pure or not (for example, whether a menstruating woman previously sat on it), it will be assumed that the bench was impure and the person who sat on it will also be rendered impure; but if one sat on a bench in the street or in the marketplace, the person who sat on it will be rendered pure.[123] Once again, this seems completely counterintuitive: surely there is greater likelihood for a bench on which two hundred people sit in one day to be impure than for a bench in someone's private quarters, and surely there is greater chance to encounter sources of impurity in the bustling public domain than in the confined space of one's own home, which can be monitored much more closely. Here too the mishnaic principle does not propose an account of what is most likely to have taken place, but rather functions as a green light for the subjects of the Mishnah to *ignore* what may have taken place so as to be able to maintain a state of purity in situations in which it seems most impossible to do so.

These two principles, then, serve as formal legalistic means to inhibit the full implications of the mishnaic system itself. Were the rabbis to follow the logic of their own system all the way through, it would indeed be very difficult to find a time and a place in which one or one's possessions cannot be at least *suspected* to have contracted impurity, and thus to be impure by default. The rabbis prevent purity from becoming an entirely lost cause by creating a critical distinction between situations and settings that are at least partially in one's control and situations and settings that are entirely beyond one's control, allowing a freer pass for purity in cases of the latter sort. To emphasize, the principles described above pertain only to cases of doubt: if one knows *for a fact* that a person or an object contracted impurity, it makes no difference at all in which domain this took place or what the mental capacities of the person are. But by declaring that in situations which one cannot control there is no *default* assumption of impurity as there is in situations that one can control, the rabbis turn the maintaining of oneself in a state of purity from an impossible task to a sisyphic yet feasible task. It is in this distinction between controllable circumstances and incontrollable circumstances, I propose, that the key to understanding the rabbis' stakes in ritual purity as an aspired ideal can be found.

## Impurity and the Making of the Mishnaic Subject

The classification of persons, things, places, and bodily conditions as either pure or impure was a critical part of the conceptual framework that the rabbis inherited from their biblical and postbiblical predecessors. This classificatory enterprise is not just a manifestation of an intellectual desire for order and systematization; it also has strong normative implications, since it entails by its very nature an expectation that one should avoid impurity to the extent that this is possible, or otherwise get rid of it as soon as possible. This is not to say that the ritually impure was in any way identified with the immoral or unethical,[124] or that concern with purity was expected to override any other legal or social considerations: obviously there are legitimate and even highly condoned activities that generate impurity, such as childbirth or care of the dead, and there is no reason to believe that people refrained (or were encouraged to refrain) from such activities so as not to contract impurity.[125] But regardless of how meritorious the situation in which one contracted impurity was, the very condition of being impure was an undesirable condition that, as is evident in all textual sources concerned with ritual impurity, one should want to change. When the rabbis create an elaborate body of knowledge on the workings of impurity as they do in the Mishnah, explaining exactly how it is transmitted and in what situations it is likely to be contracted, the underlying message of this body of knowledge, so obvious that it does not need to be explicitly stated, is "try to be pure." In this respect, the Mishnah is not different from earlier and much more concise impurity codes, as we find in the Hebrew Bible and in the texts from Qumran. What does make the Mishnah different, however, is the circumstances to which the implicit-but-obvious injunction "try to be pure" pertains. Whereas in the biblical and the Qumranic systems impurity is consequential mainly for those who function as primary sources of impurity, and at most to those in their most immediate vicinity, in the Mishnah impurity is consequential for *everyone, all the time*. As I put it above, for the rabbis impurity is an ongoing reality, whereas for their predecessors it is a noticeable event. In the mishnaic discourse, then, the injunction "try to be pure" has bearing not only on the way one conducts oneself after intercourse, for example, or after handling the dead, but also on the way one walks in the street, the way one interacts socially, the way one buys food in the market, the way one mends clothes, and so on. The concern with impurity encompasses every aspect of the mishnaic subject's life, and is manifested in all his actions.

Since the injunction "try to be pure" is the normative pivot of the Mishnah's discourse of impurity, it seems evident to me that when the rabbis elaborate on the various daily activities and behaviors that make the contraction of impurity likely, they also implicitly discourage certain activities and behaviors and endorse others. To take two simple examples, by drilling the notion that things left unattended are immediately taken to have become impure, the Mishnah discourages its subjects from leaving things unattended, and by making the point that one who eats impure food becomes as impure as what one eats, the Mishnah discourages its subjects from consuming food of whose origin and purity they are not certain, or for that matter from dining with persons of whose purity they are not certain. In constructing a world in which even the most mundane and banal actions have repercussions in terms of impurity, the rabbis also construct an idealized subject who conducts himself with heightened awareness of these repercussions, and whose effort to avoid impurity and maintain his body and possessions in a state of purity underwrites every minute aspect of his life. In other words, the rabbinic discourse of purity and impurity not only constitutes a picture of the lived world, but constitutes—and prescribes—*a way of being in the world.*

In light of the rabbis' construction of a way of being in the world through their impurity discourse, and in light of their emphasis on the behaviors and actions that the individual takes on in the course of his daily engagement with impurity, we can gain further understanding of the two counterintuitive rulings discussed above. As we have seen, impurity is the default in a case of doubt, but only in situations in which one has some control over the environment in question (that is, the private domain) or over the transmitters or contractors of impurity at hand (ones who "have a mind to be asked"). Whenever this is not the case, and one has no control over the situation, the rabbis dismiss the possibility of impurity unless one knows in certainty that it has been contracted. The rabbinic decision consciously to disregard situations in which one might be considered impure by default because of circumstances that are entirely beyond one's control speaks to the rabbis' directed attention to the *actions and choices* of the individual, more so than to questions of the probability and likelihood of impurity. Simplistically put, the rabbis can ignore the possibility of doubtful impurity in situations that are beyond one's control because these situations cannot be seen as manifestations of one's commitment to purity and of one's choice of a way of life.

Does this mean that the rabbis turn impurity into a completely artificial construct, a "nominalistic" concept as scholars like to call it,[126] which only serves to assess one's intentions and actions and thus can be tweaked and toyed with as the rabbis desire? Certainly not. Let us be reminded that the rabbis' lenient rulings that I described above pertain to cases of doubt, that is, to cases in which no decision can be reached based on the facts alone, and therefore a formal legal consideration is warranted. A case of uncertain impurity is no different from a case of disputed property: in both cases the rabbis assume that there is a factual truth out there (one contracted or did not contract impurity, one is or is not the owner), but this truth is not accessible, and thus a formal overarching principle must be applied to solve the case (for example, "in a case of doubt in the public domain, [it] is pure" or "disputed property will be shared").[127] More generally, as I will point out in various junctures in this book, I do not see any way in which the rabbis' emphasis on subjectivity, thought, and intention detracts from the "realness" of impurity.[128] What this emphasis does do, however, is establish the *self* as a new focal point in the discourse of impurity. The mishnaic self, it should be made clear, does not control the workings of impurity as such: he only controls, to a limited extent, how his own body and his own possessions operate in the realm of impurity. As the following chapters will show, it is in this limited space of control, in which the relations between the self, his body, and his environment are actively constituted, that the rabbis are most avidly interested, and where the most innovative aspects of their impurity legislation emerge.

2

# Subjecting the Body

A reader who is accustomed to associating the concepts of purity and impurity with states of mind or heart, as one who is versed in Jewish and Christian liturgical or moralistic literature might be, could perhaps be surprised by the extent to which purity and impurity in the Mishnah pertain strictly to material entities. In the Mishnah there is no such thing as impure thoughts or pure intentions, an impure soul or pure love. Rather, the rabbinic realm of impurity consists only of concrete physical objects, visible and palpable, which are made impure through direct physical contact with material sources of impurity (or through particular bodily situations), and which dispose of their impurity through a series of distinctly physical actions. As Jonathan Klawans showed in detail, in their halakhic writings the rabbis "compartmentalized" the entire range of moral and behavioral meanings of purity and impurity that can be found in the Hebrew Bible (for example, the notion that the land becomes impure as a result of murder or that evil doings make one impure), and presented instead a systematic view of impurity as an entirely natural phenomenon.[1] Indeed, the rabbinic preoccupation with impurity as a pervasive and ever-present possibility, which I described in the previous chapter, is directed solely toward one's engagements with the material world and not toward one's actions, thoughts, or inclinations, except for actions, thoughts, and inclinations that, as I will argue in the sixth chapter, have to do with the management of ritual impurity itself. Human beings, needless to say, can contract and convey impurity in this system only insofar as they are themselves material objects, namely, only insofar as they are *bodies*.

It should be noted, however, that "the material world" in which impurity transpires and with which one's engagement must be carefully monitored, according to the Mishnah, is in fact quite limited in terms of its constituents. I have already mentioned that the primary sources of impurity are very few in number and that the rabbis do not add any further sources to those mentioned in the Priestly Code, but there are also only a few kinds of entities that are capable of *contracting* impurity upon contact with one of these sources. For one, no natural element that has not yet been processed by human beings can contract impurity. Fountains, rocks, soil,[2] trees, air, and so forth are completely beyond the reach of impurity and are all categorically pure.[3] Similarly, all living animals (except for humans) are completely "immune" to impurity—they cannot contract it and cannot transmit it further. Finally, anything that is firmly connected to the ground is categorically pure, which means, for example, that houses cannot contract impurity.[4] In short, the only things that are susceptible to impurity are human beings, artifacts (that is, inanimate objects processed by humans), liquids (drawn or contained by humans), and foodstuffs.

The ongoing management and monitoring of impurity that, as I argued, underwrite the daily life of the mishnaic subject as constructed by the rabbis can thus be examined through the lens of the relations between the subject and these four elements. Put simply, the effort to stave off or at least be cognizant of ritual impurity manifests itself in the manner in which one interacts with or approaches the bodies, artifacts, liquids, and foods in one's environment: in the manner in which one watches them, handles them, exposes them to the touch of others, and so on. However, a closer look at the ways in which the rabbis parse, subclassify, and develop each of these four categories of things susceptible to impurity reveals that these categories themselves are profoundly shaped and defined by human subjectivity. The mishnaic subject not only determines (to the extent that this is in his control) whether and how to have contact with potentially impure things, but also determines—if only to a limited extent—which things actually constitute the material world of impurity that surrounds him.

To prevent any misunderstanding at the outset, this does not mean that the subject can control impurity through his volitions or desires in such a way that one will not become impure if one decides not to become impure. Undeniably, one's desire not to contract impurity has no more impact on his purity status than one's desire not to get wet when it is raining has on him actually getting wet. Rather, it is the very inclusion of an object in the impurity system (that is, its definition as *susceptible* to impurity) that depends on the relation between the subject and the object. As I will show in this chapter and the next, the rabbis introduce a revolutionary perception, according to which the mental investment of a person in a thing is a condition for the inclusion of this thing in the realm of impurity. Thus, while the Mishnah describes the material world as pervaded with impurity, it also makes clear that this material world is shaped, defined, classified, and governed by human consciousness and through dependence on human mental processes.

In the chapters that will follow, we will see how this notion of subjective investment as a condition for susceptibility to impurity unfolds and gains prominence in the mishnaic discourse. Before I turn, in the next chapter, to explore the multifaceted ways in which subjective investment determines the susceptibility of inanimate objects to impurity (most notably artifacts, but also liquids and foods), I dedicate this chapter to discussing the most central and yet the most complex object that occupies the world of impurity—the human body. As I will suggest, in the Mishnah's discourse of impurity the (living) human body functions as a paradigm for all other potentially impure objects, and it is by examining the most immediate form of relations between the subject and the material world—namely, the relation *between one and one's own body*—that we can begin to understand the weight and function of subjectivity in shaping the world of impurity.

Here I must account for the very distinction or divide between "one" and "one's body" that I put forth here and that will underlie my analysis in this chapter. To be sure, the divide or duality I am pointing to is by no means akin to a Platonic or Cartesian duality of body and soul or body and mind, and such a duality is not in any way implied in the vocabulary or rhetoric of the Mishnah.[5] As several scholars have showed, even when various rabbinic sources do mention body and soul as two distinct entities (with the latter seen as what animates the former), they also make clear that these two entities are inextricably linked and codependent, thus not leaving any room for a view of the soul as one's "real" or pristine self as we find in the Platonic heritage.[6] In the Mishnah, moreover, a distinction between body and soul is especially irrelevant and indeed does not appear: given the general nature of this work as a legal code, the Mishnah is concerned with what people do or do not do, rather than with the way they are constituted as persons, and internal divisions or tensions within the individual are not addressed in any way.

Nevertheless, there is absolutely no denying that mishnaic law assumes that each individual has an aspect of will, intention, and self-reflection, as well as an object-like aspect (that is, a material body) in which he or she is not different from animals and inanimate objects, and that these two aspects are not necessarily commensurate. Both these aspects of the human are expressed in the Mishnah through the same single word—*adam*, meaning "person," or "mankind," but an examination of all the occurrences of this word in the Mishnah reveals that *adam* can be used in two fashions. The word *adam* is most commonly used to denote a human agent as a legal subject, in such phrases as "a person should not go," "a person must bless," "a person can make a vow," and so on, but it can also be used to denote a human body to which things happen without any will or deliberation on the person's end. In cases of the latter sort, in which "person" means strictly "human body," the word *adam* almost always appears in conjunction with either artifacts *(kelim)* or animals *(behema),* making the object-like nature of humans in the given context quite apparent. To take a few typical examples: "If one threw [an item] in order to cause a wound, whether in a person or in an animal"; "They immerse artifacts before the Sabbath and [they immerse] persons on the Sabbath"; "Whether one rented a person or an animal or artifacts, the rule of paying on the same day applies";[7] and many more such examples can be found. Through these and similar conjunctions, the Mishnah reflects an underlying distinction between a person as a willing, active, self-reflective entity and a person as an object-like body, even though it does not map out this distinction by pointing to two separate constituents of the human being.

The distinction I am offering here between "one" and "one's body," then, is a distinction between the aspect of the person that is self-reflective, willing, and deliberative, an aspect to which I refer as "self" or "subject,"[8] and an aspect of the person that is object-like and is classified in the Mishnah alongside other objects. Again, my intention is not to say that the mishnaic subject is somehow immaterial or nonbodily: I submit that there is no way in which the subject can be in the world, perceive it, and act within it except through a body.[9] This does not allow us, however, to ignore the fact that the body is often experienced as disparate from the self, as something one has to care for and maintain like one would a car or a coffeemaker, and as an entity that does not always comply with one's own wills or desires. In the concise words of Bryan Turner, "Our bodies are an environment which can become anarchic, regardless of our subjective experience of our government of the body."[10]

Nowhere in the Mishnah is the nature of the body as "an environment that can become anarchic" more pronounced than in the context of bodily impurity,[11] the emergence or contraction of which is, by definition, something that happens to one's body despite one's will.[12] Whether one's body is deemed impure as a result of a physical condition (such as menstruation or scale disease) or as a result of contact with a source of impurity, the entire experience of detecting, managing, and ridding oneself of impurity is underwritten with a tension between the body as an unruly or passive object and the self as a committed and active legal subject.[13] Thus, I begin my investigation of the construction and development of subjectivity in the Mishnah's impurity discourse by exploring the mishnaic body—first, as a central site in which the drama of impurity contraction takes place, and then, as a site that the rabbis attempt to make more manageable and more commensurate with the self by introducing subjectivity as a principle that governs its impurity.

## THE BODY UNBOUND

In the Mishnah, as in the Priestly Code, the most immediate, urgent, and prominent way in which impurity can affect one's daily life is through his or her very body. First, one's body might itself be a source of impurity as a result of various physical conditions, thus requiring him or her to take certain measures and to avoid certain places and encounters for as long as the bodily condition persists. Second, one's body might contract impurity as a result of contact with a primary source, and thereby require rites of immersion and purification, as well as be subject to various limitations regarding access to the holy. Simply put, the first thing that one needs to monitor and watch, whether for signs of primary impurity or for contraction of secondary impurity, is one's own body, and the purity of one's own body is the condition for the purity of everything else that one wishes to maintain in a state of purity—one's possessions, one's food, holy articles, and so on. It is quite obvious, then, that the subject's engagement with impurity is first and foremost an engagement with one's own body. In order to understand, however, what this engagement means in the mishnaic context, we must first try to characterize what I will call the "body of impurity" of the Mishnah, that is, the way in which the human body is seen to function, interact, and be transformed in its encounters with impurity. As we shall see, the rabbis construct a body that is both extremely fluid in terms of its boundaries and highly modular in terms of its constitution, and these two qualities critically define the way impurity as a bodily phenomenon is shaped in the Mishnah.

## Contact and Connectivity

In her seminal work *Purity and Danger,* Mary Douglas put forth the paradigm that has become almost axiomatic in the study of purity and impurity, namely, that the concept of "impurity" (as well as "pollution" or "uncleanness") fundamentally pertains to the breaching of boundaries. For Douglas, the body is the ultimate bounded system,[14] and as such it can serve as a symbol for any group or society: it is a self-contained, well-defined unit, whose only vulnerable points are its points of exit and entry, that is, the orifices, and it is through these exit and entry points that impurity makes its way from and into the outside world.[15] Several scholars of purity and impurity in ancient Judaism largely adopted Douglas's paradigm, albeit sometimes with the necessary reservation that Douglas's location of the bodily drama of impurity at the orifices applies only partially to the biblical scheme (in which the only orifices that are closely identified with impurity are the genitals, and other orifices do not play a role in the impurity system).[16] A close examination of the rabbinic "body of impurity," however, strongly challenges the Douglasian paradigm of impurity as a breach of bodily boundaries, since it reveals a body that can hardly be said to be well bounded in the first place. Rather than depicting the body that contracts impurity as a neatly enveloped entity into and out of whose orifices impurity oozes, the rabbis depict the human body as an extremely fluid entity whose boundaries are constantly transformed, and which becomes impure not only through penetration but also and especially through direct and indirect *touch.* This depiction of bodily boundaries as highly unstable, I suggest, is informed by central mindsets and ideas in Graeco-Roman medical discourse, and speaks to the way in which the rabbis integrated frames of thought from their surrounding intellectual culture into the system of impurity they inherited.

How does one's body become impure, then, in the mishnaic scheme? If we leave aside for the moment cases in which impurity transpires independently in one's body due to a physical condition, the Mishnah makes clear that the primary way in which one becomes impure is through contact with a source of impurity, either direct physical contact or indirect contact that the rabbis construe as direct contact, such as shift or overhang. Penetration through an orifice, to be sure, is one possible form of contact: for example, a menstruating woman makes a man who has intercourse with her impure, and impure food renders the one who eats it impure. The most common and prominent form of contact through which impurity is conveyed, however, is what we may call "surface contact," that is, touching the source of impurity, whether another person's body or another person's bodily fluids, a dead animal or person, and so on. And yet the question remains: How exactly does surface contact transmit impurity from one entity to the other, in such a way that one body *changes* as a result of touching another? What is the nature of the process that the rabbis have in mind when depicting the contraction of impurity?

We might have been compelled to dismiss this question as unanswerable and to determine that the rabbis are simply adhering to the notions of impurity contraction they inherited from the Pentateuch, if it were not for several passages in the fifth chapter of tractate *Zavim* of the Mishnah. This chapter, which concludes the mishnaic tractate dedicated to the impurity of genital discharges, presents a series of five rulings regarding the way impurity is transmitted through various forms of contact. These rulings help reveal an underlying perception of contact between bodies as a form of physical connection, in the course of which two bodies become one and partake in the same qualities.

These five rulings discuss the degree of impurity of a person who had contact with a primary source of impurity, and put forth a curious distinction: during the time of contact itself, that is, as long as the secondary contractor is still touching the source, the degree of impurity of the toucher is *identical* to the degree of impurity of the source. Only after the two have separated, and the secondary contractor is no longer touching the source, does his or her impurity become "once-removed" and attenuated (that is, weaker in its force and shorter in its duration) in accordance with the paradigm I presented in the previous chapter. To put this simply, for as long as one is physically attached to the source of impurity, they both share the exact same level of impurity, and the secondary contractor functions like the source itself. The following two mishnaic passages demonstrate this principle:

> One who touches a man or a woman with genital discharge, and a menstruating woman, and a parturient, and person with scale disease, and a litter and a seat [of the

> aforementioned people]—*makes two impure and disqualifies one. Once he has separated himself—he makes one impure and disqualifies one.* The same is the case for one who touches, one who shifts, one who carries, and one who is carried.[17]
>
> One who touches the emission of a man with genital discharge, and his saliva, and his semen, and his urine, and menstrual blood—*makes two impure and disqualifies one. Once he has separated himself—he makes one impure and disqualifies one.* The same is the case for one who touches, and for one who shifts. R. Eliezer says: it is also the case for one who carries.[18]

The general purpose of these passages and those that follow them is to divide different sources of impurity into different categories according to the mode of contact through which they convey impurity. The most obvious form of contact is direct physical touch *(maga)*, but there are also two forms of indirect contact: carriage *(masa)*, in which one can become impure by either carrying the source of impurity or being carried by it, and shift *(heset)*, in which one can become impure by either causing the source of impurity to move or being made to move on account of it. Those divisions notwithstanding, the same basic rule applies in all cases: at the actual moment of physical contact, whoever touches the source of impurity "makes two impure and disqualifies one."[19] This is the mishnaic manner of saying that whoever touches these sources of impurity *has the same force to convey impurity as the source of impurity itself*, that is, it becomes "a father of impurity" that makes whatever it touches a "first" of impurity, whatever touches the "first" a "second" of impurity, and whatever touches the "second" disqualified for use (if it is a heave-offering).[20] For example, if Jill is menstruating, and Jack touches Jill, then for as long as he is touching her, Jack is impure in the same degree as Jill. If he touches a bowl at the same time that he is still touching Jill, the bowl will become impure in the once-removed degree; if the bowl contains flour, the flour will become impure in the twice-removed degree, and if the flour will then touch a heave-offering it will disqualify it. Thus Jack makes two (the bowl and the flour) impure, and disqualifies one (the heave-offering). In contrast, once the source of impurity and whatever touched it are no longer in contact, the toucher's impurity is attenuated in such a way that it is rendered a "first of impurity" that "makes one impure and disqualifies one." That is, if Jack touches the bowl after he separated himself from Jill, he will make the bowl "second of impurity," and if the bowl will be used to contain a heave-offering, the heave-offering will be disqualified. Thus Jack, once separated, makes one (the bowl) impure and disqualifies one (the heave-offering).

By distinguishing the force of impurity at the moment of contact from the force of impurity after separation, a distinction that has no trace in biblical or postbiblical purity legislation, the rabbis indicate that in the realm of impurity physical contact should be understood as *connectivity*. The moment of contact is a moment in which the items in question are one in terms of their ritual impurity status, as though the source of impurity annexes the thing that has contact with it and makes this thing a part of itself. In other words, for the rabbis impurity is not transmitted as much as it is *shared*. This notion, according to which physical contact turns different objects into one in terms of impurity so that they all share the same impurity status, can be illuminated through the following passage, which concerns the way in which pieces of dough contract impurity from one another:

> If a piece of dough was "first" (that is, impure in the once-removed degree), and one attached other [pieces of dough] to it, they are all "first."
> 
> If they were separated, [the piece that was initially impure] is "first," and all the rest are "second" (that is, impure in the twice-removed degree).
> 
> If [the initial piece] was "second," and one attached other [pieces of dough] to it, they are all "second."
> 
> If they were separated, [the piece that was initially impure] is "second," and all the rest are "third."[21]

As this passage clearly indicates, when several separate pieces of dough are physically connected (note: not mixed together into one lump, but merely touching one another, *noshkhot zo ba-zo*) and one of them is impure, they all effectively share the impurity status of the impure piece, since they are all considered to be *one piece* for as long as the contact persists.[22] This is the exact logic, I propose, that guides the mishnaic rulings we have seen in tractate *Zavim*, which consider physical contact to be a manner through which disparate bodies can share the same status of impurity.

I do not suggest, of course, that the rabbis thought of human beings and pieces of dough in the exact same way, or that they actually conceived of contact between humans or humanlike things as generating one physical body. The fact that the logic of contact as connectivity underwrites the rabbinic depiction of the contraction of impurity in tractate *Zavim* does not need to be taken as an indication that the rabbis considered bodies in contact to be *ontologically* one body, but rather it should be taken as an indication of how *conceptually flexible* the human body was for the rabbis, and how they were able to utilize this flexibility in their construction and explanation of the phenomenon of impurity and of the body's function within it. Attempting to account for the fundamental operative principle of the biblical impurity system, according to which touch generates "contagion" and an annexation of the toucher unto the source in terms of impurity, the rabbis created a paradigm of contact that rests on a particular view of the body as a fluid and malleable entity, whose boundaries temporarily "melt" whenever it touches another body, and thus created an explanatory scheme for the very phenomenon of the contraction of impurity. This explanatory paradigm is, of course, never articulated as such, but it is traceable, as I proposed, through the innovative notion that during the moment of contact two separate entities function as one and share, as it were, one body.

The question does remain why, according to the rabbinic paradigm of contact I attempted to uncover here, the impurity force of the toucher is eventually diminished upon its separation from the source. Presumably, one could assume that once the impurity has been "shared" and the toucher becomes like the source, the toucher's force of impurity would remain unchanged even after the separation. Here, I believe, the rabbis are bound by the logic of the biblical purity system, in which the explicit and recurring paradigm is that whatever touches the source of impurity always becomes impure in an *attenuated* degree. The rabbis essentially retained the biblical logic, but restricted it to the level of impurity *after* separation.

How did the rabbis' understanding of the mechanism of the contraction of impurity and their explanatory paradigm of contact as a form of "sharing" a body emerge? It is plausible that this view of contact as connectivity at least partially reflects the impact of Graeco-Roman medical and popular-medical mindsets.[23] The notion that touch, either direct body-to-body touch or the touch of bodily emanations and effluvia, can cause two people to share a condition was apparently quite prevalent in popular conceptions of disease contemporaneous with the rabbis, especially in the Latin-speaking world. Vivian Nutton traced the uses of the word *contagio* or *contagium,* literally "to touch together," in Roman texts, and showed that it is used not only to denote the spread of disease through contact, but also to describe the detrimental moral or cultural influence brought about by physical contact with dubious people.[24] Interestingly, the Greek word *synanachrosis,* which Nutton identifies as the closest counterpart to the Latin *contagio,* literally means "to color/dye together," suggesting that the source of pollution, so to speak, transforms the thing it touches so that the latter changes its qualities and becomes identical to the pollutant.[25] The resemblance to the rabbinic perception of impurity transmission is immediately apparent. Here it is also important to note that Greek and Roman authors considered not only direct physical contact but also mere *proximity* to a noxious entity to be a channel through which the body can be detrimentally affected,[26] a view that can help us understand why in the rabbinic paradigm it is not only touch that is seen as generating a "sharing" of impurity, but also indirect forms of touch, such as carriage and shift.

The impact of Graeco-Roman views on the permeability of the body to its surroundings, and on the body's fluid and malleable constitution, can perhaps be traced not only in the rabbinic notion of impurity-sharing through contact, but also in the rabbinic understanding of the effect of food on the body. As I mentioned in the previous chapter, the idea that one who eats impure food (that is, kosher food that was touched by a source of impurity) becomes as impure as this food has absolutely no biblical precedent.[27] Moreover, the very notion that one can *ingest* impurity at all is widely incongruent with the biblical view, and as both John

Poirier[28] and Yair Furstenberg[29] convincingly showed, it is exactly this notion that stands at the center of Jesus' famous controversy with the Pharisees in Mark 7:1–23.[30] When Jesus attacks the Pharisaic practice of hand-washing (which is geared, as Furstenberg observed, to protect the food, and thereby the eater, from the impurity of the hands), he declares "nothing outside a man can make him unclean [koinōsai] by going into him" (Mark 7:15), thus representing the traditional biblical perception in defiance of the Pharisaic (and later, rabbinic)[31] approach.[32] Here too, I believe, the notion that one becomes impure by consuming impure foods reflects the influence of Graeco-Roman views on the way food transforms one's body. According to the prevalent humoral theory, which dominated Graeco-Roman medicine during the time of the High Empire, one's body consists of four humors (blood, phlegm, black bile, and yellow bile), and the balance between these four humors is the decisive, if not the only factor, in the state of one's physical and mental health. Since all food that one consumes either increases or decreases each of the humors, one is, quite literally, what one eats: one's body is immediately affected by what one ingests, and one's bodily constitution is transformed in accordance with the ingested substance.[33] It seems plausible, then, to understand the rabbinic (or protorabbinic) innovative notion that one becomes impure by digesting impurity in light of broader cultural concepts regarding the impact of food on the eater.[34]

Clearly, the rabbinic impurity discourse and the Graeco-Roman medical discourse are concerned with very different phenomena and establish very different conceptual tools to approach these phenomena. What these two discourses do have in common, however, is an underlying perception of the body as a fluid and mutable entity, which is constantly transformed through its contact with its human and nonhuman environment. It is a fair assessment, in my view, that the rabbis conceptualized the body and the modes in which it is affected by other things and other persons in light of popular medical ideas and doctrines on the body that prevailed in their time.[35] This absorption of Graeco-Roman perceptions does not indicate that the rabbis necessarily thought of impurity in terms of hygiene and health,[36] but rather that their understanding of the mechanisms through which one body can affect another was largely shaped by the culture that surrounded them. In this culture, the body was anything but a well-bounded or stable entity; rather, it was seen to be in ongoing flux and to be constantly transformed and changed through contact with other persons and things.[37] In the concise words of Dale Martin, "For most people of the Graeco-Roman culture the human body was of a piece with its environment.... The self was a precarious, temporary state of affairs, constituted by forces surrounding and pervading the body."[38] The rabbinic "body of impurity," that is, the human body that the rabbis constructed through their impurity discourse, was thus woven from a biblical fabric, but its seams and stitches are recognizably Graeco-Roman.

By understanding the fluid and unstable nature of the body as construed in the rabbinic purity discourse, and especially by realizing how this body is constantly transformed through contact, we may gain further insight into the rabbinic depiction of impurity as a constant concern and daily preoccupation. For the mishnaic subject, ritual purity is by definition a temporary state, because his own bodily constitution is, in an important sense, temporary: as the body rapidly changes, so does, at least potentially, its purity status. Simply put, if the body does not have clear boundaries, it is also exceedingly difficult to protect it.

### The Body as a Modular Mechanism

The notion that two separate bodies can become one, which according to my analysis underlies the rabbinic view of the contraction of impurity, indicates that the rabbinic body is not only fluid and unstable, but also to a certain extent *modular*. That is to say, the individual body can change its qualities and constituency by having other external parts, such as another body, added to it: when the two bodies are connected, they conceptually form (at least in terms of impurity) one shared body, and when they are no longer connected, each of the bodies functions as a separate unit.

In this regard, the human body is no different from other modular inanimate objects to and from which parts can be added or removed. The rabbis refer to such parts that can be removed or added as *hibburim*, "appendages," a term they use to discuss things that are detachable from a specific artifact and yet when connected to it function as one unit with it (for example, the drawers of a chest or the handle of a pan). When the "appendage" is connected to the item in question, they form one unit for the purpose of contraction and conveyance of impurity: if the appendage becomes impure, then all of the object will become impure, and if the object becomes impure, the appendage will also become impure. The rabbis of the Mishnah dedicate lengthy discussions to sorting the different components of various artifacts in order to figure out whether and which of these components are "appendages,"[39] and they similarly use this term when discussing different components of particular foodstuffs.[40] Thus, the same principle that we have seen in regard to bodily contact between persons also pertains to the transmission of impurity from one artifact to another, for example:

> If a bed was impure on account of treading (*teme'a midras*, that is, an impure person stepped or leaned on it), and one appended a mattress to it, all of it (that is, the bed and the mattress) is impure on account of treading. Once [the mattress] was separated, [the bed] is impure on account of treading, and the mattress is impure on account of touching [that which is impure on account of] treading *(maga midras).*[41]

The same mechanism of impurity-sharing, then, is evident both in the case of human bodies and in the case of inanimate objects: as long as the two components are "appended," they function as a single unit in terms of impurity, and they both share the impurity status of the source. Once the physical connection is undone, the "appendage"—whether a person or object—is only residually impure, in such a way that the impurity degree of the person or object is once-removed from that of the source.

The rabbinic view of the human body as a modular mechanism, from and to which things can be removed or added, is evident not only in the notion that two bodies can be "connected" so as to constitute, in terms of impurity, one body, but also in the rabbinic consideration of several bodily components within a *single* body as "appendages." This term is used, in the context of human bodies, to refer to hair, nails, and teeth, three bodily constituents with which one is not born and that are disposable throughout one's life, in such a way that their pertinence to the body is seen as secondary. These three components partake in the impurity of the body as long as they are connected to it, but are no longer impure once they are separate from it: for example, the teeth, hair, and nails of a corpse convey corpse impurity as long as they are connected to the corpse, but not once they are set apart from it.[42] Accordingly, we find in the Mishnah statements such as this one:

> If the appendages of the impure [person] were on the pure [person], or if the appendages of the pure [person] were on the impure [person]—[the pure person] is impure.[43]

This passage concerns carriage as one of the modes in which impurity is conveyed by persons with genital discharges: as a rule, persons with genital discharges convey impurity to everyone that they carry and to everyone that carries them. The question at hand is what happens if the body parts that are being carried are parts that are considered to be "appendages" of the body. Since they do not fully belong to the body, can they be said not to convey or contract impurity in this situation? While the Mishnah does not explain what it means by "appendages," it is reasonable to understand this passage in light of the Tosefta, which specifies that the discussion relates to teeth, hair, and nails.[44] We see, then, that the human body is not a fixed, unified, and monolithic entity: it is seen as consisting of various parts, and its different constituents are subject to different rules when it comes to the contraction and conveyance of impurity.

This perceived modularity of the human body is what enables, I suggest, one of the most perplexing rabbinic (or protorabbinic) innovations, namely, the ruling that one's hands are constantly impure (in a low degree) regardless of the impurity status of the person as a whole. One's entire body can be certifiably pure, but unless one has just washed one's hands this very instant, his hands are considered to be "second to impurity" in such a way that they disqualify a heave-offering just by touching it, and if one's hands are wet, they also transmit impurity to ordinary food.[45] The reason for this constant status of impurity, as stated in the Mishnah, is that the hands always "busy themselves" *(she-ha-yadayim 'asqaniyot)*, that is, one's hands are likely to do things and touch things of which their "owner" is not aware.[46]

In other words, the rabbis assume a certain dissociation of the hands from the rest of the body insofar as the hands have "a will of their own," and therefore ascribe to the hands an impurity status that is independent of the rest of the body. This partial dissociation between hands and body brings to the fore situations such as the following:

> If one was eating fig-cake with unwashed hands *(yadayim mus'avot)* and he put his hand inside his mouth to remove the waste, R. Meir renders [the fig-cake] pure, and R. Yehuda renders it impure.[47]

The case here is of a person who is overall pure, but his hands are unwashed and thus impure in a low degree. As long as his hands are dry, they do not transmit impurity to the fig-cake he is eating, since his hands' impurity is too minor to impact it, but once he moistens his hand, his saliva transmits impurity from the hand to the fig-cake and renders the fig-cake itself impure (as we may recall, liquids function as duplicators of impurity). Thereby, once the person ingests the impure fig-cake, he himself becomes impure. The controversy between R. Meir and R. Yehuda seems to pertain to the question of whether one's saliva can indeed function as such "duplicating" liquid when it is still in one's mouth, but for our purposes the striking notion here is that a person's own hands can serve as "external" entities which can, through the mediation of liquids and foods, make the very same body to which they are attached impure. While I cannot get into the very complex and contested history and development of the notion of the impurity of hands here,[48] I do wish to point out that the rabbis could not have ascribed an independent impurity status to hands had they not held a broader perception of the human body as a modular mechanism, that is, as an entity with different constituent parts that, while operating together as one, also have independent existence. Of course, the rabbis did not consider one's hands to be "appendages" of the body in the same manner as hair and nails, but they did consider the body to be a *divisible* entity, which can be parsed and subclassified by drawing distinctions between the parts of which it consists.

The status of one's saliva, which I mentioned in passing above, is an even more radical case in point for the modularity of the rabbinic body of impurity. The rabbis maintain that one's saliva is part of the body as long as it is "attached" to one's mouth, and thereby it partakes in whatever the body's impurity status may be. However, once saliva is detached (that is, extracted from the palate), even if it is still contained in the mouth, it becomes separate from the body and functions as an independent entity. The following passage demonstrates this view:

> If a menstruating woman put coins in her mouth and went down and immersed, she is pure of her [menstrual] impurity, but impure on account of her saliva.[49]

The admittedly bizarre case described here is of a woman who is going to immerse for purification at the end of her menstrual period. Before she immerses, she puts coins in her mouth for whatever reason (perhaps she is afraid they will be stolen?), as a result of which saliva is detached from her palate and is attached to the coins. Now this woman is in an odd state: her body is overall pure, due to the immersion, but in her mouth there is saliva that was detached from her palate while she was still impure (that is, before the immersion). In other words, we have a pure woman in whose mouth there is the saliva of an impure woman, and this saliva actually renders this woman impure *again,* albeit now as a secondary contractor of impurity and not as a source of impurity. The woman in this passage becomes impure by part of her own body, a seemingly absurd situation, which is made possible because of the modular nature of the rabbinic body, because some of its constituents can be seen as parts of the body in certain circumstances and as external to the body in other circumstances.

As I will now turn to argue, it is exactly this perception of the body as modular, and the readiness to distinguish between its constituent parts, that allowed the rabbis to introduce subjectivity and consciousness into the relations between one and one's body. While the modularity of the rabbinic body, that is, its ability to be "annexed" to sources of impurity at any given moment, is what makes the body so precarious in terms of impurity, it is also this body's modularity and the ability to "remove" parts of it that allow the body's impurity to become more governable and manageable, and that enable the body to become more commensurate with the self.

## THE RABBINIC MAP OF BODILY SUBJECTIVITY

At the outset of this chapter, I argued that bodily impurity at its very core is a state of affairs that entails a heightened tension between one and one's body. I suggested that in the realm of impurity there is an implicit rupture between an active legal subject, whose aim is to maintain a state of purity, and the physical object he or she inhabits, which either passively contracts impurity from others or produces its own impurity. Indeed, the Mishnah's rhetoric regarding the management of impurity seems to suggest that, from the point of view of the subject, the body is yet another thing one owns to which one needs to attend, and that one's responsibility to purify one's own body is not fundamentally different from one's responsibility to purify one's property.[50] In terms of its function in the realm of impurity, the human body is *something one has,* like a chair or a cup or a satchel, which must be governed, managed, and put up with as part of one's sisyphic quest for purity. At the same time, the Mishnah leaves little room for doubt that the body is not only something that one has but is also *what one is.* Completely devoid of a language that distinguishes body from soul or mind, and practically devoid even of a designated word for body as such, the Mishnah knows no other way for a subject to proclaim that his body is impure except by saying "*I* am impure." The Mishnaic purity discourse thus assumes an identity between self and body, despite the notable awareness of the incongruity between the body's condition and the subject's will.

This assumed identity between body and self is largely due to linguistic conventions, as well as to the evident notion that there is no other way for the self to be present in the world, in terms of impurity or otherwise, except in a body, which seems to underlie the early rabbinic nondualistic worldview. Nevertheless, I would like to argue that the identicality of the self and the body in the Mishnah is not only assumed by the rabbis but also *constructed* by them, through a variety of rulings that define the physical body through subjectivity. As I will show, in several contexts the Mishnah puts forth a division or mapping of the human body which indicates that there are some parts in one's body that one identifies with oneself more than others, and that only parts that one tends to identify with oneself are included in the realm of bodily impurity. In other words, every part of the mishnaic subject's body is something that he *has*, but not every part of his body is something that he *is*, something that he sees as an inseparable part of himself. Impurity in the Mishnah, I argue, has repercussions only for the body that one *is*, that is, for the parts of the body in which one has some subjective investment. Thus, while impurity is clearly constructed in the Mishnah as entailing disharmony between the subject and his body, the Mishnah also presents bodily impurity as dependent on one's identification with one's body.

At the basis of the distinction between different parts of the body in terms of their susceptibility to impurity or their need for purification stands the fundamental view of the human body as a modular mechanism. The rabbinic body is not of one piece, but consists of various components, which at times can be—in actuality or conceptually—detached from the bodily mechanism and seen as units unto themselves. Such is the case for bodily components that can be physically removed from the body, such as hair, nails, and saliva, but such is also the case for hands, which while not removable can be conceptually taken as independent units. As we will see, the rabbis propose other criteria according to which certain parts can be conceptually removed from the body and be excluded from the realm of bodily impurity, all of which pertain in one way or another, I will suggest, to one's subjective relation to the body part in question.

The mishnaic subject, then, not only reflects on his body's impurity, responds to it, is frustrated by it, decides to act to remove it, and so forth; he also *determines* it through his own consciousness and through his own mental dispositions toward his body, since the very body that does or does not contract impurity is to a certain extent defined and shaped by the subject who inhabits it. In what follows, I will delineate three central rabbinic principles that exclude certain body parts from the realm of impurity, and argue for the crucial role of human subjectivity in each of these principles.

## The Externalized Interior

Most commonly, as we have seen, the drama of impurity contraction takes place at the external surface of the body, that is, on the skin, since it is transmitted (or more accurately, shared) through touch or touch-like interactions. However, by introducing the revolutionary notion that impurity can be contracted also through *ingestion* of impure substances the rabbis integrated a whole new arena into the realm of bodily impurity, namely, the interior part of the body. If impurity, according to the rabbis, can *enter* the body, then the body is transformed from two-dimensional to three-dimensional: impurity can actually reside within it and not just "on" it.

The notion that impurity can reside within the body immediately raises the problem of purification. How can one be purified by washing the external part of the body—the mandated procedure for purification—if impurity resides within him? Can immersion be effective if the impure substance is still in one's bowels? Should one wait until one is sure that the impure substance has fully passed through his system to immerse? How can it be known when this has in fact taken place? And considering the fact that the food we eat ultimately becomes part of our bodily constitution (as it builds bones, blood, muscle tissue, and so on), can one ever assume that the impure substance has really been fully expelled?

A conceivable way for the rabbis to overcome these problems could have been to prescribe a fixed temporal time frame for ingestion, after which the impure substance could be assumed to have passed through one's system, and to determine that after this time has passed the source of impurity is no longer in the body. In fact, this is exactly what the rabbis did in the case of animals that swallowed impure substances and then died: they determined that the digestion process in different animals lasts about three days, and thereby determined that an impure substance swallowed by an animal can be safely assumed to have left its body after this period of time.[51] However, in the case of humans, the rabbis devised a completely different solution to the problem of ingested impurity: they submitted that once the source of impurity has entered the body, it is no longer consequential in any way. In other words, they conceptually removed the interior part of the body from the map of bodily impurity.

According to the Mishnah, even though the impure substance renders the entire body impure as it is being swallowed, once it can no longer be seen it has no bearing on the body. Thus, one can immerse for purification *immediately* after having consumed the impure substance and become fully pure then and there, even if the impure substance is still inside him. The Mishnah demonstrates this principle through the following example:

> [If] one swallowed an impure ring, he immerses and [may] eat his heave-offering.
> [If he] vomited it—it is impure, and it made him impure.[52]

As this passage makes clear, once the impure substance has disappeared inside the body, the one who swallowed it can fully purify himself by ritual immersion, just like he would purify himself from external contact with a source of impurity, and this immersion suffices to render him pure enough to consume the consecrated heave-offering. Thus, according to the Mishnah, once the impure substance becomes invisible and inaccessible, one is considered to be ritually separated from it, like a person who has brushed away a creeping-crawling thing that touched him. This ruling is not based on a simplistic assumption that what has been ingested no longer exists: as can be inferred from the second clause of this passage ("[If he] vomited it—it is impure"), the rabbis maintain that not only does the impure substance stay in the body for a while, but it also remains impure, that is, ritual immersion has no impact whatsoever on the impurity status of things inside the body. For as long as the impure ring is in the body it is inconsequential, but if the person vomits the ring and thus has direct physical contact with it again (when it passes through his throat), he is rendered impure again by this impure ring. The same principle applies not only to artifacts that are clearly not meant to be swallowed by humans, but also to substances made for human consumption: "[If] one ate impure foodstuffs and drank impure liquids, [subsequently] immersed and [finally] vomited them—they are impure, since they are not pure in the body."[53]

The Mishnah suggests, then, that one can have an impure substance inside one's body and still be pure (provided that ritual purification has been performed after the substance is swallowed). It is not that the ingestion process obliterates the impurity of the ingested substances; rather, the interior part of the body is conceptually removed from the body, in such a way that the substances within it are seen as though they are residing separately, in an external container. This conceptual separation of the interior parts from the rest of the body works both ways: in the same way that the body cannot be affected by impure substances inside it, pure substances inside the body cannot be affected by the overall impurity of the body. Thus, even if one's body has contracted impurity, whatever is inside the body remains pure:[54]

> [If] one swallowed a pure ring, entered the tent of the dead, sprinkled [purifying water] and [sprinkled] again, [subsequently] immersed and [finally] vomited it—it [the ring] is as it was.[55]

As this example illustrates, ingested substances do not contract impurity when the rest of the body contracts impurity: if a person has a pure ring in his bowels and he then becomes impure by a corpse, absolutely nothing happens to the ring. If this person would have vomited the pure ring prior to the completion of the full ritual purification process (which includes two sprinklings and an immersion), the ring would have become impure when being projected out of his throat, only as a result of its direct physical contact with a person who is still impure. Once the purification ritual is completed, however, the ring is "as it was" when it was swallowed: it was pure then and it is pure now, and none of what the body in which it was contained went through in the interim affected it. It might as well have been contained in a drawer in a chest.

The same principle, according to which whatever is contained inside the body is inconsequential in terms of impurity, is also manifested in the rabbinic ruling that a dead fetus, for as long as it is still in its mother's womb, does not convey corpse impurity to its mother. This view, it should be noted, is uniquely rabbinic and runs contrary to the law in the *Temple Scroll* from Qumran, which emphatically renders the mother impure for the entire time that the dead fetus is inside her.[56] When tracing the rationale of this ruling, we ought to distinguish between two rabbinic traditions. According to one tradition, which is attributed to R. Ishnamel in the Midrash *Sifre* to Numbers and also appears as an anonymous majority opinion in the Tosefta, the dead fetus cannot convey impurity to anyone or anything before it has fully emerged out of its mother's womb.[57] As Vered Noam noted, this position can stem either from a view that the fetus is not its own entity for as long as it is in its mother's womb, or from a view that whatever is contained in the interior part of the body does not convey impurity at all. According to another tradition, however, which appears anonymously in the Mishnah and is attributed to R. Aqiva in the *Sifre zutta* to Numbers and in the Babylonian Talmud, the dead fetus cannot convey impurity to its mother, but can convey impurity to others who are capable of touching it:

> If a woman has a dead fetus in her bowels, and the midwife reaches with her hand and touches it, the midwife is impure for seven days and the woman (that is, the mother) is pure until the fetus comes out.[58]

The distinction between the midwife and the mother presented in this passage, according to which the former can become impure by a dead fetus that is still in the womb but the latter cannot, provides an important insight into the rabbinic exclusion of the interior of the body from the realm of impurity. The decisive question, as it is framed in this mishnaic tradition (although admittedly not in the corresponding Tosefta tradition), is not where an object is contained but whether and to whom it is *accessible*. The interior part of one's body is excluded from the realm of impurity insofar as it is unreachable, and if it is reachable to one and not reachable to another it will have repercussions in terms of impurity for one and not for the other.

Here I would like to take one step further and argue that physical reachability is inextricable from mental reachability. That is to say, the areas in one's body that one cannot touch are also the areas in one's body that are least controllable by the self and least knowable to the self. What do we really know about the processes that take place in our lungs, liver, or spleen? To what extent are we even aware of their existence at a given time, let alone feel that we have any control over them? After all, when one thinks of oneself in bodily terms, one is hardly likely to include one's interior parts in the mental picture that emerges before one's eyes. In the concise words of the philosopher Drew Leder, "My inner organs are, for the most part, neither the agents nor objects of sensibility. I do not perceive through my liver or kidneys; their intricate processes of filtration and excretion proceed mainly beneath the reach of conscious apprehension. . . . The Visceral cannot be properly said to belong to the subject: it is a power that traverses me, granting me life in ways I have never fully willed nor understood."[59]

I suggest that the rabbis conceptually detached the interior part of the body from the realm of impurity because they did not consider it to be fully part of the self, and they did not consider it to be fully part of the self because the subject has no access to it, neither physical and sensorial access nor, for the most part, cognitive access. Fundamentally conceiving of the human body as a multipart mechanism that can be divided and dismantled rather than as one indivisible whole, the rabbis set the interior part of the body aside, thus allowing the physical body to become not only more manageable and governable in terms of impurity (since one need not worry about impurity that is contained beyond one's reach), but also more commensurate with what the subject tends to identify with himself and what others identify with him.[60] As I will continue to show, the same approach, which excludes from the realm of impurity bodily parts in which one is not subjectively invested, can be traced in other mishnaic rulings.

### Visibility as Condition for Impurity

The detachability of the interior part of the body from the rest of the body can be viewed as part of a broader rabbinic tendency to exclude the invisible from the realm of impurity. As a rule, whatever is located in what the rabbis call "a hidden place" *(bet ha-starim)*, both in human bodies and in inanimate objects, is inconsequential in terms of impurity. This inconsequentiality manifests itself in two ways: first, if a source of impurity is located in an invisible place, it does not convey impurity; and second, whatever is located in an invisible place does not constitute a "barrier" in ritual immersion, that is, it does not obstruct the direct contact between body and water that is required for purification. For example, if an arrow is stuck in a person and is protruding from his flesh, this arrow constitutes a barrier in immersion, and if the arrow is impure it renders the person impure. However, if the arrow has penetrated the body in such a way that it is now invisible, one can immerse and be purified as if the arrow is not there.[61]

The centrality of visibility in the mapping of bodily impurity is manifested not only in mishnaic discussions on impurity contracted from external sources, as we have seen until now, but also in relation to impurity generated by one's own body. In tractate *Nega'im* of the Mishnah, which concerns the impurity brought about by scale disease, we find a list of various places in the body that cannot be made impure by skin afflictions. According to this list, there are places in one's body that are considered to be "protected" from skin abnormalities that are usually diagnosed as a source of impurity, in such a way that even if such abnormalities appear in these places they will not generate bodily impurity:

> The following places in a person do not contract the impurity of discolorations:
> 1. The inside of the eye, the inside of the ear, the inside of the nose, the inside of the mouth,
> 2. The wrinkles and the wrinkles of the neck, under the breasts, and the armpits,
> 3. The foot,
> 4. The [finger/toe] nails,
> 5. The head and the beard,
> 6. The boil, the scald, and the wound while festering.
>
> [All of the above] do not contract the impurity of skin afflictions.[62]

While one could take the heading "the following places in a person do not contract the impurity of discolorations" to mean that discolorations never appear in these areas in the first place, it is made clear in the beginning of the following chapter of the tractate that it is quite possible for a discoloration to appear in a wrinkled area, on the head and the beard, or in a place that is scalded or wounded, but this discoloration would be considered categorically pure.[63] Hence the list does not suggest a descriptive account of the body's dermal topography, but rather a prescriptive division of the body into areas that are consequential in terms of skin affliction impurity and areas that are not.

The list of bodily areas that do not contract the impurity of discolorations is guided by two principles: first, the area in which a discoloration appears has to be considered "skin" (since discolorations are pronouncedly *skin* afflictions); and second, the area has to be visible. The items in clauses 4, 5, and 6 of the list are clearly governed by the former principle: while all those areas are perfectly visible, they cannot be said to be "skin" in the full sense of the word. The items in clause 2, conversely, are clearly governed by the principle of visibility: while areas that are wrinkled (so that one fold of skin covers the other) or hidden by other bodily areas clearly fall under the category of skin, the fact that they are not immediately visible excludes them from the realm of impurity. The items in clause 1—the inside part of the eye, ear, nose, and mouth—could be seen as governed by either of these principles: they are both not entirely "skin" and not entirely visible.[64] Similarly, the commentators of the Mishnah disagreed on whether the bottom part of the foot is impurity-proof because it is so rough that it is not quite "skin,"[65] or because it is normally not visible.[66] The partial overlap of the categories of skin and visibility is not surprising: after all, since the skin is the external surface of the body, it is largely identical with its visible dimension.[67]

As this list indicates, the rabbis' definition of invisibility is not limited only to bodily areas that are completely beyond our reach, such as the entrails, but even to bodily parts that are not usually visible but can be observed with a minor effort (by spreading the skin, lifting one's arm, and so on).[68] In the same way that objects that are not apparent to the eye cannot make the body impure, so body parts that are not effortlessly visible cannot be seen to generate bodily impurity (with one important exception, which will be discussed momentarily). Additionally, in accordance with the same logic that excludes the invisible from the realm of impurity, invisible bodily areas are also excluded from purification. "The hidden place" *(bet ha-starim)* and "the wrinkled place" *(bet ha-qematim)* are said to be exempt from the requirement of having direct contact with the purifying water in the process of ritual immersion, even though such contact is not impossible.[69]

Through these rulings, according to which whatever one cannot see cannot make one impure and does not behoove purification, the rabbis make the point that in terms of impurity, *what we see is what we are*. In the bodily map of impurity, what constitutes a source of impurity is not what there is but what one sees and what one perceives, and whatever is beyond one's or another's immediate sight (even if it is not beyond one's knowledge) is considered as though it does not exist.

On the face of it, this approach could be understood in a strictly pragmatic vein, that is, as a way of exempting the subjects of the Mishnah from attending to parts of their bodies that they cannot see and therefore have greater difficulty in controlling and managing. While such pragmatic drive is likely to inform the rabbinic exclusion of the invisible from the realm of impurity to some extent, I suggest that this exclusion should be understood also as part of a more consistent rabbinic effort to define the body (and the material world in general, as will be emphasized in the next chapter) in accordance with human subjectivity. That is to say, the rabbis consider invisible body parts to be inconsequential not only because they are more difficult or cumbersome to manage, but also because one does not consider invisible body parts to be quite as much part of oneself as visible bodily parts.

The crucial role that the identification of body parts as fully belonging to the subject plays in the determination of impurity becomes especially evident upon examination of the one exception to the "visibility" rule. The female genitalia, while considered in all respects to be a "hidden place" and are even explicitly referred to as such,[70] are highly consequential in terms of impurity. Most notably, menstrual blood renders a woman impure before it emerges from her body, while it is still contained in the vagina, whereas men are made impure by genital discharges only after the actual emission.[71] In addition, women are made impure by seminal emission after having intercourse even though the semen is still contained in their "hidden place,"[72] and the Mishnah states that a woman who has had intercourse and has immersed for purification without first thoroughly wiping her *internal* genital area is considered as if she had not immersed at all.[73] Finally, while the Mishnah's ruling is that contact with the purifying water during ritual immersion is not required for hidden areas, in the Tosefta we find a statement that the "hidden place" in a woman can constitute a barrier in immersion (that is, if the woman's genital area is not thoroughly cleaned before the immersion, the immersion will be considered invalid since there is an obstruction between the body and the water).[74] This ruling indicates that at least in some tannaitic opinions, direct contact of the genitalia with the purifying water was seen as a requirement for women.[75] The Mishnah's overall exemption of "hidden places" from purification was thus considered by certain rabbis as incongruent with the basic notion that the female genitalia *cannot* be excluded from a woman's body and rendered inconsequential in terms of impurity.

The inclusion of the female genitalia in the bodily map of impurity, despite their invisibility and interiority, can be understood in light of Charlotte Fonrobert's observations on the systematic metaphorization of the female body as an architectural structure.[76] According to Fonrobert, the fact that the rabbis refer to the interior of the female body as a house and divide it into "a room," "a chamber," "a vestibule," and so forth indicates that for them the female genitalia were *accessible for entrance*; they were in fact *made* to be entered. The genitalia were not only considered to be an integral part of the female body, but in many respects they were seen as the essence of the female body, which was defined on the whole as a container or a house.[77] Thus, although a woman's genitalia are invisible, they are still a quintessential part—perhaps *the* quintessential part—of her body. Accordingly, we can understand the importance of visibility in the impurity-mapping of the body as part of a more general principle: the parts of the body that can become impure and that need to be purified are *the parts through which the person's bodily self is defined*, the body parts that we or others consider to be "us." Clearly, the parts in which we are most invested are our visible parts; however, the inclusion of the female genitalia in the map of bodily impurity indicates that the rabbis saw these parts as so essential to the female corporeal being that they invested them with the significance usually reserved for visible areas.

The different zones of susceptibility to impurity into which the rabbis divided the human body can thus be seen as *zones of subjective investment*. Certain body parts can be conceptually removed, detached, or ignored insofar as humans are not likely to consider them to be accessible, important, or worthy of attention—in other words, insofar as they do not consider them to be quintessential parts of *themselves*. In the Mishnah, then, the ability of body parts to contract or convey impurity serves as a marker of their consequentiality to the subject that inhabits the body. As we shall see, a similar principle, which closely ties together impurity with subjective investment, is at play in the rabbinic notions of artifacts' susceptibility to impurity, which will be discussed in the next chapter.

Before moving on, however, it is important to clarify that by "subjective investment" I am not referring to individual subjectivity, but rather to what we may call *standardized* subjectivity. That is to say, the rabbis by no means maintain that the question of what parts of the body are susceptible to impurity is given to the discretion of every single individual and is dependent upon each individual's attitude toward his or her body. Rather, the rabbis put forth principles that accord with what they consider to be reasonable states of mind and mental dispositions that are common (in their view) to most people, and they apply these principles to all persons, whether their individual states of mind and attitudes are commensurate with the rabbinic standard or not. Obviously, there could be individuals whose approaches toward their own body parts are different from the ones assumed by the rabbis—for example, it is not inconceivable that there are people out there for whom the bottom of the foot is a highly important part of their own and others' bodies—but discolorations that appear at the bottom of these people's feet would nonetheless not be considered impure.[78] An analysis of one last mishnaic principle for mapping the body will lucidly illustrate the standardized nature of subjectivity in the rabbinic legislation regarding the body, and will provide further evidence for the crucial role of subjectivity in parsing and managing the body in terms of impurity.

### Barriers in Immersion and "Fastidiousness"

In the rabbinic system, purification from impurity in any of its minor or major forms, whether for humans or for artifacts, inevitably entails ritual immersion in water. In order to be properly purified, the rabbis stipulate that three basic conditions must be met in the process of immersion. First, one can only immerse in a reservoir of naturally contained water, collected without human intervention. Second, the immersion pool must hold enough water to cover fully the entire body or object in question, an amount that the rabbis determine to be forty *se'a* (about eight hundred liters). Third, there must not be any barrier *(hatzitza)* between the surface of the body or object and the water. This last requirement, as simple as it sounds, raises a whole array of questions and problems, since it forces one to define what, exactly, constitutes such a barrier. It goes without saying that clothing items or jewelry are considered to be barriers, but what about elements that are physically attached to the body in one way or another, such as dirt or makeup? What should be considered as part of the body for the purposes of immersion, and what should be considered as an external addition and thus as a barrier? As the mishnaic passages that list possible barriers indicate, the answer to this question is far from being self-evident:

> The following constitute a barrier in persons: [ . . . ][79] Tangled hair of the chest and of the beard, and of the hidden place (that is, the genitalia) in a woman, secretion outside the eye and a scab outside a wound, and the bandage on it, and dry resin and crusts of excre-

ment on one's flesh, and dough under the nails, and clots of filth, and miry mortar and potter's mortar and road mortar. [ ... ][80] One must not immerse with dust on his feet, and one must not dip a kettle [when it is covered] in soot, unless he scraped [it].[81]

The following do not constitute a barrier: The tangled hair of the head and of the armpits, and of the hidden place in a man. R. Eliezer says: [the rule is] the same for a man and for a woman. All that one is fastidious about constitutes a barrier, and that one is not fastidious about—does not constitute a barrier.

Secretion inside the eye and a scab on a wound, and moist resin, and filth of excrement on one's flesh, and excrement under the nails, and a dangling fingernail [do not constitute a barrier].[82]

Looking closely at these lists, we can divide the items in these passages into three subgroups:

(1) Bodily elements connected to the skin (tangled hair, dangling fingernail, scab on a wound)
(2) Bodily elements that are not connected to the skin but are merely placed on it (eye secretion, scab outside a wound, residues of excrement)
(3) External elements that are "attached" to the skin so that they have to be scraped or peeled off (resin, dust, dough, mortar, bandage)[83]

Interestingly, the rabbis were not inclined to delineate a clear-cut general rule to determine what passes as part of the body for the purpose of immersion and what does not. While they could have devised a principle according to which semiattached elements are to be or not to be deemed barriers (for example, "everything that originates in the body is not a barrier" or "everything that can be scraped off is a barrier"), the rabbis did not do so. Rather, they examined different "attachments" to the human body on a case-by-case basis, suggesting that items belonging to all of the above three categories can constitute barriers or not, depending on different variables such as location, moisture, degree of attachment to the skin, and even the gender of the person in question. As will become evident, all of these variables point to a single question that guides the rabbis in determining what constitutes a barrier: does the person *mind* that this thing is attached to his or her skin or not. In other words, the decisive criterion in deciding what constitutes a barrier and what does not, for the purposes of ritual immersion, is the person's own bodily experience and relation to the potential "barrier" in question.

This criterion, known as "fastidiousness" (*haqpada*), is stated explicitly in M. Miqva'ot 9.3, at which we will now take a closer look:

1. The following do not constitute a barrier: The tangled hair of the head and of the armpits, and of the hidden place in a man.
2. Rabbi Eliezer says: [the rule is] the same for a man and for a woman.
3. All that one is fastidious about constitutes a barrier, and that one is not fastidious about—does not constitute a barrier.

The principle "all that one is fastidious about *(maqpid 'alav)* constitutes a barrier, and that one is not fastidious about does not constitute a barrier" is the most explicit rabbinic statement regarding the decisive role of subjectivity in the impurity system that we find in the Mishnah.[84] It suggests, simply, that whatever is on one's body and does not bother him or her can be seen as part of one's body and is therefore not a barrier. Indeed, subjective relation to one's body and body parts is the only prism through which the distinction between men and women's pubic hair presented in this passage can be understood. There is no difference between the pubic hair of a man and the pubic hair of a woman except that, in the view of the rabbis, women are expected to keep their genital area kempt and tidy, whereas there is no such expectation from men. That such social expectation was seen as part of a woman's general obligation to be attractive to her husband[85] is implied in a comment we find in MS Vienna of the Tosefta, according to which "the hidden place" constitutes a barrier in immersion (if it is not clean) for married women, but not for unmarried women.[86] This ruling indicates that this area was seen as significant and consequential, both in terms of aesthetics and in terms of impurity, only for women in whose bodies this area was regularly visited, so to speak. Thus, the question of whether tangled pubic hair is considered a barrier or not is inherently dependent on the question of whether the fact that it is tangled *matters* or not.

Once again, for the rabbis represented in the anonymous voice in this passage, the question is not whether any particular man or woman *actually* cares about the state of their pubic hair: since there are certain accepted aesthetic norms, it is simply assumed that people care or do not care about certain things, whether or not specific individuals abide by these norms or not. "Fastidiousness" is another form of standardized subjectivity, in that it is the rabbis who decide what one is fastidious about and what one is not. This is especially manifest in the laws that pertain to barriers in artifacts, which are also governed by the principle of "fastidiousness." The rabbis assert that the question of whether tar, clay,[87] or other forms of dirt constitute barriers in artifacts depends on who owns or uses these artifacts. For instance, "on the beds of a house-owner, [tar and clay] constitute a barrier, and [on the beds] of a poor person, they do not constitute a barrier."[88] For the wealthy, who are more careful to keep their belongings clean, dirt constitutes a barrier, whereas for the poor, who do not have this privilege, the exact same kind of dirt on the exact same kind of object does not constitute a barrier. One's subjective relation to one's belongings, just like one's subjective relation to one's body, is determined through external criteria like class and gender, not through one's individual and private dispositions. In this sense, through their purity and impurity discourse the rabbis are also enforcing and reaffirming social norms of cleanliness, aesthetics, and bodily maintenance.[89]

The principle of fastidiousness as a determining factor in the purification process provides another example, then, of the crucial role that subjectivity plays in the rabbinic mapping and construction of the human body. By maintaining that only what one does not wish to have on one's body constitutes a barrier in immersion, the rabbis define the body in accordance with persons' perception of their bodies, that is, in accordance with one's bodily sense of self. We may thus conclude and say that for the rabbis subjective dispositions profoundly shape and determine the constitution of the physical body in terms of impurity: things that originate outside one's body can be considered, if one does not experience them as disruptive, as part of one's body, and things that are integral to the body, such as one's entrails, can be considered as separate from the body. What defines the rabbinic body's function in the realm of impurity is not a prefixed concept of unchanging bodily boundaries, but rather the way the body is conceived and experienced by its (standardized) inhabitant.

Having begun this chapter by pointing out that the body can become impure only insofar as it is a material object, I conclude it by arguing that for the rabbis, the body can also become impure only insofar as it is a subject. By suggesting that the parts of one's body that are consequential for impurity and purification are the parts of the body that one identifies with oneself, thereby largely excluding from the bodily map of impurity inaccessible, invisible, or unnoticeable parts, the rabbis are unifying the subject with the object that is his body. That is to say, the rabbis establish a concept of bodily impurity that allows one to identify what happens to his body with what happens to *him*: the body that one thinks of when one thinks of oneself and the body that functions in the realm of impurity are largely congruous with each other. Thus, while a state of impurity accentuates the disparity between one and one's body (as it becomes impure although one does not want it to), it is also a manifestation of the identity between one and one's body.

The notion that only that which one identifies with oneself can become impure, as we will see, profoundly shapes not only the rabbis' views on the impurity of one's immediate human body, but also their views on what I will define as one's extended or nonhuman body. It is to this nonhuman extended body, which consists of inanimate objects, to which I now turn.

3

# Objects That Matter

One of the more notable features of the rabbinic impurity discourse, to which I have already pointed on several occasions, is the unapologetic presentation of human beings and inanimate objects not only as comparable, but also as interchangeable. Beyond the notion that objects that have come into contact with a human source of impurity sometimes function as if they were this human source itself, we have seen that the Mishnah often couples "person" *(adam)* and "artifacts" *(kelim)*[1] together in its accounts of the ways in which impurity is contracted and is ridden of. The parity between humans and artifacts is especially pronounced in the context of purification, in many passages in which specific immersion procedures for humans are juxtaposed with identical procedures for artifacts,[2] and in the mishnaic depiction of both humans and objects as equally passive and motionless in the immersion process.[3] Perhaps even more striking is the rabbinic manner of discussing human bodies in the context of impurity while using terminology and categories that seem to pertain only to objects. We have already seen the use of the term *appendages* to parse the human body into its modular constituents,[4] in the same way that it is used to describe beds, pots, vegetables, and the like. In addition, in various contexts the Mishnah discusses human beings, alongside other inanimate objects, in terms of their potential function as "tents" (that is, as creating a shared space for impurity by overshadowing other things),[5] as dams that can stop a flow of water in order to create an immersion pool,[6] and even (through a somewhat complicated mechanism) as seals for cracks in the ceiling.[7] In short, in the Mishnah the human body is clearly and emphatically a thing among things.

This "objectification" of human beings in the mishnaic discourse may seem disturbing to the modern reader, who is likely to have been raised with the Kantian notion that human beings, unlike inanimate objects, should always be considered as ends in and of themselves rather than in terms of their usability and function. We usually think of the equation of persons with objects, or even of a mere juxtaposition of the two without explicitly acknowledging the unbridgeable differences between them, as demeaning to the persons in question and as robbing them of their humanity. Coming from this perspective, one could suggest that the notable parity of humans and objects in the rabbinic purity discourse stems from a deep alienation toward the body: presumably, if the rabbis repeatedly relegate the body to the level of cloaks and jugs, they indicate that in their view the body is an inferior entity, fully disparate from the self. Such a reading, however, which rests on the distinctly modern view of inanimate objects as utterly expendable and disposable, is at odds with the thought-world of the Mishnah, and with the ways in which the rabbis saw the role and function of artifacts in human life in general and in the impurity system in particular. Rather, I will argue, the rabbis did not "relegate" bodies to the level of artifacts as much as they "elevated" artifacts to the level of bodies, or more concisely, they did not objectify humans as much as they humanized objects.

In this chapter, I will venture to illuminate key concepts and ideas in the rabbinic view of inanimate objects as central actors in the world of impurity, and to situate these concepts and ideas in correspondence with the rabbinic notions on the human body that I explored in the previous chapter. I will argue that the comparability and even interchangeability of inanimate objects and human bodies in the rabbinic impurity discourse derive from a view of both human bodies and artifacts as entities of the same kind, namely, as *material objects invested with subjectivity*. In the same way that the rabbis define certain areas of the body, as we have seen, as insusceptible to impurity since they are not physically or mentally accessible to the subject who inhabits the body, and thus define consciousness and subjectivity as determining factors in constituting the realm of impurity, so they do in the case of artifacts. The Mishnah presents an elaborate system of classification according to which inanimate objects are susceptible to impurity, first of all, only insofar as they are man-made, usable artifacts (that is, function as extensions of the human body), and second and more importantly, only insofar as their owner invested *thought* in them and consciously deliberated to use them. Put simply, as in the case of bodies, so (and much more pronouncedly) in the case of inanimate objects: only that which *matters* to human beings can partake in impurity.

In what follows, I introduce the central principles for the categorization and classification of inanimate objects in the rabbinic impurity system, starting from the biblical foundations and continuing to the rabbinic development of these foundations. Focusing on the elaborate and detailed treatment of the notion of usability in the Mishnah, I show that the rabbis established subjective investment in artifacts, in the form of deliberate intention and will to use them, as a decisive factor in the susceptibility of artifacts to impurity, thus revealing the underlying principle that the ability to contract impurity is a marker of *importance for humans*. I then continue to discuss the rabbinic principles for determining the susceptibility of foodstuffs to impurity, and highlight the prominent role of thought, intention, and personal disposition that is at play in these principles. Taken as a whole, then, this chapter sets out to demonstrate the extent to which the entire material world that is governed by humans—bodies, artifacts, and foods—was conceived by the rabbis as one interrelated system, assessed and deciphered in terms of impurity through the prism of human consciousness.

## ARTIFACTS AND THE HUMANIZATION OF THE MATERIAL WORLD

### Biblical Foundations

As I mentioned in the previous chapter, one of the fundamental principles in the biblical (and therefore also the rabbinic) purity system is that the natural world is fully protected from contracting impurity. As long as various material entities—be they (living) animals, trees, water, minerals, soil, and so on—are in the state in which they are found in nature, unmanipulated and untransformed by human beings, they remain insusceptible to impurity.[8] In contrast, once human beings put labor into a natural element, change it, and designate it for their own purposes in such a way that it becomes a usable artifact *(keli)*, food *(okhel)*, or drink *(mashqe)*, the object is introduced into the realm of impurity and is susceptible to the contraction of impurity in the same way that human beings are.[9] This overarching principle is derived from the following biblical passage, concerning the impurity conveyed by creeping and crawling creatures:

> (31) ... Those are for you the unclean among the things that swarm on the earth; whoever touches them when they are dead shall be unclean until evening.
>
> (32) And anything on which one of them falls when dead shall be unclean: be it any article of wood, or a cloth, or a skin, or a sack—any such article that may be put to use shall be dipped in water, and it shall remain unclean until evening; then it shall be clean.
>
> (33) And if any of those falls into a clay vessel, everything inside it shall be unclean, and it itself you shall break.
>
> (34) As to any food that may be eaten, it shall become unclean if it came into contact with water; and any liquid that may be drunk from any vessel shall become unclean.
>
> (35) Everything on which the carcass of any of them falls shall be unclean: an oven or a stove shall be smashed. They are unclean, and unclean they shall remain for you.
>
> (36) However, a spring or a cistern in which water is collected shall be clean [if such a creature falls into it], but whoever touches such a carcass in it shall be unclean.

(37) If such a carcass falls upon seed grain that may be sown, it is clean;
(38) But if water has been put on the seed and a carcass falls upon it, it shall be unclean for you.[10]

For the Priestly author, the most immediate and consequential contractors of impurity are human beings, who may come into contact with sources of impurity through their very bodies: he thus begins his account by first declaring that "swarming creatures" convey impurity to any person who touches them (v. 31). He then continues to go beyond the human body per se and states that artifacts, foods, and liquids are (under certain conditions) as susceptible to impurity through contact as human beings are (vv. 32–35). Finally he notes, by way of contrast, that springs, cisterns, and seeds remain pure despite direct contact with such impure creatures, and that seeds (a term that perhaps refers to plants more generally)[11] do not contract impurity until water is placed on them, presumably for the purpose of preparing them for human use (vv. 36–38).[12] While I will touch upon some of the specific details of this biblical passage throughout this chapter, for the time being I wish to propose that the susceptibility of nonhuman objects to impurity is indicated in this passage to be dependent upon a certain degree of *humanization*. The ability to contract impurity is primarily, as we see through the order and organization of the passage, a quality of human beings, and the paradigmatic object to which impurity applies is the human body. Inanimate things—artifacts, foods, liquids—can become impure only insofar as they have been designated for human purposes ("may be put to use,"[13] "may be eaten," "may be drunk"), whereas things that remain in their natural state, such as cisterns and untouched seeds, are immune to impurity.[14] Thus, in order to become susceptible to impurity a material object must be actively incorporated into the human realm: it must be handled by humans and adjusted for their use.

In this reading of the investment of labor in natural objects as a form of "humanization" of nature, I am deeply influenced by Karl Marx, who offered, to my mind, a highly astute definition of tools and artifacts as extensions of the human body. According to Marx, when human beings put labor into natural resources and process them in order to use them, nature in effect becomes "man's inorganic body" and thereby becomes humanized.[15] When we fill a cup with water from a fountain, the cup functions as an extension of our mouth; the clothes we wear are an extension of our skin; the plow we use is an extension of our hands and feet; and so on. We see whatever we do with artifacts as if it were done by *us,* and do not say "my gun shot him" or "my pencil drew the picture" but rather "I shot him" or "I drew the picture," thus identifying inanimate objects that we use with ourselves.[16] I propose that the Levitical passage quoted above, which presents, albeit in a rather rough form, a distinction between man-made or man-handled objects and natural unhandled objects, and maps susceptibility to impurity onto this distinction, is guided by a view similar to the one fleshed out by Marx. Impurity, the passage suggests, affects the nonhuman natural world only insofar as this world is appropriated by humans, insofar as natural objects have effectively become part of the paradigmatic contractor of impurity, the human body. As I will argue, the notion that objects can only contract impurity in their capacity as extensions of human beings is also critically at play in the rabbinic discourse of impurity, but the rabbis present a unique and highly ingenuous take on the process that objects must undergo in order to be seen as "humanized" in terms of impurity.

### The Rabbinic Construction and Classification of "Artifacts"

The rabbis utilized Leviticus 11:32–38 as a constitutive text for addressing the impurity of artifacts and foodstuffs at large, applying the distinctions and principles expressed in this biblical text not only to impurity conveyed by carcasses and carrion, which is the explicit topic of this passage, but also to other forms of impurity, such as corpse impurity and the impurity of genital discharges. However, the rabbis developed a highly elaborate classificatory system for distinguishing, in terms of susceptibility to impurity, not only between natural and man-made objects, but also between different kinds of man-made objects. The sizable mishnaic tractate *Kelim* (Artifacts), on which I will focus in this part of the chapter, sets out from Leviticus 11:32–35 with three working premises: first, that not all man-made objects contract impurity in the same way or are purified in the same way; second, that not all man-made objects even contract impurity to begin with; and third, that even man-made objects that are susceptible to impurity in principle are not automatically susceptible in actuality, but rather can be deemed "not yet susceptible" or "no longer susceptible." Operating with these three premises, which I will explain below, the makers of tractate *Kelim* impressively (and quite tediously) classified and scrutinized almost every conceivable artifact under the rabbinic sun, from furniture to garments to kitchenware to working implements to musical instruments, determining whether, how, and at what point each artifact becomes susceptible to impurity or stops being susceptible to impurity. It is particularly the development of the third premise, as I will argue, that reveals the immense weight that subjectivity and consciousness bore for the rabbis in their recomposition of biblical purity laws.

The first premise, according to which not all man-made objects contract impurity in the same way or are purified in the same way, is rather straightforwardly derived from the biblical text. Leviticus 11:32–33 distinguishes between artifacts made of wood, cloth, skin, and sackcloth, which become impure when the source of impurity falls *on* them and are purified by immersion in water, and articles made of clay, which become impure when the source of impurity falls *into* them and cannot be purified by water but must be broken.[17] Following this distinction, the rabbis determine that clay artifacts contract impurity *only* from within, whereas all other artifacts contract impurity *only* from without (that is, if the source of impurity is inside them but does not touch their surface, they remain pure).[18] In addition, already going beyond the biblical edict, the rabbis put forth a distinction between artifacts that can be used as receptacles (that is, that have an "inside") and artifacts that cannot be used as receptacles, and they determine that artifacts made of certain substances (specifically wood, leather, bone, and glass) can only contract impurity when they are in the form of receptacles.[19] Determining which material(s) an artifact is made of and whether it functions as a receptacle or not is thus the first stage for the rabbis in figuring this artifact's mode of contraction of impurity and mode of purification.

The second premise, according to which some man-made objects are not susceptible to impurity at all, relies on two criteria that can be traced in the biblical text, but are considerably developed by the rabbis through exacting exegetical moves. The first criterion for susceptibility to impurity pertains to the substance that the artifact is made of: the rabbis determine that only substances that are explicitly mentioned in the Hebrew Bible as requiring purification are indeed susceptible to impurity.[20] This list also includes, in addition to wood, cloth, skin, and sackcloth (which are mentioned in Leviticus 11:32), artifacts made of metal and of bone, which are mentioned in Numbers 31:20–23.[21] While the rabbis did end up also including glass in the list of substances susceptible to impurity, admittedly without scriptural basis[22] and perhaps because of pressing economic considerations,[23] they notably excluded three kinds of substances from this list: stone, earth, and dung. Artifacts made of these three materials were deemed insusceptible to impurity even when fully formed and used by humans,[24] conceivably not only because they are not explicitly mentioned in the Bible but also because they were seen as especially close to nature, and thus not "man-made" to a sufficient extent.[25] This view regarding the categorical inability of certain substances to contract impurity accounts for the notable popularity of stone vessels among Jews during the Second Temple period and thereafter, which I have already mentioned.[26]

Much more radical and far-reaching is the rabbis' construction of the second criterion for susceptibility to impurity, which concerns the usability of the object in question. As we may recall, the biblical text asserts that "any article which may be put to use" is susceptible to impurity. In its context in the Leviticus passage, it is plausible to read this clause simply as offering an explanatory definition of the general term *article (keli)*, namely, as clarifying that an *article* is something that is put to use. The rabbis, however, interpreted this clause as restrictive, maintaining that *only* articles that can be put to use are susceptible to impurity. This restricting and exacting reading led the rabbis to the third premise, which I will discuss momentarily, according to which artifacts that are *not yet* usable or artifacts that are *no longer* usable are not susceptible to impurity; but it also led them to identify certain kinds of artifacts as categorically pure (that is, not susceptible to impurity) regardless of their state. Such is the case with artifacts for which human beings cannot find a use of any sort (for example, a piece of cloth smaller than three fingers on three fingers),[27] as well as with artifacts that are not meant to be used directly by human beings but are designated for the use of animals or as supplements for other artifacts (for example, rings for animals[28] or protective covers for tools and vessels[29]). In addition, the Mishnah indicates that articles that are not actively used by human beings but merely serve decorative purposes, such as painted sheets that are hung on the wall, are not susceptible to impurity.[30] Perhaps most interesting in this regard is the rabbinic ruling that artifacts that are too large to be moved around, for instance, a commode big enough to contain forty *se'a*,[31] are categorically insusceptible to impurity.[32] These rulings speak, I suggest, to the rabbis' understanding of usability as a criterion that pertains not only to the question of whether an artifact has a certain function for humans, but also to the question of to what extent humans can manage this artifact and "do things" with it, or, in Marxist terms, to what extent the artifact can be seen as an extension of their bodies.

Derived from the same rigorous interpretation of the biblical definition of an artifact as that which "may be put to use," the third premise that guides the rabbis in their classification of artifacts is that even artifacts that do meet the above requirements for susceptibility to impurity cannot start contracting impurity until they are complete and ready to use, and similarly they stop conveying impurity once they are no longer usable. The notion that susceptibility to impurity is a *dynamic* rather than a static feature of artifacts, and has both a starting point and an end point, underlies a significant portion of the Mishnah's discussions in tractate *Kelim*. In addition to sorting, for example, what types of baskets (or beds, or fishnets, or saddles, and so on) are susceptible to impurity based on their material substance, shape, function, designation, and so on, the rabbis also put forth elaborate guidelines for assessing whether a *particular* basket (or knife, or hair comb, or ladle, and so on) of one of the generally susceptible types is indeed susceptible to impurity in its current state or not. The rule of thumb is simple: artifacts do not become susceptible to impurity until their production is complete, and once they are damaged in a way that significantly compromises their usability they are no longer susceptible to impurity. The application of this simple rule to the myriad of different artifacts that inhabit the human world, however, is not a simple matter, and the Mishnah contains lengthy lists that delineate the point of completion and the point of destruction (that is, the beginning and end points for susceptibility to impurity) for different artifacts that are grouped together according to similar physical and functional traits. To illustrate this briefly, here are excerpts from two such lists, the first pertaining to the point of completion of wooden objects, and the second pertaining to the point at which metal objects are no longer considered usable:

> Beds and cots [become usable, that is, susceptible to impurity] once one rubs them with fish-skin.... Wooden baskets—after one binds their rims and trims their edges.... A case for bottles and a case for cups, even if one did not trim their edges from the inside.[33]
>
> A shovel whose blade was removed is impure (that is, remains susceptible to impurity) because it is like a hammer.... A saw that has lost one tooth out of every two is pure (that is, becomes insusceptible to impurity), but if a length of one *sit*[34] [of teeth] has remained in one place, it is [still] impure. If an adze, scalpel, chisel, or drill were damaged they are [still] impure, but if they lost their sharp edge they are pure.[35]

We see, then, that the rabbis took the general biblical reference to usability as the quality that defines artifacts, interpreted it in a highly exacting and restrictive way, and made it, in many ways, the center of their inquiry into the impurity of inanimate objects. For them, in order to be sufficiently incorporated into the human realm so as to partake in impurity, artifacts need not only be man-made, and need not only be usable in principle: they need to be usable *right here, right now,* and in a way that makes a palpable difference in the lives and function of human beings.

Mishnaic lists such as the two above and dozens of others like them serve not only as a dizzyingly rich inventory of the material culture of Palestine in the first centuries C.E., but also as an important reminder of the value and cost of artifacts in the ancient world, and of the reluctance of people to dispose of them.[36] Underlying the rabbis' very elaborate treatment of artifacts in the Mishnah is the assumption that people normally strive to keep using artifacts even after they are broken or damaged, and to find new uses for artifacts that can no longer be used for their original purpose.[37] Thus, for example, the Mishnah points out that a chest with one of its sides missing is still susceptible to impurity because it can be used for sitting,[38] and that a torn bedsheet is still susceptible to impurity because it can be used as a curtain.[39] As strange as this may seem to denizens of the affluent first world of the twenty-first century, who are surrounded by more objects than they are even aware of and who dispose of usable artifacts on a daily basis, in the ancient world people were profoundly dependent on the few artifacts they owned, which were purchased or made through considerable effort, and wished to hold on to them and make use of them for as long as possible.

Being mindful of the scarcity and high cost of artifacts in antiquity, we may begin to understand better the stakes that the rabbis and their contemporaries had in the artifacts they possessed, and moreover, we may gain a better grasp of the perspective I suggested above, according to which artifacts are in some way an extension of the body and partake in the realm of impurity in this capacity. When a person has only one garment to wear, which was not at all rare in the rabbinic period,[40] this garment is like a second skin to her and is indeed part of her: if this garment becomes unusable, this person literally has nothing with which to cover herself. When the sickle that a person uses to reap his field breaks, if he does not have the means of replacing this sickle or fixing it, he and his family might end up starving. In the ancient world (as is still the case in less well-off societies) one's few garments, furniture, working implements, and so on were one's dignity, one's livelihood, one's comfort, and one's well-being. As such, they constituted not only part of one's habitat, but also part of one's self-perception and part of one's making as a person.[41]

It is only by realizing the investment that the rabbis assumed persons to have in their artifacts that we may fully grasp the most remarkable innovation of the rabbis' in their construction of the impurity of inanimate objects, namely, the concept of *thought*, to which I now turn. As I will show, in their development of the third premise mentioned above, that is, that susceptibility to impurity has a beginning point and an end point, the rabbis introduced the principle that the actual beginning point of susceptibility to impurity comes into effect only through the deliberation of the person intending to use the artifact. In other words, the rabbis constructed the "humanization" of objects required for the contraction of impurity as dependent upon subjective *mental* investment on the side of the owner, and not only upon investment of physical labor. As I will argue, the correspondence between the role of subjectivity in the susceptibility of artifacts to impurity and the role of subjectivity in the susceptibility of body parts to impurity, which I explored in the previous chapter, allows us to understand better the parity between humans and objects which is expressed in multiple places in the Mishnah.

## THOUGHT, WILL, INTENTION, AND SUSCEPTIBILITY TO IMPURITY
### *"All Artifacts Descend into Impurity through Thought"*

So far, when discussing the process through which natural substances are transformed into artifacts and are thus incorporated into the human realm and become susceptible to impurity, I referred only to the human investment of physical labor in objects. As we have seen, raw substances that have not been handled or manipulated by human beings lie beyond the realm of impurity altogether, and according to the rabbis, even artifacts that are half-made or almost-fully-made are not yet susceptible to impurity. Rather, for every kind of artifact there is a definitive action that marks the end of its manufacture process, and it is only after this action has been performed that the artifact is a "candidate" for impurity. This definitive action, which is termed "completion of labor" *(gemar melakhah)*, varies from artifact to artifact: for leather satchels, it is the adding of straps;[42] for clay pots, it is their baking in a kiln;[43] for knives, it is their sharpening;[44] and so on. Whatever the specific form of "completion of labor" may be, it is a critical and indispensable step in the transformation of an object and its introduction into the human world of impurity. However, the physical labor put into an object, even when topped off with the appropriate "completion of labor," is not enough. According to the rabbis, the action that effectively determines the transition of an artifact into the realm of impurity is a mental action, which they call "thought" *(mahshavah)*.[45]

"Thought" is, in essence, a *decision* to put an artifact into use. While such a decision is perhaps most clearly manifested through one's actual use of the object, thought is construed in the Mishnah primarily as an act of will and deliberation that can take place well before the artifact is ever actively used, and that without which the artifact does not become susceptible to impurity.[46] Simply put, an artifact has no ability to contract impurity before someone actually *wants* to use it. To be sure, thought has no effect on the susceptibility to impurity of an object before it is fully produced, but once it is fully produced it is only following thought that impurity comes into play. This principle is most clearly stated in the following passage:

> In any case in which there is no lack of labor (that is, nothing else remains to be done in the manufacturing process), thought renders [artifacts] impure.
> But in any case in which there is a lack of labor (that is, something remains to be done in the manufacturing process), thought does not render [artifacts] impure.[47]

Furthermore, "thought" transforms objects and introduces them into the realm of impurity not only before they are initially used, but also after they have gone out of use. Thus the Mishnah maintains that if an artifact was damaged in such a way that it is no longer usable and therefore no longer susceptible to impurity, a person's "thought" to use the damaged artifact or part of it reinstitutes its susceptibility to impurity:

> A [three-legged] table that one of the legs of which was removed—is pure (that is, insusceptible to impurity).
> If the second one was removed—it is pure.
> If the third one was removed, it becomes impure once he thinks about it *(tame ke-she-yahshov 'alav)*.[48]

While a two-legged or a one-legged table cannot be used for anything and is thus categorically pure, the tabletop can possibly be used for other things, and thus can potentially become susceptible to impurity. For this to happen, however, someone must actively *want* to use this tabletop.[49] Thought, then, is not only the power that transforms "not yet usable" objects into usable objects (in terms of susceptibility to impurity), but also the power that transforms "no longer usable" objects into usable objects, provided, of course, that there is in fact a conceivable new use for them.

The concept of thought adds another dimension to the rabbis' highly developed and exacting notion of usability. In the innovative rabbinic recomposition of the

Levitical text, an object is not deemed susceptible to impurity simply because it *can* be put to use, but rather because a human being is personally invested in it. For the rabbis, then, usability resides not only within the object itself (that is, it is not determined only by its physical qualities), but also, and perhaps primarily, in the *relations* between the object and its owner. Indeed, the Mishnah makes clear that it is only the actual owner of an artifact that is capable of making it susceptible to impurity through thought: artisans who produce artifacts for the purpose of selling them cannot render what they produce susceptible to impurity, even if they do think of using it; and even thieves do not render the artifacts they have stolen susceptible to impurity until it can be asserted that the original owners have "given up" and become disinvested in the artifact.[50] In the Mishnah the susceptibility of an object to impurity is a marker of its being owned, and more importantly, it is a marker of a certain *mindset* on the side of its owner, that is, of the mental investment of the owner in the artifact he possesses, which is manifested in his will to use it. The connection between definitions of ownership and personal investment in the thing owned is also evident in another area of rabbinic legislation, namely, in the laws pertaining to the retrieval of lost objects: the halakhic principle known as "despair" *(ye'ush)*, to which I just alluded, determines that once an owner "despairs" of an article that was lost or stolen, that is, *severs his or her mental ties to it*, the object no longer has an owner and can legally belong to whoever finds or takes it.[51] A mental dissolution of attachment thus eventually means a dissolution of ownership, and vice versa: the establishment of attachment constitutes ownership and thereby inscription into the human realm and susceptibility to impurity.

By putting forth the concept of "thought" as a determining factor in the inclusion of artifacts in the realm of impurity, the rabbis present a unique take on what I referred to above as the "humanization of nature." Already in the Priestly Code, I suggested, it is implied that human beings are the paradigmatic contractors of impurity, and that inanimate objects can become impure only insofar as they are somehow incorporated into the human realm, that is, are transformed from natural elements to things designated for human use. The rabbis clearly follow this notion, but for them the incorporation of objects into the human realm is effected not through labor (although labor is, to be sure, a sine qua non), but through *subjective investment*. To put it again in Marxist terms, in the Mishnah an artifact becomes part of one's extended body not when one makes it or uses it, but when one establishes oneself as its owner by deliberating to use it and, consequentially, by mentally constituting this artifact as something that *matters* to him. For the rabbis—and herein lies their revolutionary view—the road to the human realm inevitably passes through human consciousness.

It is important to note that despite the central role of subjectivity and thought in determining the susceptibility of artifacts to impurity, their power only works in one direction: in the words of the Mishnah, "All artifacts descend into their impurity by thought, and do not ascend from their impurity except by a change of action (*shinui ma'ase*, that is, actual change)."[52] One can "think" things into impurity but cannot "think" them out of impurity. While the mere will to use an object suffices to make it susceptible to impurity (provided that its manufacture is complete), a decision to stop using an artifact has absolutely no impact on its susceptibility to impurity. Rather, only an actual change in the object rendering it unusable will make it insusceptible to impurity. This ruling can be understood in strictly pragmatic terms: while it is quite easy to pinpoint the initial decision of a person to use an artifact (which would usually be at the moment of purchase, or at the very least at the moment preceding the first actual use), the moment in which one decides to *stop* using something is more difficult to locate (how many of us hold on to things for years and years, thinking that we might use them some day?). Alternatively or additionally, this ruling may point to an overarching assumption on the side of the rabbis that people do not usually decide to stop using things that are still in working condition, an assumption that seems, as I mentioned above, quite realistic in the context of the world in which they lived.

There is notable correspondence between the role of subjectivity in determining the susceptibility of objects to impurity and the role of subjectivity in mapping the human body in terms of impurity. As I argued in the previous chapter, the rabbis construct the human body as a modular mechanism, to and from which parts can be conceptually added or removed, and determine that certain bodily areas are effectively excluded from the realm of impurity. Thus, for instance, the internal part of the body functions as an isolated unit that is protected from the impurity dramas that take place on the surface of the body, on the one hand, and does not affect the rest of the body if impurity is contained within it, on the other hand. Other invisible bodily areas are likewise excluded from various forms of impurity. I have argued that behind this exclusion of parts that are physically or mentally inaccessible from the realm of bodily impurity stands a view that these are parts that one does not strongly identify with oneself, that is, these are parts in which one is not subjectively invested. If this analysis is correct, we may now suggest that in the context of impurity, the rabbis conceive of body parts and artifacts in the same fundamental way: they consider both to be material objects toward which human beings develop a mental relation, and they consider this mental relation to be the key for the determination of susceptibility to impurity. In other words, both bodies (with their various constituent parts) and artifacts are incorporated into the realm of impurity insofar as they *matter* to the subject who inhabits or owns them. This is of course not to say that the rabbis did not acknowledge critical differences between human bodies and inanimate objects or that they treated them identically, but it is to say that the comparability of the two, which is so often emphasized in mishnaic texts, stems from the same rabbinic innovation. Since the rabbis considered the entire material world—human and nonhuman alike—to be governed, in terms of susceptibility to impurity, by human consciousness, they constructed susceptibility to impurity as a marker of *objects that matter*, thereby creating parity between different kinds of objects in which humans are invested. This pertains not only to bodies and to artifacts but also, as I will show in what follows, to food.

## Subjectivity and "Thought" in the Impurity of Foodstuffs

Until now, I have focused almost exclusively on the rabbinic reconstruction of the Priestly laws regarding the impurity of artifacts (Leviticus 11:32–33), according to which objects are susceptible to impurity insofar as they may be "put to use," and showed how the rabbis interpret the concept of usability in far-reaching ways, placing their emphasis on the consciousness and subjectivity of the owner. I now move on to discuss the role of deliberation and "thought" in the rabbinic remaking of the biblical clause regarding the impurity of foods and liquids, which according to Leviticus 11:34 pertains only to "food that may be eaten" and to "liquid (literally drink, *mashqe*) that may be drunk." As in the case of usability, the rabbis construct the "edibility" of foods for impurity purposes as ultimately dependent upon human consciousness, stressing one's mental disposition toward the food in question as a significant if not a decisive factor in determining its susceptibility to impurity.

The biblical reference to "food that may be eaten" and "liquid that may be drunk" is most readily understood as referring to substances that human beings are likely to eat and drink (for example, not shells, peels, pits, waste, and so on),[53] and probably also indicates that the substances in question must be processed in some way so as to function as food or drinks: presumably animals are only considered "food" after they have been slaughtered and cooked, water is only considered "drink" after it has been drawn, and so forth. In regard to the susceptibility of liquids to impurity, the rabbis did not significantly develop the biblical edict except by presenting a complete list of all the "drinkable" liquids that are to be considered susceptible to impurity (only, to be sure, after having been disconnected from their source and handled by humans). This list consists of seven liquids:[54] dew, water, wine, oil, blood,[55] milk, and honey, which are all deemed susceptible to impurity except when they are so putrid that they cannot be consumed.[56] In regard to food, however, we find a more intricate and complex development.

The Mishnah presents a categorical distinction between food "designated for human beings" (*meyuhad la-adam*) and food not designated for human beings, and puts forth a general rule regarding the susceptibility to impurity of foods in each category:

> Whatever is designated to be eaten by human beings is impure (that is, susceptible to impurity), until it becomes unfit to be eaten by dogs.
>
> Whatever is not designated to be eaten by human beings is pure (that is, not susceptible to impurity), until one designates it for human beings (or: for *a* human being).[57]

This ruling distinguishes between substances that are commonly designated for persons, that is, that most people consider to be "food" without hesitation, and substances that are not usually identified as food but can still conceivably be consumed by persons, which become "food" only when one actually makes a point of using them as such. Human flesh, raw flesh cut off from animals, and generally inedible weeds, thorns, and flowers are mentioned in the Mishnah as some examples of such unlikely foods, which are not considered "designated for human beings" until one actually designates them.[58] To be clear, this distinction has nothing to do with laws of *kashrut* and forbidden foods: the rabbis fully acknowledge that even substances that are prohibited for consumption, such as animal carrion, rabbits, pigs, and so on, are eaten by many, and they are thus considered "designated for human beings."[59] Furthermore, the Mishnah is explicit that one can make a point of giving something that he himself cannot eat (or will not eat) to a Gentile, and thereby deem it "designated for a human being."[60]

Interpreting the Levitical ruling that impurity affects only food "that may be eaten," the rabbis determine that substances that are not commonly designated for human consumption are not susceptible to impurity, that is, they remain pure even if they come into contact with a source of impurity. However, the rabbis also determine that such substances *can* become susceptible to impurity if one in fact decides to eat them (or to have someone else eat them). The act through which nonfood is transformed into food and thereby becomes susceptible to impurity is called, as in the case of artifacts, "thought" *(mahshavah)*, here referring to a conscious decision to treat the substance in question as food.[61] In contrast, foods that are ordinarily consumed by humans are said not to require active "thought," that is, one does not need to *decide* that they will be eaten in order to introduce them into the realm of impurity.[62] The very fact that most people consider a certain substance as food functions as a form of automatic "thought" for this substance, in such a way that this substance is, as it were, "preapproved" for impurity.

Interestingly, the rabbis acknowledge that different communities might have different norms as to what constitutes food, and maintain that these norms indeed determine susceptibility to impurity: for example, the same thing can require "thought" in the countryside, where it is not commonly eaten, but not require "thought" in urban areas.[63] The transition of food into the realm of impurity is thus effected through human consciousness, and specifically through the formation of a relation between the person and the substance in question: by deciding that something will be used as food, one renders this substance consequential and important for oneself, and thereby introduces it into the realm of impurity, which consists, as I argued above, only of objects that *matter*. In what follows, I will attempt to suggest a conceptual paradigm for understanding the rabbinic emphasis on thought, ownership, and subjective investment in the constitution of the world of impurity.

## The Impurity of What We Care About

In an extensive study on the decisive force of thought and intention in rabbinic legislation, in which he also dealt with aspects pertaining to the susceptibility of artifacts and foods to impurity, Howard Eilberg-Schwartz ventured to account for the worldview that stands behind the rabbis' notion that human consciousness can shape reality.[64] He argued that in all the cases in which will and intention actively change the status of things in the world, the process through which the change takes effect is a process of *naming*. That is to say, human beings transform the qualities of objects when they call these objects a different name. Thus, for instance, a substance that is not susceptible to impurity becomes susceptible when people call it "food," and random pieces of wood or metal become susceptible to impurity when people call them "furniture" or "vessel." According to Eilberg-Schwartz, the view that naming has the power to transform reality derives from the first two chapters of the book of Genesis, which serve, in his view, as the theological infrastructure of the Mishnah. At the center of these biblical chapters, argues Eilberg-Schwartz, stands God's role as the one who puts the world into order by classifying, categorizing, and giving names to its components. This role is then bestowed upon Adam, who names all the animals as an agent or proxy of God (Genesis 2:19–20). Following Genesis 1–2, the rabbis hold that through the prerogative of naming, humans partake in the divine will and serve as secondary creators: human will has the power to change reality since it is an extension of the divine will, which can shape and change reality.[65]

Eilberg-Schwartz's argument is compelling insofar as it captures the centrality of naming in the rabbinic system. As he convincingly showed, the susceptibility of objects to impurity is often decided by determining what people *call* the object in question.[66] He is also surely correct in identifying usability as the main criterion according to which humans call objects and substances "artifacts" and "food" and thereby render them susceptible to impurity. However, I find Eilberg-Schwartz's explanation to be somewhat limited, as it does not account for the *mental mechanism* through which an object acquires its new "name" and thus becomes susceptible to impurity in its capacity as "artifact" or "food." As we have seen, for the rabbis an object can be entirely worthy of the name "artifact" as far as its material and functional qualities are concerned, and yet it cannot become susceptible to impurity—or, in Eilberg-Schwartz's terms, it does not acquire the name "artifact"—until it has an owner, and until the owner actively wants to use it. If susceptibility to impurity is a function of "naming," why is this naming not dependent upon the inherent traits of the object in question but upon the human *relation* to this object, and more importantly, why is only the owner of an artifact empowered to "name" it? Why am I, as a human being capable of divine-like thought and volition, not in a position to name my neighbor's new purchase "a table" or "a skillet" and thereby render it susceptible to impurity? The piece that is missing from

Eilberg-Schwartz's explanation is that the ability to render an artifact susceptible to impurity is a prerogative not of all of mankind vis-à-vis all material objects, but rather only of an owner of an object vis-à-vis what he or she owns.

In order to understand the nature of the process that makes a specific human being capable of introducing a specific object into the realm of impurity, I wish to suggest a different conceptual paradigm for the role of thought and intention in rabbinic notions of susceptibility to impurity. I propose that the way in which humans incorporate objects into the world of impurity is by *caring* about them, that is, by seeing them as things that *matter*. To disambiguate my use of the term "care" here, I turn to the work of the philosopher Harry Frankfurt, whose classic article "The Importance of What We Care About" significantly augmented my understanding of the role of subjectivity in the rabbinic discourse of impurity.[67]

Caring, according to Frankfurt, has to do with the question of what is important to us. This question, he emphasizes, must be distinguished from the ethical question "what is morally right?" Even if identifying something (or someone) as important can ultimately lead to certain ethical decisions, there are many things about which one cares without this caring generating any sort of moral obligation. The essence of caring, Frankfurt maintains, is identifying something *as making a difference,* that is, thinking that it matters whether this thing does or does not exist, and what sort of characteristics it does or does not have.[68] Caring about something thus must not be confused, Frankfurt's stresses, with liking something or wanting something; it also does not mean judging that something is universally valuable or important. Rather, it is a self-reflexive process in which one identifies a relation between the thing she cares about and herself: "A person who cares about something is, as it were, invested in it. He *identifies* himself with what he cares about in the sense that he makes himself vulnerable to losses and susceptible to benefits depending upon whether what he cares about is diminished or enhanced. Thus he concerns himself with what concerns it, giving particular attention to such things and directing his behavior accordingly."[69] Frankfurt's definition of caring helps us better understand, I propose, the central role of thought, intention, and will in the determination of susceptibility to impurity in the Mishnah. The principle that underlies all the rulings we have seen thus far is that one must have personal *stakes* in the object in question in order to make it susceptible to impurity. Only an owner who decides to use an artifact, that is, who is personally interested in the durability, function, and performance of this artifact, can deem an artifact susceptible to impurity; only one who decides to consume some substance as food, and for whom thereby the smell, taste, texture, and so on of this substance make a difference, can deem it susceptible to impurity; and similarly, only body parts that humans identify with themselves, of which they are cognizant and aware, can partake in the realm of impurity.

The rendition of an object as susceptible to impurity effectively means allowing this object to make a difference in the ritual sphere: a difference in the purity status of humans and objects that come into contact with it, and a difference in the way in which it is approached and handled in the course of everyday activities. By incorporating thought and intention into the determination of an object as susceptible to impurity, the rabbis put forth the notion that for an object to make a difference in the realm of purity and impurity, it must first of all make a difference to its owner on a day-to-day basis, that is, its owner must be invested in this object's existence and in its condition. According to the rabbinic view, then, an object about which one does not care, which is inconsequential for its owner as a usable tool or as edible food, is by necessity also inconsequential in terms of purity and impurity. In the Mishnah, human subjectivity constitutes the material world insofar as it determines which components of the material world *matter,* and it constitutes the world of impurity insofar as only that which matters can partake in purity and impurity.

The examination of the centrality of subjectivity, thought, and intention in constituting susceptibly to impurity in the Mishnah cannot be complete without considering the crucial role that personal mindsets and subjective dispositions play in one particular halakhic arena, namely, in the rendering of food susceptible to impurity by placing liquids on it, to which I now turn. While the workings of intention and thought in this halakhic arena cannot be subsumed under the paradigm of "caring," they do speak to the tremendous and unprecedented role of human consciousness and deliberation in shaping the world of purity and impurity in the Mishnah, which I will continue to explore in the chapters to follow.

### *Will, Intention, and Contentment in "Activation" of Impurity through Liquids*

In my discussion above on the susceptibility of foodstuffs to impurity, I mentioned that whereas substances that are not commonly designated for human consumption require "thought" in order to become susceptible to impurity, foods that are ordinarily consumed by humans require no such active mental transformation, since they are seen as automatically "thought" into impurity. However, even common or ordinary food is not considered in the Mishnah to be inherently susceptible to impurity, without the need for additional mental or physical actions. Rather, ordinary food acquires its susceptibility to impurity only after going through what the rabbis refer to as "activation through liquids" *(hekhsher mashqin).*

The concept of "activation through liquids" rests on the stipulation made in Leviticus 11:34: "As to any food that may be eaten, it shall become unclean if it came into contact with water." This is joined by a similar assertion in Leviticus 11:38: "But if water has been put on a seed and a carcass falls upon it, it shall be unclean for you." Behind these stipulations, according to which foodstuffs (made of both plants and other things) become susceptible to impurity only after contact with water, stands the notion that water functions as the lubricant of the "impurity machine," so to speak. Moisture establishes contact: it obfuscates the boundaries between separate entities since it makes one thing cling to the other, thereby enabling impurity to be transmitted from the source to the secondary contractor. Early Jewish interpreters, as I mentioned in the first chapter, significantly developed this notion by suggesting that liquids duplicate impurity ad infinitum and thus allow two things that would normally not affect each other to contract impurity from each other.[70]

The process in which liquids come into contact with foods and plants (provided that the latter have already been picked or harvested) and thereby make them susceptible to impurity was termed *hekhsher tum'a* by the rabbis, an idiom that can be translated as "activation for impurity," or perhaps more literally as "making-appropriate for impurity." The more common rabbinic code word for activation for impurity through liquids is *ki yutan*, "if water has been put," pointing to Leviticus 11:38, quoted above.[71] The Mishnah asserts that all foods, whatever their kind, require contact with liquids in order to be rendered susceptible to impurity, whether they are normally designated for human consumption (in which case they require activation through liquids but not "thought") or not normally designated for human consumption (in which case they require both "thought" and activation through liquids).[72] The only exception to this rule is foodstuffs that are impure to begin with, such as carrion meat or meat from unclean animals, which do not require activation for impurity because they are impure by nature.[73] According to the rabbis it is not only water, which is explicitly mentioned in the biblical verse, that functions as such an "activator," turning foodstuffs from categorically pure to susceptible to impurity; it is also the six other liquids included in the list of "liquids that may be drunk" (dew, oil, wine, blood, milk, and honey) and even bodily substances that are "derivatives" *(toladot)* of water, such as saliva, tears, and urine.[74] The Mishnah also clarifies that foods can be made susceptible to impurity by coming into contact with the liquids contained inside them, at the point where these liquids come to the surface: thus, for instance, meat is made susceptible to impurity through the blood that covers it in the slaughtering process, and olives become susceptible to impurity when the oil that is inside them oozes and covers them.[75]

On the face of it, "activation through liquids" seems like a completely mechanical procedure: once food comes into contact with liquids of any sort, whether this happened intentionally or accidentally, it becomes susceptible to impurity. Admittedly, this mechanism is quite troublesome: imagine someone who left freshly picked peaches outside during a night in which it happened to rain, and in the morning discovered that they were covered not only in rainwater, which made them susceptible to impurity, but also with some dead mosquitos, which made them impure (and foodstuffs that have become impure cannot be purified in any way). The Mishnah is replete with instructions and guidelines for protecting foodstuffs, especially fruits and vegetables, from moisture and thereby from impurity for the longest time possible,[76] but it also introduces a revolutionary idea, according to which "activation" for impurity depends upon the *will and mindset* of the owner of the foodstuffs. Thus tractate *Makhshirin* (Activators) of the Mishnah opens with the following rule:

> Any liquid that was [put on food, and the contact of food with this liquid was] initially according to [the] will [of the owner], even though it was not according to [the] will [of the owner] in the end—
>
> And [any liquid] that was [put on food, and the contact of food with this liquid was] according to [the] will [of the owner] in the end, even though it was not according to [the] will [of the owner] initially—
>
> This is a case of "if water has been put" (*ki yutan*, that is, the food is made susceptible to impurity).
>
> Impure liquids render [whatever they touch] impure both according to one's will and not according to one's will.[77]

Will or "satisfaction" *(ratzon),* this passage proclaims, is a key component in the process of "activation though liquids": in order to render food susceptible to impurity, it is required that at some point in the course of contact between food and liquids, even if not throughout all of it, the owner must be actively interested in this contact or pleased with it. To return to our previous example, the person who left the freshly picked peaches outside might be initially content with the rainfall, thinking with satisfaction that the rain will wash off the dust and dirt from the peaches, and only later realizing with annoyance that it will also make the peaches susceptible to impurity. However, this moment of initial contentment suffices to deem the contact of the peaches with the water as taking place "according to his will" and thus render the peaches susceptible to impurity. Whether the owner's assent to the contact between food and liquid was at the beginning, at the end, or throughout the process, it is clear that without such assent, food does not become susceptible to impurity. This view is evident from multiple other mishnaic passages as well: for example, the Mishnah relates an anecdote about the people of Jerusalem who hid their fruits in water for fear that violent robbers *(sikarin)* would take them away, and the Sages deemed these fruits insusceptible to impurity, since they were clearly not placed in water according to the "will" of their owners (while the owners initiated it, they were clearly not content with this arrangement).[78] Simply put, the rabbinic position expressed in these passages is that random physical contact between food and liquids in and of itself is not enough: the ability of liquids to function as "activators" depends on the *state of mind* of the owner of the food.

In addition to the concept of "will," we find in the mishnaic treatment of activation through liquids several explicit and implicit references to "intention" *(kavanah),* that is, to the motivation behind a person's actions. The underlying assumption here is that if the contact between liquids and food took place unintentionally, without the owner's deliberation, the liquids do not activate the food for impurity. To take two examples:

> If one was picking weeds when the dew was still on them in order to cover wheat with them, this is not a case of "if water has been put" (*ki yutan*, that is, the wheat does not become susceptible to impurity).
> If he intended that (that is, he wanted the wet weeds to moisten the wheat)—it is a case of "if water has been put."[79]

> If one took his fruits up to the roof on account of aphids (that is, to protect the fruits from insects), and dew fell upon them—this is not a case of "if water has been put."
> If he intended that (that is, he wanted the dew to fall upon them)—it is a case of "if water has been put."[80]

This principle, according to which only contact between food and liquids that takes place with the mindful deliberation of the owner establishes susceptibility to impurity, is most forcefully expressed in a statement attributed to R. Yehoshua,[81] who urges his audience to realize that no liquid whatsoever can make food susceptible to impurity, except for liquid that one intentionally places on food (*ad she-yitkaven ve-yiten*).[82]

It is important to note that "intention" is not necessarily something that must be proclaimed, but is assumed in the Mishnah to be divulged by the way in which one conducts oneself. Behavior that attests to a willingness or readiness for contact between food and liquid to take place is construed in the Mishnah as an indication of "intention" regardless of what exactly was going on in the mind of the owner at the time.[83] Furthermore, there are controversies between the rabbis on whether one's state of mind of assent in itself suffices to make food susceptible to impurity, or whether this state of mind must be accompanied by an action that will make this state of mind manifest. For example:

> If one was walking [with] wheat to the miller, and rain fell upon it [on the way], if he was content by this—this is a case of "if water has been put" (that is, the wheat becomes susceptible to impurity).
> R. Yehuda says: It is impossible not to be content, but [the wheat does not become susceptible to impurity] unless he stood.[84]

> If donkey-drivers were passing through the river and their bags fell into the water, if they were content by this—this is a case of "if water has been put" (that is, the produce in the bags becomes susceptible to impurity).
> R. Yehuda says: it is impossible not to be content, but [the produce in the bags does not become susceptible to impurity] unless they turned them.[85]

In both cases described in these passages (as in several other similar cases), food products come into contact with liquids without the owner's intention, but this contact nonetheless pleases the owner. According to the anonymous *tanna*, the very fact that the owners are pleased by this turn of events is sufficient to render the food products susceptible to impurity. In contrast, R. Yehuda maintains that the owners must manifest their state of mind of contentment thought their actions, for instance, by standing still so that the wheat is fully exposed to the rain, or turning the bags in the water so that they absorb water from all sides. According to both opinions, however, it is the owners' *mental disposition* toward the contact with liquids that generates or does not generate susceptibility to impurity. Whether or not it is divulged through actions, it is one's consciousness that ultimately "activates" things for impurity: liquids in and of themselves do not have the power to do so.

While the view that will and intention are decisive factors in the process of activation for impurity may not have been accepted by all the rabbis,[86] and may have fully developed only in the later stages of the making of the Mishnah,[87] it nonetheless features prominently in the mishnaic text as it stands before us today, and provides a further indication of the centrality of subjectivity and consciousness in the rabbinic discourse of impurity as a whole. As in the case of artifacts and of normally inedible substances, the rabbis maintain that in order to be incorporated into the realm of human beings and to thus become susceptible to impurity, even substances that are normally designated as food must actively pass through the consciousness of a human agent. Here, indeed, the mechanism that inscribes ordinary foods into the realm of impurity is not one of mental investment (since the owner of the food may be displeased with the contact of food with liquids exactly *because* he or she cares about this food), but rather a mechanism of assent or contentment. Nevertheless, the perception at the core of this mechanism is the same revolutionary perception we have seen above: the susceptibility of an object to impurity is determined not solely based on the intrinsic qualities of the object or on its physical state, but also and most crucially based on a human relation with and disposition toward this object.

Bodies, artifacts, and foodstuffs are all subsumed, then, albeit in different forms and with different emphases, under the same overarching view of susceptibility to impurity as a subjectively generated trait. This view, which looms so large in the rabbinic impurity discourse, means that in the Mishnah human beings not only respond to the world of impurity (that is, to the ongoing presence of impure things and people in their vicinity) by choosing how to conduct themselves in relation to it, but also *construct* the world of impurity by forming or not forming mental investments in objects and by reacting to what happens to these objects in particular ways. To be sure, the critical role of subjectivity and mindsets in the mishnaic world of impurity does not make this world in any way less "real" for the rabbis. The very fact that the Mishnah dedicates so much attention to the workings of susceptibility to impurity and to the ways in which it is established attests to the rabbis' fundamental view that once an object has been rendered susceptible to impurity, it is in a very real and constant risk of actually becoming impure and must be handled accordingly.[88] What the rabbinic emphasis on will, intention, and thought does do, however, is recenter the world of purity and impurity around the human subject who perceives them and reacts to them, instead of around the physical sources of impurity.

How did this rabbinic emphasis on human consciousness and will as what constitutes the world of impurity emerge? On one level, the kernel of this rabbinic view can be traced back to the biblical stipulations regarding "article[s] that may be put to use" and "food that may be eaten": these clauses, as I noted above, make the point that objects need to become part of the human realm in order to become susceptible to impurity. We may thus suggest that the rabbis essentially applied this requirement thoroughly and systematically, identifying incorporation into the human world with the subjective investment of humans. On another level, it is possible to detect certain resonance, albeit not a conclusive direct connection, between the rabbinic discourse of purity and impurity and the intellectual context of the Graeco-Roman world of the first to the third centuries,[89] in which themes of subjectivity, mindsets, and personal disposition were becoming rapidly more prominent.[90] While fully acknowledging that the rabbinic notion of subjectivity is markedly different from the notions of subjectivity that emerge from Greek and Latin literature,[91] we cannot ignore the fact that the rabbis' preoccupation with what people think, feel, intend, see, and want as formative components in the making of the halakhic world speaks to a vested interest in human consciousness, which they significantly shared with other contemporaneous authors. This interest, as I hope to have made evident by now, profoundly transforms the biblical impurity system that the rabbis inherited, and creates a radically new form of legal discourse, in which impurity is located not within things, but in the *relations between people and things*.

The centering of the world of impurity on the human subject, and the consideration of humanness as the condition for partaking in the world of impurity, will continue to engage us in the next chapter, in which I turn to discuss the corpse as one of the more perplexing objects that inhabit this world, an object located somewhere between the human and the nonhuman.

4

# On Corpses and Persons

For the rabbis, as I mentioned in the first chapter, impurity is by definition the ability to make *others* impure, and to contract impurity from a person or object effectively means to acquire the ability to impart impurity to something or someone else. Accordingly, since impurity can travel well beyond the primary source, every contractor of impurity is also a potential conveyor of impurity, if only in an attenuated degree. Interestingly, the premise that a secondary (and sometime even tertiary) contractor of impurity in turn becomes a source of impurity in and of itself also operates in the reverse direction, since the rabbis construct the ability to convey impurity as almost inevitably preceded by the contraction of impurity. Simply put, the premise in the Mishnah is that if something or someone is now impure (in such a way as to be able to make others impure) it is because something or someone else initially made *it* impure. Impurity, in this view, is not an intrinsic quality but always (or, as I will point out momentarily, almost always) the result of contact with an external source. This view is quite self-evident in the case of inanimate objects (artifacts, foods, and liquids), which the Priestly Code explicitly mentions only as secondary sources of impurity and never as primary sources: a loaf of bread, for example, can under no circumstances generate its own impurity; it can only be impure if it has contact with an impure substance. However, the rhetorical formulae used in the Mishnah to refer to states of bodily impurity indicate that the rabbis applied the same premise—namely, that a state of impurity is by necessity a result of the contraction of impurity rather than an intrinsic quality—even to persons whose state of impurity is a result of their own bodily condition.

In the Mishnah, when a person effectively functions as a primary source of impurity due to his or her bodily condition, as in the case of genital discharges and skin afflictions, the rabbis use the passive-reflexive form of the verb "to make impure" to refer to this person, presenting the state of being impure as a result of *having being made* impure. The usage of the passive verb form "is made impure" *(mitame)* in reference to persons with impurity-generating bodily conditions paints a picture in which the bodily condition *unto itself* is the source of impurity and the person experiencing this condition in effect contracts his or her own impurity from the bodily condition, as it were, in the same manner in which a loaf of bread contracts impurity from an impure person that touches it.[1] Thus a menstruating woman is said to be "made impure by menstruation" *(mitam'a be-niddah)*,[2] a man (or a woman) with genital discharge is "made impure by genital discharge" *(mitame be-ziva)*,[3] and afflicted areas in the body are "made impure by skin afflictions" *(mitam'in bi-nega'im)*.[4] Bodily conditions are presented in these formulae as external sources of impurity that make one impure through contact: one is "made impure by (one's own) skin afflictions" in the same way that persons or artifacts are, for example, "made impure by the dead" *(mitam'in ba-met)* when touching it or sharing a space with it.[5] The rabbis, then, construct the function of the human body as a conveyor of impurity—even of the primary impurity that stems from its own condition—as the result of the contraction of impurity from something that cannot be identified with the body itself.

There is, however, one subgroup of sources of impurity among those mentioned in the Priestly Code that does not lend itself to the rhetoric of passive contraction of impurity from an external entity. This subgroup consists of various dead creatures—human corpses, animal carrion, and carcasses of creeping and crawling creatures—that cannot be said to have "contracted" impurity, but must be considered as *identical* with the impurity they convey. Unlike the impurity of persons with genital discharges or skin afflictions, which can be seen as contracted from the affliction or the discharge itself,[6] the impurity of dead creatures cannot be traced back to any specific source except for "death" as such, which is too abstract to play a part in the highly concrete rabbinic impurity circuit. The dead is the only entity that can convey impurity to others without having first contracted it from something else,[7] an oddity that generates the paradoxical comment found in Midrash *Sifre zutta* to Numbers: "The one who touches the dead is impure, but the dead himself is not impure *(ein 'atzmo shel met tame)*."[8] In the rabbinic framework, in which impurity is primarily a contracted feature, the dead cannot be considered properly "impure" because he or she did not actually contract impurity from anyone or anything. Accordingly, the *Sifre zutta* asserts that if the dead are resurrected, they do not require purification of any sort when coming back to life, and can even immediately handle holy articles and foods (whereas those who touched them when they were still dead require a week-long purification procedure).

This unique quality of dead bodies, which are not in "a state" of impurity but rather perpetually and incorrigibly *embody* impurity in their very being, has been an ongoing source of fascination for readers and interpreters of the Hebrew Bible, who attempted to fathom what is it that makes dead creatures—and most notably the human corpse—the epitome of impurity. A prominent idea that recurs in many of the explanations proposed for the intense impurity of the corpse in the biblical tradition is that the impurity of the corpse is a manifestation of its *loss of personhood*. Such view was expressed already by the Jewish-Hellenistic philosopher Philo of Alexandria (d. ca. 50 C.E.), who wrote: "For the soul of man is a valuable thing, and when that has quitted its habitation, and passed to another place, everything that is left behind by it is polluted as being deprived of the divine image."[9] Almost two thousand years later, the Bulgarian-French psychoanalyst Julia Kristeva defined the polluting power of the corpse as deriving from its being, in her terms, a "non-subject":[10] "A body without a soul, a non-body, disquieting matter, it is to be excluded from God's *territory* as it is from his *speech*."[11] Their very different conceptual language and intellectual orientations notwithstanding, both Philo and Kristeva associate the impurity of the corpse with its lack of subjectivity: they maintain that it is only an illusion of a human being, since it is devoid of what makes human bodies into persons.

In this chapter, I will argue that the Mishnah's treatment of corpse impurity presents a close engagement with the question of personhood, and that the rabbis consider the extent to which the corpse can be regarded as a person as the key to the discernment and determination of its power to convey impurity. However, I will show that the paradigm that underlies the rabbinic reconstruction of biblical corpse impurity is exactly opposite to the view presented above: for the rabbis, a corpse can convey impurity only insofar as it can *still* be considered a person, and the less a corpse can be identified as a person, the less capable it is of conveying impurity. Like Philo and Kristeva, the rabbis saw the corpse as a deteriorated shadow of a living person, although the rabbis focused on the deterioration of the physical body itself rather than on the soul's presumed abandonment of the body. But whereas for Philo and Kristeva (as well as for others)[12] the growing dissimilarity between the living person and the corpse is the *cause* of the corpse's impurity, for the rabbis this growing dissimilarity is exactly what *diminishes* the corpse's impurity. Put differently, for the rabbis the impurity of the corpse depends not on its disparity from a body that we can identify with ourselves, but rather on its *similarity* to a body that we can identify with ourselves.

At the center of this chapter stands the rabbinic development of a graded system of corpse impurity, in which some corpse parts have greater ability to convey impurity than others, and some corpse parts have no ability to convey impurity at all. I begin by examining the mishnaic classification and categorization of different corpse fragments, and show that in the rabbinic system corpse parts are considered impure only insofar as they can function as signs or symbols of a whole human being, whereas corpse parts that do not have such signifying power are considered ritually pure. I then continue to argue that the body that these fragments are thought to signify is distinctly a *living* body: corpse fragments are assessed according to the extent to which they can function in a body that is still alive, and the less commensurate with a living body that a corpse fragment is, the less impurity it can convey. Impurity is thus construed in the Mishnah as a quality that depends on personhood, and personhood is construed as a quality that depends on life. I conclude this chapter with an excursus in which I briefly discuss the concept of "rot impurity," a category that was developed in rabbinic literature as a way of setting particularly high standards of personhood and integrity for corpses, thus creating an almost unattainable ideal of "a perfect corpse."

## SIGNIFYING FRAGMENTS

In the Priestly Code, the corpse stands out as the most powerful source of impurity.[13] Its force to convey impurity to everything and everyone around it exceeds the force of any other source of impurity, both in the modes in which impurity is transmitted and in the duration of this impurity. The corpse is the only entity that conveys impurity through shared space as well as through direct contact,[14] and the impurity it conveys lasts seven days rather than one day, which is the standard duration of secondary impurity.[15] The rabbis of the Mishnah continued to emphasize that the impurity of the corpse is greater than that of all the other sources of impurity,[16] not only by substantially expanding the category of shared space or "overhang," but also by pointing to the power of the corpse to duplicate its impurity through contact with artifacts.[17] However, while many facets in the rabbinic concept of corpse impurity can largely be seen as part of a systematic development of the biblical model, the rabbis introduced a new and unique view on the seemingly trivial question of what a corpse *is*.[18]

In tractate *Oholot* of the Mishnah, a lengthy tractate that deals in great detail with the ways in which corpse impurity is conveyed and contracted, the rabbis are preoccupied with the uncanny but unavoidable question of the distinction between dead bodies and the physical environment in which they are placed and into which they often unrecognizably coalesce. Openly and matter of factly discussing processes of decomposition and decay, in which the corpse rapidly loses its human form, dissolves into its surroundings, and eventually becomes almost indistinguishable from other organic matter, the rabbis construe the corpse as an entity in gradual transition from the human to the nonhuman, at the end of which it essentially disappears and becomes one with its environment. Since the rabbis saw corpses as steadily disintegrating, the paradigmatic corpse in the Mishnah is *a body in ruins:* the corpse is conceived of and described not as an intact seemingly human entity, but as an assemblage of fragments (bones, bits and pieces of flesh, residues of blood, dregs of decayed matter, and so forth). The rabbis' task in their reconstruction of the biblical laws of corpse impurity is to determine at which point a dead body in its fragmented and ruined state is still a "corpse" that can convey impurity, and at which point it is so disintegrated and decomposed that it can only be seen as organic matter, incapable of conveying impurity any longer. This task is taken on by creating a graded scale of corpse purity, onto which corpse parts and fragments are mapped as having different degrees of ability to convey impurity.

### The Graded System of Corpse Impurity

The biblical account of corpse impurity mentions two ways in which the impurity of the corpse is conveyed. If the corpse is contained in a confined space, it transmits impurity to everything within this space; but if the corpse lies in an open space, one must have direct physical contact with it in order to become impure. The same applies for any human bone and for graves, which convey impurity to anyone who touches them in the same way that corpses do:

> This is the law [that applies] when a person dies in a tent: anyone who enters the tent and anyone who is in it will be unclean for seven days, and every open container without a lid fastened on it will be unclean.
>
> Anyone out in the open who touches someone who has been killed with a sword or someone who has died a natural death, or anyone who touches a human bone or a grave, will be unclean for seven days.[19]

In the biblical account, the distinction between impurity conveyed by touch and impurity conveyed by a "tent" (which the rabbis expanded to include any kind of shared overhang with the dead) does not pertain in any way to the nature of the corpse in question, but only to its location. The same corpse will convey impurity by overhang when in a tent and by touch when out in the field, and presumably a bone in a tent will convey impurity by overhang, in the same way that a bone in an open field conveys impurity by touch. In all likelihood, the bone was mentioned only in the context of outdoor corpses since bones, like graves, are normally not found in confined spaces.

The rabbis of the Mishnah, however, utilized the biblical distinction between impurity conveyed by overhang and impurity conveyed by touch to construct a distinction between different types of corpse fragments. They submitted that the question of whether a part of a corpse conveys impurity by touch or by overhang depends not only on its location, but also on its *degree* of impurity: the ability to convey impurity by overhang is a quality that requires greater impurity-force, so to speak, than the ability to convey impurity by touch. The Mishnah thus introduces a graded system of corpse impurity, in which different kinds of bodily fragments are divided into three groups: fragments that convey impurity by overhang as well as by touch, fragments that convey impurity only by touch (as well as by indirect carriage, which is considered to be a form of touch) but not by overhang, and fragments that do not convey impurity at all. The assumption that underlies this graded system is that corpse fragments must meet certain standards in order to function like an actual corpse in terms of impurity.

The second chapter of tractate *Oholot* of the Mishnah,[20] which is the principal rabbinic text dedicated to examining and redefining the corpse, and which will stand at the center of my discussion in this chapter, commences with a list of items that convey impurity by overhang, that is, that meet the most stringent requirements for corpse impurity:

> The following convey impurity by overhang:
> The dead [body], and a volume of an olive [of flesh] of the dead, and the volume of an olive of congealed flesh, and a ladle-full of rot;
> The spine and the skull;
> A limb from the living and a limb from the dead [body], that have sufficient flesh on them;
> A quarter [of a *qav*] of bones from the majority of the skeletal frame or its numerical majority, and the majority of the skeletal frame or its numerical majority, even if they are less than a quarter [of a *qav*]—are impure. And how much is one's numerical majority? One hundred and twenty five [bones].
> A quarter [of a *log*] of blood and a quarter [of a *log*] of mixed-blood [convey impurity by overhang] . . .[21]

The passage begins by stating the obvious: "the dead" is the quintessential conveyor of impurity by overhang.[22] We can only assume that by "the dead" the Mishnah is referring to a whole corpse, whereas all the other items in the list are fragments "of the dead" *(min ha-met)*. One might wonder why it was considered necessary to include "the dead" here as an independent category when clearly a whole dead body includes flesh, bones, and so on, which are sources of impurity in and of themselves.[23] I suggest that by including the obvious category of "the dead" in this list the Mishnah implies that the yardstick against which all corpse parts are assessed is the body when it is whole, and that the parts included in this list are emblematic, as I will argue, of a human body as such.

Looking closely at the list in this passage, we can identify three major categories of corpse components: flesh, bones, and decayed matter ("rot"). If we add the first item in the following mishnaic passage (M. Oholot 2.2), we have a fourth category, blood.[24] The category of bones further comprises four subgroups: (i) skull and spine; (ii) limbs detached from dead persons; (iii) limbs detached from living persons;[25] (iv) all other bones. For some of the items in the list, the Mishnah stipulates that they must meet a *quantitative* standard, that is, that a certain minimum amount of them is required to convey impurity by overhang. For flesh, a very small amount of an olive-bulk (around thirty-five cc) is enough to convey impurity, and the same is the case with congealed, gel-like flesh *(netzel)*.[26] For "rot" *(raqav)*, that is, decayed matter that was crushed into powder, a larger quantity, a "ladle-full," is required. For blood, the required amount is a quarter of a *log* (about ninety ml).[27]

As for the fourfold division of bones, here the picture is more complex. All bones can convey impurity by overhang if they meet a strictly quantitative standard, which is expressed by a measure of volume—one quarter of a *qav* (around four hundred cc). However, this volume has to consist of the bones of *one person only*: in the language of the Mishnah, the bones in question must constitute either part of the numerical majority of bones in one's body or part of the skeletal frame that comprises most of one's height. Scattered fragments of bones from multiple people will not convey impurity by overhang, according to this passage, even if their quantity is a quarter of a *qav* or more.[28] Alternatively, bones that actually constitute more than half the numerical amount of bones in the body (which according to M. Oholot 1.8 is 248, making its "more than half" 125), or that comprise most of one's skeletal frame, convey impurity even when their volume is less than a quarter of a *qav* (for example, in the case of the skeleton of a child). In contrast, the spine and the skull and individual limbs are assessed not based on quantity but based on wholeness. The skull and the spine are units unto themselves, whose impurity, as we shall see momentarily, depends on their being intact. The same requirement for intactness applies to limbs, either from the living or from the dead, which convey impurity as long as they are whole and have some flesh on them. "Limb" here refers to any of the 248 bones that compose the skeleton according to M. Oholot 1.8: any one of those bones, when whole, even if very small, can convey impurity by overhang. We can thus identify two different criteria according to which corpse fragments are classified in the Mishnah: a criterion of size or volume, and a criterion of unit integrity.

What happens when corpse fragments of the four said categories (flesh, rot, blood, and bones) are either diminished in quantity or compromised in integrity in such a way that they no longer meet the requirements put forth in the above list? In the case of the first three, the answer is simple: the Mishnah specifies that less than an olive-bulk of flesh or congealed flesh, less than a ladle-full of rot, and less than a quarter *log* of blood do not convey impurity at all.[29] Rather, they are simply dismissed as nonexistent and have absolutely no bearing on their surroundings. In the case of bones, however, the picture is once again more complicated: here the rabbis create not a binary division (conveys impurity/does not convey impurity) but rather a *ternary* division. According to the Mishnah, only bones that meet the criteria of volume and integrity mentioned above can convey impurity by overhang (that is, like an entire corpse). However, no bone that originates in a dead person can stop conveying impurity altogether until its size is less than that of an ear of barley.[30] Thus, bones that do not meet the requirements for conveying impurity by overhang (due to insufficient quantity or because they are not intact) but

| Body part | Conveys impurity by touch, carriage, and overhang | Conveys impurity only by touch/carriage | Does not convey impurity at all |
|---|---|---|---|
| Flesh/congealed flesh | The volume of an olive-bulk or more | — | Less than the volume of an olive-bulk |
| Rot | Ladle-full or more | — | Less than a ladle-full |
| Blood | Quarter of a *log* or more | — | Less than quarter of a *log* |
| Bones | | | |
| Spine and skull | When whole | When lacking | Less than the size of an ear of barley |
| Limbs from the dead | When whole with sufficient flesh | When whole without sufficient flesh | Less than the size of an ear of barley |
| Limbs from the living | When whole with sufficient flesh | When whole without sufficient flesh | When not whole |
| Nonspecific bones | Quarter of a *qav* (from one person) *or* the numerical majority or the majority of the skeletal frame (from one person) | The size of an ear of barley or more | Less than the size of an ear of barley |

are still larger than the size of an ear of barley are classified into a third, intermediate category, and are declared to convey impurity by touch but not by overhang.[31] This intermediate category, which includes a lacking skull or spine, whole limbs without sufficient flesh on them, or any other bone down to the size of an ear of barley, rests on an exacting reading of the biblical verse "anyone who touches a human bone . . . will be unclean for seven days," taking it to mean that a nonspecific bone (that is, a bone that is not substantial enough in either amount or integrity) can convey impurity *only* through touch.

The Mishnah establishes, then, a graded system of corpse impurity, in which the ability of corpse parts to convey impurity is diminished as they disintegrate and become more fragmented. The table above summarizes this graded system according to the classification of corpse parts in M. Oholot 2.1–5.[32]

How did this graded system of corpse impurity, which has no trace in the Priestly Code, emerge in the rabbinic discourse, and what are the fundamental perceptions regarding the essence of the corpse and its power to convey impurity that underlie it? On the face of it, the rabbis' enterprise here, namely, the determination and specification of minimum standards that must be met for a legal category (in this case, corpse impurity) to take effect, is not different from their enterprise in a myriad of other halakhic discussions. Just as the rabbis set four cubits as the minimum distance of travel that constitutes a violation of the Sabbath, or ten handbreadths as the minimum height for a sukkah, or one out of sixty as the minimum quantity at which forbidden food disqualifies permitted food, so they set certain minimum quantities for determining what is still "enough of a corpse," so to speak, to convey impurity. Once the rabbis put forth the notion that corpse parts can convey impurity just like entire corpses (a notion that is already implied in the biblical reference to bones), it is only reasonable that they would set minimum requirements that all corpse parts must meet in order to be considered consequential in terms of impurity. Nevertheless, the complex treatment that bones receive in this classificatory system indicates that there is more going on here than a standard pragmatic attempt to affix minimum quantities.

As they do in the case of blood, flesh, and rot, the rabbis set a minimum quantity below which bones cannot convey impurity: this quantity is the size of an ear of barley. Unlike in the other cases, however, meeting this minimum quantity is not a sufficient condition for a bone to convey impurity by overhang (that is, like an entire corpse). Rather, the standards that bones have to meet to convey impurity by overhang are much higher: their volume must be significantly more substantial than that of an ear of barley, or alternatively, they must comprise identifiable bodily units and be intact as such. The very division of the general category of bones into further subcategories is curious, considering that the minimum quantity of an ear of barley applies to all of them (with the exception of a limb from the living), and even more curious is the rabbis' establishment of an "intermediate" degree of impurity for bones that meet the minimum size requirement but do not meet other standards. This distinction between different kinds of bones and the notion that different kinds of bones convey impurity in different degrees depending on their physical condition and not just depending on their quantity strongly suggest that the classification of corpse parts in the Mishnah is guided by a principle that goes beyond quantity per se. In what follows, I will attempt to uncover this principle, and will offer some implications of this principle for understanding the rabbinic concept of corpse impurity more broadly.

## Corpse Impurity and Symbolic Personhood

The Mishnah itself does not provide us with any explicit explanation for its graded system of corpse impurity or for the logic behind its ternary categorization of corpse parts. However, an extremely helpful key for understanding the principle that underlies the classificatory system of the Mishnah is found in the *Sifre zutta*, an early rabbinic Midrash to the book of Numbers, which is contemporaneous with or slightly later than the Mishnah.[33] The Midrash expounds on the word *person (adam)* in the biblical ordinance starting with the words *when a person dies in a tent,* and derives from this word that anything that has the capacity to bring about impurity in a tent must be tantamount to a whole person:

> "This is the law, when a person dies in a tent." If by saying "person" the intention is to exclude animal carcasses, this has already been taught; therefore, what must I maintain—that [the word] *"person" is meant to include another thing that conveys impurity like an entire corpse.* What do I include—the spine and the skull, and half a *log* of blood and half a *qav* of bones and a limb from the living and a limb from the dead with sufficient flesh on them, and a quarter *qav* from the majority of the skeletal frame and a quarter *qav* of the numerical majority and a quarter from the majority of the height of the body[34]—those convey impurity by touch, carriage, and overhang.[35]

There are several discrepancies between the list of corpse parts in the *Sifre zutta* and the corresponding list in the Mishnah. Most notably, the list in the *Sifre zutta* does not mention the categories of flesh, congealed flesh, and rot,[36] and the volumes it specifies for bones and blood are larger than the quantities stipulated in the Mishnah (half a *qav/log* rather than a quarter).[37] Nevertheless, the two lists are similar enough, especially in their classification and subdivision of bones, to allow us to use the *Sifre zutta* to illuminate the Mishnah. The *Sifre zutta* prefaces its list by stating that in order to convey impurity by overhang—that is, in order to convey impurity like an entire corpse—a fragment of a corpse must be able to stand for a person *(adam),* so as literally to comply with the biblical edict commencing with "when a *person* dies in a tent" (Numbers 19:14). Accordingly, we may define the determinant requirement that corpse parts must meet in order to convey impurity as *symbolic personhood,* that is, as the ability of a part of a corpse to invoke a mental image of a whole human being.[38] Every one of the corpse fragments mentioned in the Mishnah and in the *Sifre zutta* as capable of conveying impurity by overhang, then, is a fragment that by way of synecdoche can represent the human body in its entirety.

The notion that corpse parts can represent the bodily whole is, of course, not unique to the rabbis. The cultural prevalence of this notion was observed by Philippe Ariès, who noted that "the skeleton need not be whole in order to play its role. It may be dismantled and divided into small pieces; each of its bones possesses the same symbolic value."[39] It is exactly the view of corpse parts as bearing the significance of the entire body that underlies the practice of relic veneration in different traditions, a practice that relies on the premise that a bodily fragment can capture the entire essence of the person.[40] A particularly interesting and relevant manifestation of this idea can be found in the Roman custom of *os resectum* (severed bone), in which a bone, usually a digit, was cut off from the dead body prior to its cremation. As Emma-Jayne Graham explains, the bone functioned as a symbol for the body in all the changes that the dead was seen as going through: whereas the actual body had to be disposed of rather quickly, the severed bone could be subject to elaborate rituals of purification and veneration, and thus symbolically enable a more gradual transition for the person into the world of the dead.[41] Most resonant with our discussion here is Varro's comment that "if the bone of the dead was set aside for the household's purification, until it is interred into the purifying ground... the household remains polluted" *(si os exceptum est mortui ad familiam purgandam, donec in purgando humo est opertum... familia funesta manet).*[42] Varro's comment indicates that for the Romans, the fragment that signified the dead held within it the polluting power of the dead in its entirety.

However, the rabbinic system of graded corpse impurity emphasizes not only the potential ability of corpse fragments to signify entire persons, but also the notion that fragments must meet certain criteria in order to serve as such signifiers. Above I identified two alternative criteria according to which the force of different corpse parts to convey impurity is determined, namely, quantity and integrity. I now propose that these two criteria serve as two ways of assessing the fragment vis-à-vis the whole body, which are used to decide whether this fragment can be seen as significant enough to stand for an entire person or not. For items such as blood, flesh, and nonspecific bones, the Mishnah requires a quantity substantial enough to signify the entire amount of these substances in the body, in such a way that a small quantity represents the larger quantity. Certain bones in the body, however, which are quintessentially human in their shape (that is, the skull, the spine, and limbs that still have flesh on them), have the power to signify personhood unto themselves.[43] These specific bones, as long as they are discernible and whole, can serve as synecdochic representations of the whole body.

With the principle of symbolic personhood in mind, we are now in a better position to understand the complex treatment of bones in the mishnaic reconstruction of corpse impurity, particularly the subdivision of bones into different categories and the surprising establishment of an intermediate category of impurity. Bones are the only parts of the corpse that are explicitly mentioned in the Priestly Code as capable of conveying impurity like an entire corpse. Whereas the biblical text mentioned only "bone," without referring either to quantity or to integrity, thus implying that *any* bone is equivalent to an entire corpse, the rabbis interpreted the biblical edict to cohere with their requirement that the fragment should represent an entire person. Since the unspecified bone was mentioned in the Bible in the context of touch, the rabbis limited the impurity-force of a nonspecific "bone the size of an ear of barley" to touch and carriage, and maintained that in order to convey impurity by overhang bones must be able to stand for the body as a whole. They also specified that there are several different ways in which bones can represent the body. One way is, of course, by quantity: a quarter *qav* of bones (or half a *qav,* according to the *Sifre zutta*) is a substantial enough amount to signify the entire body, as long as it is from a single person. Another way is by proportion: if the bones at hand comprise most of the bones in one's body, either in number or in their constitution of the skeletal frame, they can also stand for the entire person. Finally, specific bones that are discernibly human, like the skull, the spine, or limbs with flesh on them, can be emblematic of an entire person and convey impurity by overhang in and of themselves. Since a common burial practice during the time of the Mishnah was *ossilegium* (burial of bones only, after allowing the body to decompose), in which bones were seen as identical with the person herself,[44] it should not surprise us that the rabbis thought out several ways in which bones can be taken as representing the whole body.[45]

The idea that corpse parts that are significant either in size or in shape can symbolically represent the entire body is interestingly reflected in the Mishnah's discussion on the impurity of apertures in a house. As a rule, if a person dies in a house, all the apertures (such as windows and doors) in the house and all that is in them are deemed impure, because the corpse can potentially pass through any of them on its way out of the house. However, if a specific aperture was designated as the one through which the dead will be taken out of the house, only the designated aperture becomes impure, and the other apertures remain pure. According to the Mishnah, if one wishes to designate a specific aperture through which to take out the dead from the house, the height of the designated aperture has to be determined in accordance with the amount that remains of the corpse in question. If an olive-bulk of flesh remains from the corpse, the height of the aperture designated for removing it from the house must be at least one handbreadth *(tefah)*, but if an *entire* dead body is to be taken out of the house, the height of the designated aperture has to be at least four handbreadths. The Mishnah then says:

> [An amount] greater than the volume of an olive-bulk is like the [entire] dead (that is, requires an aperture of four handbreadths).
> R. Yose says: The spine and the skull are like the [entire] dead.[46]

The parallel Tosefta passage adds:

> Others say in the name of R. Nathan: All the impurities that depart from the dead are like the [entire] dead, and [the height of] their [designated] aperture [must be] four handbreadths.[47]

In these passages it is suggested that if the amount of corpse-matter is substantial enough to convey impurity by overhang, any amount greater than this amount (according to the anonymous Mishnah) or even equal to this amount (according to R. Nathan) is considered as an entire dead body, insofar as it requires the same height of aperture as a whole corpse. Thus, in what concerns corpse impurity the part not only represents the whole, but actually *functions* like the whole.[48]

An important facet of the rabbinic principle of symbolic personhood, albeit a contested facet, is the requirement that the fragments in question come from one and only one corpse. As we have seen, the Mishnah specifies that a quarter *qav* of bones must be either from the numerical majority or from the skeletal majority, that is, even if the bones are scattered and broken they must all be from the same body and not from multiple corpses. This requirement, which is expressed anonymously in M. Oholot 2.1, notably follows the opinion of the House of Hillel in a controversy brought forth in tractate *Eduyot*:

> The [disciples of the] House of Shammai say: A quarter [*qav*] of bones from [any] bones [conveys impurity by overhang], be it from two or three dead bodies.
> 
> The [disciples of the] House of Hillel say: A quarter *qav* [conveys impurity by overhang only if it is] from one dead body, from the majority of the skeletal frame or the numerical majority.
> 
> Shammai says: [A quarter *qav* conveys impurity] even if it is from one bone.[49]

For the disciples of the House of Shammai, the only decisive parameter in the determination of the impurity-force of bones is volume. They maintain that as long as more than a quarter of a *qav* of bones in any shape or form can be found in one place, these bones convey impurity like an entire corpse whether they are from one body or from several bodies. In contrast, the disciples of the House of Hillel maintain that the required volume of bones must originate from one corpse and only from one corpse. For the Hillelites, the frame of reference through which bones are assessed is emphatically an entire human body as one discrete unit, and it is according to their ability to represent a single human body that the impurity-force of corpse fragments is determined. This controversy of the two houses resonates with another series of controversies that appears in tractate *Oholot*:

> The spine and the skull from two dead bodies, and a quarter [*log*] of blood from two dead bodies, and a quarter [*qav*] of bones from two dead bodies, and a limb from the dead from two dead bodies, and a limb from the living from two persons—R. Aqiva renders them impure, and the Sages render them pure.[50]

The controversy between R. Aqiva and the Sages seems like an expansion or broader application of the controversy between the houses in tractate *Eduyot*, with R. Aqiva uncharacteristically siding with the House of Shammai. According to R. Aqiva, as long as there is a sufficient amount of corpse-matter to convey impurity by overhang, this corpse-matter conveys impurity even if it originates in more than one body. For example, if the minimal requirement for impurity is a quarter *log* of blood, and in one place there can be found an eighth *log* of blood from one corpse and an eighth *log* of blood from another corpse, together these two eighths constitute a quarter *log* that conveys impurity. Conversely, the Sages maintain that corpse-matter conveys impurity only if the entire required amount originates in one and only one dead body.[51]

While the view that only corpse fragments from a single corpse can convey impurity by overhang was clearly a matter of ongoing tannaitic dispute,[52] it is quite evident that this is the position endorsed by the redactors of the Mishnah, as it is presented anonymously in M. Oholot 2.1 (regarding bones) and in M. Oholot 2.2 (regarding blood), and is associated with the majority opinion of "the Sages" in M. Oholot 2.6.[53] The prominence of this position in the redacted Mishnah indicates that for the redactors, corpse fragments were seen as capable of conveying impurity only insofar as they represent not only the generic species of human beings, but actually a *particular* human being.[54] Put differently, it was not enough for them that the amount of corpse-matter at hand constitutes a significant enough amount of bodily substance as such; rather, they insisted that corpse fragments must constitute a synecdochic representation of the actual body from which they came.

Whence emerged the principle that I call here "symbolic personhood," that is, the idea that corpse fragments can convey impurity only insofar as they can stand for whole persons? One conceivable answer to this question is that the rabbis were motivated by a pragmatic decision to reduce the ubiquity of corpse impurity. By maintaining that corpse parts must be substantial enough in quantity or in shape to convey impurity, the rabbis effectively restricted the pervasiveness of corpse impurity and significantly decreased one's chance of becoming impure simply by inadvertently overshadowing, for example, a tiny piece of human bone. While such an explanation is essentially unverifiable, the fact that we have seen several instances in which the rabbis clearly operate with the intention of making impurity more manageable and controllable[55] suggests that similar pragmatic considerations may have guided the rabbis in their restrictive interpretation of corpse impurity as well. Alternatively, another way of accounting for this principle and for the graded system of impurity that is guided by it is to see this principle as deriving from a rather straightforward interpretive process, similar to the one delineated in the *Sifre zutta*. Since Scripture specifically mentions a "person" *(adam)* as the source of corpse impurity, the rabbis, who were aware of the inevitable fragmentation of the body after death, attempted to discern to what extent corpse fragments can be construed as "person." They thus developed the criterion of symbolic personhood—that is, the ability of a fragment to represent the whole—in order to comply with the biblical ordinance in the most literal way possible.

While it is very plausible that the rabbis were guided here by a combination of pragmatic and hermeneutic motivations,[56] I wish to call attention to the premise that seems to be underlying their innovative construction of graded corpse impurity, which is that the full power of the corpse to convey impurity depends on the extent to which it still recognizably belongs to the human realm. This premise resonates with the view I identified in the previous chapter in respect to inanimate objects, according to which objects must be invested with human subjectivity and actively transformed into part of a human being's extended body in order to partake in the circuit of purity and impurity. The case of corpses is, of course, different from that of inanimate objects, insofar as impurity is seen as intrinsic to the corpse rather than as a state to which it is susceptible or insusceptible, but the notion that the corpse loses its force to convey impurity as it is further removed from discernible human form speaks, I believe, to the same essential rabbinic view. Here I should mention that a similar principle which closely ties together the ability to convey impurity and recognizable humanness can be found in the Mishnah's discussion regarding the impurity of the parturient woman, in which the Sages rule that an aborted fetus cannot render its mother impure as a parturient unless this fetus had the discernible form of a human being.[57] It seems, then, that the rabbinic insistence that a corpse or corpse fragment must be able to stand for a person to convey full impurity has to do not only with pragmatic and hermeneutic considerations, but also with a fundamental perception of impurity as a marker of pertinence to the human world.

But what, exactly, is the "person" against which all corpse parts are assessed, and what is the mental image they are supposed to invoke? What constitutes the quality of personhood for the rabbis in their view that personhood is what gives corpses and corpse parts power in terms of impurity? In order to answer these questions, we must delve a little deeper into the particularities of the rabbinic criteria according to which corpse parts are classified. Following my analysis of these particularities, I will argue that the idea of a person by which the rabbis were guided in discussing corpse impurity is emphatically, and quite surprisingly, the idea of a *living* person.

## THE LIFE OF THE DEAD

### *The Diminished Impurity of Lacking Corpses*

So far I focused mainly on the list of corpse parts that convey impurity by overhang, that is, body parts whose capacity to convey impurity is maximal and is comparable to that of an entire corpse. However, the rabbinic graded system of corpse impurity in general, and the principle of symbolic personhood in particular, cannot be fully understood without an examination of the second list in the same mishnaic chapter, which enumerates items that can convey impurity by touch and carriage, but not by overhang. This curious intermediate category, as I will show, provides us with a key to a more comprehensive understanding of the rabbinic notion of corpse impurity and, ultimately, to uncovering an important aspect of the rabbis' concept of a person.

The list of items that convey impurity in the "intermediate" degree reads as follows:

> The following convey impurity by touch and carriage, but not by overhang:
> A bone the size of an ear of barley;
> And the land of the nations, and the plowed grave-field;

> A limb from the living and a limb from the dead that do not have sufficient flesh on them;
> And the spine and the skull that are lacking (that is, not whole).
> How much is a lack in the spine? The [disciples of the] House of Shammai say: Two vertebrae. The [disciples of the] House of Hillel say: Even one vertebra.
> And [how much is a lack] in the skull? The [disciples of the] House of Shammai say: A gimlet-full. The [disciples of the] House of Hillel say: [An amount that] if taken away from the living would cause him to die.[58]

This mishnaic passage lists two kinds of items: bones that do not meet the requirements specified in M. Oholot 2.1, and items that are not mentioned in the Bible and convey impurity only by the power of a rabbinic decree. The latter items ("the plowed grave-field" and the "land of nations") are in fact not corpse fragments as such, but rather physical spaces that are suspected to contain corpse fragments.[59] The rabbis utilized the category of corpse impurity conveyed by touch and carriage and not by overhang to express different kinds of attenuated or partial impurity, whether this attenuation derives from diminished quantity or compromised integrity of the item itself, or from the inferior position of the rule regarding this item in the rabbinic legal hierarchy.[60]

In terms of its classification of human bones, the list in M. Oholot 2.3 has two central functions. First, it asserts that bones of any sort continue to convey impurity in a lesser degree (that is, only by touch and carriage) even if they do not meet the requirements brought forth in M. Oholot 2.1, as long as they are larger than an ear of barley. Second, it specifies under what circumstances distinctly human and uniquely shaped bones (the skull, the spine, and limbs) are no longer capable of conveying impurity by overhang, but are rather to be considered like any other bone larger than an ear of barely. In other words, the list specifies at which point these "special" bones lose their intensified symbolic personhood and become just plain pieces of bone. According to the Mishnah, the quality that allows skulls, spines, and limbs to convey impurity like entire corpses—that is, by overhang—is lost when the spine and the skull are not intact and are missing parts of themselves, and when limbs no longer have sufficient flesh on them. How do these physical flaws rob from skulls, spines, and limbs the ability to convey impurity by overhang, and what, if any, is the connection between these flaws and symbolic personhood? A direction for answering this question, I suggest, can be found in the Hillelites' definition of a "lack" in the skull.

Whereas the disciples of the House of Shammai stipulate the actual minimal size of a hole in the skull that constitutes, in their view, a "lack" that will preclude the skull from conveying impurity by overhang ("a gimlet-full"), the disciples of the House of Hillel choose a more abstract and general definition. They submit that any amount that "if taken away from the living would cause him to die *[she-yinatel min ha-hai ve-yamut]*" constitutes a substantial enough lack in the skull to not allow this skull to convey impurity by overhang.[61] They thus maintain that the impurity force of the skull is determined by asking the following question: had the skull of a living person been in such a state, would this person still be able to live? If the answer to this question is positive, the skull conveys impurity by overhang; if the answer is negative, the skull conveys impurity only by touch and carriage.

The exact same kind of question also determines the impurity-force of limbs from the living and from the dead, as the Mishnah indicates in the following passage, which is part of a larger survey of impurities that originate in the human body:

> A limb that does not have sufficient flesh on it conveys impurity by touch and carriage, and does not convey impurity by overhang.
> And if there is sufficient flesh on it—it conveys impurity by touch, carriage, and overhang.
> *The amount of sufficient flesh [is an amount that is sufficient] for it to heal.*
> R. Yehuda says: if there is enough flesh in one place to encompass it with a woof-string, there is [enough] in it to heal.[62]

The decisive factor in determining the impurity-force of a limb, whether from a dead or a living body, is the amount of flesh on it, which should be sufficient for the limb of a living person to regenerate. Just like in the case of the skull, the point of reference is the living body. In order to determine whether a detached limb can convey impurity or not, the question that is being asked is, had this limb been connected to a living person, would this limb still be able to "live"? If the answer to this question is positive, the limb conveys impurity by overhang; if the answer is negative, the limb conveys impurity only by touch and carriage.

I propose, then, that both for limbs and for the skull (according to the Hillelites' view), the critical quality that the items in the intermediate category are lacking is the quality of *life,* and this is what sets them apart from items that are capable of conveying impurity by overhang. Admittedly, this does not seem to be the case for the spine, since I doubt that the lack of one or two vertebrae was associated with death for the rabbis; here the definition of "lack" indeed seems to be more technical. However, the rabbis' reference to the living body when determining the impurity-force of corpse fragments is not restricted to skull and limbs: two rabbinic sources suggest that the minimal quantities required for impurity by overhang are distinctly the quantities that are vital for the sustenance of life. In the Tosefta, we find a statement by Abba Shaul according to which "a quarter [*log*] is the beginning of the blood of a child," that is, life does not begin until there is a quarter *log* of blood in the body.[63] Similarly, we find in the *Sifre zutta* that "an olive-bulk of the dead is impure, for this is the beginning of his creation."[64] While both of these explanations may be seen as attempts to account for the details of the mishnaic list after it had already been formed, it is not inconceivable that these traditions rely on common views on the physical constituency of embryos and infants, and that these views are what guided the rabbis in setting those quantities as minimal requirements for impurity in the first place.[65]

In the rabbinic classification of corpse parts, then, the principle of symbolic personhood is of two facets: it requires not only that the fragment will invoke the mental image of a whole person, but also that this person will be a *living* one. Put differently, the greater the distance between a corpse part and the living body, the less capable this corpse part is of conveying impurity. The yardstick against which all corpse parts are measured is thus not the intact and whole corpse, as we could have expected, but rather the living body. Indeed, a powerful indication that the rabbis understood the very category of person, *adam*, as pertaining to a living person can be found in the Midrash *Sifre* to Numbers, in a passage that sets out to include both limbs from the living and limbs from the dead in the biblical reference to "a bone of a person" (Numbers 19:16):

> "Or any one who touches a bone of a person" *(o be-etzem adam)*. This refers to a limb from the living.
> Is it possible that it actually refers to a bone the size of an ear of barley [from the dead]?
> When it says "or any one who touches a bone"—this refers to a bone the size of an ear of barley [from the dead]. Why was it said "a bone *of a person*"?—[because] this refers to a limb from the living.[66]

According to this midrashic passage, if the biblical reference to a bone were meant to include only the bones of the dead, it would have been enough to mention only the word *bone* in the verse. The very fact that the verse makes a specific reference to the bone *of a person* indicates, for the rabbinic exegetes, that the category of bone also includes a bone from the living. The interpretive move in this passage, in which the word *person* is read as necessarily referring to a *living* person, strongly suggests that the perception that *person* equals *living* stood at the core of the rabbinic understanding of the workings of corpse impurity.

The idea that the corpse and its parts are essentially measured and assessed against a living person is further developed in the Tosefta, which goes beyond the Mishnah in subcategorizing the corpse. While the Mishnah only distinguishes between different fragments of corpses, the Tosefta also distinguishes between different kinds of whole corpses, ultimately suggesting that corpses that are not sufficiently "alive" do not qualify as corpses in the full sense of the word:

> A lacking [corpse] has no occupancy of graves *(tefisat qevarot)* and no neighborhood of graves *(shekhunat qevarot)*.
> And which is a lack? Rabbi says: [An amount that] if taken away from the living would cause him to die.[67]

According to the Tosefta, corpses that are not fully intact (for example, that are missing an arm or a leg) are subject to less strict rules than corpses that are intact. For intact corpses, if they are transferred from their grave, the dust of the grave must be transferred with them; this "claim" that corpses make on their immediate surroundings is known as "occupancy of graves." Lacking corpses, in contrast, have no such "occupancy of graves" and one need not transfer the dust of the grave along with the corpses if they are moved to another grave. Similarly, the rabbis rule that if one finds three of more corpses buried in the same area, this is a "neighborhood of graves" and the graves there must not be evacuated; however, if one of the corpses is not intact, it does not count as one of the three in declaring this area a "neighborhood of graves." The Tosefta thus takes the Mishnah's requirement of the integrity of corpse fragments one step further: while in order to convey impurity by overhang corpse parts must *represent* a whole person, to be considered as a corpse for all intents and purposes corpses must *actually* be whole. Rabbi's definition of a "lack" that compromises the corpse's integrity is an exact replication of the Hillelites' definition of a lack in a skull that precludes it from conveying impurity by overhang: "[An amount that] if taken away from the living would cause him to die." In the Tosefta's tradition, then, the entire corpse, and not just particular body parts, is assessed against a living person, and it is suggested that only corpses whose physical state would allow them to live had they not been dead are indeed corpses to which all the rules regarding corpses apply. The ultimate dead, according to this view, is one who most closely resembles the living.[68]

Interestingly, the Tosefta's ruling regarding "lacking" corpses is identical with its ruling regarding miscarried fetuses *(nefalim)*. Although dead fetuses convey impurity by overhang like any other dead (as long as there are sufficient quantities of flesh, blood, and so on in their bodies), they have neither occupancy of graves nor a neighborhood of graves.[69] Here too, I believe, this ruling can be explained in light of the general rabbinic view that fetuses are not fully alive creatures, and thus not full persons.[70] The questionable personhood of fetuses in rabbinic law stems not only from the rabbis' view that unborn babies are essentially part of their mothers,[71] but also from the view that a fetus who has not been carried in the womb for at least eight months is unlikely to survive even if it did happen to be born alive.[72] The notion that a fetus that came out (dead or alive) before completing its term is not quite a person is evident from the mishnaic ruling that if such fetus is killed, the one who killed it is not liable for murder.[73] The quality that fetuses who did not go through an entire term of pregnancy lack, and that denies them full personhood, can be inferred from the rabbinic expression used to denote the opposite of miscarried and premature-born fetuses, which is "viable beings" *(benē qeyama,* literally, "beings of existence"), a phrase that indicates that fetuses are *not* viable beings, that is, unlikely to survive.[74] In the context of corpse impurity, since the fetus was never seen as truly alive, and therefore was never seen as a full person, the dead fetus does not function like a corpse in all possible respects. Once again, we see that full "corpsehood," so to speak, depends upon full personhood, and full personhood depends upon being alive.

### The Paradox of the Living Corpse

The notion that the corpse must be as "living" as possible to convey impurity and to function fully as a corpse is, admittedly, profoundly paradoxical. According to this notion, while a body must be unequivocally dead to convey corpse impurity,[75] this impurity depends on the body's hypothetical ability to live. Put differently, corpses and corpse fragments are assessed by examining whether the body or body parts in question would have been able to live had they not been dead.

As strange as this idea sounds, it closely resonates with another rabbinic principle, which concerns the definition of forbidden meat. In addition to the prohibition of eating carrion *(nevelah)*, that is, animals that died a natural death, the Pentateuch also prohibits the eating of *terefah*, literally "torn" or "devoured" animal.[76] The rabbis interpret the latter category as pertaining to animals that would have died within a year of the time they were slaughtered, on account of some disease or injury.[77] The practical implication of this interpretation is that every animal that was slaughtered for the purpose of human consumption must be physically examined for different possible defects and diseases, in order to determine whether or not this animal would have been able to keep on living had it not been slaughtered. Only if the animal is indeed certified as "living" enough may it be eaten.

The parity between the principle that governs the classification of animals as *terefot* and the principle that governs the classification of corpse parts for the determination of impurity was not lost on the later rabbis. In the Palestinian Talmud we find the ruling that if one's leg was severed above the knee, the rot from his corpse (a category on which I will expand in the excursus at the end of this chapter) cannot convey impurity, whereas if his leg was severed below the knee, the rot from his corpse can convey impurity. This is one of the quintessential distinctions between animals that may be eaten and animals that may not be eaten: "An animal whose legs were severed, below the knee—it is kosher, above the knee—it is defiled" (M. Hullin 4.6). Both the ruling regarding animals and the ruling regarding corpses are guided by the premise that if the leg is severed above the knee, the animal or the person will inevitably die, but if the leg was severed below the knee, the person or animal is likely to survive. The same distinction is also at play in determining the likelihood that a person has died in order to allow his wife to remarry: in M. Yebamot 16.4 the story is told of a person who fell into the sea, and only his leg was pulled out. The Sages decreed that if the leg was severed above the knee, it can be assumed that the person died and his wife should be allowed to remarry, but if it was severed below the knee, he may still be alive and she may not remarry. In all these cases, a leg severed above the knee is an indication that had this person or animal not been dead already, they would have died on account of the severed leg. The certainty that such injury would result in death renders animals that are injured in this way nonkosher, and renders human corpses that are injured in this way less than fully capable of conveying impurity.

The comparability of the case of corpse impurity to the case of slaughtered animals is instructive: just as the rabbis' ultimate kosher animal is a healthy, that is, living, animal, even though they are of course prohibited from eating living animals, so their ultimate dead person is a living one, even though a living person cannot convey corpse impurity. Impurity in the Mishnah is first and foremost a quality of *persons,* and only those who are alive can be truly and fully seen as persons. This view is lucidly reflected in a mishnaic passage that enumerates ten degrees of impurity whose origin is the human body.[78] The title of this list is "Ten Impurities Depart from the Person" *(porshot min ha-adam),* and it continues to mention the various human sources of impurity, such as the person with genital discharge, the person with scale disease, and so on, in an ascending order of impurity-force. When this list gets to the highest level of bodily impurity, that is, to corpse impurity, it does not attribute it to corpses, but rather to *limbs from the living* (which, indeed, convey impurity like a corpse). This seems to be a clear indication that for the rabbis a "person" who is a source of impurity is distinctly and pronouncedly a *living* person, even if the impurity in question is corpse impurity.

By ultimately assessing corpses and corpse parts against a paradigmatic living body, and by putting forth the notion that the more "dead" the corpse, the less capable it is of conveying impurity, the rabbis, in a way, turned the biblical picture of impurity on its head. Whether or not one would argue, like Jacob Milgrom, that all impurity in the Priestly Code is fundamentally death-related, and that all the bodily states and substances that are said to convey impurity involve a symbolic or actual loss of life,[79] it is undeniable that impurity in the Bible is closely associated with physical deficiency or vulnerability and with mortal danger or dead creatures. In the Priestly Code, the body's ability to convey impurity is clearly enhanced as it comes *closer* to death, not as it goes further from it. The rabbis, of course, accept the biblical list of bodily conditions that bring about impurity as a given, but they completely subvert the frame of thought that underlies it: for them, the ability to convey impurity is not a marker of a human body's partial or utter loss of life, but rather a marker of the amount of life that is still within this body. Thus, while the Mishnah does not contest the biblical notion that the dead is the most forceful source of impurity, it effectively subordinates the impurity of the dead to the impurity of the living, maintaining that the former's ability to convey impurity is a derivative of its resemblance to the latter.

This radical reconceptualization of the biblical idea of corpse impurity is strikingly articulated in a mishnaic passage in tractate *Eduyot.* This passage introduces a controversy between R. Eliezer and R. Yehoshua regarding the ability of a limb from the dead to convey impurity. Whereas R. Yehoshua states that both limbs from the living and limbs from the dead convey impurity by overhang (the position that was ultimately endorsed in the anonymous Mishnah), R. Eliezer insists that only a limb from the living conveys impurity, whereas a limb from the dead does not:[80]

> R. Yehoshua ... testified regarding a limb from the dead that it is impure, for R. Eliezer says: They (that is, his masters) only said so in respect to a limb from the living.
> [The Sages] told [R. Eliezer]: But it (that is, R. Yehoshua's opinion) is derived *a fortiori*! If it is the case that for the living, who is pure, a limb that departs from him is impure, does it not follow that for the dead, who is impure, a limb that departs from him is impure?
> He said to them: They only said so in respect to a limb from the living.
> An alternative explanation: *The impurity of the living is greater than the impurity of the dead,* for the living causes the litter and seat from underneath him to make persons and garments impure [ ... ] which the dead does not.[81]

The statement "the impurity of the living is greater than the impurity of the dead" (*merubah tum'at ha-hayim mi-tum'at ha-metim*) capsizes the prevalent view that the dead is the most impure thing to be found (which is mentioned explicitly in the Mishnah itself).[82] The technical "advantage" of the living over the dead, which is raised here as support for this statement, is not as important as the actual redefinition of the living rather than the dead as the ultimate source of impurity. This rhetorical inversion of the hierarchy of impurity is perhaps the culmination of the systematic rabbinic move we have seen in this chapter, in which the living person is placed as the defining center of the purity system, as the yardstick against which impurity is assessed and determined.

The question of personhood, and the close interconnectedness between impurity and pertinence to the human realm, will continue to engage us in the next chapter, at the center of which will stand the purity status of Gentiles. As we will see, the rabbis of the Mishnah oscillated between viewing Gentiles as persons and as nonpersons, thereby generating a unique perspective on the place and function of non-Jews within the impurity system. It is to the rabbinic development of the concept of Gentile impurity that I now turn.

## EXCURSUS: "ROT" AND PERSONHOOD BEYOND THE MISHNAH

Among the different mishnaic categories of corpse parts that are significant enough in quantity or shape to convey impurity (mentioned in M. Oholot 2.1), the category of rot *(raqav)* stands out as perhaps the least congruent with the principle of symbolic personhood that I analyzed above. Not only is rot, that is, decayed flesh crushed into powder, hardly likely to be associated with a living human being, it is also barely discernible from other organic matter and is often unrecognizably mixed with its surroundings. In truth, the ability of rot to invoke a mental image of a person is quite limited. While the anonymous voice of the Mishnah nonetheless maintains that rot in the amount of ladle-full or more conveys impurity by overhang, perhaps because rot was conceived by those who included it in the list as close enough to flesh, in other compilations of rabbinic literature we can identify persistent attempts to make the category of rot effectively inapplicable. Attempts to reinterpret and restrict the category of rot impurity so as ultimately to dismiss it altogether can be found already in the Mishnah itself, but are especially prominent in the Tosefta and the two Talmuds, and these attempts provide an important indication of the centrality of the principle of symbolic personhood not only for the creators of the Mishnah, but also for its interpreters.

The first indication of the problematic nature of the category of rot appears in the Mishnah itself, in a controversy between R. Shimon and the anonymous Mishnah:

> More than a ladle-full of grave-dust is impure; R. Shimon renders it pure.[83]

The underlying premise of this controversy is that as the corpse decays, the decayed matter, which the rabbis refer to as "rot," coalesces with the dust in which it is buried.[84] Thus, an amount of more than a ladle-full of dust from a grave can be assumed to contain at least a ladle-full of rot, which conveys impurity by overhang. On the face of it, the question at hand is whether the fact that the rot is indistinguishable from the dust precludes it from conveying impurity (R. Shimon's position), or whether the fact that the required amount of rot is nonetheless contained in the dust is enough to render the mixed dust impure like a corpse (the anonymous position). In actuality, however, the controversy pertains to the very applicability of corpse impurity to the category of rot. If, according to R. Shimon, rot does not convey impurity when mixed with its surroundings, it is admittedly quite difficult to find rot from a corpse that *does* convey impurity, since rot is almost by definition barely distinguishable from other organic matter. In other words, R. Shimon's insistence that only rot that is visibly discernible from its environment conveys impurity effectively makes the notion of impurity conveyed by rot untenable.

Clearly, the redactors of the Mishnah rejected R. Shimon's position, presenting it as a minority opinion that contrasts with the authoritative anonymous voice, and maintained that rot in a sufficient amount can convey impurity even when indistinguishable from its surroundings. In the Tosefta, however, not only is R. Shimon's position presented anonymously as the sole ruling on the question of "grave-dust," but it is also taken a significant step further. Whereas in the Mishnah R. Shimon asserts that if rot is *already* mixed with dust from the grave it cannot convey impurity, the anonymous Tosefta submits that the very fact that rot from a corpse *might eventually* be mixed with something else precludes this rot from conveying impurity:

> Which is a corpse that has rot? [One that was] buried naked, in a sarcophagus of stone, on a [stone] floor, or on a table of marble.
> But [one that was] buried in a garment, in a sarcophagus of wood, or in the dust, has no rot. [If] one takes the dust from underneath it, this is "more than a ladle-full of grave-dust" [which does not convey impurity].[85]

The Tosefta expands the notion of grave-dust to include other substances, in addition to dust, that can coalesce with the decayed corpse, such as garments and wood from the sarcophagus. It suggests that rot may only convey impurity when it is known to be entirely unadulterated. According to the Tosefta, the very fact that a corpse was buried with items that will eventually decay and mix with it denies its rot from *ever* conveying impurity, whether or not the rot from this corpse is discernible from its surroundings at a given point or not.[86] It should be noted that according to the literary and archeological evidence, the burial practices that were mentioned in the Tosefta as denying the possibility of rot impurity were the most common ones in Palestine of the second and third centuries C.E.: the dead were usually buried in their own garments or in shrouds, and for the most part in wooden caskets, whereas stone or marble sarcophagi were available only to the wealthiest.[87] Following on R. Shimon's position, but significantly expanding his ruling, the Tosefta effectively removes rot from the list of corpse parts that are capable of conveying impurity.

The Tosefta's more radical innovation, however, lies in the very rhetorical question with which its ruling is introduced, namely, "which is a corpse that has rot" *(eize hu met she-yesh lo raqav)*. This rhetorical question suggests that while all dead bodies "have" rot insofar as they eventually decay, *only certain kinds of dead bodies have the ability to convey impurity through rot*. The Tosefta presents the ability of rot from a corpse to convey impurity as an indication of the corpse's distinguishability from other substances, thereby turning such distinguishability, I suggest, to another facet of personhood. The Tosefta thus adds another mode of impurity conveyance to the two mentioned in the Mishnah (overhang and touch/carriage), and introduces this mode of conveyance as another marker of the corpse's resemblance to a living person: in the same way that the ability to convey impurity by overhang depends on the intactness and lifelikeness of the corpse or corpse parts, the ability to convey impurity through rot depends on its distinguishability from other substances.

The notion that the ability to convey impurity through rot is a litmus test for the corpse's personhood is significantly developed in postmishnaic literature. In the two Talmuds, the Palestinian and the Babylonian, we find traditions that drastically expand the requirement of distinguishability as a prerequisite for impurity conveyance through rot. These traditions introduce the curious term *galgalin* or *ganglion*,[88] which refers to any object, even one very insignificant in size or substance, that was buried together with the dead, and the rule that any such object denies this corpse the ability to convey impurity through rot. The etymology of the term is not clear, nor is its exact literal meaning: it may derive from the Greek *gangamon* (net) or from the Latin *cingulum* (belt or girdle),[89] and it may also derive from the Hebrew root *glgl*, which connotes adding-on or wrapping. Either way, this noun clearly refers to some sort of external addition to the body. The Palestinian Talmud brings forth a tradition in the name of R. Yohanan, according to which "if [something] was buried with [a corpse], even a small *gilgalin*, this is not rot."[90] R. Yohanan thus expands the Tosefta's requirement that the dead be entirely unadulterated in order to convey impurity, and asserts that even the most insignificant items that might "mix" with the dead exclude its rot from the circuit of impurity.

Furthermore, in the two Talmuds we find the ruling that even another corpse constitutes *galgalin* that precludes one's rot from conveying impurity: "R. Yasa in the name of R. Yohanan [said]: two dead [bodies] that were buried one next to the other become each other's *galgalin*."[91] That is to say, even a human body mixed with another human body is adulterated in such a way that it cannot convey impurity through rot. This ruling resonates with the anonymous Mishnah's requirement that the designated minimal amount of corpse-matter distinctly originate from one and only one dead body; however, the redactors of the Mishnah were not concerned with the intermingling of two corpses unto itself, but only with the requirement that there be a sufficient quantity from one corpse in a given setting. In contrast, R. Yohanan rules that even two *intact* corpses cannot convey impurity through rot if they were buried together in such a way that they will eventually coalesce. The level of distinguishability required to convey impurity through rot is thus much higher than the level required to convey impurity by overhang.[92] The rabbis of the Talmud, I suggest, shared the mishnaic rabbis' view that a person is by definition *one* and that corpse parts must represent a particular person, but utilized the category of rot to express this view in a much more emphasized way, by asserting that the mixed bodies of two persons do not have the same impurity-force as the body of one person.

Finally, the category of rot is used in the Talmuds as a litmus test not only for the corpse's distinguishability, but also for the corpse's other trait of personhood, namely, its resemblance to a living person and its hypothetical ability to "live." Above I mentioned the Tosefta's ruling: "A lacking [corpse] has no occupancy of graves and no neighborhood of graves."[93] The same ruling appears both in the Palestinian Talmud and in the Babylonian Talmud, with one notable addition:

A lacking [corpse] *has no rot,* and no occupancy of graves, and no neighborhood of graves.[94]

In the talmudic tradition, the lesser personhood of the lacking corpse is also expressed by its inability to convey impurity through rot. The ability to convey impurity through rot, then, is reserved only for corpses in an impeccable state, or, to put it in the term I have been using throughout this chapter, to corpses with the highest degree of symbolic personhood. The same idea is introduced in a Palestinian talmudic tradition to which I alluded above: "If his leg was severed above the knee, he has no rot. Below the knee—he has rot."[95] As I explained, in the rabbinic view the distinction between a leg severed above the knee and a leg severed below the knee is tantamount to the distinction between death and life: it is assumed that one whose leg was severed above the knee would not be able to continue to live, whereas one whose leg was severed below the knee would be able to continue to live. The fact that a body with a leg severed above the knee is by definition a body that cannot live attenuates the impurity-force of a corpse in this state, and this attenuated impurity-force is manifested through this corpse's inability to convey impurity through rot.

The talmudic rabbis thus continued to develop the tannaitic notion that personhood is a prerequisite for impurity, and utilized the category of "a corpse that has rot" to present standards of personhood that are even more stringent than the ones presented in the Mishnah. Thereby they constructed the ability to convey impurity through rot as a marker of a "perfect" corpse, that is, a corpse that is almost identical with a living body.

5

# The Duality of Gentile Bodies

The rabbinic notion that both inanimate objects and body parts must meet certain conditions in order to be able to convey and contract impurity, which I ventured to demonstrate in the last three chapters, oddly turns impurity into something of a *prerogative*. The ability to be impure is constructed in rabbinic discourse not as an inherent and unchanging trait, but rather as a trait that can only materialize when certain standards are met. In contrast, purity in the Mishnah is the unmarked state: it is the neutral status of that which no longer meets the requirements for impurity or does not yet meet them. The rabbis' insistence that objects—whether human body parts (living or dead), artifacts, or foods—that are either not consequential for humans or not identifiable with the human realm are categorically pure establishes a unique paradigm, in which the insignificant, the derelict, the defective, and the lacking are pure, and the significant, the complete, the functioning, and the whole are impure. Needless to say, this paradigm seems to run against the intuitive identification of purity with the whole and the holy, and of impurity with the abject, the disdained, and the flawed, an identification that is firmly rooted, as shown by Mary Douglas and others, in the Priestly rhetoric.[1]

There is perhaps no area of rabbinic impurity legislation in which this counterintuitive construction of impurity as a marker of completeness and consequentiality and of purity as a marker of incompleteness and inconsequentiality is as pronounced as it is in the case of Gentile impurity. According to the Mishnah, non-Jews who experience the bodily conditions that bring about ritual impurity (menstruation, scale disease, and so on) or have contact with various sources of impurity *do not become impure on account of them*. Just like cistern water or unusable artifacts, the bodies of Gentiles are categorically pure and reside outside the realm of impurity altogether; and just as cistern water cannot become impure until it is drawn and inanimate objects cannot become impure until they are fully usable, so Gentiles cannot become impure until they convert to Judaism. The dichotomy of purity and impurity is thus used in rabbinic discourse, as it is used in multiple other cultures, as a means of defining group identity and of distinguishing "us" from "them." However, it does so exactly in the manner opposite to what we would expect: the favored group is marked by the rabbis as (potentially) impure, whereas those excluded from it are marked as pure. Establishing what Vered Noam called "an inverted hierarchy,"[2] the rabbis create a system in which impurity is not a testament to the inferior position of "them," but to the superior position of "us."

This is not to say, of course, that the rabbis turned the intuitive paradigm of purity and impurity on its head, and celebrated impurity rather than purity as the preferred state of either humans or objects. There is no question that for the rabbis ritual impurity is a predicament, an undesirable condition that one must seek to undo as quickly and efficiently as possible, and that ritual purity is—or should be—the goal and quest of the mishnaic subject. An actual state of ritual impurity as such is clearly a disadvantage compared to a state of ritual purity, but the *ability* to become impure, which depends upon wholeness and significance, situates the object or person in question as more complete, perfected, and consequential than objects or persons that are incapable of becoming impure. The rabbinic scheme indeed creates an inverted hierarchy insofar as Gentiles are always in the preferred state of purity, whereas Jews are sometimes pure and sometimes impure, but this inverted hierarchy is to a great extent an optical illusion, or more accurately, a semantic illusion. Whereas a Jew is "pure" *(tahor)* in the sense that she attains or maintains a state of purity, a Gentile is "pure" because she is outside the realm of impurity altogether. The difference between saying "the Gentile is pure" and "the Jew is pure" is like the difference between saying "the wall does not see" and "the man does not see": the predicate is identical, but the meaning is completely different.

While the inverted hierarchy of Jews and Gentiles in the impurity system strikes us at first blush as highly counterintuitive, it does, I will argue in this chapter, correspond with two interrelated notions to which I have pointed in the previous chapters, according to which the participation of a body or an object in the realm of impurity depends either upon personhood (as in the case of corpses) or upon investment in this body or object on the side of a subject. I will argue that since the rabbis did not hold Gentiles to be persons in the full sense of the word, they also did not consider them to be subjects who are capable of rendering their own bodies (or their own possessions, for that matter) susceptible to impurity through their mental investment.

But this inverted hierarchy is not the entire story. Alongside the identification of Gentiles as categorically pure, that is, insusceptible to impurity, the Mishnah also introduces the exact opposite and more predictable paradigm, according to which Gentiles are categorically *impure*. While Gentiles cannot contract or convey impurity in the same ways that Jews can (by undergoing certain bodily conditions or having contact with sources of impurity), they are considered to be *inherently* impure due to the very fact that they are not Jews, and this inherent impurity cannot be gotten rid of until the Gentile actively converts to Judaism. Accordingly, if a Jew or a Jew's property comes into physical contact with a Gentile, the Jew or her property is immediately rendered impure, regardless of the physical state of the Gentile. Strangely enough, then, in the rabbinic system Gentiles are both categorically pure and categorically impure.

This perplexing duality led several scholars to determine that the two incongruent rabbinic paradigms regarding Gentile impurity stem from different time periods, and that one of those paradigms is necessarily more authentic than the other. Conversely, I argue that both of these paradigms are equally and uniquely rabbinic, and can only be understood within the rabbis' intricate and distinctive development of notions of purity and impurity. While these two paradigms are unquestionably in tension with each other, a more nuanced analysis of the rabbis' concept(s) of impurity will show that they are not actually contradictory but rather, ultimately, complementary.

My purpose in this chapter is twofold. First, I set out to disentangle the complexity of the Gentile's dual purity status in the Mishnah, and to provide an explanatory scheme that will account for the identification of Gentiles as both pure and impure. Second, I attempt to decipher how the rabbis utilized both the notion of categorical Gentile purity and the notion of categorical Gentile impurity to define and solidify Jewish identity and, specifically, to construct an idealized Jewish subject. I will suggest that the rhetoric and imagery that are used in the Mishnah to describe both the impurity and the purity of Gentiles allow us to trace what qualities, according to the rabbis, make Jews superior to Gentiles and, thereby, to understand what qualities the rabbis championed, valorized, and urged their intended Jewish audience (whether real or imagined) to cultivate.

The rabbis, I argue, deploy the concepts of Gentile purity and impurity to construct the Gentile as a nonsubject and, thereby to construct, by way of contrast, an idealized Jewish subject as its oppositional counterpart. On the one hand, the Mishnah explains the categorical purity of Gentiles in terms of a lack of legal subjectivity, maintaining that the bodies of Gentiles are insignificant within the system of purity and impurity because these bodies are not inscribed by the law. Thereby the rabbis put forth the idea that for Jews to become full subjects, they must know the law and submit to it. On the other hand, the categorical impurity ascribed to Gentiles is analogized specifically to the impurity of persons with abnormal genital discharges, that is, to a type of impurity closely associated with effeminacy and loss of masculinity, which in the cultural context of the rabbis is by and large akin to a loss of subjectivity. As the categorical impurity of Gentiles is constructed as a marker of femininity, the ability of Jews to be pure is constructed, by way of contrast, as closely dependent upon and indicative of masculinity. Thus, through their characterization of Gentiles as nonsubjects or lesser subjects, using both categorical impurity and categorical purity, the rabbis develop a notion of an idealized rabbinic subject, an ideal that "others" can never fully attain.

## DISENTANGLING GENTILE IMPURITY

Undoubtedly, one of the most efficient ways to erect boundaries between different groups is by using rhetoric of impurity, identifying outsiders as incorrigibly polluting.[3] The intricate cultural connection between impurity and disgust promises that by labeling a person or a group as ritually impure this person or group is also marked as repulsive, uncanny, and even dangerous, and thus as one from which one should want to stay away.[4] If we consider the prevalent Jewish concern, in different times and places, with too close of an interaction with non-Jews, it is not surprising that various works of Jewish literature are replete with references to the Priestly laws of purity and impurity meant to debase non-Jews and to express revulsion toward them. As Alexandra Cuffel showed, medieval Jewish authors often claimed, in an attempt to slur and disparage Gentiles, that Gentiles' failure to observe the laws of menstrual purity makes them physically abhorrent, and that Gentiles are more prone to bodily conditions considered as sources of impurity, such as leprosy.[5] An association of Gentiles with biblical impurities can be traced already in the talmudic and midrashic literature, in which we find comments on the corrupt nature of Gentile bodies as a result of the consumption of impure foods, and references to the proneness of Gentiles to detrimental bodily conditions.[6] In light of this, it would have only been expected of the rabbis of the Mishnah to declare that the bodies of Gentiles are perpetually impure because Gentiles do not regularly purify themselves in the same way that Jews do.[7] However, the Mishnah, alongside other tannaitic sources, paints a radically different picture: the rabbis unequivocally assert that Gentiles *cannot* contract and convey the impurities mentioned in the Priestly Code.

While we do not find a sweeping rabbinic ruling that Gentiles are not susceptible to any sort of ritual impurity, several tannaitic passages explicitly exclude Gentiles from specific kinds of impurity. Thus it is stated that Gentiles cannot contract the impurity of skin afflictions,[8] nor can garments or houses owned by Gentiles become impure by mildew.[9] Similarly, one mishnaic passage makes clear that the menstrual blood of Gentile women does not convey impurity,[10] and another passage asserts that the seminal emission of Gentile men does not convey impurity to women who have intercourse with them.[11] In addition, Gentiles are mentioned alongside domestic animals as incapable of contracting impurity from corpses,[12] and as requiring no purification after contact with the dead.[13] Finally, the most curious statement regarding Gentiles' inability to become impure concerns the impurity of abnormal genital discharges:

> Gentiles and resident aliens are not made impure by abnormal genital discharge *(ziva)*. But even though they are not made impure by abnormal genital discharge, they are impure like persons with abnormal genital discharge in every respect.[14]

This passage introduces the perplexing ruling that while Gentiles who have abnormal genital discharges are *not* rendered impure on account of those discharges, all Gentiles convey impurity *like* Jews who have an abnormal genital discharge. Put differently, Gentiles are considered to be perpetually impure, but pronouncedly *not* because they do not purify themselves of the various impurities mentioned in the Bible; in fact the biblical sources of impurity do not have any impact on them. The ruling that Gentiles convey the same impurity as persons with abnormal genital discharges is echoed in numerous passages in the Mishnah and the Tosefta, which refer to the impurity of the innocuous bodily fluids of Gentiles (namely, urine and saliva), a form of impurity associated with persons in this condition.[15]

The view of all non-Jews as impure is neither surprising nor unprecedented: advocates of Jewish separatism during the Persian and Hellenistic periods made substantial use of this notion in their cries against assimilation,[16] and it is not implausible that the rabbis, being familiar with some earlier uses of this idea, endorsed such a view to express their disdain and hostility toward non-Jews. What does require explanation, however, is why the rabbis stressed that the impurity of Gentiles is *not* the same as the impurity of Jews and, moreover, that the things that make Jews impure emphatically do not make Gentiles impure. If the general assumption among the rabbis was that Gentiles are impure, why did they make a point of saying that their impurity was statutory in nature, merely "likened" to the impurity of abnormal genital discharges, rather than take the more obvious path and submit that Gentiles are perpetually impure because they fail to purify themselves of actual impurities?

The first scholar who grappled with this question was Adolf Büchler,[17] who argued that the "original" halakhic view, which derives directly from the Bible, is that Gentiles do not contract or convey any kind of impurity. However, according to Büchler, during the first centuries B.C.E. and C.E. the rabbis gradually started attributing impurity to Gentiles in order to discourage Jews from contact with them, and this process culminated with a decree issued shortly before the Great Revolt (in the mid-sixties of the first century C.E.) according to which all Gentiles are inherently impure, regardless of their actual physical state.[18] In contrast, Gedalyahu Alon argued that the view of Gentiles as inherently impure dates back to the biblical period, and that this impurity stems not from the ritual sources of impurity, but from the Gentiles' engagement with idols.[19] According to Alon, the two rulings of the rabbis regarding Gentile impurity are equally based on the Bible:

Gentiles have always been considered ritually pure as far as bodily impurities are concerned, and have always been regarded as inherently impure on account of idol worship. Alon's approach was rejected by Jonathan Klawans[20] and, more recently, by Christine Hayes,[21] both of whom argued that there is no trace of the idea of inherent Gentile ritual impurity, on account of idolatry or on account of anything else, in the Pentateuch. They both subscribed to Büchler's view that the notion of categorical Gentile impurity is not commensurate with the biblically inherited legal system, as well as to his view that this idea first emerged during the first century c.e. as a political tool.

My own view on the evolvement of the two notions of Gentile impurity and on the relation between them is different. I would like to suggest that both the ruling that Gentiles are insusceptible to impurity and the ruling that they convey impurity like persons with abnormal genital discharges are rabbinic innovations, and that each of these rulings rests on a different set of meanings of the concepts of purity and impurity as those were understood and developed by the rabbis.

In order to gain a more nuanced understanding of the two seemingly contradictory rulings regarding Gentile impurity, it is important to distinguish, right at the outset, between the two different meanings of the terms *pure (tahor)* and *impure (tame)* as those are used in rabbinic literature. These terms are used to refer both to the *actual* ritual state of an object (which depends, for the most part, on whether it had contact with a source of impurity or not) and to the *susceptibility* of an object to impurity (which depends on the qualities and traits of the object and, most prominently, on the way human beings perceive of it). Depending on the context, a sentence such as "the bed is impure" could mean either that the bed contracted impurity from something and is now in a status of ritual impurity until someone purifies it,[22] or that this bed is sufficiently usable and consequential to its owner so that *if* it were to have contact with a source of impurity it *could* become impure in such a way that it would require purification.[23] Likewise, the sentence "the bed is pure" could mean either that the bed did not actually have contact with a source of impurity (or, alternatively, that it has already been purified), or that this bed cannot be considered usable and thus cannot become impure should it come into contact with a source of impurity.

These two meanings of the terms *pure* and *impure* are also at play in the rabbinic rulings regarding Gentile impurity, with the ruling regarding categorical purity exclusively utilizing one of the meanings, and the ruling regarding categorical impurity exclusively utilizing the other. In terms of *actual ritual status*, Gentiles are impure: they convey impurity to all their surroundings and are barred from having contact with the holy. In terms of their *susceptibility* to impurity, however, Gentiles are pure, since any impurity to which they are exposed does not affect them. In this respect, the case of Gentiles is reminiscent of the case of corpses, which I discussed in the previous chapter: corpses (and other dead creatures) are insusceptible to impurity insofar as they do not contract impurity from other things, yet they are impure insofar as they convey their own intrinsic impurity to others. It is not technically impossible, then, for an object or person to function as a source of impurity in and of itself and yet not be susceptible to impurity contracted from others, but we must nonetheless account for the fundamental rabbinic views on Gentiles and their place in the impurity system that underlie these two rulings.

Whence emerged the principle that Gentiles are not susceptible to impurity, and cannot contract the same impurities to which Jews are susceptible? Scholars who engaged with this question assumed that this principle is already biblical in origin, but most of them did not provide substantiation for this claim. Attempting to find a biblical anchor for this ruling, Christine Hayes argued that since the biblical commandments pertaining to ritual impurity all commence with the words "speak unto the children of Israel," it is clear that the Priestly Code excludes Gentiles from the circuit of impurity, and that the rabbis simply followed the biblical precedent in doing the same.[24] However, the biblical picture is hardly so unequivocal. First, it is never mentioned in the Hebrew Bible that only Israelites become impure by the various sources of impurity: it is only stated that if Israelites become impure, it is their duty to conduct themselves in a certain way. It is not unreasonable to assume that in the Priestly view impurity is an all-encompassing natural phenomenon affecting all human beings alike, but that the Priestly author is concerned with the Israelites as a particular group and thus legislates specifically for them. Furthermore, the biblical text explicitly states that alien non-Israelites who live among the people of Israel *(gerim)*[25] are required to purify themselves from the impurity of carcasses[26] and from corpse impurity,[27] and it is also mentioned that Gentile war captives[28] must be purified of corpse impurity.[29] Finally, as Vered Noam convincingly showed, there are traces of the idea that Gentiles *do* contract corpse impurity even in early rabbinic halakhah, and the debate on whether Gentiles are in fact excluded from this impurity persisted well into the second century.[30]

The consistent anonymous position that we find in the Mishnah, according to which Gentiles do not contract any of the impurities mentioned in the Pentateuch, can hardly be said, then, to be a simple application of the biblical precedent (if any application of a biblical precedent is ever "simple"). To the extent that there even is a biblical precedent that pertains to Gentile impurity, it seems to lead in a direction opposite to that of the official line of the Mishnah. How are we to explain, then, the dominant rabbinic view of Gentiles as insusceptible to ritual impurity?

I propose that the view of Gentiles as incapable of contracting impurity should be understood as guided by the same principle according to which the rabbis distinguish between objects that are susceptible to impurity and objects that are not susceptible to impurity.[31] As I have showed, for the rabbis the ability of artifacts, foods, and even body parts to contract impurity depends on the extent to which these things *matter* to human beings, in such a way that their inclusion in the circuit of impurity is indicative of the human subjectivity invested in them. The principle according to which what does not matter cannot contract impurity, which is a distinct rabbinic innovation, allowed the rabbis to use the theme of insusceptibility to impurity to express what they perceived as the *insignificance* of Gentiles. Within a system in which whatever is not susceptible to impurity is for the most part flawed, lacking, or in some other way lesser than whatever is susceptible to impurity, the ruling that Gentiles are unable to contract impurity effectively presents them as inferior to other humans who *are* able to contract impurity, that is, to Jews. The presentation of Gentiles as insusceptible to impurity is thus a way of affirming the advantage of Jews over Gentiles, an advantage that is comparable, in the rabbis' view, with the advantage of complete and functioning artifacts over incomplete or defective artifacts. In the next section of this chapter, I will suggest in what sense Gentiles were perceived as disadvantaged compared to Jews and in what way the rabbis saw Gentiles as divested of human subjectivity. For the time being, I wish only to make the point that the rabbis did not inherit the idea that Gentiles are insusceptible to impurity from the Priestly Code, but rather incorporated Gentiles into the larger map of susceptibility to impurity that they developed, in order to make a statement about the qualitative difference between Jews and non-Jews.

Whereas the notion that Gentiles are categorically pure (that is, insusceptible to impurity) rests on the uniquely rabbinic view of impurity as a marker of significance and is nowhere implied in prerabbinic literature, the notion that Gentiles are impure is by no means a rabbinic invention. The rabbis are likely to have inherited the basic concept of overarching Gentile impurity from their predecessors in the Persian and Hellenistic periods, and to have endorsed it as part of their general attempt to set distinctions between Jews and Gentiles while emphasizing the superiority of the former over the latter.[32] However, while the essential identification of all Gentiles as impure is hardly an innovation of the rabbis, the definition of Gentiles' impurity as *statutory*, that is, as merely analogous to the impurity of persons with abnormal genital discharges rather than as actually stemming from any recognized source of impurity, is unprecedented. This unprecedented rabbinic ruling should be understood, I argue, against the more general background of the rabbinic restrictive interpretation of the biblical concepts of impurity, and be taken as a result of an attempt to uphold a notion of Gentile impurity in a system in which such a notion technically has no place.

As Jonathan Klawans showed, in the biblical discourse of purity and impurity we can distinguish between two different forms of impurity: ritual impurity, which stems from natural-like physical phenomena and is gotten rid of through physical rites of purification, and moral impurity, which stems from abominable deeds and sins and is gotten rid of through repentance and a change of one's ways.[33] Whereas the Pentateuch is ambiguous as to the ritual impurity of Gentiles (although, as

I argued, it gives us no real reason to think that ritual impurity does not pertain to them), it uses the strong rhetoric of moral impurity to condemn the detestable acts of the Canaanites and the Egyptians, which range from idol worship to sexual misdeeds.[34] It is unclear whether this impurity is invoked literally or metaphorically, and whether the impurity of those peoples is taken to be intrinsic or contingent upon actions and lifestyle, in such a way that if they were to change their ways they would also cease to be impure. However, in the Persian and Hellenistic periods the Priestly notion of the moral impurity of specific non-Israelite peoples was conflated with the Deuteronomic notion that only the people of Israel are to be considered innately holy,[35] ultimately leading to the premise that Gentiles are inherently and irrecoverably impure because they are not part of the holy seed of Israel.[36] The Gentiles' abominable deeds came to be seen as a manifestation of their unchanging unholiness, and thereby the impurity associated with these deeds came to be seen as intrinsic and fixed.[37] It was against this cultural background that the rabbis shaped their own view of Gentile impurity.

While the rabbis of the Mishnah were heirs to the prevalent notion that Gentiles are inherently impure, they had constructed their own impurity system in a way that did not leave much room to incorporate Gentiles as actual sources of impurity. The tannaitic notion of impurity, as we have seen, is purely ritual and has no trace of moral considerations in it whatsoever: only natural phenomena bring about impurity, and only physical means can be used to dispose of impurity.[38] In this framework, there is no rubric into which impurity caused by abominations and misdeeds (whether performed by Jews or by non-Jews) can fit, nor is there place for what Christine Hayes called "genealogical impurity," that is, impurity brought about merely by non-Jewish family descent.[39] The utter exclusion of any impurity except for the physical-ritual from the rabbinic system, then, made it impossible for the rabbis to incorporate Gentiles as sources of impurity into their system by using the paradigms of Gentile impurity that they had at their disposal, whether moral or genealogical. The only other path through which Gentiles could be identified as sources of impurity within the strictly ritual rabbinic framework would have been to maintain that Gentiles are constantly impure because they fail to purify themselves from the various impurities mentioned in the Pentateuch, but such a ruling would run against the principle "that which does not matter cannot become impure." If the rabbis wanted to retain the notion that Gentiles are not significant enough to convey impurity, they would have to give up on the notion that Gentiles are perpetually impure, and vice versa. In other words, the rabbis had to choose between marking Gentiles as inferior through the theme of insusceptibility to impurity, and marking Gentiles as inferior through the theme of everlasting impurity.

The rabbis, I argue, chose not to choose. They wanted to maintain the prevalent view that Gentiles are impure within a system that only acknowledges ritual impurity, and they also wanted to retain the notion that Gentiles are insusceptible to impurity, which they derived from their association of susceptibility to impurity with completeness and consequentiality. The result of this attempt to hold the rope at both ends was the paradoxical ruling that Gentiles are effectively ritually impure even though they are not *actually* ritually impure. Their impurity is akin to an existing type of physical impurity because physical impurity is the only kind of impurity that the rabbis acknowledge, but it is pronouncedly *not* a result of the Gentiles' actual physical state. The rabbis identified this ruling as a rabbinic decree, "from the words of the Scribes" *(mi-divre sofrim)*,[40] since it was obvious to them, as it is to us, that this hybrid notion of ritual impurity which does not stem from natural sources or conditions is not biblically based. This does not mean, however, that before this decree was put forth Gentiles were considered to be pure. Rather, it seems more plausible to me that by this decree the rabbis attempted to ground an already existing notion of Gentile impurity, with its roots probably in the Second Temple period, in their own system.

Why was it so important for the rabbis to maintain that Gentiles are impure, even at the price of creating such an anomaly within their own system? Like Christine Hayes, I doubt that this ruling was intended primarily as means to a practical end, that is, as a way of preventing Jews from interacting with Gentiles.[41] Not only is the Mishnah replete with indications that such interactions took place on a daily basis and were not discouraged by the rabbis, it is also never assumed in the Mishnah that interaction with impure people more generally is to be avoided. Rather, the rabbis' insistence that Gentiles are categorically impure seems geared toward cultivating a particular way of *thinking* about Gentiles more than toward cultivating a particular way of dealing with Gentiles (although the two are inevitably connected).[42] The rabbis, like all their other contemporaries and predecessors, used a language of purity and impurity in their discourse on identity and group boundaries because of the power of these concepts to invoke immediately positive and negative connotations, respectively. The rabbinic ruling that Gentiles are perpetually impure was designated to express a view of Gentiles as profoundly unholy, and to emphasize the difference between Jews and Gentiles while asserting the superiority of the former.

The rabbis, then, use both the theme of categorical impurity and the theme of categorical purity to debase Gentiles, and to accentuate the Jews' advantage over them. But what is the essence of this advantage, and how did the rabbis delineate the critical difference between Jews and Gentiles that yields them a different status and a different function in the impurity system? As I will suggest in the remaining parts of this chapter, a close look at the rabbis' rhetoric and imagery in their discussion of Gentiles' purity and impurity reveals some of their views on the (imagined) nature of Gentiles as opposed to the (idealized) nature of Jews. The discourse of purity and impurity thus serves the rabbis to create an idealized Jewish subject, which is diametrically opposed to the Gentile.

## SUSCEPTIBILITY TO IMPURITY AS LEGAL SUBJECTIVITY

Throughout my discussions on the decisive role of subjectivity and personhood in the rabbinic mapping of the world of purity and impurity, I stressed several times that the rabbis constructed the circuit of impurity first and foremost as a *human* circuit. For them, the paradigmatic contractor and conveyor of impurity is the living human body: other objects can only partake in impurity to the extent that they can be seen as appropriated by humans, or to the extent that they themselves can be identified with the living human body. If we consider that in the rabbinic impurity system humans are so notably "the measure of all things," to use this famous phrase of Protagoras, it is quite surprising that the rabbis emphatically assert that certain living human beings—that is, non-Jews—are excluded from the realm of impurity altogether. This ruling inevitably raises an unpleasant but unavoidable question: did the rabbis not conceive of Gentiles as human beings?

In her study on corpse impurity in ancient Judaism, Vered Noam suggested that this indeed might be the case.[43] She noted several cases in which Gentiles are juxtaposed with domestic animals or prematurely born babies as examples of objects that do not contract corpse impurity,[44] and analyzed this juxtaposition as implying that Gentiles, animals, and prematurely born babies were all seen as nonhumans or, at the least, as less than fully human. Furthermore, Noam pointed to several rabbinic disputes regarding the question of whether the corpses of Gentiles convey impurity by overhang or merely by touch and carriage, like animal carcasses: at the core of these disputes, she suggested, stands the question of whether the bodies of Gentiles can be seen as fully human or rather as akin to the bodies of animals.[45] In a recent article, Ishay Rosen-Zvi and Adi Ophir argued that this implied denial of personhood to Gentiles in the tannaitic impurity discourse resonates with various explicit statements in rabbinic literature, according to which whenever the word *adam* appears in Scripture only Israelites are intended, since Gentiles do not qualify as "persons."[46]

I am in agreement with Noam and with Rosen-Zvi and Ophir that the exclusion of Gentiles from the rabbinic impurity circuit effectively constructs Gentiles as nonpersons or lesser persons, and that this indeed resonates with the prevalent rabbinic theme according to which Gentiles are not implicated in the concept of *adam* and are commonly classified alongside animals.[47] However, I wish to stress that this exclusion of Gentiles from the category of persons is not reflective of an *ontological* position on the side of the rabbis, but rather of a *discursive* technique (which has, nonetheless, far-reaching legal consequences, such as the notion that one who kills a Gentile is not liable for murder).[48] That is to say, the rabbis cannot be taken to have held a view according to which Gentiles are physically different from human beings in the same way that animals are different from human beings: the very fact that they held that conversion is a viable option, that is, that a non-Jew can turn into a Jew, precludes such an understanding.[49] Moreover, we do find occasional rabbinic references to Gentiles specifically under the category of "human beings," for instance, in the ruling that if one designated food that one cannot eat to a Gentile, this is considered to be a case of "designation for humans," which makes the food susceptible to impurity.[50] Rather than constructing the nonpersonhood of Gentiles as an intrinsic quality, the rabbis emphatically construct it as a *changeable* quality, which depends not upon one's physical being but upon one's pertinence to one ethnoreligious group and not to the other, and which serves to delineate the boundaries of these groups and the superiority of one vis-à-vis the other. In other words, the rabbis acknowledge full well that Gentiles are, realistically speaking, just as "human" as they are, but they do not bestow *personhood* upon Gentiles—that is, as I will propose momentarily, they do not see them as subjects within the legal system—for as long as they remain in their ethnoreligious otherness.

In what follows, I will show that the rabbis constructed the personhood of Gentiles—that is, in our context, their ability to be classified alongside humans in the impurity system rather than alongside animals and other inconsequential beings—as dependent upon their legal subjectivity, or put differently, upon their subordination to the Torah. I will argue that the bodies of Gentiles were not viewed as ontologically different from the bodies of Jews, but rather as bodies that are not "activated" within the impurity system because they are not inhabited by an actual subject. In the same way that an artifact is not susceptible to impurity until a person is invested in it and wants to use it, the body of a Gentile is not susceptible to impurity until it is inhabited by a person, and one does not actively become a person, as far as the rabbis are concerned, until one subordinates oneself to the law. In this view, I am echoing an alternative explanation for Gentiles' insusceptibility to impurity proposed by Vered Noam, according to which Gentiles are excluded from the impurity system *in their capacity as human beings,* because they are not bound by the law. Noam follows here a tradition found in the Babylonian Talmud, according to which Gentiles cannot contract impurity because they cannot be purified.[51] While the talmudic tradition itself does not explain why Gentiles are denied the possibility of purification, Noam takes this tradition to mean that Gentiles cannot become impure because they are not bound by the array of commandments and ordinances by which Jews are bound. According to Noam, since Gentiles are under no *obligation* to purify themselves, the states of impurity that require purification do not pertain to them. While Noam's reconstruction remains somewhat vague on this point and she does not explain why a lack of obligation to be pure also rules out the possibility of impurity, I believe that her identification of commitment to Jewish law as a key factor in the determination of susceptibility to impurity captures an important aspect of the rabbinic understanding of the workings of impurity.

Noam identified her second explanation, according to which Gentiles are excluded from the impurity system because they are not bound by the law, as pronouncedly incongruent with her first explanation, according to which Gentiles are excluded from the impurity system because they are not considered to be persons, and presented her two explanations as mutually exclusive. However, if we hold that the rabbis considered personhood to be dependent upon legal subjectivity, that is, if we take the implied rabbinic view that Gentiles are nonpersons not as an ontological claim but as a claim about *subordination to the law as what constitutes personhood,* Noam's two explanations are not mutually exclusive but rather complementary. In this vein, I will now turn to show that in the rabbinic view the susceptibility of humans to impurity—and by implication their personhood—is determined by their relation to the law and by their commitment to the commandments. This commitment manifests itself in the person's physical body through the body's ability or inability to contract impurity, in such a way that those who have not subjugated themselves to the law cannot partake in the realm of impurity. The rabbis construct the transition into legal subjectivity as fundamentally transformative of one's body, so much so that conversion to Judaism—that is, self-subjection to the law—is presented as an acquisition of a new body: when one's subjective relation to the law changes, his or her body changes as well.

### *Gentile Bodies as Legally Invisible*

In the second chapter I discussed one of the key principles in the rabbinic determination and discernment of ritual impurity, according to which whatever is effectively invisible is excluded from the realm of impurity. This principle, I showed, pertains not only to "swallowed" objects (for example, a ring in one's intestines or an arrow under one's skin), but also to parts of the body that are not immediately visible, such as one's armpits or areas of the body covered with folds of skin. I suggested that the premise behind this principle is not that invisible objects or parts of the body are nonexistent, but rather that because they are inaccessible (mentally if not physically), they are also inconsequential. Interestingly, when we come to consider the exclusion of Gentiles from the circuit of impurity, we see that this exclusion was presented in the Mishnah as analogous to the exclusion of invisible body parts from the circuit of impurity, thus suggesting that the state of Gentiles within the impurity system can be perceived as a state of invisibility. This invisibility, to be sure, should not be understood in physical terms but rather in legal terms: while Gentile bodies may be empirically visible, they have no consequence in the ritual system of purity and impurity. The transition from invisibility to visibility, the Mishnah indicates, depends on a transition into the realm of the law.

Immediately following the mishanic passage in tractate *Nega'im* which lists the parts of the body that are not susceptible to the impurity of discolorations, the seventh chapter of the tractate commences with the following ruling:

> The following discolorations are pure: [those] that were in one before the giving of the Torah, in the Gentile before he converted, in the child before he was born, in the

wrinkle before it was revealed, in the head and the beard [before they became bald], in the boil, the scald, and the wound that were festering [before they healed].[52]

This passage discusses situations in which bodies or body parts that were previously insusceptible to impurity were transformed in such a way that they are now susceptible to impurity. These transformations can be classified into three groups: (i) bodily areas that were previously "nonskin" have now become "skin" (head and beard became bald; wounds and boils healed); (ii) bodily parts that were previously invisible have now become visible (wrinkled areas were smoothened or revealed); (iii) human beings who were previously not subordinate to the law (the Israelites before receiving the law, Gentiles before they converted) have now become subordinate to the law. The case of a child who was born can be classified into either of the two latter groups, since birth entails both a transition from invisibility to visibility and a transition into a group that is defined by subordination to the Torah.[53] For all these cases, the rabbis introduce the same principle: any discolorations that were previously considered pure (that is, inconsequential), either because they were in a body that is insusceptible to impurity or because they were in a bodily area that is insusceptible to impurity, remain pure even after the body or bodily areas have changed and become susceptible to impurity.

In all these transitions, there is emphatically a lack of continuity between the pretransitional body and the posttransitional body: any skin conditions that preceded the transition are regarded as nonexistent even though they persist after the transition.[54]

The grouping together of hidden areas in the body, unborn babies, the Israelites before the reception of the Torah, and Gentiles before conversion indicates that the rabbis distinguished well between ontological reality and legal reality. All of the above are capable of being *physically* afflicted with skin afflictions, but their afflictions have no legal consequences—namely, a ritual status of impurity—until they become visible to the law. In the case of hidden areas and unborn babies, their empirical visibility also generates their legal visibility; in the case of Israelites and Gentiles, in contrast, their legal visibility depends on willful subordination to the law. For as long as Gentiles have not converted and are not inscribed by the law, their status is akin to that of fetuses: while they are certainly existent and recognized as physical beings, they are viewed as effectively invisible in legal terms and thus as inconsequential in matters of purity and impurity. Simply put, for as long as one is not a subject of the law, one's body is conceptually sealed from the effects of impurity, as if this body were a swallowed ring within one's intestines, invisible and inaccessible and therefore of no impact.

The transition from invisibility to visibility, however, is not conceptualized in the Mishnah simply as an emergence out of a sealed compartment (as, for example, in the case of a ring being vomited), in such a way that what was excluded from the realm of impurity is now included in it. Rather, this transition is conceptualized as the acquisition of a new body altogether.[55] When one subordinates oneself to the Torah, the body he or she inhabited prior to the conversion *remains* legally invisible: bodily phenomena that took place in that body are considered inconsequential in terms of impurity even if they still persist after one's conversion, and only bodily phenomena that transpired after the conversation are assessed in terms of purity and impurity. To illustrate this with a simplified example, if a skin affliction appears on a Gentile's arm on Monday, he converts on Tuesday, and a new skin affliction appears on his leg on Wednesday (without the affliction on his arm from Monday ever disappearing), then when the convert comes to have his affliction(s) examined on Thursday the affliction from Monday is simply ignored, whereas the affliction from Wednesday is inspected carefully for signs of impurity. Converts, and likewise, according to the Mishnah, Israelites after the reception of the Torah and newborn babies, thus inhabit two bodies within one: the old body, prior to the transformation, which has no consequences in terms of impurity, and the new body, after the transformation, to which the laws of purity and impurity fully apply. The distinction between these two bodies is not physical but temporal: one body ends when the other begins, and to the extent that the old body still exists—that is, to the extent that one's physical body still harbors the signs of things that happened prior to the transformation—this old body is still seen as "sealed" and contained, protected from the effects of impurity.

The same notion of the temporal bifurcation of the convert's body into two separate bodies, one consequential in terms of impurity and the other not, appears in the Mishnah in regard to the impurity of genital discharges:

> One who sees a seminal emission is not rendered impure by abnormal genital discharge for twenty-four hours *(me-et le-et)*. R. Yose says: [during that same] day. A Gentile who has seen a seminal emission and [then] converted is immediately rendered impure by abnormal genital discharge.[56]

At the basis of this passage stands the distinction between normal seminal emission *(qeri)* and abnormal genital discharge *(zov)*. The mishnaic rule here is that if one had a normal seminal emission, whatever abnormal discharge he may have in the twenty-four hours after the emission (or during the same day, according to R. Yose) will be considered as a residue of the seminal emission and not as an abnormal genital discharge that will render him impure. The Mishnah then mentions the case of a Gentile who had a normal seminal emission, converted, and then had an abnormal genital discharge. The ruling is that since the seminal emission took place before the conversion, it is not taken into consideration in the determination of his impurity status, and if the convert has an abnormal genital discharge within twenty-four hours of the seminal emission, it *will* render him impure. In short, everything that happened to the body of the convert prior to conversion is inconsequential: it does not matter that the abnormal genital discharge could be the aftermath of the seminal emission, since for all intents and purposes the seminal emission and the abnormal genital discharge took place in two different bodies.[57]

Thus, the Mishnah presents a picture in which converts (or Israelites after receiving the Torah, for that matter) still *have* the same bodies as they did before, but legally and conceptually they *are* new bodies. What generates this new body, and along with it visibility and susceptibility in terms of purity and impurity, is one's subordination to the Torah, that is, one's emergence as a *legal subject*. The connection between legal subjectivity, which subordination to the law establishes, and the ability to contract bodily impurity or to render one's possessions susceptible to impurity ties back into the principle I identified in previous chapters, according to which body parts and objects can only become impure insofar as a subject is actively invested in them. As I will propose in what follows, the inability of Gentiles to contract impurity can be understood as a manifestation of the Gentiles' lack of legal subjectivity: because they are not subordinate to the law, they cannot be considered subjects, and because they cannot be considered subjects, they cannot render themselves or their possessions impure.

### *The Mishnaic Self as a Legal Subject*

The construction of an intricate connection between subordination to the law and consequentiality within the realm of impurity serves the rabbis to set a sharp distinction between Jews and Gentiles through the language of purity and impurity, and to accentuate the "incompleteness," so to speak, of the latter. The implicit analogy between Gentiles who have not converted to Judaism, babies who have not been born, and artifacts that are not usable, all of which are in a state of insusceptibility to impurity until they undergo a certain transformation, places Gentiles as fundamentally lacking compared to Jews, as devoid of a quality that makes objects and persons matter.

What is it that makes objects, whether human or nonhuman, matter? In the previous chapters, I argued that this has to do with subjective investment, that is, with the extent to which an object can be identified with a human, conscious agent. For artifacts to matter (and hence be susceptible to impurity), one has to want to use them and consider them as extensions of oneself; for food to matter, one has to think of it as edible for humans; for body parts to matter, one has to conceive of them as integral to oneself; and for corpse parts to matter, they must significantly resemble a living person, that is, an entity that one can identify as a subject. In this paradigm, the inability of Gentiles to become impure suggests that they are *divested of subjectivity*. However, my analysis above indicates that Gentiles are insusceptible to impurity as long as they are divested of a very particular kind of subjectivity, namely, *legal* subjectivity. Gentiles may be subjects insofar as they think, plan, perceive, wish, and so on, but because they are not subjects of the law, they are considered to be nonsubjects in what concerns purity and impurity.

This construction of subjectivity, as the quality that yields one effective presence in the realm of impurity, in terms of subordination to the law, has important implications not only for the way the rabbis conceived of Gentiles, but also for the way the rabbis conceived of Jews and, more imperatively, for the way they wanted Jews to conceive of themselves. By depicting non-Jews as invisible in the realm of impurity, the rabbis are making the point that to exist as a significant person, as a person who *matters,* is to exist as a subject of the law. Moreover, in order to make *other* things matter through subjective processes such as thought, intention, and so on, and thus render them susceptible to impurity, one must be a legal subject. To be sure, in the same manner that Gentiles' bodies cannot become impure, inanimate objects owned by Gentiles are also not susceptible to impurity, and they only become susceptible to impurity when they are transposed to Jewish ownership.[58] The exclusion of Gentiles from the realm of impurity suggests that the power of human beings to shape reality through their consciousness critically depends on their subordination to the Torah. Put differently, in order to govern the world, one must be governed by the law.

Herein lies, I contend, the critical message that the rabbis wish to communicate to their audience: *in order to be a subject, one must be subjected.* The notion that Gentiles are not susceptible to impurity serves the rabbis not only to demarcate the difference between Jews and Gentiles, and not only to define Gentiles as inferior to Jews, but also and perhaps especially to tell Jews something about what they are and what they ought to be: that which turns them into agents, that which allows them to act as willful and conscious subjects and thus partake in the shaping of the world, is their subordination to the Torah.

In this vein, my analysis of the mishnaic discourse of purity and impurity ties in well with recent studies on rabbinic notions of subjectivity more largely. In his study of the rabbinic ethics of the subject in comparison to Greek and early Christian traditions, Ron Naiweld argued that the rabbinic self, unlike the Hellenistic self, is defined not through its relation to its own internal better part, but rather through its relation to the external authority of the law. Thus, the rabbinic subject, according to Naiweld, constitutes itself by actively fulfilling the commandments, which perpetually establish the link between the self and the law.[59] Similarly, Joshua Levinson showed that in rabbinic narratives in which the protagonists are engaged in self-reflection, they always assess themselves, their moral choices, and their behavior vis-à-vis the law: in rabbinic literature, Levinson argued, one's relation to the law reflects the innermost world of the actor.[60] In the sixth chapter I will return to some of these observations, and discuss at length how the rabbis create a discourse of self-reflection and self-making through the theme of one's relation to purity and impurity. For the time being, however, it will suffice to emphasize that the rabbis' identification of Gentiles as categorically pure plays a crucial part in their construction of Jewish (or, perhaps more accurately, rabbinic) selfhood and subjectivity. Through the notion that Gentiles are inconsequential because they are not subjects of the law, the imagined or real addressees of the Mishnah are to realize that their own agency as human subjects depends on their subordination to the law and thereby, presumably, also on their subordination to the rabbis.

Like the ruling that Gentiles are categorically pure, the ruling that Gentiles are categorically *impure* also plays a critical part in the rabbinic construction of selfhood and subjectivity. Here too, I will argue, the rabbis identify the inability of Gentiles to be pure as a manifestation of their lesser or defective subjectivity, and here too, by presenting Gentiles as nonsubjects, the rabbis indicate what, in their view, ideally constitutes Jews as subjects.

## GENTILE IMPURITY AND DEFICIENT MASCULINITY

Above I argued that while the basic notion that Gentiles are inherently impure was by no means a rabbinic innovation, the presentation of Gentiles' impurity in ritual and statutory terms, through its analogization to the impurity of abnormal genital discharges, is a rabbinic innovation through and through, which stems from the rabbis' self-imposed limitations in their treatment of the biblical impurity system. Since the rabbis did not acknowledge moral atrocities or genealogical descent as sources of impurity in and of themselves, and since they refrained from adding new sources of ritual-physical impurity to those mandated by the Priestly Code, any new sources of impurity they wished to introduce into the system had to be explained either as derivatives of the biblical sources of impurity or through analogies to these sources. The only manner, then, in which Gentiles could be incorporated into the system of purity and impurity was by making them tantamount to an already existing source of impurity. While this is evident enough, the question does arise of why the rabbis systematically and consistently analogized the impurity of Gentiles to the impurity of persons with abnormal genital discharges *(zavim)* and not to any other kind of impurity.[61] Why is it specifically this impurity that is attributed to Gentiles and not, for instance, the impurity of corpses or animal carcasses?

One dimension of the analogy of Gentile impurity to the impurity of abnormal genital discharges might be the pertinence of the modes in which such impurity is conveyed to the modes of interaction between Jews and Gentiles in the mishnaic world. Unlike dead creatures, with whom one must have direct physical contact (or, in the case of human corpses, be with them in the same confined space), persons with abnormal genital discharge convey impurity through their bodily fluids, not only through their actual genital discharges but also through their urine and saliva.[62] Since in the world of the ancient Mediterranean urination and spitting in streets and marketplaces were not out the ordinary, inadvertent contact with others through the bodily fluids they left behind was seen to take place constantly in the public arena, of which Gentiles were obviously a part.[63] To this we may add the notion that persons with abnormal genital discharge have the capacity to convey impurity both by "treading" (leaning, sitting, or lying on objects) and by "shift" (causing another person or object to move), so that the mere sharing of objects and of daily activities with persons with abnormal genital discharges is enough to make one impure. A form of impurity that is conveyed in such ways was perhaps seen as particularly germane to the living situation of Jews and Gentiles, which probably did not include much direct skin-to-skin physical contact, but included numerous daily interactions in the public sphere.[64]

However, the appositeness of the modes through which persons with abnormal genital discharges convey impurity to the ways in which Gentiles and Jews interacted in the mishnaic world does not fully account for the rabbis' decision to analogize Gentiles *specifically* to persons with abnormal genital discharges. As we may recall, persons with abnormal genital discharge are not the only ones who convey impurity through bodily fluids and through treading and shift: in the rabbinic system, these modes of conveyance also pertain to persons with scale disease, as well as to menstruating and parturient women. Practically speaking, of course, it does not matter whether Gentiles are compared to persons with abnormal discharges or to other sources of impurity that operate identically, but the analogy to persons with abnormal genital discharge has a very different *rhetorical* effect and cultural connotations than would, for instance, an analogy to persons with skin afflictions. I suggest, then, that in order to understand the construction of Gentile impurity in the rabbinic discourse, we must consider the impurity of abnormal genital discharges not only in terms of the ways it is conveyed, but also in terms of the cultural meanings with which it is charged. If we gain a better understanding of the way the rabbis perceived the bodies of persons with abnormal genital discharge, we will be in a better position to explain their choice to ascribe this condition to the bodies of non-Jews.

### *The Cultural Meaning of Male Abnormal Genital Discharge*

Chapter 15 of the book of Leviticus mentions different forms of impurity brought about by genital emissions of various sorts. The chapter begins by discussing abnormal genital discharge in men (vv. 1–15) and continues to discuss briefly the normal male genital discharge, namely, seminal emission (vv. 16–18). Then it turns to discuss the genital discharges of women, this time starting with the normal phenomenon of menstruation (vv. 19–24) and continuing with the abnormal case of an ongoing flow of blood (vv. 25–31). At first glance, it seems that the chapter's chiastic structure is pointing to a parity between men and women with abnormal discharges, and men and women with normal discharges;[65] however, a closer look at the wording and the particulars of these laws points in a different direction. The man with abnormal genital discharge and the two women—both the one with normal menstrual flow and the one with abnormal discharge—all convey impurity in the exact same way (by touching persons or things and by lying or sitting on things), and they are all referred to with the same participle, *zav* or *zava* (literally, "oozing" or "dripping"). The only difference between the menstruating woman and the man and woman with abnormal discharges is that the latter two are required to wait for seven days after their discharge disappears and then bring a sacrifice, whereas the menstruating woman is not required to do so.[66] In contrast, a man who has a seminal emission cannot convey impurity further to anything or anyone, and the word *zav* is not mentioned in regard to him. In rabbinic discourse, it should be noted, the words *zav* and *zava* are used only to denote men and women with abnormal discharges, whereas the word *niddah* is exclusively used to denote a menstruating woman.

The Priestly Code, then, only seemingly groups together normal/abnormal male discharges as opposed to normal/abnormal female discharges, or alternatively normal male/female discharges as opposed to abnormal male/female discharges. Rather, it groups together all continuous and uncontrollable genital discharges, whether in men or in women, on the one hand, and momentary and (for the most part) controllable genital discharge—which pertains only to men, of course—on the other hand.[67] The man with abnormal genital discharge, that is, an ongoing discharge that is emitted from a flaccid rather than an erect penis, is thus a man whose form of impurity is comparable to that of a woman.

Rabbinic references to different forms of impurity brought about by genital discharges strongly indicate that the rabbis, following in the footsteps of the Priestly author, classified male abnormal discharges alongside female genital discharges, normal and abnormal, while they considered the impurity of normal male seminal emission to be a category unto itself, subject to completely different laws.[68] The rabbis often group men with abnormal genital discharges together with three types of impure women (parturient, menstruating, and women with ongoing blood flow): for example, like these impure women, a man with abnormal genital discharge (*zav*) is prohibited from consuming the consecrated dough-offering,[69] is excluded from the Temple Mount,[70] may not partake in the Passover sacrifice,[71] and so forth.[72]

Furthermore, several rabbinic sources suggest that the *zav* is not just a man comparable to women, but is in certain ways a man who has *turned into a woman*. The rabbis assert that men with abnormal genital discharges must adopt life habits that are normally prescribed only for women (whether pure and impure), that is, they must constantly scrutinize and examine their genitalia in the same way that women do. According to the Mishnah, even women who have regular menstrual cycles must examine themselves daily to see whether they have any sort of uterine bleeding, and they must examine themselves every single time after they have intercourse.⁷³ The Mishnah emphatically states that the requirement for regular genital self-examination is incumbent upon women and not upon men: "Every hand that performs multiple examinations—in women it is praised, and in men—it should be severed."⁷⁴ As the Tosefta explains, the reason for this strong reservation is that a man might arouse himself by constantly examining his penis.⁷⁵ However, the same Tosefta passage also makes clear that this reservation applies only to men who examine themselves to see whether they have had a normal seminal emission; but men with abnormal genital discharges are encouraged to examine themselves as frequently as women do.⁷⁶ In another place, the Mishnah rules that men with abnormal genital discharges must examine themselves every day in the same way that women do.⁷⁷ Thus, a man with abnormal genital discharge is not only physically comparable to a woman, but also performs the same actions as a woman, as if taking on a feminine way of life.

The notion that abnormal genital discharges in men entail a gender transformation of sorts is strongly implied in the Mishnah's discussion on the status of a person who has experienced a single abnormal discharge. The rabbis rule that a person must have an abnormal discharge at least twice in order to be considered a *zav* according to the biblical definition, and at least three times in order to be obligated to bring a sacrifice. The question remains, however, of what one's status after having a discharge only once is. Here we find a dispute between the House of Hillel and the House of Shammai. According to the House of Shammai, the status of a man who has had a single discharge is comparable to that of a woman who has seen blood at a time not during the days of her menstruation: this woman is impure and conveys impurity during the same day and the next day, but if during the next day she does not see blood again, at the end of it she will be rendered pure. Conversely, according to the House of Hillel, the man's status is comparable to that of a man who has had a seminal emission, who is impure during the same day only, and does not convey impurity to anything else.⁷⁸ The question that underlies this dispute is, ultimately, whether the appropriate analogue for a man who has had a single abnormal genital discharge is (still) a man or (already) a woman. Is a man in this condition more like a woman with a similar kind of discharge (that is, uncontrollable and ongoing), or more like a man with a completely different kind of genital discharge (that is, momentary and for the most part controllable)? While it is unquestionable to the rabbis that a man who has already had two or three genital discharges is analogous to a woman, the man who has had such discharge only once is a hybrid of the two gender categories. He is at a liminal point between manhood and womanhood, and his status will be decided according to what happens next: if he has another genital discharge, he will be transposed to the realm of women, and if he does not have another discharge, he will return to the realm of men.

The association of abnormal genital discharge with the loss of masculinity and virility can be understood in light of the rabbis' view that a penis that emits uncontrollably when it is flaccid is "dead" in essence, and thus that a man in this condition is effectively penis-less. In the Tosefta the distinction between normal seminal emission and abnormal discharge is defined in the following terms: "An abnormal discharge *(zov)* comes from the dead flesh, and a seminal emission *(qeri)* comes from the living flesh."[79] This statement closely resonates with the distinction drawn by the Greek physician Aretaeus of Cappadocia, who lived in the first century C.E., between men with "living seed" *(zōousa thorē)* and men without it. According to Aretaeus, the "living seed" is what turns men into men, allowing them to exhibit distinctly masculine qualities such as "agility, affectivity, roughness, a manly voice, and courage." In contrast, the seed of men who suffer from *gonorroia* (flow of seed) is dead seed, and accordingly such men are "weak, full of wrinkles, have a shrill voice, are without hair, beardless and effeminate."[80] To be clear, for Aretaeus, men with genital discharges, or *gonorroia,* are not simply similar to women in that they have an ongoing and uncontrollable flow: *they actually acquire the physical attributes of women.* As many scholars have noted, in Greek and Roman medicine the dominant paradigm was that a woman is a lacking or a deficient man.[81] Correspondingly, if the "living seed" is what actively turns a person into a man, then the lack thereof denies one of the qualities of men, thereby turning one into a woman. The ultimate proof that a lack of "living seed" makes one effeminate, according to Aretaeus, is the womanly features of eunuchs,[82] but he asserts that every man who experiences an ongoing genital flow is going through a similar process of feminization as men who were actually castrated.[83]

In this view, Aretaeus closely follows the scheme put forth by Aristotle, according to which masculinity and femininity are a matter of degree rather than of essence. Aristotle identified the key difference between men and women as a difference in temperature, and maintained that men are hot and dry whereas women are cold and wet. One who is biologically male but whose body is getting colder (whether due to dietary and lifestyle choices or due to pathological conditions) is turning into a woman, and one who is biologically female but whose body is getting hotter is turning into a man.[84] The degree of one's heat is manifested in the thickness and concentration of one's seed (a category that pertains both to men and to women), which are the indications of one's virility: the colder one is, the more liquid and runny his or her seed, and thereby, the more one is a woman rather than a man. Accordingly, Aristotle maintained that a man who is lacking sufficient heat loses the ability to produce potent semen and effectively becomes a woman, the ultimate example for such men being those who suffer from *gonorroia.*[85]

While there are several indications in rabbinic literature that the rabbis endorsed the Aristotelian view of gender as volatile and subject to change,[86] the Mishnah does not suggest that a man with genital discharge is *actually* transformed into a woman, but merely asserts that in terms of impurity he is akin to a woman. However, it is impossible to ignore the fact that in the cultural world in which the rabbis created and operated, men with abnormal genital discharges were stigmatized as semiwomen, and that this stigma was, to be sure, a demeaning one.

In light of this, we can begin to understand the cultural meaning of the association of Gentiles with the impurity of abnormal genital discharges. In the world of the rabbis, this particular physical condition was marked not simply as humiliating, but also as a condition that turns the one undergoing it from what they perceived as a complete human being (that is, a man) to what they perceived as a lacking or deficient human being (that is, a woman).[87] It is worth noting that the analogue that the rabbis proposed for Gentiles was not women (that is, they did not identify the impurity of Gentiles as the impurity of menstruating women, for example), but *effeminate men*. In this regard, the rabbinic rhetoric of Gentile impurity resonates with the more general tendency in the ancient and late ancient world to discuss femininity as a negative and condemned trait of *men* rather than of women.[88] The language of ritual impurity is thus used by the rabbis in order to assess *men* disparagingly, in this case non-Jewish men. Of course, Gentile women are also considered to be perpetually impure, but their impurity is implicated in the impurity of the men with whom they are associated, and on whom the rabbis' rhetorical and conceptual attention focuses, since for the rabbis the category of "Gentiles," like the category of "Israel," in effect pertains to men. By identifying Gentiles as womenlike men in terms of impurity, the rabbis essentially turn Gentiles into nonsubjects or lesser subjects.

The perpetual association of Gentile men with abnormal genital discharges is interestingly complemented with a sustained effort to refrain from ascribing this impurity to Jewish men. The rabbis were noticeably reluctant to render Jewish men impure on account of abnormal genital discharge, and did their utmost to provide alternative explanations for what might seem like such discharges. I have already mentioned that one must have at least two episodes of discharge within a given time span to be rendered impure,[89] as well as that any genital discharge that takes place within twenty-four hours after a normal seminal emission is immediately seen as a result of the seminal emission and not as indication of abnormal genital discharge.[90] More remarkably, the rabbis prescribe a series of "examinations" for a person who had a genital discharge. The purpose of these examinations is to discern whether the discharge in question can be explained as a result of some incidental bodily occurrence, rather than as a result of a pathological condition:

> In seven ways they examine the man with abnormal genital discharge, before he has been certified by genital discharge (that is, before he has seen two consecutive discharges, which would render him unequivocally impure):
> In food, in drink, in carriage, in jumping, in sickness, in sight [of a woman], and in contemplation [of a woman], whether he contemplated without seeing or saw without contemplating.

R. Yehuda says: Even if he saw an animal or a bird meddling with each other, [and] even if he saw colorful garments of a woman.

R. Aqiva says: Even if he ate any kind of food, whether bad or good, or drank any kind of drink.

They told him: So there are no men with abnormal genital discharge here from now on!

He said to them: The responsibility for men with abnormal genital discharge is not upon you.[91]

The Mishnah mentions seven possible causes of genital discharge, which one must take into consideration before deciding that a certain person in fact suffers from the ongoing abnormal condition, which is a source of impurity according to the Bible. Genital discharge can be explained as a result of certain foods or drinks, physical activities, disease, or sexual arousal, and in all those cases it will be dismissed as incidental and not as an indication of a pathological condition. It is especially notable that even the slightest sexual arousal, either through thought or through sight, is sufficient to rule out the possibility of an abnormal condition, and it is quite plausible that the very ability to be aroused was seen by the rabbis as an indication that the person in question can function like a man, and thus should not be diagnosed with a condition defined by demasculinization.

While the anonymous Mishnah suggests that it is possible to explain away genital discharges so that they will not render one impure, R. Aqiva takes a significant step further and makes the striking comment that *anything* can be used to dismiss genital discharges as incidental. According to R. Aqiva, one can simply say that the discharge was brought about by the food or drink that this person consumed, without even assessing whether such food or drink is likely to cause a discharge. As R. Aqiva's interlocutors immediately point out, the implication of his position is that no man will ever be diagnosed with abnormal genital discharge. To this R. Aqiva responds that it is not the responsibility of the rabbis to ensure that there are persons with genital discharges out there. His blunt response implies that this is exactly the underlying purpose of his ruling: to obliterate the possibility of impurity due to abnormal genital discharges altogether.[92] It seems hardly incidental that both the anonymous rabbis and, in a more extreme form, R. Aqiva attempt to make sure that Jews are not considered to be impure with the same impurity that the rabbis made the trademark of Gentiles.

This rabbinic attempt to associate non-Jews with deficient masculinity is of particular interest in light of the prevalent Graeco-Roman tendency to identify subjugated or "barbarian" peoples as effeminate. As Benjamin Isaac showed in detail, both Greek and Roman writers constructed an elaborate physiognomy of the foreign subjects of their empires, emphasizing—especially in regard to Eastern peoples—their effeminate traits.[93] By identifying Gentiles with a form of impurity that signifies a lack of masculinity, the rabbis adopted the Graeco-Roman gender hierarchy: they identified the superior group (in their view) with masculinity and the inferior group with femininity, while clearly positing the Jews on the masculine side of this equation.[94] According to Isaac, the Jews were the only Eastern people (along with the Parthians) that the Romans did *not* characterize as feminine,[95] and it is possible that the Jews similarly perceived themselves as more masculine than the peoples by which they were surrounded. However, in the Roman scheme of things, the very fact that a certain group was subjugated rendered its members effeminate, since by being conquered this group was marked as the passive or penetrated side in the relations with the conqueror.[96] In a sense, by identifying their "others"—including the Romans themselves—as effeminate and thus inferior to them, the rabbis also offered a form of cultural resistance to the common identification of the Jews as inferior to their subjugators.[97]

### Manliness and the Idealized Mishnaic Self

As I argued in regard to the rabbinic construction of Gentiles' insusceptibility to impurity, by delineating how Gentiles are different from Jews the rabbis are also making a normative statement on what Jews are and what they ought to be. The same applies for the rabbis' ruling that Gentiles convey impurity like persons with abnormal genital discharges: by identifying the "others" as incorrigibly effeminate, the rabbis also implicitly portray their own idealized subject as a distinctly masculine man, and thereby urge their intended audience (which they, to be sure, take to be strictly male) to cultivate certain qualities, which they associate with manliness, and to condemn others. In order to consider what those qualities might be and what role the association of impurity with effeminacy plays in the broader rabbinic discourse of selfhood and subjectivity, let us very briefly consider the cultural concepts of femininity and masculinity in the world of the rabbis.

I have already mentioned the prevalent Aristotelian view of women as lacking or deficient men. In this "one sex" model, as Thomas Laqueur called it,[98] the deficiency of women (or otherwise of effeminate men) was thought to manifest itself in certain attributes and character traits, all of which were disapproved of and all of which, as Anne Carson showed, were associated with one central quality: the lack of self-control.[99] According to Carson, since women were considered to be cold and wet in the Aristotelian paradigm, their bodies were perceived as constantly oozing and leaking, incessantly overflowing and traversing their own boundaries and the boundaries of others. Ancient medical and philosophical writers, in accordance with their view that one's personality is directly constituted by one's biological features, saw women's lack of control over their physical bodies as reflected in their inability to control their emotions, their desires, and their behavior. They thus identified undesirable character traits such as irrationality, cowardliness, impulsivity, lustfulness, and so forth as quintessentially feminine.

In his study on manliness in rabbinic literature, Michael Satlow convincingly showed that the rabbis largely adopted the identification of manliness with self-control and of womanliness with the lack thereof, and that they built a great deal of their ideology of Torah study upon this theme.[100] Furthermore, Satlow commented that the imagined rabbinic Jewish male, who is distinguished by his insurmountable self-control, is contrasted in rabbinic literature not only with women, but also with Gentiles:[101] "Gentiles, like women, are portrayed by the rabbis as totally lacking the ability to control themselves. To be a woman or a Gentile is essentially to be in a natural state. To be a rabbinic man of God is to be transformed, to rule over those natural tendencies that women and Gentiles manifest."[102] With the aid of Satlow's observations, we can now see the rabbinic notion of Gentile impurity in its greater cultural context and as part of a more general rhetorical effort to construct Jewish (rabbinic) identity. Through the language of purity and impurity, the rabbis established an inextricable link between Gentiles and effeminacy, and by way of contrast, between Jews and masculinity. The identification of Gentiles with an "effeminate" bodily phenomenon, which epitomizes a lack of self-control, can be seen as part of a broader rabbinic attempt to valorize and champion the cultivation of self-control as the unique trademark of the idealized Jewish male. To say that Jews possess greater self-control than Gentiles do is not simply to make a metaphysical claim: it is primarily to make a normative claim and to require Jews to *become* men by adhering to certain practices and behaviors.

It is important to note, however, that the rabbinic discourse on Gentile impurity establishes not only a connection between self-control and Jews on the one hand and effeminacy and Gentiles on the other hand, but also a connection between self-control and *purity* and effeminacy and *impurity*. In other words, the identification of Gentiles as categorically impure constructs ritual impurity as a state that is in some way indicative of a lack of self-control, and constructs purity as a state that is indicative of laudable self-control. Purity and impurity, then, seem to acquire through this discourse an added dimension as manifestations of the virtues, or the lack thereof, of the subject in question. This role of purity and impurity in the shaping of the rabbinic ethics of the self will be the topic of the final chapter of this book.

# 6

# The Pure Self

Throughout this book, I have showed that some of the most central innovations that the rabbis introduce into the biblical impurity system have to do with subjective mindsets and mental processes. I emphasized that the rabbis turned one's personal investment in an object or even in one's body parts into a condition for susceptibility to impurity, and thereby remapped the world of purity and impurity through the prism of human consciousness as manifested in processes of thought, intention, deliberation, and contentment. By this point, then, I hope to have persuaded the reader that the rabbis positioned the *self*, the conscious agent who is capable of mental activity and, no less importantly, of reflection on his or her mental activity, as a new and critical pivot in their discourse of purity and impurity. To be sure, impurity for the rabbis does not become an utterly mental construct that takes place solely within the mind, and it is still presented in the Mishnah as a natural-like phenomenon, operating in a way that mirrors the physical laws of motion and transferability, to a large extent without any regard for human will. Nevertheless, the rabbis established the domain of impurity qua natural-like phenomenon as a domain created primarily through human consciousness.

In a recent article, Joshua Levinson surveyed some of the legal contexts (among them purity and impurity) in which the rabbis introduce thought and intention as central components in determining legal outcomes, and juxtaposed these legal contexts with midrashic narratives in which self-reflection plays a prominent part. He argued that the unprecedented rabbinic emphasis on self and subjectivity, which is manifested in these legal and narrative texts, should be understood in light of the rise of the self as a major preoccupation in late antiquity, discernible both in Graeco-Roman (particularly Stoic) writings and in early Christian writings.[1] Identifying a profound correspondence between the preoccupation with the self in the greater cultural world of which the rabbis were a part and the new developments in rabbinic legal discourse, Levinson argued that these rabbinic legal innovations are "based upon a new inward turn," in which the self is "an object for investigation and training."[2]

I fully concur with Levinson that the rabbinic emphasis on subjective processes of thought and intention closely resonates with the general interest in the self in the rabbis' surrounding culture, and I am fairly convinced that this emphasis speaks to the impact, if not direct influence, of the rabbis' greater intellectual environment on their legal (and narrative) creation. In one important respect, however, the leap from the critical role of thought and intention in generating certain legal outcomes to identifying a Graeco-Roman-like "inward turn" in rabbinic legal literature is problematic. As many scholars have noted, the essence of the discourse on the self in antiquity and of the exercises geared toward the cultivation of the self in this period is *ethical*.[3] The self preoccupies Stoic authors insofar as it is a rational entity that in its rational capacity can and should endorse right views and right behaviors, and it preoccupies early Christian authors insofar as it is an entity with (or without) free moral will, oscillating between sin and salvation.[4] The "inward turn" and the heightened attention to states of mind and heart in Graeco-Roman and early Christian literature are guided by one very distinct question, namely, what is good for man to do and to be. This is hardly the case in the mishnaic discussions on the role of thought and intention in the realm of impurity, as we have seen. There is no underlying ethical component to the question of whether a three-legged table is susceptible to impurity, or to the question of whether one is content with his produce becoming wet: one's subjective investment in objects generates certain results in term of impurity, but it has nothing to do with what is good or what is right. The rabbis' notable engagement with the workings of the subject, then, seems to be motivated by directed attention to human consciousness as a constitutive factor in the world, which indeed characterizes many of their contemporaries, but not by the same ethical concerns that guide their contemporaries in this attention.

Nevertheless, if we broadly conceive of ethics as the field of human reflection on what is good to do and be, there is one important ethical dimension to the prominence of subjective processes and states of mind in the rabbinic discourse of purity and impurity, to which I pointed in the previous chapter. As I argued, in order to be considered a subject in the first place, that is, in order for one's subjective processes and states of mind to "count" in the world of purity and impurity, one must be a subject of the law. The ruling that Gentiles are not susceptible to impurity in any way and have no legal agency to make either their bodies or their possessions partake in impurity powerfully makes the point that for the rabbis subjectivity is legal subjectivity and that the rabbinic self is defined by subordination to the Torah.

As both Jonathan Schofer and Ron Naiweld showed, the rabbis perceived of the Torah not simply as a "code" of ethics but as the only path through which right views and right behaviors could be begotten and upheld.[5] Accordingly, the rabbis construct their subjects' ethical disposition through an emphasis on one's relations with the *law,* equating the question of "what is right to be and do" with the question of "how one should adhere to the Torah." We can thus certainly say that rabbinic discourse establishes agency in terms of purity and impurity as congruent with, or dependent upon, ethical subjectivity, since ethical subjectivity is identical, for the rabbis, with subordination to the law.

The ability to act and make a difference in the realm of purity and impurity is thus contingent, according to the rabbis, upon one's relations with the law: but is there anything in their discourse of purity and impurity that constitutes the rabbinic subject as one who, as Levinson argued, has a particular relation with *oneself* as a subject of the law?[6] What, if anything, in the mental processes of thought and intention pertaining to purity and impurity corresponds with Graeco-Roman accounts of self-formation, at the center of which lies an attempt to *become* a particular kind of subject and to guide oneself actively toward what is right and good?

In this final chapter, I will argue that the rabbinic purity discourse does, indeed, have a critical ethical dimension to it, in which one's engagement with purity and impurity is shaped as a site through which one forms oneself as a subject and constitutes a certain relation to oneself. Moreover, I will argue that purity is constructed in the Mishnah as attained through practices that resonate with Graeco-Roman *askesis,* that is, modes of self-training. This ethical dimension, however, does not lie in the mishnaic subject's thoughts or intentions regarding *things,* despite the centrality of thought and intention in one's power to introduce objects and bodies into the world of impurity. Rather, it lies in one's fundamental commitment to maintain oneself and one's possessions in a state of purity in the face of the considerable effort this requires, which is manifested through certain daily practices, physical and mental alike. These practices, as I will show, bear great resemblance to the practices that stand at the center of ancient forms of *meditatio,* which consists, as Shadi Bartsch concisely put it, of "self-questioning, self-command, self-exhortation, and self-review."[7] In the context of the Mishnah, the obvious and immediate purpose of such practices is, of course, the actual attainment of ritual purity, and their ultimate purpose is full adherence to the law as an all-encompassing way of life. However, I will argue that through the performance of these practices one was seen as exhibiting *mental dedication* to the pursuit of purity, dedication that in several contexts is presented as tantamount to ritual purity per se. The pursuit of purity thus emerges in the mishnaic discourse not only as a path toward a desired ritual status, but also as a path through which one shapes oneself as a subject according to a particular cultural and religious ideal.

To be clear, by referring to the ethical dimension of the rabbinic discourse of purity and impurity, I am not suggesting in any way that the rabbis associated ritual impurity with sin or described treacherous activities or indecencies in terms of impurity, nor did they equate justice, piety, and religious devotion with ritual purity. As I stressed, the rabbis restricted these concepts to the physical-like effect of the few natural sources mentioned in the Priestly Code. What I am suggesting is that the rabbis constructed the realm of purity and impurity as a site through which one's merits as a subject of the law are manifested, and that they thereby implicitly encouraged their subjects, real or imagined, to try to strive for ritual purity not only in order to achieve a particular cultic status, but also in order to enhance as well as to exhibit these merits.

With this chapter, then, I come to a full circle with the first chapter, in which I suggested that by making impurity an ever-pervasive presence in everyday life, the rabbis of the Mishnah turned the management of impurity into a critical component of one's most quotidian interactions and activities. In what follows, I explore how the daily life of the mishnaic subject was to be practically shaped, according to the rabbis, by the preoccupation with impurity, and I examine the practices that the rabbis prescribed as indispensable to the attainment of purity, so as to decipher what kind of subject is being constituted through the ongoing engagement with purity and impurity. As I will show, the pursuit of purity is presented in the Mishnah as dependent upon constant examinations of one's actions and one's body, and furthermore, upon reflections on one's *attention,* or mental dedication, to purity. The rabbis thus shape the pursuit of purity as taking place not only in one's interaction with and management of the physical lived world, but also and perhaps primarily in one's interaction with and management of *oneself,* in such a way that the effort to maintain a state of purity also generates a particular kind of self-reflective subject. I propose that through the presentation of the attainment of purity as dependent upon constant self-examination, and through the presentation of ritual purity itself as a manifestation of one's commitment to purity, the rabbis give purity and impurity a new ethical substance. They redirect their audience from the desired results of the attainment of a status of purity—access to the Temple, membership in an elitist self-selecting group, and so on—to the *quest* for the attainment of purity, constructing the daily effort to maintain a state of purity not just as a means, but as an end in itself, through which one both nurtures and displays one's devotion to the law.

## SELF-EXAMINATION AS A WAY OF LIFE
### *The Mishnaic Subject and Its Oppositional Counterparts*

In the first chapter, I argued that the rabbis depicted the pursuit of purity as an unending everyday task, which is undertaken in a world pervaded with impurity.

The Mishnah's discussion of the management of impurity throughout one's daily activities and interactions, as presented particularly in tractate *Tohorot*, is guided by two underlying assumptions. First, the person for whom the rabbis are designating their rules and guidelines strives (or should strive) to be in a status of purity to the extent that this is possible; and second, this person is inevitably and constantly surrounded by impure people. At the basis of the mishnaic discourse of impurity, then, lies a pronounced opposition between the intended subject of the Mishnah, who is led by a quest for ritual purity, and different kinds of persons who are identified as categorically different from this subject (or, if you will, as nonsubjects or lesser subjects), and are marked by perpetual impurity that is a hindrance to the subject's own purity. Accordingly, the first step in exploring how the Mishnah constructs and champions a particular kind of subject through its purity discourse is to approach the mishnaic subject by way of negation, that is, to examine this subject by contrasting him with those who are presented as fundamentally different from him. In what follows, I will mention three distinct social categories that the rabbis contrasted with their intended subject and identified as perpetually impure. Toward the end of this chapter I will discuss the implied gender of the intended subject of the Mishnah and the ambivalent place of women in the rabbinic notion of the idealized self.

First and most obviously, the intended subject of the Mishnah is contrasted, as we have seen in the previous chapter, with Gentiles. This subject's quest for ritual purity and his very ability to attain a status of purity stand in opposition to the irrevocable impurity of Gentiles, which cannot be obliterated by any means save conversion. The rabbis, I argued, emphasize the discrepancy between Jews and Gentiles by identifying Gentiles with the impurity of genital discharges, thus associating them with effeminacy and a lack of bodily self-control, and thereby implicitly suggesting that the exact opposite qualities are those that allow the intended Jewish subjects of the Mishnah to be pure.

In addition, the rabbis identify groups of Jews who do not adhere to rabbinic authority as perpetually impure, in this case not because of an intrinsic unchangeable quality as in the case of Gentiles, but rather because their failure to comply with rabbinic teachings and their choice to follow different legal traditions do not allow them to be seen as pure according to rabbinic standards. A famous mishnaic passage states that Kuthian (that is, Samaritan) and Sadducean women are always in a state of menstrual impurity, and their husbands are always in a state of impurity on account of having intercourse with menstruating women.[8] The reason for this ruling is that Kuthian and Sadducean women do not "walk in the ways of Israel," that is, do not accept the rabbinic distinction between pure uterine blood and impure uterine blood. Rather, they assign themselves seven days of purification for every genital bleeding they see.[9] As a result, the entire management of impurity by members of these groups is flawed (in the rabbinic view). Submitting that any way of approaching purity and impurity which is not commensurate with rabbinic teachings and not performed through appeal to the knowledge of the sages is destined to result in a series of mistakes, this tradition not only excludes those who do not comply with the rabbis from the community of "Israel,"[10] but also excludes them from the possibility of ever being pure. Thereby, the Mishnah distinctly shapes the ability to attain a status of purity as a marker of subordination to the authority of the rabbis.

The presence in the public sphere of Gentiles and nonrabbinic Jews, both of whom are defined by their perpetual impurity, is an important component in the rabbinic depiction of public spaces as permeated with impurity, and in the construction of everyday activities and interactions as entailing inevitable contact with sources of impurity.[11] However, the most ubiquitous conveyors of impurity in the Mishnah, who stand in opposition to the intended mishnaic subject in the most stark and emphasized way, are Jews who are categorized as *am ha-aretz*, the "People of the Land." While scholars have suggested various theories regarding the identity of the People of the Land as a particular social or religious group,[12] the exact nature of these people and the historical origins of this appellation are not critical to the analysis I am proposing here. For our purposes, it will suffice to note that throughout the Mishnah, the most consistent and dominant characteristic of the People of the Land, whomever and whatever they may be, is their notable carelessness regarding impurity, at least according to rabbinic standards, that is, in comparison to the intended subject of the Mishnah.[13]

The People of the Land, as depicted in the Mishnah, are not entirely oblivious to the requirements of ritual purity. For instance, they are assumed to be cautious in what concerns the purity of holy articles and foodstuffs,[14] and in some contexts they are also described as careful in regard to corpse impurity.[15] However, they are notably lax regarding more common impurities, such as menstrual impurity, and regarding nonconsecrated articles. Therefore, almost any contact with them or with their possessions, inadvertent or advertent, results in the contraction of impurity. Whereas in the case of Gentiles and nonrabbinic Jews the otherness of these groups is manifested in these groups' perpetual impurity, in the case of the People of the Land these people's perpetual impurity, which is a result of their insufficient efforts to maintain a state of purity in their everyday lives, is what essentially constitutes their otherness. Unlike Gentiles, the People of the Land are not incapable of being pure. Rather, they *choose* not to be pure, or, more accurately, they do not choose to be pure, since it is the choice to be pure that requires effort and deliberation, whereas one need not actively do anything in order not to be pure.[16]

As in the case of Gentiles and nonrabbinic Jews, then, a perpetual (albeit not irrevocable) status of impurity serves to identify the People of the Land as quintessentially other, and indeed inferior, to the subjects of the Mishnah. However, whereas in the case of Gentiles their otherness lies in their ethnoreligious identity and in the case of nonrabbinic Jews their otherness lies in their wrongful traditions and failure to comply with the rabbis, in the case of the People of the Land their otherness lies in their *mental disposition* toward impurity, namely, in the fact that they are not attentive to impurity at all times. Put differently, if Gentiles are impure on account of a lack of subordination to the law, and if nonrabbinic Jews are impure on account of a lack of subordination to the rabbis as the self-proclaimed representatives of the law, the People of the Land are impure on account of their slack *attitude* toward the law to which they are subordinated.

The inattentiveness to impurity of the People of the Land, to be sure, is not identified in the Mishnah as deriving from malice or from disrespect to the law as such.[17] In fact, in the tannaitic literature the People of the Land are usually described as decent persons who are overall committed to the law and do not wish to transgress it, and accordingly they are considered to be trustworthy in regard to more grave purity issues, particularly what concerns the Temple and the sancta. However, the People of the Land do not take upon themselves the elaborate daily practices that are required of one who wishes to maintain a state of purity during everyday life,[18] and as a result they are not constantly preoccupied with impurity in the same way that the mishnaic subject is assumed and urged to be. Whether they knowingly choose not to be preoccupied with impurity on account of laziness or carelessness, or whether they are simply not familiar with the intricate requirements of purity,[19] the People of the Land, as a consequence of their inattentiveness to impurity, are described in the Mishnah as childlike figures who touch and meddle with everything in their vicinity without giving thought to the repercussions that this might have in terms of the contraction and conveyance of impurity. The following two passages illustrate this well:

> If one leaves artisans (who are assumed to be from among the People of the Land) inside his home, the house (that is, everything in the house) is impure, the words of R. Meir.
>
> And the Sages say: [It is impure] up to the place where [the artisans] can reach with their hands and touch.[20]
>
> If a wife of a member (*haver*, presumably one who is cautious in the observance of purity)[21] leaves the wife of [one of] the People of the Land to grind in her house, once the [voice of the] millstone ceased—the house (that is, everything in the house) is impure.
>
> If the [voice of the] millstone did not cease—it is only impure up to where she can reach with her hand and touch.
>
> If there were two of them (that is, women from among the People of the Land), either way the house is impure, for one is grinding and the other one is touching and meddling *(memashmeshet)*, the words of R. Meir.
>
> And the Sages say: It is only impure up to the place where they can reach with their hands and touch.[22]

Both of these passages describe cases in which a person lets in one or more of the People of the Land into his or her home and leaves them unattended as they perform a specific task that presumably keeps them occupied. The unquestionable assumption in those cases is that the minute the People of the Land are left unattended, they will start to touch and meddle with the homeowner's properties, not in order to harm them and certainly not in order to steal them, but out of a simple uncontrollable childlike curiosity. The controversy between R. Meir and the Sages pertains to the question of whether the People of the Land will only meddle with things in their immediate vicinity, which they would be able to do even while still performing the task they were left to perform, or whether they will touch everything in the house, thus rendering all that is in it impure. All agree, however, as we see in the second passage, that if the person in question actually ceases from the activity he or she was performing, everything in the house is impure. This depiction of the People of the Land as "meddling" with everything they see resonates with a mishnaic ruling that since it is a child's way to touch whatever it sees, whenever a child is found next to dough, the dough should be considered impure.[23] Like children, then, the People of the Land conduct themselves in respect to impurity in a way that can be best described as *mindlessness*.

The intended subject of the Mishnah, as constructed by the rabbis, is emphatically one who is different from the People of the Land and who strives to maintain a clear dividing line between him and them.[24] The Mishnah prescribes specific guidelines for interacting with the People of the Land in commercial, personal, and neighborly settings,[25] thus presenting these people as markedly different from the person to whom these guidelines are directed and as requiring various measures of caution when approached. The positioning of the intended subject of the Mishnah as pronouncedly contrasted to the People of the Land points us to a quintessential characteristic of this intended subject, a characteristic that sets him apart from the People of the Land and thereby makes the possibility of purity tenable for him: if the People of the Land are marked by their mindlessness of impurity, then their oppositional counterpart is marked by being ever mindful of it. What distinguishes the potentially pure from the perpetually impure, in this scheme, is the former's incessant concern for purity and the extent to which it shapes his daily activities. In what follows, I will discuss the ways in which the concern for purity manifests itself in the lives of those who are constantly cognizant of it as they were imagined in the Mishnah, and argue that the main expression of one's commitment to purity is a recurring process of *self-examination*.

### Examination of the Day and Examination of the Body

As has become clear by now, it is the premise of the Mishnah that impurity is, on the whole, an unavoidable and inseparable part of life. Purity cannot be an ongoing and unchanging state, and the pursuit of purity is by definition a cyclical process:

one contracts impurity, purifies oneself, contracts impurity again, and so on. While it is the act of ritual immersion that effectively constitutes the transition from impurity to purity within this cycle, for this transition to take place one must first *realize* that he or his possessions have (or may have) become impure, and it is upon this initial realization of impurity that the process of purification depends. Thus, one's commitment to purity is manifested not simply in one's readiness to purify oneself upon contraction of impurity, but primarily in constant self-scrutiny so as to know if purification is in order. Accordingly, the main difference between the intended subjects of the Mishnah and the People of the Land is that the latter do not make the mental effort to discern whether they and their belongings have become impure or not. It is not that these people are impure and decide not to take measures to rectify this; rather, they do not care enough, or do not know enough, to ask themselves constantly whether they are impure at a given moment or not, and as a result, of course, they are taken to be impure all the time. The most crucial aspect of a life governed by a pursuit of purity, then, and the task to which the Mishnah dedicates a great deal of its discussions about purity and impurity, is the discernment of the purity status of one's body and possessions. As I will argue, the everyday life of the intended subject of the Mishnah is defined by recurring processes of self-examination of two sorts, which correspond with the two modes in which one can become impure, namely, as a result of contact with another person or object, and as a result of a bodily condition.

In the first chapter I discussed at length the possibility of contracting impurity inadvertently, through contact with primary sources of impurity (or even secondary sources, in some cases), and showed that the Mishnah's discussions on the inadvertent contraction of impurity rest on the premise that every object upon which one stumbles, every person against which one brushes, and even certain spaces and places can turn out to be impure and thereby to have conveyed impurity to whoever and whatever came into contact with them. In order to determine whether one has indeed contracted impurity during such quotidian encounters, one must be able to give a full account of his actions and interactions throughout the day, and to recount for himself whom he met, what he ate, what he touched, whether or not he washed his hands before eating, where he went, whether he left his belongings unattended, and so on. Indeed, the Mishnah makes the point that if one is not capable of answering such questions with certainty, the result is usually a status of impurity by default, except in a number of exceptional cases (for instance, if one of the people involved is mentally incapacitated, or if the questionable impurity is in the public domain).[26] The very fact that the Mishnah dedicates special discussions to cases in which one *cannot* say whether he touched an object or not, or on which path he was walking, or whether the loaf of bread that he ate was pure or not[27] suggests that for the most part people were expected to have definite answers for such questions. Thus, one aspect of the self-scrutiny required of those who strive to maintain a state of purity is what I will call here *examination of the day:* an ongoing effort to give oneself an account of all of one's activities and encounters that could have exposed one or one's possessions to impurity.

Impurity, however, is not only contracted from external sources, but also generated by one's own body, which becomes a source of impurity as a result of various physical conditions. Therefore, the Mishnah also prescribes elaborate practices of *self-examination of the body,* the purpose of which is to find signs that will attest to a bodily state that renders one impure. The most common and recurring physical self-examinations in the Mishnah are performed to find traces of genital discharge in both sexes, that is, of seminal emission in men and of uterine blood in women.[28] Alongside these regular examinations for normal genital discharges, the Mishnah also prescribes self-examinations for men and women with abnormal genital discharges, which they must conduct daily after the abnormal discharge ensues, in order to make sure that they go through seven full days without discharge.[29]

As I mentioned in the previous chapter, women are guided to check themselves internally using pieces of cloth that are referred to as "witnesses" *('edim)* in order to discern whether any blood is contained in their vaginas (since women start to convey menstrual impurity before the blood is emitted to the outside).[30] Even women who have regular menstrual cycles, the Mishnah asserts, and even women who are not likely to menstruate at all (like pregnant or postmenopausal women) must examine themselves twice a day, at dawn and at dusk, as well as after they have intercourse.[31] In addition, women are expected to look for traces of blood in their urine,[32] and look for bloodstains on their sheets, garments, and skin,[33] as possible indications of uterine bleeding.

In the case of men, the main practice that the Mishnah prescribes is scrutinizing one's urine for traces of semen. Since semen is a source of impurity in itself, the rabbis rule that men become impure not only by actual seminal emission, as mentioned in the Priestly Code,[34] but also by contact with incidental residues of semen. Therefore, the Mishnah suggests practical guidelines for identifying traces of semen in one's urine based on the urine's color, consistency, and flow: white or cloudy urine is a sign of residues of semen, as well as urine that is not flowing out freely but intermittently.[35] While the Mishnah does not specify the frequency with which one ought to scrutinize one's urine, it is reasonable to assume that this must be done at least in the first few urinations after the emission of semen, and perhaps even every time one urinates. In addition, another passage in the Mishnah mentions that if one had sexual thoughts during the night and his "flesh was warm" in the morning, even if there are no traces of semen in sight, this person is assumed to have emitted at least a few drops of semen and to have become impure as a consequence.[36] Thus, one is required not only to scrutinize one's urine, but also to keep track of his sexual thoughts in order to monitor his potential impurity.

The two kinds of self-examinations that the intended subject of the Mishnah is assumed or expected to conduct regularly, namely, examinations of the day and examinations of the body, are only the first stage in the discernment of impurity. After one establishes the "facts" of the day (that is, the encounters and activities that took place in its course) or of the body (that is, indications of genital emissions), one also needs to decipher the meanings of these facts in terms of impurity: Did a particular encounter or activity indeed result in the contraction of impurity? Is the trace of semen or blood that one found actually a sign of bodily impurity? And so on. Sometimes the translation of the facts into an impurity status is straightforward, but in many cases, the Mishnah presents the determination of impurity as dependent upon an elaborate body of knowledge that not everyone can be taken to possess, and whose proficient bearers are the rabbis.

### Self-Examination and Appeal to Rabbinic Expertise

By expanding the realm and repercussions of impurity in substantial ways, the rabbis also made the process of determining whether one contracted impurity or not infinitely more complicated than it is in the Priestly Code. In many cases, one's ability to discern his or her purity status depends on thorough acquaintance with the complex principles of impurity conveyance through liquids, with the classification of different artifacts and their parts, with the counterintuitive principles regarding doubtful impurity, and with other aspects of the highly intricate rabbinic "science" of impurity. In short, the rabbis created a system of impurity so complicated that their mediation is bound to be necessary for those who wish to maintain a state of purity in accordance with the rabbinic interpretation of biblical law (which the rabbis, of course, promulgated as the only legitimate interpretation). It is unsurprising, then, that the Mishnah suggests that the process of self-examination, at least in some cases, can only be completed upon consultation with a sage.

The Mishnah, it should be made clear, never states that one is *expected* to turn to a sage in order to determine his or her purity status: presumably, anyone who is familiar with the workings of impurity can do so independently. However, several mishnaic discussions describe situations (albeit probably hypothetical situations) in which one relays his or her actions during the day to the sage and asks him to determine his or her impurity status,[37] and in one context we even find that the process of determination of impurity is described like a court procedure held in front of a sage and includes the hearing of different testimonies.[38] Furthermore, while there are not many narrative accounts of cases in which the rabbis were consulted in regard to impurity, the few case stories that we do find in tannaitic sources suggest that referral to rabbinic authority was not an uncommon part of the attempt to maintain a state of purity. Thus we find references to consultations with sages regarding the contraction of corpse impurity and regarding the impurity of particular artifacts,[39] and in the Tosefta we also find several narrative accounts of cases in which the rabbis were consulted by persons who attempted to maintain a certain object in a state of purity and wanted to confirm that the object indeed remained pure.[40] We may therefore infer that the daily concern with purity was expected to manifest itself not only in self-examination, but also, at times, in appeal to rabbinic knowledge. Such appeal was not mandated, and was certainly not always necessary, but it did constitute part of a life guided by commitment to purity as such a life was imagined by the rabbis.

Whereas the Mishnah and the Tosefta provide only scattered indications that the rabbis were consulted (or were expecting to be consulted) following examinations of the day, that is, after one had detected a possible encounter or event that may have rendered him or his possessions impure, the textual evidence for consultation with rabbis following examinations of the body is far more explicit. In particular, the Mishnah suggests that the sages were regularly consulted in order to decipher whether women were in a state of menstrual impurity or parturient impurity or not.[41] Such consultations, to be sure, do not replace the physical examinations that women are supposed to conduct for themselves; rather, they follow and complement these examinations, since women are assumed to consult a sage when they are unsure whether the blood that they have seen in the course of their self-examination is a sign of impurity. As both Charlotte Fonrobert[42] and Chaya Halberstam[43] noted, the very fact that women might be uncertain whether their genital bleeding is an indication of impurity or not is a result of the rabbis' development of an elaborate system of categorization and classification of genital blood, in which not every kind of blood is necessarily a sign of impurity.[44] Again, nowhere in the Mishnah is it stated that women must consult with a sage on their issues of blood, or that they are incapable of discerning their impurity on their own, but the intricate system that the rabbis created made women who comply with rabbinic authority highly dependent on the rabbis' knowledge. Furthermore, Charlotte Fonrobert persuasively argued that compliance with rabbinic authority and pertinence to the group that aligns with the teachings of the rabbis were presented by the rabbis as *manifested* in readiness to consult with a sage on matters of menstrual impurity: "Walking in the ways of Israel means walking over to the next sage in the neighborhood to consult with him about purity and impurity."[45]

A similar process, in which the rabbis develop an intricate body of knowledge regarding the bodily impurity of women, thereby making the discernment of impurity dependent upon their own specialty and expertise, takes place in regard to parturient impurity, specifically in the case of miscarriage. As a rule, a woman is considered to be impure as a parturient if she had a miscarriage, and in accordance with the biblical laws in Leviticus 12, she is in a state of impurity for forty days if the fetus was male and for eighty days if it was female. However, according to the Mishnah not all miscarriages render the woman impure as a parturient: it depends on the form and shape of the fetus, on the condition of the placenta, on the stage of the pregnancy when the miscarriage took place, and so on.[46] As a result, laypeople are less likely to be able to determine whether a particular miscarriage brought about parturient impurity or not, and consultation with a sage becomes almost unavoidably necessary.

While in later rabbinic traditions it is suggested that sages actually *inspect* the bodily issues of women,[47] there is no indication of such practice in tannaitic sources.[48] In fact, it seems that the very elaborate descriptions of colors of blood and shapes of miscarried fetuses in the Mishnah were meant to serve as a "dictionary" that would help rabbis make sense of the accounts that women gave of what they themselves had seen. It is important to observe, then, that consultation with a sage does not obviate the process of self-examination, but actually makes it more rigorous: women were expected to collect all the information possible on their bodily condition and discharges to provide the sages with the most accurate and comprehensive account. Even if we do assume, however, that sages were actually examining the bodily issues themselves, they were still relying on women's ability to give an account of various details pertaining to the issue at hand, and obviously the very decision of a woman (or of her husband) to approach the sage would be a result of self-examination of some sort. The consultation with a sage is thus depicted in the Mishnah as complementary to the process of self-examination and as what enables the individual to pursue ritual purity.

All the examples I have mentioned so far for consultation with sages in regard to bodily impurity pertain to women, and in truth, rabbinic literature does not suggest any accounts in which men consult with a sage regarding their discharges. This discrepancy is not wholly surprising: First, since menstrual impurity is of relevance not only for those who wish to maintain a state of ritual purity but also for those who wish to avoid sexual intercourse with a menstruating woman, which is mentioned in the Bible as a transgression in and of itself,[49] this was probably the kind of impurity with which people were most concerned.[50] Second, the rabbis may have been particularly invested in the process of identification and certification of menstrual impurity since this constituted a way of supervising and monitoring female sexuality.[51] It is also possible, as I will suggest in greater detail toward the end of this chapter, that women were conceived of by the rabbis as less capable of understanding and managing the workings of their own bodies, and thus as more dependent on the sages' knowledge and guidance. One passage, however, indicates that men were also occasionally consulting with sages (or expected to consult with sages) in order to determine whether they were impure or not. As we have seen in the previous chapter, M. Zavim 2.2, which commences with the words "in seven ways they examine the man with genital discharge," prescribes a process of interrogation for men who have experienced one or two genital discharges in order to check whether their discharge(s) can be attributed to incidental factors such as food, drink, physical exertion, disease, and so on. While it is not explicitly stated who performs the interrogation in such cases, the use of the third person plural *bodqim* (they examine) makes it clear that other people—in all likelihood the sages—are the ones who determine the purity status of the man in question, and not the man himself. This passage thus seems to reveal a premise that not only women but also men might seek the counsel of a sage in order to discern whether they are pure or impure, and that for both sexes the process of regular self-examination is complemented, at least on occasion, with an appeal to the specialized knowledge of the rabbis.

The combined process of self-examination and consultation with a sage serves as a manifestation of the two commitments that distinguish the intended subject of the Mishnah from his perpetually impure counterparts. Self-examination demonstrates the constant concern for purity, which distinguishes this subject from the People of the Land, and consultation with a sage demonstrates subordination to rabbinic authority, which distinguishes this subject from "heretical" Jewish groups. The appeal to the knowledge of the sage, however, is not simply an exhibition of complacency with the rabbis (although it is certainly also that). As I stressed, the basic assumption in the Mishnah is that people are capable of discerning their own purity status, provided that they have full knowledge of the relevant facts and of the workings of impurity. The only case in which a person is actually *obligated* to consult an expert and cannot decide his purity status for himself is that of skin afflictions, which the Pentateuch makes clear must be inspected by a priest,[52] but in all other cases consultation is entirely optional. Therefore, the choice to seek a sage's counsel is portrayed in rabbinic texts as part of a personal and self-motivated quest for purity, rather than as submissive compliance with authority. It is self-evident, I believe, that the rabbis promoted the practice of consultation with a sage at least partially in order to bolster their own authority and to claim religious and legal power, but they did so by presenting consultation with a sage as something that laypeople themselves voluntarily initiate. The sage is not presented as subordinating the one who seeks his council, but as the one who helps him or her to pursue their own commitment to purity, and thereby, as I will now continue to argue, fills a supporting role in one's active formation as a subject of the law.

## Self-Examination and Self-Formation

The daily processes of self-examination that the intended mishnaic subject is expected to conduct, both of bodily phenomena and of actions and encounters, are of course directed toward one pragmatic goal: maintaining oneself and one's surroundings in a state of ritual purity to the extent that this is possible. However, by presenting the attainment of this goal as dependent upon constant self-scrutiny, the rabbis constructed their idealized subject as one who is distinguished from others not only by his relations with other people and things (for example, by his choices to avoid certain people or objects, to prepare food in a particular way, and so on), but also by his relations with *himself*. A life governed by concern for purity and impurity, according to the Mishnah, is defined by heightened self-awareness and self-command, in such a way that the mishnaic subject can be seen as effectively divided: it is as if the person who inhabits a body, works, eats, roams in public spaces, encounters other people, and so on is continuously watched and assessed by an internalized purity-oriented authority. What distinguishes the mishnaic subject from his oppositional counterparts, and especially from the People of the Land, is the dominance of this internalized authority, the purity-oriented part of the self, in one's mental constitution.

The critical role that self-examination and self-scrutiny play in the mishnaic construction of a life geared toward purity and the shaping of the mishnaic subject as one who is, or should be, constantly overseen by an internalized authority closely resonate with Greek and Roman (particularly Stoic) accounts of the ongoing self-examination required as part of philosophical training. As Pierre Hadot showed, in the ancient world philosophy was not seen merely as a contemplative activity, but was considered an all-encompassing commitment to self-improvement and self-perfection, ultimately aspiring toward harmony with the perfect order of the cosmos. Hadot sees ancient philosophical circles as developing therapeutic approaches, designated to heal the self from weakness, passions, pains, treacheries, and other forms of malaise, so as to allow the self to be governed by its better part, namely, by reason, and thus to align with nature.[53] The therapeutics of the self in antiquity consists of a variety of both mental and physical exercises, all of which can be classified under the heading *askesis,* that is, rigorous training of the body and the soul. While *askesis* includes many activities such as reading, fulfillment of duties, conversations with others, and more,[54] a fundamental aspect of *askesis* is constant self-scrutiny, which Hadot calls "examination of the conscience." Examination of the conscience is not limited to the question "have I been bad or good?" but concerns the broader question of how one stands vis-à-vis the ideal that one put forth for oneself.[55]

The prominence of self-examination in a philosophical life is especially lucid and developed in the writings of Seneca, who dedicates much attention to the Stoic exercise of *meditatio* (the Latin equivalent of *askesis*), and describes an ongoing dialogue that one conducts with oneself about oneself as a quintessential part of this exercise. In the course of *meditatio,* as Shadi Bartsch explained, one essentially holds a conversation with one's own better self (which in Stoicism is tantamount to the *hegemonikon,* the governing power of reason), and allows oneself to be reviewed, chastised, and judged by this superior self.[56] In Bartsch's words, "One participant in the dialogue is conceived as already holding the keys to Stoic wisdom, and thus leading along his lagging partner, who is invariably less advanced, more prone to passion and to error, more in need of direct instruction."[57] At times,

Seneca suggests, this superior participant in the dialogue can actually be the internalized figure of a Stoic teacher or wise man,[58] which functions as a concrete manifestation of one's own *hegemonikon*.

A famous passage in Seneca's *De ira* (On Anger) specifically suggests that one form that this commitment to ongoing self-scrutiny should take is the habit of an *examination of the day*, that is, a recapitulation of all of one's activities and encounters during the day and a reflection on the way one conducted oneself throughout them.[59] The mind, writes Seneca, must be called every day to give an account, and thus nothing is more worthwhile than the habit of self-inspection before one falls asleep. As James Ker observed, while the idea of a daily examination of one's conscience can be found already in Pythagorean writings,[60] Seneca takes the call for self-examination in a new direction by associating it with self-control.[61] The purpose of the examination of the day, according to Seneca, is not simply to assess one's moral progress, but to shape one's character and behavior in an active way, since by knowing that one is "brought before the judge" daily *(ad iudicem esse veniendum)*, one is inclined to be more conscious of oneself throughout the day and therefore govern oneself better. In other words, Seneca recommends that one examine his day not just in order to evaluate his performance, but also because the very process of examining motivates one to behave better and enhances one's self-mastery.[62]

For Seneca, then, the very commitment to undergo self-examination and self-scrutiny changes one's actions and responses, since one begins to conduct oneself as if watched at all times, and the fact that the one watching and the one being watched are ultimately the same person does not detract from the transformative power of this internalized gaze.[63] Moreover, this commitment is in and of itself an indication of self-transformation. One who is willing to reflect on oneself and to assess oneself as if through the gaze of another has already consciously subordinated himself to his better part, and has thus already actively begun to be transformed. In the words of Seneca, "He who came to the mirror so as to change himself, has already been changed" *(Qui ad speculum venerat ut se mutaret iam mutaverat)*.[64]

The theme of self-examination in Greek and Roman literature pertains not only to one's conscience but also to one's body, since the therapeutic regime of philosophy included care for both mental and physical aspects of the self, which were seen as inseparable from each other. Accordingly, the careful management of one's habits of eating, drinking, bathing, exercise, and engagement in sexual activity was seen as part and parcel of philosophical *askesis*.[65] As Andrew Crislip noted, one of the manifestations of this concern with the well-being of the body was the habit of conducting physical self-examinations on a daily or semidaily basis.[66] A notable example of the interrelatedness of examinations of the day and examinations of the body in Roman Stoic culture can be found in Marcus Aurelius's letters to

Fronto, which include detailed accounts of the author's thoughts, encounters, and activities, as well as of his physical sensations and his efforts to nurse his ailments.[67] While some have argued that this incessant self-scrutiny of his body attests to Marcus Aurelius's own hypochondriac tendencies, Judith Perkins persuasively argued that for Marcus Aurelius, as well as for others of a similar persuasion, constant attention to the workings and vicissitudes of the body was a philosophical activity, a way of reflecting about the self and communicating it to others.[68] Self-reflection, which was the sine qua non of an ethical life, thus meant consciousness of one's body as well as consciousness of one's actions, and as in the case of examinations of the day, readiness to perform physical self-examinations marked the subject as distinct from others who, much to their detriment, ignored the well-being of their bodies and souls.

Unquestionably, the rabbinic practices of self-examination for the detection of impurity and the philosophical practices of self-examination prescribed as part of *askesis/meditatio* could not be more different. The former are geared toward the attainment of a ritual status of purity, focus on one's physical engagement with the material world, and have no apparent ethical undertone to them (except for the general edict to comply with the laws of the Torah), whereas the latter are geared toward liberation from passions and accord with reason, focus on one's moral and social behavior and one's physical and mental well-being, and strictly concern one's standing and function as an ethical agent. Neither the practices of self-examination themselves nor the motivations behind them nor their desired results are in any way comparable between the Mishnah and the ancient philosophical corpus. What is comparable, however, is the kind of subject that these practices both assume and generate, that is, *a subject distinguished by his self-command and self-consciousness*, who conducts himself as if divided into two separate entities, one a supervisor and one a supervisee. In other words, although the ultimate goals of the mishnaic subject (in the context of purity) and of the philosophical subject are utterly different and unrelated, the qualities, mental constitution, and relations of one with oneself that both of these subjects must bolster and nurture to achieve these goals are quite similar. Furthermore, both the rabbis and the Stoics emphasize the critical role that sages (rabbis/wise men) play in helping one conduct and complete these self-examinations and in enabling one to pursue one's ultimate goal, in such a way that subordination to the sage, whether internalized or externalized, is in and of itself part of one's constitution as a subject. In this respect, both in rabbinic and in philosophical texts, *self-examination is also self-formation.*

While I am by no means suggesting any direct line of influence between philosophical and rabbinic writings, and certainly do not see the rabbinic discourse of purity as an *askesis* manual in disguise, I do contend that the rabbis and their Greek and Roman intellectual contemporaries had similar notions of an idealized self. The greater questions of what is good and right for one to do and be were approached and dealt with very differently by the rabbis and the Stoics, with the former essentially turning to the Torah and the latter turning to the cosmic power of reason, but the kinds of qualities one was seen as needing to display and cultivate in order to attain the good were parallel. This close resemblance between the idealized rabbinic self and the idealized philosophical self, which were both considered to be formed through recurring processes of self-examination, does attest, in my view, to an infrastructure of shared cultural values between the rabbis and their Graeco-Roman contemporaries.

What kind of self, then, are the rabbis forming through the recurring self-examinations that they prescribe, and more broadly, what are the defining traits of the subject that the rabbis imagine to be fully committed to the pursuit of purity? At this point, it is fair to say that a critical quality that characterizes this subject is *self-control*, a quality to whose importance I already pointed in the previous chapter. The ability to control oneself, mentally and physically, is the main trait that distinguishes the idealized mishnaic subject from his oppositional counterparts: as we have seen, the rabbis presented the perpetual impurity of Gentiles as akin to the impurity of abnormal genital discharges, thus identifying Gentiles with a bodily phenomenon defined by a loss of self-control, and similarly the People of the Land are depicted as conducting themselves with a mindlessness that resembles that of children, lacking any sense of self-control. The life of the mishnaic subject, in contrast, is underwritten by regimented self-examination that, as Seneca observed, yields self-mastery since one learns to shape one's behavior so as to avoid the exhortation of one's internalized overseer. To this end, the pursuit of purity (as well as, one might argue, adherence to Jewish law in general) not only depends on one's capacity for self-control, but also actively enhances this capacity. In what follows, I will argue that self-control is intertwined in the mishnaic discourse of purity and impurity with *self-knowledge,* and will propose that by portraying these two inextricable qualities as what enables the pursuit of purity, the rabbis gave the quest for ritual purity a new ethical substance, which allowed it to resonate with the cultural values that dominated their world.

## "IT WAS IN MY HEART TO GUARD IT": SELF-CONTROL, SELF-KNOWLEDGE, AND THE QUEST FOR PURITY

### Attention and Attention to Attention

Impurity, as I have emphasized time and again in this book, is conceived in the Mishnah as a phenomenon that operates in the material world through concrete modes of contagion and contraction. In accordance with this view, the effort to stave off impurity consists of concrete actions taken to make sure that the object in question, whether one's body or one's possessions, will not have physical contact with known or suspected sources of impurity. However, several tannaitic sources suggest that such actions are not enough. Rather, the effort to manage the object at hand physically so that it does not contract impurity must be accompanied by a *mental* effort, that is, by concentration on the object in question and by conscious deliberation to keep it pure.[69] Accordingly, I will argue that part of the process of self-examination, which is so central to the pursuit of purity, is an examination not only of one's actions and body, but also *of one's mental dedication to purity*. This emphasis on the mental dimension of the pursuit of purity provides us with a key, I propose, to reconstructing the Mishnah's idealized self as it is shaped through the rabbinic discourse of purity and impurity, and ultimately, to understanding the ethical substance that the rabbis give to this discourse.

The most straightforward expression of the notion that mental dedication to purity is required in order to stave off impurity appears in a passage that concerns the attempt to eat one's meals in a state of purity. The passage mentions two different forms of purification that one might undertake in preparation for a meal: first, ritual immersion for the purpose of full-body purification, and second, washing one's hands immediately before eating, a custom which rests on the assumption that one's hands are impure in a minor degree at all times, even if one's body is otherwise pure. The Mishnah addresses two cases in which one attained a state of purity (of the entire body and of the hands) in preparation for a meal, but then got distracted and therefore did not immediately begin to eat:

> If one was pure, and he drove his heart away from eating *(hisi'a libo mi-le'ekhol)*—R. Yehuda renders him pure, because it is the way of the impure ones to separate themselves from him; and the Sages render him impure.
>
> If one's hands were pure and he drove his heart away from eating, even though he said: "I know that my hands have not become impure"—his hands are impure, for the hands are continuously busying themselves *(she-ha-yadayim 'asqaniyot)*.[70]

The first case here presents a controversy between R. Yehuda and the Sages regarding the purity status of a person who, as he was about to eat, was distracted and took his mind off of the meal. According to R. Yehuda, this person's purity status is maintained, since even if he was not careful to avoid sources of impurity during the time in which he was distracted, others were surely careful not to expose him to their impurity. The Sages, in contrast, hold that this person's distraction from his intention to eat immediately undoes his purity status, presumably because in their view whenever one is not fully attentive to purity one inevitably contracts impurity and other people cannot be counted on to distance themselves from him.

There seems to be no controversy between the rabbis, however, that one's *hands* can only remain pure for as long as one is actively conscious of keeping them in this state. Thus, according to the second case, if one sat down to eat with pure hands and was then distracted from his original intention to eat, thereby briefly ceasing to be mindful of the requirement to eat with pure hands, his hands are immediately rendered impure. Even if this person is convinced that he did not actually come into contact with any source of impurity, the very fact that he was mentally inattentive to impurity renders his hands impure. Yair Furstenberg explained the rationale behind this ruling lucidly: "A lack of attention brings about a lack of control . . . once one takes his mind off of [the requirement of purity], his hands operate uncontrollably, as if of their own accord."[71] There is notable correspondence between the notion that one's hands, once not given to one's scrutiny and supervision, are assumed to touch whatever is around them and the depiction of the People of the Land as meddling with everything they see: lack of attentiveness manifests itself in lack of self-control, and lack of self-control inevitably results, as I indicated above, in impurity.

Furthermore, several tannaitic texts make the point that one is required not only to be mindful of impurity, *but also to be mindful of one's mindfulness*. Put differently, one needs to be held accountable not only for what one touched and what one did, but also for whether one was mentally *conscious* of one's commitment to maintain a state of purity at a given moment or not. This notion is remarkably illustrated in the following two accounts:

> It once happened that one woman was weaving a garment in [a state of] purity, and she came before R. Ishmael so that he would examine her.
> She told him: Master, I know that the garment has not become impure, but it was not in my heart to guard it *(lo haya be-libi leshomro)*.
> In the course of the examinations that R. Ishmael was conducting, she told him: Master, I [now] recall that a menstruating woman came in and pulled the rope [of the weaving loom] with me.
> Said R. Ishmael: how great are the words of the Sages, who said, "If one did not intend to guard [an object in a state of purity], it is impure."[72]
>
> It again happened that one woman was weaving a tablecloth in [a state of] purity, and she came before R. Ishmael and he was examining her.
> She said to him: Master, I know that the tablecloth has not become impure, but it was not in my heart to guard it.
> In the course of the examinations that R. Ishmael was conducting, she told him: Master, I [now] recall that a thread was torn and I have tied it in my mouth.
> Said R. Ishmael: how great are the words of the Sages, who said, "If one did not intend to guard [an object in a state of purity], it is impure."[73]

In both of these narratives, R. Ishmael is described as "examining" the weaving woman in order to assess whether the garment and tablecloth in question can be considered pure. Both women took it upon themselves to weave in purity, that is, to ensure that the fabric would not come into contact with any source of impurity; however, a thorough investigation is required to determine whether the product can actually be certified as pure or not. Both women admit that while they took measures to weave in purity, they were not deliberate about maintaining the fabric in a state of purity at all times, that is, at some point they were distracted from the constant concern for purity. The statement that recurs in both stories, "I know that the garment (or the tablecloth) has not become impure, but it was not in my heart to guard it," is noteworthy: the women are expected to give an account not only of what happened to the object in question, but also of what their mental disposition toward this object was at the said time. Indeed, once it is established that these women were not *mentally* attentive to protecting the object from impurity, it is quickly revealed that they have also *actually* failed to protect it from impurity. In the first case, a menstruating woman appeared and participated in the act of weaving, and in the second case the weaver moistened one of the threads in her mouth, thus making the tablecloth vulnerable to impurity (since once something has become moist, it can "duplicate" the impurity of whatever touches it). Again we see that when one takes one's mind off of something, one immediately relinquishes his or her control over it. As R. Ishmael comments at the end of each of these narratives, these cases affirm the rabbinic principle that whatever one is not attentive to inevitably becomes impure: as well intended and as committed to purity as both of these women were, by failing to perform on a mental level they also failed on a practical level.

These two passages serve as yet another powerful example of the ways in which the process of consultation with a sage is constructed in rabbinic literature as an integral part of the process of self-examination and as enhancing and enabling the individual's quest for purity. The consultation with the sage is structured here in the form of a dialogue, through which the consulter acquires a more comprehensive knowledge of the events that she herself reports, in such a way that she realizes that her previous account of these events was in fact flawed. R. Ishmael was clearly not present at the time and place that either of these women engaged in weaving, and his only knowledge of the situation comes from the women themselves, but nevertheless he is able, in both cases, to uncover an event that the women themselves were initially not aware of, and to determine the impurity status of the object in question in a way that the women could not. These two cases, however, also reveal a new dimension of the two interrelated practices of self-examination and consultation with a sage: they suggest that one is expected to produce not only an account of what one did, but also an account of one's mindset while one did it. In other words, mindfulness of purity and impurity, which is the distinctive mark of the intended subject of the Mishnah, is not just manifested in attention to what one does and in attention to one's body: it is also manifested in *attention to attention itself.*

The emphasis that these passages place on mental attention, by explicitly referring to the state of the heart *(hisi'a libo, haya be-libi)* and its disposition toward the pursuit of purity, is resonant with the central notion of attention (Greek *prosochē*, Latin *attentio*) that we find in Stoic writings, particularly in the works of Epictetus.⁷⁴ As Pierre Hadot explains, attention is "a continuous vigilance and presence of mind, self consciousness which never sleeps, and a constant tension of the spirit."⁷⁵ Essentially, it is ongoing awareness of what one does and how one does it at the very time of doing. Unrelenting attention is championed not only by Stoic writers, who advocate it as crucial for a philosophical life, but also by writers such as Plutarch and Cicero, who emphasize the importance of attention for the public speaker,⁷⁶ and by Jewish-Hellenistic authors such as Philo of Alexandria and the author of the Wisdom of Solomon, who see it as quintessential for the worship of God.⁷⁷ Particularly relevant for our purposes is Epictetus's comment that by ceasing to be fully attentive, even briefly, one immediately loses control over oneself: "Do you not see," asks Epictetus, "that when you have let your mind loose, it is no longer in your power to recall it either to propriety or to modesty or to moderation, but you do everything that comes to your mind in obedience to your inclinations?"⁷⁸ Self-control, then, closely depends on attention; however, attention also depends on self-control, since only by being in full mastery of oneself can one become fully attentive and not allow oneself to be distracted.

Therefore, as Ciarán Mc Mahon explained, attention is both an exercise (that is, a form of *askesis*) and the goal of the exercise.⁷⁹ The capacity for attention is the trademark of the philosopher, and it can only be acquired through constant striving for full attention as an end in and of itself. In Stoic writings, attention usually means attention to the present moment, that is, a complete and utter dedication of the mind to the thing in which one is engaged at this very instant.⁸⁰ However, Epictetus puts forth the idea that the highest form of attention is attention to attention itself: "Give me a man who cares how he shall do any thing, not for the obtaining of a thing, but who cares about his own energy *(tēs energies tēs autou)* ... who, when he is deliberating, cares about his own deliberation *(bouleuomenos autēs tēs boulēs)*, and not about obtaining that about which he deliberates."⁸¹ Epictetus's idealized subject is focused not only on what he can achieve through attention, but also on attention for its own sake.

The valorization of the capacity for attention in Greek and Roman culture and particularly the championing of attention as what allows one to exert control over oneself again point to the shared values of the rabbis and their contemporaries in what concerns an idealized notion of the self. The rabbinic view that one has to monitor one's own attention to purity and keep it in check, and that part of self-examination for impurity is self-examination of the *heart* for its mental dedication to purity, indicates that for the rabbis the ideal of self-control, to whose prominence in the purity discourse I pointed above, was inextricable from the ideal of *self-knowledge*. Putting forth the notion that one is expected to make a conscious decision to be attentive to purity, and that one must be constantly aware of the extent to which he or she succeeded or did not succeed in being attentive, the rabbis suggest that caring about purity also means caring about caring about purity; in other words, the rabbis construct a discourse in which *attentiveness to purity is, in a sense, attentiveness to the self*. Thus they present the ability to attain a status of purity as necessitating an investigation of the workings of one's heart, and shape the pursuit of purity as requiring a fulfillment of the famous Delphic imperative *gnōthi sauton*, "know thyself."[82]

In Greek and Roman culture, the two qualities of self-knowledge and self-control were closely intertwined, and were often viewed together as constituting the ideal of *sōphrosynē*, loosely translated as "temperance" or "soundness of mind." While the concept of *sōphrosynē* is too complex and multifaceted for me to discuss it at length here,[83] for our purposes it will suffice to note that this admired trait was thought to be manifested in abstention from any kind of excess, in moderate and balanced behavior, and in the ability to master one's desires. As Helen North and others showed, *sōphrosynē* comprises exactly the combination of self-knowledge and self-control, in such a way that each of these qualities nurtures and enhances the other.[84] In order to be able to master oneself, one needs to keep oneself in check constantly, to become intimately familiar with one's own dispositions and tendencies, and to keep close track of one's mental vicissitudes; at the same time, in order to be able to investigate oneself thoroughly, one needs self-discipline and mental dedication.[85] The idealized self that the Mishnah constructs, then, and with which it encourages its intended subjects to comply is a self that can be defined as possessed of *sōphrosynē*.

My identification of self-knowledge and self-control as the constitutive qualities of the Mishnah's idealized subject, and of the Greek ideal of *sōphrosynē* (or its Roman counterparts *temperantia* and *continentia*)[86] as that by which the rabbis are consciously or unconsciously guided in imagining this subject, suggests that for the rabbis there was an intricate connection between purity and masculinity. As various scholars pointed out, both the Greek *sōphrosynē* and its Latin cognates were essentially synonyms for manliness,[87] and the ability to present the esteemed combination of self-knowledge and self-control was not only a manly trait, but in many ways the very *definition* of manliness.[88] If the ability to attain and maintain a state of purity is restricted, in rabbinic discourse, to those with a notable capacity for self-knowledge and self-control, which are quintessentially defined as masculine traits, then the status of purity itself becomes in this framework a manifestation of masculinity. Here the rabbinic discourses on the irrevocable impurity of Gentiles and on the ongoing pursuit of purity expected of Jews converge to promote the same cultural ideal of masculinity: Gentiles are identified with a condition that emphatically renders them unmanly and that robs them of any ability to be pure, whereas for Jews the attainment of purity depends on qualities that were identified as epitomizing manliness.

This close association of purity with manliness confronts us, inevitably, with the question of how women fit into the mishnaic notion of the self, and of how the rabbis envisioned and constructed the pursuit of purity by women. While these questions merit a more elaborate discussion than I am able to offer here, in what follows I will suggest a number of observations on the place of women in the mishnaic portrait of a life inscribed by an ongoing commitment to purity, and on the implied gender of the idealized mishnaic subject.

### Women and the Subject of the Mishnah

As the sources that were discussed in this chapter have clearly demonstrated, the management of impurity is portrayed in the Mishnah as a defining part of the lives of women just as much as, and perhaps even more than, it is a defining part of the lives of men. Menstruation is a recurring source of impurity with which women deal regularly, and the examination and monitoring of menstrual impurity, as we have seen, are prescribed for women as a daily routine. In addition, the fact that women are the ones primarily concerned with the preparation of food, both consecrated and nonconsecrated, makes them chiefly responsible for preserving foodstuffs in a state of purity, and in general, the prominent role of women in the household places them as the ones upon whom the purity of the human habitat heavily depends. The expectation that women be fully devoted to the pursuit of purity is indicated not only in the notion that they must make efforts to examine their own bodies and to give an account of their actions, but also, as the stories of the two weaving women clearly illustrate, in the notion that they are required to be entirely attentive while engaging with pure substances. One could deduce, then, that the mishnaic discourse of purity and impurity was equally directed to men and to women, and that both men and women partook in the rabbinic notion of an idealized self.

In truth, nothing in the Mishnah explicitly suggests that this is not indeed the case, or that women were not seen as displaying and cultivating the valorized qualities of self-knowledge and self-control through their effort to maintain themselves and their surroundings in a state of purity. The fact that these qualities were commonly identified as masculine does not preclude women from striving to attain them: as several scholars have noted, although *sōphrosynē* was identified as a distinctly manly trait, it was expected of men and women alike.[89] It is reasonable to assume that the rabbis esteemed the purity practices of women as manifestations of their merit and of their devotion, and encouraged these practices for women as they did for men. However, the rabbis leave little room for doubt that the intended subject of the Mishnah, the one whom its makers have in mind when depicting a person committed to purity, is a man and not a woman. This is not simply because the Mishnah was unquestionably created for men by men, but also because the purity of women in the Mishnah is always presented as instrumental to the purity of men. Women are never depicted, for instance, as actually consuming food in a state of purity, washing their hands before meals, and so on, but rather only as preparing food in purity, food that will, presumably, be consumed by men.[90]

Moreover, the rabbis of the Mishnah define women's commitment to purity strictly in terms of the commitment of their male guardians, either their husbands or their fathers. In M. Tohorot 7.4, which was discussed above, we have seen that the rabbis contrasted a woman who is lax in regard to purity with a woman who is stringent in regard to purity by identifying the former as "the wife of [one of] the People of the Land" *(eshet 'am-ha-aretz)* and the latter as "the wife of a member" *(eshet haver)*. While this way of characterizing women by the men with whom they are associated can be seen as mere linguistic convention and is a common way of creating feminine epithets in the Mishnah,[91] in the Tosefta we find the more explicit view that women and slaves essentially comply with the standard set for them by others and do not have a standing of their own in matters of purity.[92] Accordingly, a woman's scrupulousness in the observance of purity is always a derivative of the scrupulousness of either her father or her husband, and is assumed to be abandoned immediately when the woman is no longer under the guardianship of a scrupulous man.[93] Women's commitment to purity is thus presented and discussed in tannaitic texts not as a personal self-motivated piety, but as a derivative of the commitment of their husbands or fathers. This is not to say, of course, that there were not women who were devoted to purity as a personal form of piety in the mishnaic world, but it is to say that women were of interest to the rabbis only insofar as they enabled or impeded men's quest for purity.

The point that the Mishnah (as well as the rest of rabbinic literature) was designated for men, and that women were only of concern to it to the extent that they affected the lives of men, was cogently made by Ishay Rosen-Zvi in his work on the "inclination" towards transgression *(yetzer)* in rabbinic literature. Rosen-Zvi showed that while it can be deduced from rabbinic sources that women deal with illicit desires (sexual and nonsexual alike) in the same way that men do, the rabbis take extremely little interest in the desires of women, for the simple reason that their purpose is to provide guidance for men. The enterprise of the rabbis is not to present a comprehensive account of the mental world of human beings, but to cultivate certain habits and qualities in their audience, which is unequivocally an audience of men.[94] Following Rosen-Zvi, I suggest that while the pursuit of purity was in multiple ways relevant for women's lives and for women's self-formation as subjects of the law, the rabbis constructed their discourse of purity and impurity as a discourse for men and about men. Thus, even though women can potentially strive to develop the qualities of the mishnaic idealized subject, this ideal subject is clearly a male.

Here it is important to raise one more point. While women were certainly expected to make efforts to maintain themselves and their environment in a state of purity, there are some indications in rabbinic texts that they were seen as less capable of succeeding in attaining this goal than men. It is perhaps not incidental that the stories of the weaving women, through which the Tosefta demonstrates the importance of constant mindfulness of purity, present women rather than men as failing to be fully attentive, and thus as losing control over themselves and their surroundings in such a way that the task of weaving in purity was not accomplished. These stories can be taken as affirming the view that was prevalent in the Greek and Roman world, according to which women are less capable of self-control than men.

The notion that women are less capable of self-control than men, and that their tendency to follow their inclinations and desires mindlessly might in fact compromise their attempt to maintain an object in a state of purity, is blatantly expressed in M. Tohorot 7.9. This passage describes a case in which one woman goes out for a while, and when she comes back she finds that another woman is feeding coals to a fire under a pot containing a heave-offering. R. Aqiva rules that in such a case, even if the pot was covered when the first woman got back, the heave-offering in the pot is to be rendered impure. His ruling is explained as guided by the premise that "women are gluttonous (*gargeraniyot*), and she (the second woman) is suspected to have uncovered the other woman's pot, to see what she was cooking." This characterization of women as unable to restrain themselves from touching what they are not supposed to touch corresponds with the way in which the People of the Land are described as constantly meddling with things, as well as with the statement that children are in the habit of touching whatever they see, as we have seen above. Women, the People of the Land, and children are all identified in the Mishnah as possessed of diminished self-control, and thus as less capable of maintaining a state of purity.

As I mentioned in the previous chapter, in Greek medical thought the overall characterization of women as less capable of self-control was closely related to the view of their bodies as "leaking" and as constantly traversing boundaries.[95] A similar perception of women's bodies as uncontrollable and uncontained can be observed in the Mishnah, in which women are depicted as if they might start exuding uterine blood and as if their breasts might start leaking milk involuntarily at any given moment.[96] The seeping and unruly nature of women's bodies makes them more prone to impurity not only because such bodies are harder to control, but also because such bodies are more difficult to *know*. The elaborate system of knowledge of the female body that the rabbis constructed, which is not paralleled by a similar system of knowledge of the male body, rests on the premise that the female body is far from being self-explanatory and that its workings are so complex that the help of an expert is required to fathom it.[97]

A particularly striking statement regarding the inability of women to monitor and understand their bodies (and thereby their impurity) by themselves can be found in a passage that discusses the possibility of women miscounting the number of days that they are in a specific state of purity or impurity. The rabbis divide the female cycle into segments of eighteen days: genital blood emitted during the first seven days of this cycle is considered to be normal menstrual discharge *(dam niddah)*, whereas genital blood emitted during the following eleven days of this cycle is considered to be abnormal discharge *(dam zavah)*. Different rules apply if a woman sees blood during the first seven days or during the following eleven days; therefore, it is quite important for a woman to know at which point in this eighteen-day cycle she has seen the blood. After presenting different scenarios in which women might not be sure whether their discharge took place during the "normal" phase or the "abnormal" phase,[98] we find the following statement:

> Said R. Yehoshua: While you (masc. pl.) are repairing the mentally inept ones, repair the competent ones *('ad she-atem metaqnim et ha-shotot taqnu et ha-piqhot)*.[99]

In this statement, R. Yehoshua seems to be alluding to a rule we find earlier in the tractate (M. Niddah 2.1), according to which mentally inept women, who cannot take charge of their own menstrual impurity, are examined and managed by mentally competent women *(piqhot)*, who serve as the ones who "repair them" *(matqinot otan)*.[100] R. Yehoshua makes the point that since even competent women are likely to make mistakes while counting their days of purity or impurity, they require supervision and guidance no less than mentally inept women. However, while in the anonymous statement (M. Niddah 2.1) it is other women who "repair" the mentally inept women, in R. Yehoshua's statement (M. Niddah 6.14) it is his interlocutors, the rabbis, who "repair" women, inept and competent alike. This presentation of male experts as the ones who are capable of knowing and understanding the bodies of women in ways that women themselves are incapable of closely resonates with Rebecca Flemming's description of Greek and Roman medical writings about women: "The female self is entirely absent from a text that establishes a relationship between those in whose care and control the girls fall and the wayward and problematic bodies of their charges."[101]

Thus, women are depicted in the mishnaic discourse as lacking both in the ability for self-control and in the ability for self-knowledge, the two qualities that, according to my suggestion, the rabbis saw as quintessential for the attainment of purity. This is not to say that women were thought to be categorically incapable of these qualities and thereby incapable of purity, since this is clearly not the case. But it is to say that in the course of their pursuit of purity, men were seen as affirming and solidifying their manliness, and thereby as forming themselves in direct opposition and contrast to women (and to feminine men, for that matter). While women as they appear in the Mishnah certainly participate in the pursuit of purity and are certainly committed to purity as an ideal, they also appear as nonsubjects or lesser subjects in the mishnaic discourse, and serve as embodiments of the very qualities against which the rabbis' idealized subject is defined.

## The Mishnaic Subject and the Quest for Purity

Through their discourse of purity and impurity, I proposed thus far, the rabbis shaped and championed a particular kind of self, whom they positioned as the intended subject of the Mishnah. This subject is distinguished from various non-subjects or lesser subjects in his constant mindfulness of impurity, which translates, in the rabbinic setting, to constant mindfulness of oneself: of one's body, of one's actions and interactions, and perhaps most notably of one's mindfulness itself. This intense mindfulness both depends upon and enhances one's capacity for self-control and self-knowledge, two interrelated, highly valorized ideals in the ancient world, which were closely identified with manliness. It is fair to say, then, that the mishnaic subject was molded by the rabbis in the image of the Greek and Roman ideal of the self-governing man, and moreover, that the very ability to attain a status of ritual purity was constructed in the Mishnah as contingent upon at least partial compliance with this ideal.

However, while the mishnaic subject shares critical traits with various Greek and Roman ideals of selfhood, he is fundamentally distinguished from them in what I will call here the *teleology of the self*, namely, in the underlying purpose that guides the idealized self in his interactions with the world and in his relations with himself. The mishnaic subject does not seek to rule a polis or to prevail in battle, nor does he seek to become one with the godly nature of the cosmos. Rather, his sole purpose, as he is imagined by the rabbis, is to live in full accordance with the teachings of the law, with the Torah as it was interpreted and promulgated by the rabbis. The ideals of selfhood that prevailed throughout the Graeco-Roman world of which the rabbis were a part were thus notably appropriated by the rabbis, but underwent teleological transformation, so to speak, which repositioned these ideals as enabling full adherence to the law and extolled them as such. In this framework, self-scrutiny and self-control are laudable traits insofar as they help one avoid halakhic mishaps: they can prevent one from violating the Sabbath, from taking what is not his, from touching holy articles when impure, and so on. The idealized mishnaic subject, then, is ultimately one whose personal constitution and mental dispositions allow him to comply with the law in the most scrupulous way possible.

In this respect, the rabbinic discourse of purity and impurity is not fundamentally different from the rabbinic discourse on any other legal theme. Indeed, it is hard to think of any realm of life in which adherence to the Torah does not require self-control and self-scrutiny, and in which the rabbinic subject is not defined by his subordination to the law and by his commitment to careful fulfillment of the commandments. What makes the arena of purity and impurity especially remarkable in the general framework of the Mishnah's construction of an idealized legal subject is the prominence of recurring practices of *self-examination* as an inextricable part of the pursuit of purity. These practices, which, as I showed, closely resonate with philosophical *askesis*, are unique to the halakhic context of purity and impurity, and highlight the extent to which adherence to the law is also a process of self-formation in the Mishnah. Furthermore, the positioning of the mishnaic subject, specifically in the context of purity and impurity, in direct contrast to the People of the Land, who are characterized by a lax attitude to the law, especially stresses the role of the pursuit of purity in one's constitution as a legal subject.[102] The totality of the engagement with impurity and the pursuit of purity as an ongoing aspect of everyday life as imagined in the Mishnah thus makes the halakhic arena of purity and impurity a particularly fecund site through which to explore rabbinic notions of selfhood, although these notions can also be traced in various other contexts in rabbinic literature. The question remains, however, of whether and how the heightened emphasis on the self in the rabbinic depiction of the pursuit of purity *changes the meaning of purity itself*. In what ways, if any, does the function of ritual purity as a site for self-formation as a subject of the law transform the very concept of ritual purity?

Here I would like to propose that by presenting attention to purity, that is, mental dedication to the pursuit of purity, as a condition for the actual attainment of ritual purity, the rabbis turned ritual purity from a technical-like cultic status into a manifestation of one's *commitment* to purity. That is to say, through their emphasis on deliberation and mindfulness the rabbis reconstructed the status of ritual purity as an externalized halakhic expression of one's internal state of mind toward purity. To a certain extent, this reframing of ritual purity in terms of mental dedication to ritual purity is traceable already in the tannaitic texts according to which distraction or insufficient attention to purity immediately denies one or one's possessions the possibility of purity. However, whereas in the passages we have seen above the underlying assumption is that a lack of attention is likely to result in an actual contraction of impurity, in the two rabbinic passages I will now examine we find a radical view according to which mental dedication *suffices* to maintain an object in a state of purity, regardless of external conditions. These passages strongly suggest, I will argue, that mental dedication to purity was seen, at least by some, as tantamount to ritual purity, so much so that the concept of ritual purity could, in some contexts, be stripped of its physical aspects and become a sheer manifestation of one's state of mind.

Whereas above we have seen the rabbinic ruling that "if one did not intend to guard [an object in a state of purity], it is impure," in another passage in the Tosefta we find that this idea is complemented with the notion that if one *did* intend to guard an object in a state of purity, this object is pure. Simply put, in the same way that lack of attention to purity renders an object impure, dedicated attention to purity can render an object pure:

> If one was wearing a robe and wrapped in a cloak, and he said, "It is in my heart regarding the robe but it is not in my heart regarding the cloak"—the robe is pure and the cloak is impure.
>
> If there was a basket on his shoulder and a rake was inside it, and he said, "It is in my heart regarding the basket but it is not in my heart regarding the rake"—the basket is pure and the rake is impure.[103]

According to this passage, the impurity status of an object is determined, all things being equal, solely based on one's attention, or lack thereof, to this particular object. By presenting a situation in which a person makes a conscious decision to be attentive to one object and not to the other, when the two objects are supposedly exposed to the same sources of impurity, the Tosefta turns attention into the point toward which the entire pursuit of purity gravitates. According to this passage, attention does not just *enable* one to safeguard things from impurity: it actually *is* what safeguards them.[104] Attention is depicted in this passage as operating almost automatically: it is as if the very decision to be attentive to an object coats it with invisible proofing against impurity. Note that the Tosefta pairs the two cases specifically to belie any assumption that the object's purity status is determined according to the probability of its actually contracting impurity: in both cases we have a pair of objects, one within the other (a robe wrapped in a cloak, a rake inside a basket), but whereas in the first case the "inner" object, which is presumably less exposed to impure substances, maintains its purity, in the second case the "outer" object is the one that maintains its purity, even though it has greater exposure to impurity than that which is inside it. While it could be inferred, of course, that the decision to pay attention to something actively makes one more careful in managing it, this is not the way the Tosefta presents this. Rather, it describes the protective effect of attention as taking effect immediately, and as ensuring the purity of the object in question regardless of any external circumstances. In accordance with this view, in the Babylonian Talmud's rendition of the two stories of the weaving women we have seen above, the Sages' ruling addresses not only the detrimental effect of lack of attention, as their ruling in the Tosefta does ("If one did not intend to guard it, it is impure"), but also the protective effect of attention: "If it is in his heart to guard it, it is pure, and if it is not in his heart to guard it, it is impure."[105]

Whereas the Tosefta passage can still be taken as implying that attention to purity leads to better care of the objects at hand, even though it does not say so explicitly, the following passage in the Mishnah leaves little room for doubt that the decision to dedicate attention to the purity of an object is a *sufficient* condition for rendering it pure. According to this passage, attention not only enhances one's physical care for one's possessions, but it can actually replace it:

> If one (a priest) leaves his articles from this grape-harvest to the next grape-harvest—his articles are pure.

And with an Israelite (that is, a nonpriest), [they are impure] until he says: "It was in my heart to guard them."[106]

This passage concerns the possibility of leaving one's vessels and wine-pressing articles in the vineyard during the interim between two grape-harvest seasons. It is suggested that a priest can do so without worrying that his articles might contract impurity—presumably, since he is a priest, everyone (that is, even the People of the Land) knows that he has to maintain a high standard of purity and will be careful not to convey impurity to his possessions.[107] Nonpriests, however, must make a conscious decision to be mindful of these articles for them to remain pure during this interim. It is clearly assumed in this passage that the one who makes the decision to guard his articles in a state of purity is not actually watching them at all times (hence the word choice "one who *leaves* his articles," *ha-maniah et kelav*); nonetheless, his very attentiveness seems, in itself, to safeguard the articles from impurity.

The notion that the very decision to maintain an object in a state of purity protects it from impurity is somewhat reminiscent of the rabbinic principle that the *intention* to offer a sacrifice outside of its designated time or place suffices to defile it, even before this sacrifice is ever offered.[108] In both of these cases, one's state of mind constitutes halakhic reality: in the same way that one's intention to misuse a sacrifice is seen as tantamount to the actual misuse of a sacrifice, the decision to guard an object from impurity is tantamount to guarding it from impurity. However, whereas in the case of sacrifices the one whose state of mind determines the status of the sacrifice (namely, the priest) is also the one who is capable of physically defiling it through his actions, in the case of impurity the one who intends to guard an object from impurity is usually *not* the one who poses a threat to it. Put differently, whereas in the case of sacrifices there is an evident (albeit not inevitable) correspondence between what the priest plans to do and what actually happens to the sacrifice, in the case of purity what happens to the object in question in terms of impurity depends on multiple external forces that are not all given to the control of the owner. In the context of purity, then, we see not simply a notion that state of mind is equivalent to action, but a notion that a state of mind effectively obliterates external circumstances and solely determines the cultic status of the object. This notion, as admittedly inconspicuous in rabbinic literature as it is, points to a striking transformation in the very concept of purity within the thought-world of the rabbis, according to which ritual purity is fundamentally an expression of commitment to ritual purity, an externalized affirmation of an internal disposition. In other words, while in what we have seen so far the rabbis present the ability to attain a state of purity as dependent upon a certain state of mind, in these two passages they present this state of mind as *amounting* to ritual purity.

This finally brings us back to the ethical dimension of purity in rabbinic discourse, with which I began this chapter. The rabbis, as I stressed time and again, did not associate ritual impurity with sin and immorality, nor did they associate ritual purity with justice and goodness. Unlike many of their predecessors, they insistently referred to both of these halakhic concepts strictly in technical and physical terms. What the rabbis did create, however, is a subtle but critical shift of focus from the status of ritual purity itself to the *quest* for ritual purity, which placed an unprecedented emphasis on the process of attaining ritual purity and on the self-reflective practices it entails. Whereas earlier treatments of purity and impurity in biblical and postbiblical literature were mainly concerned with determining what sanctions ritual impurity portends and what prerogatives ritual purity allows, the rabbis' vested interest is in the things that one must do and the kind of person that one must be in order to attain ritual purity. They thereby infused ritual purity with a new ethical substance, turning this cultic status into a testament for a particular way of life, that is, a life governed by the Torah and geared toward full compliance with it. Accordingly, the rabbis did not *equate* purity and virtue, but they positioned the desire to be pure (as part of a greater desire to adhere to the law) as the ultimate virtue, and in this way established congruity between ritual purity and their own cultural values. The quest for purity, which in the Mishnah takes precedence over purity itself, thus becomes, in the rabbinic discourse, a quest for self-perfection as a subject of the law.

# Epilogue

*Recomposing Purity and Meaning*

This book set out to explore the ways in which the biblical concepts of purity and impurity, and the institutions and practices that pertain to these concepts, were reshaped and reconstructed in the Mishnah around a new focal point, namely, around the self. Throughout this study, I examined some of the critical innovations that the rabbis introduced into the system of purity and impurity that they had inherited from their predecessors, and showed how questions of subjectivity and consciousness profoundly shape the rabbinic discourse on the emergence, discernment, and management of impurity, and on the pursuit of purity. The centrality of the self in the Mishnah's discourse of purity and impurity is manifested in two central facets: first, in the notion that the ability of things (artifacts, foods, bodies) to contract impurity depends upon human relation to these things, that is, on the consciousness of the subject; and second, in the construction of one's daily engagement with impurity and one's quest for purity as processes in which mindsets, dispositions, and personal commitments play a fundamental role. One's relations with oneself, with one's body, and with one's human and nonhuman surroundings are what constitute the world of purity and impurity in its rabbinic construction, in such a way that the self, the human subject who is capable of reflection on himself and on his surroundings, is in many ways the ultimate point of reference of the discourse of purity and impurity in the Mishnah.

The story that I ventured to tell throughout this book, through the analysis of various tannaitic rulings and innovations, and through my attempts to uncover conceptual frameworks and classificatory principles that underlie these innovations, is a story of a creative enterprise of recomposition of scriptural heritage. By "scriptural heritage" I am referring not only to the Priestly Code's treatment of purity and impurity unto itself, from which the foundational edicts regarding purity and impurity derive, but also to the various ways in which these edicts were interpreted, utilized, applied, and practiced by different reverent communities from the time they were put forth until the time of the redaction of the Mishnah. I choose the word *recomposition* to describe the rabbinic treatment of purity and impurity in the Mishnah to emphasize the Mishnah's essential dependence on the biblical infrastructure of the law, on the one hand, and its striking independence of it, structurally and rhetorically as well as conceptually, on the other hand.

The intricate balance of dependence on and independence from the Bible is one of the most defining characteristics of the Mishnah as a whole. Although it is perhaps best described as presenting a systematic attempt to construct a comprehensive picture of a life guided utterly by commitment to biblical law (according to its rabbinic interpretation), the Mishnah almost entirely refrains from explicitly directing its learners to the biblical text itself. The Mishnah's order and structure are not dictated by those of the Pentateuch, but rather follow a division of topics and themes devised by the rabbis; the Mishnah rarely engages with biblical terminology or phrasing as such, but rather embeds them within rabbinic discussions without distinguishing between biblical and rabbinic terms and concepts; and perhaps most importantly, the Mishnah almost never resorts to the Bible for authority. This compilation acquires its authoritative stance neither from claiming to be given through divine revelation (like the *Book of Jubilees* or the *Temple Scroll*), nor from taking the exegetical standpoint of uncovering the hidden truths of the revealed text (like the tannaitic Halakhic Midrashim), but rather solely from itself. Thus, while biblical law unquestionably constitutes the infrastructure of the Mishnah, and while the learner of the Mishnah is assumed to be thoroughly versed in it (for if this is not the case, the Mishnah is entirely senseless), the Mishnah generally seems as though it had "swallowed" biblical law, digested it, and turned it into an unrecognizable part of the rabbis' discourse.

In this respect, although many of the rabbis' rulings in the Mishnah are clearly (albeit implicitly) informed in some way or another by interpretive readings of and direct engagement with the biblical text, the Mishnah's enterprise vis-à-vis the Bible is essentially not one of interpretation, but one of *recomposition*. Recomposition, as I use this term here, is not to be confused with *rewriting*, in which an author attempts to create a new text that imitates or complements the Bible; rather, it is a process that takes place only after the biblical text has been thoroughly *decomposed*. The Biblical laws, to return to the alimentary metaphor, have been chewed up by the rabbis of the Mishnah, cut off from their context and dissected into categories and subcategories, and mixed with an array of other substances—customs and traditions, fantasies of the past, hopes for the future, and so forth. They then reemerge in the new form of *halakhah*, a discourse that is based on biblical law but is neither akin to it nor a commentary on it.

This amalgamation of biblical edicts with various postbiblical notions, which can be traced throughout the Mishnah more broadly, is especially apparent in the mishnaic discourse of purity and impurity. Whereas in some halakhic areas the biblical infrastructure is rather negligible, if at all traceable (prayers and blessings, laws pertaining to *Eruv*, and marital arrangements come to mind as prominent examples of such areas), the Mishnah itself proclaims that "purities and impurities" *(ha-tohorot ve-ha-tum'ot)* are among "the bodies of the Torah," and defines them as areas of rabbinic knowledge that are firmly based on Scripture.[1] Since this topic receives a rather extensive treatment in the Pentateuch, the foundational elements of the rabbinic purity and impurity discourse are clearly biblical, and as I noted, the rabbis are strongly bounded by these elements. Nevertheless, the biblical teachings regarding sources of impurity and modes of conveyance of impurity and of purification are unrecognizably coalesced in the Mishnah with ideas that emerged in the Second Temple period or later on. One who studies the Mishnah without being thoroughly acquainted with biblical law has no way of knowing, for instance, that the idea that liquids duplicate impurity is not biblical, or that nowhere in the Bible is the washing of hands before meals prescribed, or that the idea that food makes the one who eats it impure is a postbiblical innovation. Biblical premises, later interpretations and developments of these premises, and popular practices that prevailed before or during the time of the rabbis all appear as part of one monolithic discourse, which, while introducing many individual rulings as expressed by specific named rabbis, presents itself to the reader as created by no one in particular, as an embodiment of *The Law* par excellence.

What I proposed in this book is that the process in which the biblical edicts of purity and impurity were recomposed by the rabbis of the Mishnah also entailed a close intermingling of these edicts with ideas that prevailed in the cultural and intellectual world of the rabbis, at the center of which stood the self. The molding together of biblical laws and postbiblical traditions and interpretations with this heightened attention to self and subjectivity generated a recomposed discourse of purity and impurity, in which the self plays a critical part and is, as I argued, in many ways the ultimate point of reference of this discourse. Again and again we have seen that the rabbis' discussions of purity and impurity present thought, intention, deliberation, and mindsets not only as part of the considerations taken into account in determining purity and impurity, but oftentimes as what essentially constitutes both the ability to contract impurity and the ability to be pure. This stress on human consciousness as the channel through which the world must pass in order to be significant in terms of purity and impurity recomposes the biblical edicts in such a way that their focus is not on the qualities of the object but on a person's relation to this object, and not on one's cultic prerogatives but on one's standing as a subject of the law.

It is quite difficult to determine whence this heightened interest in the self and the view of human consciousness as a determining force arose. I find it quite conceivable, as I cautiously proposed, that the rabbis were directly or indirectly influenced by prominent mindsets in Graeco-Roman culture that emphasized self-reflection and self-formation. Such influence, however, is almost impossible to substantiate, whether it is to be traced to direct engagement with philosophical writings and teachings (or popular adaptations of them) or to certain ideas simply being "in the air" in the Roman Mediterranean of the first centuries C.E. Alternatively, one could argue that it was the social, religious, and political changes in Jewish Palestine during the tannaitic period that led to this shift of focus from community to individual, and to the stress on intention, thought, and self-reflection. Possibly the lack of social cohesion, the lack of a place of worship around which purity practices could be centered, and a growing general sense of precariousness and instability during this period led to "an inward turn" in which the only realm that was seen as knowable and governable was that of one's consciousness. Finally, another factor that may have been at play in the rabbinic reconfiguration of purity is the emergence of the early Christian communities as competing interpreters of the biblical heritage. As those communities took on metaphorical and nonritual approaches to the concepts of purity and impurity, dismissing their practical implications,[2] the rabbis may have been compelled to offer new and vibrant interpretations for the Levitical code of purity and impurity, while emphasizing the religious merit attained specifically *through* concrete and physical purity practices. As appealing as all these conjectures are, however, they remain by and large unverifiable. My purpose in this book was thus not to try to explain why, when, and as a response to what (if it was a response to anything at all) the self emerged as a critical point of reference in the Mishnah's discourse of purity and impurity, but rather to analyze the ways in which the emphasis on self and subjectivity in the Mishnah profoundly changed the meaning of purity and impurity in rabbinic discourse.

The ability and readiness of the rabbis to mold biblical legal concepts and institutions in the image of concerns, interests, and practices that were germane to their own time gave ritual purity and impurity a new substance. It turned purity and impurity into gauges through which to sort out and map the body, to determine relations of ownership, to establish the presence of the dead in the world of the living, to distinguish between self and other, man and woman, Jews and non-Jews, and, perhaps most importantly, to express and assess one's relation to oneself and to the law. Purity and impurity acquired in the Mishnah new meanings as prisms through which to examine oneself and one's surroundings, and thereby became powerful themes in the Mishnah's construction of its own subject.

Here I wish to be very clear: as prominent as self and subjectivity are in the mishnaic discourse of purity and impurity, it is unquestionably *not* a discourse about the self, either manifestly or in disguise, but a discourse about purity and impurity. The rabbis' purpose in the Mishnah is not to delineate the inner workings of human attachment to material things, nor to pontificate on what establishes one as a subject of the law, nor to muse over the gradual transition from life to death, nor to extol the virtue of self-control. Its purpose is to create a comprehensive account of the way a life guided by an effort to adhere to the laws of purity and impurity as the rabbis understood them should look. The Mishnah is not a work of philosophy or anthropology or applied ethics: it is decidedly and unquestionably a work of law, albeit with "law" conceived somewhat more broadly than it is in our own world. However, "the way the rabbis understood" those laws cannot be extricated from the ways the rabbis understood the world, and from the way they understood the workings of human beings. It is impossible to discuss corpse impurity without certain ideas on what corpses are and what happens to them; it is impossible to explain how one ought to conduct oneself in the public sphere without certain assumptions on the people that inhabit the public sphere; it is impossible to discuss impure food without considering what turns something into "food"; and most importantly, it is impossible to create any sort of legal text without implicitly directing it to someone, real or imagined, and without having certain assumptions about and expectations of the person to whom it is directed. My attempt throughout this book was to gain a deeper and richer understanding of the Mishnah's treatment of purity and impurity by uncovering these and other unspoken assumptions.

The Mishnah, then, is a fecund site in which biblical edicts and principles are kneaded together with past and present traditions, real and invented practices, customs and decrees, imagination and anxiety, close textual interpretations and overarching ontological assumptions, and form together a complex discourse that, despite its seemingly dry and technical style, is effervescent with ideas that resonate well beyond the horizon of the particular legal topic at hand. Close engagement with the Mishnah as a text that recomposes scriptural heritage in light of the rabbis' own cultural and intellectual world allows us, I believe, not only to understand this cultural and intellectual world as such better, but also to expand our understanding of the multifaceted phenomenon of interpretation as a religious enterprise, and of the delicate dynamics between preservation and innovation in the world of late antiquity.

NOTES

INTRODUCTION

1. The earliest attestation of this common statement is in the collection of Geonic responsa *Sha'are teshuva* (§175), in a response attributed to Rav Hayya Gaon; see B. M. Levin, *Otzar ha-Geonim* (Jerusalem: Hebrew University Publication Society, 1937), 5:26–27 (on tractate *Rosh ha-shana* 16b). While the Gaon is attributing this statement to "the Sages," we do not find any statement to that effect in classical rabbinic literature. However, in the medieval Midrash *Lekah Tov* (also known as *Pesiqta zuttrata*) Tazri'a 16, a similar statement is attributed to R. Yohanan, and Louis Ginzburg conjectured that this statement is originally taken from the Palestinian Talmud to tractate *Niddah*, which did not survive. See Louis Ginzberg and Burton Visotzky, *Genizah Studies in Memory of Doctor Solomon Shechter: Midrash and Haggadah* (1928; Piscataway: Gorgias Press, 2003), 71.

2. With the exception of the laws of menstrual purity, which are still largely practiced because intercourse with a menstruating woman is an explicit biblical prohibition (Leviticus 18:19) and not just a source of impurity (Leviticus 15:19).

3. http://www.kipa.co.il/ask/show/212118. All translations from Hebrew in the book are mine, unless stated otherwise.

4. See Jacob Neusner, *The Idea of Purity in Ancient Judaism* (Leiden: Brill, 1977), 32–71; David Flusser, *Judaism of the Second Temple: The Jewish Sages and Their Literature*, trans. Azzan Yadin (Grand Rapids: W. B. Eerdmans, 2009), 8–11.

5. For an elaborate study on the ubiquity of the observance of purity laws during the Second Temple period, see Hanan Birenboim, "Observance of the Laws of Bodily Purity in Jewish Society in the Land of Israel during the Second Temple Period" [in Hebrew], PhD diss., Hebrew University, Jerusalem, 2006.

6. Babylonian Talmud (hereinafter BT) Shabbat 13a.

7. See Jonathan Klawans, "Notions of Gentile Impurity in Ancient Judaism," *AJS Review* 20, no. 2 (1995): 285–312; Christine Hayes, *Gentile Impurities and Jewish Identities: Inter-*

*marriage and Conversion from the Bible to the Talmud* (New York: Oxford University Press, 2002), 45–67.

8. See Lawrence Schiffman, "The Pharisees and Their Legal Traditions according to the Dead Sea Scrolls," *Dead Sea Discoveries* 8, no. 3 (2001): 262–77; Eyal Regev, "The Sadducees, the Pharisees, and the Sacred: Meaning and Ideology in the Halakhic Controversies between the Sadducees and the Pharisees," *Review of Rabbinic Judaism* 9 (2006): 126–40.

9. On the use of purity rhetoric in the New Testament, see Michael Newton, *The Concept of Purity at Qumran and in the Letters of Paul* (Cambridge: Cambridge University Press, 1985).

10. See Colleen Conway, "Toward a Well-Formed Subject: The Function of Purity Language in the Serek ha-Yahad," *Journal for the Study of the Pseudepigrapha* 21 (2000): 103–20.

11. As is most evident if one compares the purity corpus in the Mishnah with the copious purity-related texts from Qumran; see my discussion in the first chapter.

12. On the centrality of the Temple in the Priestly construction of purity, see Jacob Milgrom, *Leviticus 1–16: A New Translation with Introduction and Commentary*, Anchor Bible 3 (New York: Doubleday, 1991), 718–42.

13. See Birenboim, "Observance of the Laws of Bodily Purity," 159–222; see also Hayes, *Gentile Impurities*, 45–91.

14. In this respect the rabbinic treatment of purity and impurity in *Seder Tohorot* must be distinguished from mishanic discussions of purity and impurity in tractates that directly pertain to worship in the Temple, such as *Pesahim* and *Hagigah*: in the latter tractates the focal point of the discussions is unquestionably the purity of the Temple and the sancta.

15. See, for instance, Ben Zion Bokser, *Pharisaic Judaism in Transition: R. Eliezer the Great and Jewish Reconstruction after the War with Rome* (New York: Bloch, 1935); Jacob Neusner, *Ancient Israel after Catastrophe: The Religious Worldview of the Mishnah* (Charlottesville: University of Virginia Press, 1982); Avraham Aderet, *From Destruction to Restoration: The Way of Yavneh in the Rehabilitation of the Nation* [in Hebrew] (Jerusalem, Magnes Press, 1990). For a recent revisiting of this topic, see Daniel Schwartz and Zeev Weiss, eds., *Was 70 CE a Watershed in Jewish History? On Jews and Judaism before and after the Destruction of the Second Temple* (Leiden: Brill, 2012).

16. To a great extent, this intensified interest has to do with the publication of the Qumran Scrolls, in which the concern with ritual purity and impurity is overwhelmingly dominant; see, for example, Hannah Harrington, *The Purity Texts: Companion to the Qumran Scrolls* 5 (New York: T & T Clark, 2004). This interest was also invoked as a result of developments in the study of the origins of Christianity, which made scholars redraw their attention to the social and halakhic world of Jesus and his disciples, of which purity laws and practices were a central aspect; see, for example, E. P. Sanders, *Jesus and Judaism* (Philadelphia: Fortress Press, 1985); Roger Booth, *Jesus and the Laws of Purity: Tradition and Legal History in Mark 7*, JSNT Supplement Series 13 (Sheffield: JSOT Press, 1986); Thomas Kazen, *Jesus and Purity Halakhah: Was Jesus Indifferent to Impurity?* (Winona Lake: Eisenbrauns, 2010). Finally, the rather recent introduction of social-scientific perspectives to the study of ancient Judaism brought about a renewed interest in the topic of purity and impurity as a fecund site for social and anthropological explorations. Most notably, see Albert Baumgarten, *The Flourishing of Jewish Sects in the Maccabean Era: An Interpretation* (Leiden: Brill, 1997); Phillip Davies, "Food, Drink, and Sects: The Question of Ingestion in the Qumran

Sect," *Semeia* 86 (1999): 151–63; Eyal Regev, "Pure Individualism: The Idea of Non-Priestly Purity in Ancient Judaism," *Journal for the Study of Judaism* 31, no. 2 (2000): 176–202.

17. The ground for this sort of investigation was laid by the pioneering works of Adolf Büchler and Gedalyahu Alon, both of whom attempted to reconstruct a historical account of the observance of purity in the Palestinian Jewish society of the Second Temple and mishnaic periods (ultimately reaching utterly different conclusions). See Adolf Büchler, *Der galiläische Am ha-Ares des zweiten Jahrhunderts: Beiträge zur innern Geschichte des palästinischen Judentums in den ersten zwei Jahrhunderten* (Vienna: A. Hölder, 1906); Gedalyahu Alon, "The Bounds of the Laws of Levitical Cleanness," in *Studies in Jewish History in the Times of the Second Temple and the Talmud* [in Hebrew] (Tel-Aviv: Ha-Kibbutz ha-me'uhad, 1957), 1:148–76. An important landmark in the sociohistorical study of purity in ancient Judaism was Jacob Neusner, *The Rabbinic Traditions about the Pharisees before 70* (Leiden: Brill, 1971), whose conclusions were later fiercely challenged by E. P. Sanders, *Jewish Law from Jesus to the Mishnah: Five Studies* (London: SCM press, 1990), 131–254.

18. On the question of the dependence of purity laws on the Temple, see John Poirier, "Purity beyond the Temple in the Second Temple Era," *Journal of Biblical Literature* 122, no. 2 (2003): 247–65.

19. Jacob Neusner, *A History of the Mishnaic Law of Purities*, 22 vols. (Leiden: Brill, 1974–77). See also Hyam Maccoby, *Ritual and Morality: The Ritual Purity System and Its Place in Judaism* (Cambridge: Cambridge University Press, 1999), 149.

20. See Eyal Regev, "Non-Priestly Purity and Its Religious Aspects according to Historical Sources and Archeological Findings," in *Purity and Holiness: The Heritage of Leviticus*, ed. M. Poorthuis and J. Schwartz (Leiden: Brill, 2000), 223–44; Birenboim, "Observance of the Laws of Bodily Purity"; Yair Furstenberg, "Eating in a State of Purity during the Tannaitic Period: Tractate Teharot and Its Historical and Cultural Contexts" [in Hebrew], PhD diss., Hebrew University, Jerusalem, 2010.

21. Both ritual baths and stone vessels, which are quintessential to the observance of purity, are relatively less common in remains from the later mishnaic period than they are in remains from earlier periods (although they certainly did not disappear); see Ronny Reich, "Miqwa'ot (Jewish Ritual Immersion Baths) in Eretz-Israel in the Second Temple and the Mishnah and Talmud Periods" [in Hebrew], PhD diss., Hebrew University, Jerusalem, 1990, 143. For an elaborate survey of archeological findings of stone vessels and their implications, see Birenboim, "Observance of the Laws of Bodily Purity," 64–67. In his dissertation, Yair Furstenberg argued that a close textual analysis of the Mishnah leads to conclusions similar to those of the archeological investigation: he shows that earlier strata in the Mishnah preserve practical manuals meant to assist with the observance of purity, whereas later strata introduce purity mainly as a matter of concern for distinctly committed individuals and as a more theoretical subject. For a summary of this analysis, see Furstenberg, "Eating in a State of Purity," 254–62. These studies challenge the conclusions of earlier scholars, who maintained that impurity practices increased rather than decreased in the course of the second century; for this view, see Ahron Oppenheimer, *The Am ha-aretz: A Study in the Social History of the Jewish People in the Hellenistic-Roman Period*, trans. I. H. Levine (Leiden: Brill, 1977), 63–64; Aderet, *From Destruction to Restoration*, 281 and passim. It should be mentioned that Ya'akov Sussman, who examined the talmudic texts that address questions of purity and impurity, firmly maintained that laws of purity continued to be

practiced in Palestine even in the postmishnaic period; see Ya'akov Sussman, "Babylonian Sugyot for Zerai'm and Tohorot" [in Hebrew], PhD diss., Hebrew University, Jerusalem, 1969, 310.

22. See, for example, Neusner, *The Idea of Purity;* Newton, *The Concept of Purity;* Hannah Harrington, *The Impurity Systems of Qumran and the Rabbis* (Atlanta: Scholars Press, 1993).

23. See Jonathan Klawans, *Impurity and Sin in Ancient Judaism* (New York: Oxford University Press, 1999); Hayes, *Gentile Impurities;* Jonathan Lawrence, *Washing in Water: Trajectories of Ritual Bathing in the Hebrew Bible and Second Temple Literature* (Atlanta: Society of Biblical Literature, 2006); Vered Noam, *From Qumran to the Rabbinic Revolution: Conceptions of Impurity* [in Hebrew] (Jerusalem: Yad Ben Zvi Press, 2010).

24. For an astute description of the Mishnah's blending of past, present, and future, see Ishay Rosen-Zvi, *The Rite That Was Not: Temple, Midrash and Gender in Tractate Sotah* [in Hebrew] (Jerusalem: Magnes Press, 2008), 249.

25. For a concise characterization of this approach in the study of rabbinic literature, see Charlotte Fonrobert, "On *Carnal Israel* and the Consequences: Talmudic Studies since Foucault," *Jewish Quarterly Review* 95, no. 3 (2005): 462–69.

26. For some notable examples of studies oriented by such a cultural-corporeal approach, see Michael Satlow, *Tasting the Dish: Rabbinic Rhetorics of Sexuality* (Atlanta: Scholars Press, 1994); Miriam Peskowitz, *Spinning Fantasies: Rabbis, Gender and History* (Berkeley: University of California Press, 1997); Beth Berkowitz, *Execution and Invention: Death Penalty Discourse in Early Rabbinic and Christian Cultures* (New York: Oxford University Press, 2006); Ishay Rosen-Zvi, *The Rite That Was Not;* Rosen-Zvi, "The Body and the Temple: The List of Priestly Blemishes in the Mishnah and the Place of the Temple in the Tannaitic Study House" [in Hebrew], *Jewish Studies* 43 (2006): 49–87. Particularly pertinent to my own work is Charlotte Fonrobert, *Menstrual Purity: Rabbinic and Christian Reconstructions of Biblical Gender* (Stanford: Stanford University Press, 2000).

27. For but a few examples of works that challenge the very notion of the body as a fixed entity and look into the fluidity of its boundaries, its fragmentariness and heterogeneity, and its relations with the nonhuman, see Elizabeth Grosz, *Volatile Bodies: Towards a Corporeal Feminism* (Bloomington: Indiana University Press, 1994); Jeffrey J. Cohen and Gail Weiss, eds., *Thinking the Limits of the Body* (Albany: SUNY Press, 2003); Christopher E. Forth and Ivan Crozier, eds., *Body Parts: Critical Explorations in Corporeality* (Lanham, MD: Lexington Books, 2005); Margaret Lock and Judith Farquhar, eds., *Beyond the Body Proper: Reading the Anthropology of Material Life* (Durham: Duke University Press, 2008). Many of these and similar works emerged from the fields of queer studies and disability studies, disciplines that are ardently promoting radical rethinking on what "bodies" mean and how they are parsed and interpreted.

28. See, for example, Joshua Levinson, "Cultural Androgyny in Rabbinic Literature," in *From Athens to Jerusalem: Medicine in Hellenized Jewish Lore and in Early Christian Literature,* ed. S. Kottek, M. Horstmanhoff, G. Baader, and G. Ferngren. (Rotterdam: Erasmus Publishing, 2000), 119–40; Levinson, "Bodies and Bo(a)rders: Emerging Fictions of Identity in Late Antiquity," *Harvard Theological Review* 93, no. 4 (2000): 343–72; Charlotte Fonrobert, "When Women Walk in the Way of Their Fathers: On Gendering the Rabbinic Claim for Authority," *Journal of the History of Sexuality* 10, no. 3–4 (2001): 398–415; Fonrobert,

"Blood and Law: Uterine Fluids and Rabbinic Maps of Identity," in *Blood and the Boundaries of Jewish and Christian Identities in Late Antiquity*, ed. R. Boustan and A. Yoshiko Reed, special issue, *Henoch* 30, no. 2 (2008): 243–66.

29. In a work that has become a classic, Marcel Mauss traced the different meanings of the notion of self *(moi)* or person *(personne)* in various cultures, showing how diverse the referents of these terms are. See Marcel Mauss, "A Category of the Human Mind: The Notion of Person; The Notion of Self," trans. W.D. Walls, in *The Category of the Person: Anthropology, Philosophy, History*, ed. M. Carrithers, S. Collins, and S. Lukes (New York: Cambridge University Press, 1985), 1–25.

30. As Gretchen Reydams-Schils noted, a highly useful way of detecting notions of the self in ancient texts is by tracing the use of reflexive pronouns (such as *autos* or *se*); see Gretchen Reydams-Schils, *The Roman Stoics: Self, Responsibility, and Affection* (Chicago: University of Chicago Press, 2005), 15. Richard Sorabji commented that in some Greek texts the word *autos* is mentioned without an accompanying noun, indicating that it should be understood as referring to "*the* self," as in the expression *hekastos autos*, "each self." See Richard Sorabji, *Self: Ancient and Modern Insights about Individuality, Life, and Death* (Chicago: University of Chicago Press, 2006), 32.

31. For useful surveys of some of the central works in this field, see Nick Mansfield, *Subjectivity: Theories of the Self from Freud to Haraway* (New York: NYU Press, 2000); Kim Atkins, ed., *Self and Subjectivity* (Oxford: Blackwell, 2005).

32. See, for example, Henry Wheeler Robinson, *Corporate Personality in Ancient Israel* (Philadelphia: Fortress Press, 1981); Diskin Clay, "Missing Persons, or the Selfless Greeks," in *The Quest of the Individual: Roots of Western Civilization*, ed. W. Carroll, J. Furlong, and C. Mann (New York: Peter Lang, 1990), 13–22. For a similar but less radical position, see Charles Taylor, *Sources of the Self: The Making of Modern Identity* (Cambridge: Cambridge University Press, 1989); Michael Frede, "A Notion of a Person in Epictetus," in *The Philosophy of Epictetus*, ed. T. Scaltsas and A. Mason (New York: Oxford University Press, 2007), 153–82.

33. Most comprehensively, see Christopher Gill, *Personality in Greek Epic, Tragedy, and Philosophy: The Self in Dialogue* (Oxford: Clarendon Press, 1998); Gill, *The Structured Self in Hellenistic and Roman Thought* (Oxford: Oxford University Press, 2006); Sorabji, *Self*. For examples of other studies on selfhood in various contexts, see Phillip Cary, *Augustine's Invention of the Inner Self: The Legacy of a Christian Platonist* (New York: Oxford University Press, 2000); Reydams-Schils, *The Roman Stoics*; Troels Engberg-Pedersen, "Philosophy of the Self in the Apostle Paul," in *Ancient Philosophy of the Self*, ed. P. Remes and J. Sihvola (Dordrecht: Springer, 2008), 179–94.

34. Pierre Hadot, *Philosophy as a Way of Life*, ed. A. Davidson, trans. M. Chase (Oxford: Blackwell, 1995).

35. Ibid., 102.

36. For the most concise articulation of this idea, see Michel Foucault, "On the Genealogy of Ethics: An Overview of Work in Progress," in *The Foucault Reader*, ed. P. Rabinow (New York: Pantheon, 1984), 340–72.

37. See Michel Foucault, *The Care of the Self*, trans. R. Hurley (New York: Random House, 1986); Foucault, "Technologies of the Self," in *Technologies of the Self: A Seminar with Michel Foucault*, ed. L. Martin, H. Gutman, and P. Hutton (Amherst: University of

Massachusetts Press, 1988), 16–49; Foucault, *The Hermeneutics of the Subject: Lectures at the Collège de France, 1981–1982*, trans. G. Burchell (New York: Picador, 2001).

38. Pierre Hadot himself criticized Foucault for misrepresenting the Stoic investment in the self as aesthetic when it is in fact ethical in essence; see Hadot, *Philosophy as a Way of Life*, 206–13. A similar critique was raised by Martha Nussbaum, *The Therapy of Desire: Theory and Practice in Hellenistic Ethics* (Princeton: Princeton University Press, 1994), 5–6; and James Porter, "Foucault's Ascetic Ancients," *Phoenix* 59, no. 2 (2005): 121–31. From a different direction, Foucault's work was rightfully criticized as entirely disregarding women; see Page DuBois, "The Subject in Antiquity after Foucault," in *Rethinking Sexuality: Foucault and Classical Antiquity*, ed. D. Larmour, P. A. Miller, and C. Platte (Princeton: Princeton University Press, 1998), 85–103. In the same volume, Paul Allen Miller argues that Foucault presents a narrow and homogeneous picture of Roman culture, since he restricts himself only to prescriptive texts (philosophical and medical). See Paul Allen Miller, "Catullan Consciousness, the 'Care of the Self,' and the Force of the Negative in History," in Larmour, Miller, and Platte, *Rethinking Sexuality*, 171–203.

39. For a mere handful of examples of studies that examine constructions of the self in antiquity from a critical perspective and through emphasis on practice, see Maud Gleason, *Making Men: Sophists and Self-Presentation in Ancient Rome* (Princeton: Princeton University Press, 1995); Judith Perkins, *The Suffering Self: Pain and Narrative Representation in the Early Christian Era* (New York: Routledge, 1995); Yasmin Syed, *Vergil's Aeneid and the Roman Self: Subject and Nation in Literary Discourse* (Ann Arbor: University of Michigan Press, 2005); John Dugan, *Making a New Man: Ciceronian Self-Fashioning in the Rhetorical Works* (New York: Cambridge University Press, 2005); Shadi Bartsch, *The Mirror of the Self: Sexuality, Self-Knowledge, and the Gaze in the Early Roman Empire* (Chicago: University of Chicago Press, 2006); David Brakke, *Demons and the Making of the Monk: Spiritual Combat in Early Christianity* (Cambridge, MA: Harvard University Press, 2006); Shadi Bartsch and David Wray, eds., *Seneca and the Self* (New York: Cambridge University Press, 2009). Specifically in the context of the study of religion, see also Jan Assmann and Guy Stroumsa, eds., *Transformations of the Inner Self in Ancient Religions* (Leiden: Brill, 1999); David Brakke, Michael Satlow, and Steven Weitzman, eds., *Religion and the Self in Antiquity* (Bloomington: Indiana University Press, 2005).

40. Not much has been done in the field of rabbinic studies in terms of critical exploration of the self. Several scholars of rabbinic literature have attempted to present a comprehensive picture of the "person" or "human being" in this literature; see, most notably, Ephraim Elimelech Urbach, *The Sages: Their Concepts and Beliefs* [in Hebrew] (Jerusalem: Magnes Press, 1976), 189–226; Emero Stiegman, "Rabbinic *Anthropology*," in *Aufstieg und Niedergang der römischen Welt* II.19.2: *Religion (Judentum)*, ed. Wolfgang Haase (Berlin: Walter de Gruyter, 1979), 487–579. More recently, Jonathan Schofer published two studies about the rabbinic ethics of the self: Schofer, *The Making of a Sage: A Study in Rabbinic Ethics* (Madison: University of Wisconsin Press, 2005); and Schofer, *Confronting Vulnerability: The Body and the Divine in Rabbinic Ethics* (Chicago: University of Chicago Press, 2010). His studies, however, are not primarily interested in positioning the rabbinic notions of self in their greater cultural context. Conversely, two recent works by Ron Naiweld and Ishay Rosen-Zvi are particularly concerned with the correspondence between rabbinic literature and Hellenistic and early Christian literature: see Ron Naiweld, "L'anti-sujet: Le rapport

entre l'individu et la loi dans la littérature rabbinique classique," PhD diss., l'École des hautes études en sciences sociales, 2009; Ishay Rosen-Zvi, *Demonic Desires: Yetzer Hara and the Problem of Evil in Late Antiquity* (Philadelphia: University of Pennsylvania Press, 2011). All these studies, it should be noted, focus exclusively on aggadic (nonlegal) rabbinic texts.

41. Here it is important to mention Carol Newsom's pioneering work on the construction of self through disciplinary practices in the Qumran Scrolls as an important step toward the integration of early Jewish legal manuals and codes into the study of self-formation in antiquity. See Carol Newsom, *The Self as Symbolic Space: Constructing Identity and Community in Qumran* (Leiden: Brill, 2004). While Newsom focuses mainly on speech-acts and the use of language in the making of the sectarian subject, she does dedicate an extensive chapter to a discussion of embodied practices and modes of conduct in the sectarian discourse.

42. In this view, I align with several recent scholarly works on the Mishnah, which emphasize the unity and integrity of the text as a redacted whole. On this methodological perspective in the study of the Mishnah, see Christine Hayes, "What Is (the) Mishnah? Concluding Observations," *AJS Review* 32, no. 2 (2008): 291–97.

43. However, as Vered Noam showed in detail, in regard to purity there are striking incongruities between the Mishnah and the Halakhic Midrashim. Most importantly, the Halakhic Midrashim emphatically restrict the realm of purity to the Temple and the sancta alone, whereas the Mishnah assumes that purity is observed also beyond the Temple and for the purpose of consumption of nonconsecrated food. See Vered Noam, "The Bounds of Non-Priestly Purity: A Reassessment" [in Hebrew], *Zion* 72 (2007): 127–60.

44. One notable exception to this widely accepted view is the opinion of Albeck, who dates the redaction of the Tosefta to the end of the amoraic period (approximately the fifth century C.E.). However, Albeck does maintain that the actual materials that are included in the Tosefta are by and large early and contemporaneous with the Mishnah. See Hanoch Albeck, *Studies in Baraita and Tosefta* [in Hebrew] (Jerusalem: Mosad ha-Rav Kook, 1954), 87–88, 182–84.

45. This is, generally speaking, the traditional view. See, for instance, Ya'akov Nahum Epstein, *Introduction to Tannaitic Literature: Mishnah, Tosefta, and Halakhic Midrashim* [in Hebrew] (Jerusalem: Magnes Press, 1959), 242–62; Abraham Goldberg, "The Tosefta—Companion to the Mishna," in *The Literature of the Sages*, ed. Shmuel Safrai (Assen: Van Gorcum, 1987), 1:283–302.

46. See Judith Hauptman, *Rereading the Mishnah: A New Approach to Ancient Jewish Texts* (Tübingen: Mohr Siebeck, 2005).

47. See Martin Jaffee, *Torah in the Mouth: Writing and Oral Tradition in Palestinian Judaism, 200 BCE–400 CE* (New York: Oxford University Press, 2001), 39–61; Elizabeth Shanks Alexander, *Transmitting Mishnah: The Shaping Influence of Oral Tradition* (New York: Cambridge University Press, 2006), 35–55.

48. See Shamma Friedman, "Mishnah-Tosefta Parallels" [in Hebrew], *Proceedings of the 11th World Congress of Jewish Studies* C.1 (1994): 15–22; Friedman, "The Primacy of Tosefta to Mishnah in Synoptic Parallels," in *Introducing Tosefta: Textual, Intratextual, and Intertextual Studies*, ed. Harry Fox, Tirzah Meacham, and Diane Kriger (Hoboken: Ktav, 1999), 99–121.

## CHAPTER 1

1. William Robertson Smith, *The Religion of the Semites* (New York: Meridian Books, 1956), 447.

2. This idea was influentially introduced by Mary Douglas, *Purity and Danger: An Analysis of the Concepts of Pollution and Taboo* (1966; New York: Routledge, 2002). For a similar analysis, see Howard Eilberg-Schwarz, *The Savage in Judaism: An Anthropology of Israelite Religion and Ancient Judaism* (Bloomington: Indiana University Press, 1990), 177–94.

3. For a helpful survey of these various explanations, see Milgrom, *Leviticus 1–16*, 177–216.

4. See, for example, *Sifra* Ahare mot par. 9 per. 13:10 on Leviticus 18:4 (ed. Weiss 86a); BT Yoma 67b; *Pesiqta deRav Kahana* Parah 6 (ed. Mandelbaum 71). On the general form and function of such passages, see Rosen-Zvi, *Demonic Desires*, 87–101.

5. See *Pesiqta deRav Kahana* Parah 1, 7 (ed. Mandelbaum 54–55, 73–74).

6. See Jonathan Klawans, *Impurity and Sin*, 1–43, and the notes on pages 163–64.

7. The one notable exception to this rule is the use of the terms *pure* and *impure* in reference to a woman who has had intercourse with a man other than her husband (an act that ostensibly renders her *teme'a*, "impure"); see, for example, M. Kettubot 2.5; M. Nedarim 11.12; M. Sotah 1.5, 3.3, 3.6, 4.2. While the use of these terms in the context of marital infidelity is biblical in origin (see Numbers 5:13–15), it is important to note that a woman who was unfaithful to her husband is not considered among the sources of ritual impurity in the Mishnah, and cannot convey impurity to others.

8. See Klawans, *Impurity and Sin*, 92–117.

9. Leviticus 11:24–28, 39–40.

10. Leviticus 11:29–38.

11. Numbers 19:11–22.

12. Leviticus 15:16–18.

13. Numbers 19:9–10, 21.

14. Leviticus 12:1–8.

15. Leviticus 13:1–46.

16. Leviticus 15:1–15.

17. Leviticus 15:19–31.

18. Leviticus 13:47–59; 14:33–57.

19. Leviticus 11:1–23.

20. While this is not mentioned in the Priestly texts that directly discuss the sources of impurity, in Numbers 5:1–3 it is stated that not only persons with scale disease but also persons with abnormal genital discharges and persons who have been made impure by corpses must be distanced from the camp of Israel. On this, see Baruch Levine, *Numbers 1–20: A New Translation with Introduction and Commentary*, Anchor Bible 4A (New York: Doubleday, 1993), 184–86.

21. On the Priestly view of sources of impurity as capable of defiling the Temple and the camp by their very presence, see Jacob Milgrom, "Israel's Sanctuary: The Priestly Picture of Dorian Gray," *Revue Biblique* 83 (1976): 390–99.

22. Leviticus 15:4–11, 20–23, 26–27.

23. Leviticus 15:24.

24. Numbers 19:22.

25. For a helpful survey of scholarly works on the development of the biblical purity legislation in the Second Temple period, see Birenboim, "Observance of the Laws of Bodily Purity," 2-9.

26. See ibid., 9-19.

27. By the term *Qumran* I am referring here to the large collection of scrolls found in the Dead Sea caves, while being acutely aware that these scrolls are of very diverse nature, that each composition has its own history and purposes, and that the scrolls taken together do not necessarily reflect a single approach or worldview. However, since it is impossible, in the confines of this survey, to delve into the intricate questions pertaining to specific scrolls, I am following the lead of scholars who maintain that despite differences and varieties, there are certain principles and frames of thought that can be discerned throughout the Qumran corpus.

28. For but a few examples, see Harrington, *The Purity Systems of Qumran and the Rabbis*; Harrington, *The Purity Texts;* Ya'akov Sussman, "The Study of the History of Halakhah and the Dead Sea Scrolls: First Talmudic Contemplations in Light of the *Miqsat Ma'ase ha-Torah* Scroll" [in Hebrew], *Tarbitz* 59 (1990): 11-76; Birenboim, "Observance of the Laws of Bodily Purity," 223-303; Noam, *From Qumran to the Rabbinic Revolution*. It is also imperative to mention a few of the many studies of Joseph Baumgarten on this topic: "The Essene Avoidance of Oil and the Laws of Purity," *Revue de Qumran* 6, no. 2 (1967): 183-92; "Liquids and Susceptibility to Defilement in New 4Q Texts," *Jewish Quarterly Review* 85, no. 1-2 (1994): 91-101; "Zab Impurity in Qumran and Rabbinic Law," *Journal of Jewish Studies* 45, no. 2 (1994): 273-77; "The Red Cow Purification Rites in Qumran Texts," *Journal of Jewish Studies* 46, no. 1-2 (1995): 112-19; "The Halakha in Miqsat Ma'ase ha-Torah (MMT)," *Journal of the American Oriental Society* 116, no. 3 (1996): 512-16; "Tohorot," in *Qumran Cave 4 XXV: Halakhic Texts*, Discoveries in the Judean Desert 25, ed. J. Baumgarten et al. (Oxford: Clarendon Press, 1999), 79-122. For a recent survey of scholarship on purity in Qumran, see Hannah Harrington, "Purity and the Dead Sea Scrolls—Current Issues," *Currents in Biblical Research* 4, no. 3 (2006): 397-428.

29. Jacob Milgrom, "The Qumran Cult: Its Exegetical Principles," in *Temple Scroll Studies*, ed. G. J. Brooke (Sheffield: JSOT Press, 1989), 165-80.

30. See Harrington, *The Purity Texts*, 103.

31. This is the plausible reading of 4Q274 1 i 1-3, as suggested by Jacob Milgrom, "4QTohora: An Unpublished Qumran Text on Purities," in *Time to Prepare the Way in the Wilderness: Papers on the Qumran Scrolls by Fellows of the Institute for Advanced Studies of the Hebrew University, Jerusalem 1989-1990*, ed. D. Dimant and L. Schiffman (Leiden: Brill, 1995), 59-68. However, Baumgarten believes that this text concerns a person with genital discharge rather than a person with scale disease; see Baumgarten, "Tohorot," 101, and see Birenboim's discussion ("Observance of the Laws of Bodily Purity," 280-84), in which he convincingly rejects Baumgarten's reading. In rabbinic literature, the analogy between persons with scale disease and persons with genital discharges is evident in M. Niddah 10.4 and M. Zavim 5.6.

32. As shown by Vered Noam, in various places we can trace not only similar homogenizing tendencies in Qumranic and rabbinic texts, but even similar "midrashic" methods of reading. See Vered Noam, "Between Qumran and Rabbinic Midrash: Common Exegesis and Implied Polemics" [in Hebrew], *Megillot* 7 (2009): 71-98.

33. See M. Nega'im 13.7, 11–12. This ruling might stem not only from an analogy between a person with scale disease and a corpse, but also from an analogy between an afflicted house, which renders one who enters it impure, and an afflicted person.

34. See 4Q274 2 i 8, 11Q19 45.11–12, 4Q266 6 i 14–16; and see Martha Himmelfarb, *A Kingdom of Priests: Ancestry and Merit in Ancient Judaism* (Philadelphia: University of Pennsylvania Press, 2006), 98–112; Harrington, *The Purity Texts*, 103–6; Birenboim, "Observance of the Laws of Bodily Purity," 291.

35. This theory was suggested by Baumgarten based on his analysis of various purification manuals from Qumran (4Q414, 4Q512, and 4Q284); see Baumgarten, "Tohorot," 83–88. Baumgarten's view was endorsed by Esther Eshel, "Ritual of Purification," in Baumgarten, *Qumran Cave 4 XXV*, 135–54, but rejected by Birenboim, "Observance of the Laws of Bodily Purity," 274–76.

36. See my elaborate discussion in chapter 5.

37. On the impurity of outsiders in Qumran, see Aharon Shemesh, "The Origins of the Laws of Separatism: Qumran Literature and Rabbinic Halacha," *Revue de Qumran* 18, no. 2 (1997): 223–41; Harrington, *The Purity Texts*, 112–27. The view that any person who is not a member of the community is ritually impure is especially prominent in the Community Rule (1QS 6.16–22, 7.20). If one is to adopt the view that the Qumran community can be identified with the Essenes, further evidence for the impurity of outsiders in Qumran can be found in Josephus's comment that the Essenes purified themselves after every contact with foreigners (*War* 2.150). There are also several indications in Qumranic texts that Gentiles were seen as conveying ritual impurity: according to the Temple Scroll, a war captive taken by an Israelite man cannot touch pure food for seven years (11Q 19.63.15); according to the Damascus Document, a priest who was a captive among Gentiles must undergo purification (4Q 266 5 ii 5–7); and proselytes are prohibited from entering the Temple (CD 12. 8–11, 11Q19: 39.5–7). The reference to marriage with non-Jews in the *Miqtsat Ma'ase ha-Torah* Scroll (4QMMT C 49) also seems to indicate that Gentiles were seen as inherently impure; see Hayes, *Gentile Impurities*, 87–89.

38. For helpful surveys of notions of Gentile impurity in the Second Temple period, see Klawans, "Notions of Gentile Impurity," 293–302; Hayes, *Gentile Impurities*, 45–67; Birenboim, "Observance of the Laws of Bodily Purity," 69–158.

39. See T. Zavim 2.1.

40. This view was put forth most dominantly by David Flusser, "The Dead Sea Sect and Pre-Pauline Christianity," *Scripta Hierosolymitana* 4 (1958): 215–66; and Flusser, *Judaism and the Origins of Christianity* [in Hebrew] (Tel Aviv: Sifriyat Poalim, 1979), 209–39; and it has been endorsed by many different scholars. See Jonathan Klawans, "The Impurity of Immorality in Ancient Judaism," *Journal of Jewish Studies* 48, no. 1 (1997): 1–16.

41. Martha Himmelfarb, "Impurity and Sin in 4QD, 1QS, and 4Q512," *Dead Sea Discoveries* 8, no. 1 (2001): 9–37.

42. For a similar view, although more hesitant than Himmelfarb's, see Birenboim, "Observance of the Laws of Bodily Impurity," 224–32.

43. Some scholars consider excrement to be another source of ritual impurity in Qumran; see Magen Broshi, "Qumran and the Essenes: Six Realms of Purity" [in Hebrew], *Megillot* 2 (2004): 9–20; Harrington, *The Purity Texts*, 106–8. There is indeed abundant evidence in the scrolls that excrement was considered to be abominable and unholy, and

was therefore to be excluded from the city of the Temple (11Q19. 45.15, 4Q265 7 i 3) and to be avoided on the Sabbath (4Q265 6.2), as well as some suggestive evidence that the members of the community were expected to dig a pit for their excrement, in accordance with the edict in Deuteronomy 23:13–15. See Baumgarten, "Tohorot," 156. However, it is not entirely clear whether excrement was considered as an actual source of ritual impurity or just as deeply profane and incommensurate with the holy, as it is regarded also (though to a lesser extent) in rabbinic literature (for example, BT Berakhot 22b-26a). The most convincing evidence for the consideration of excrement as ritually defiling in Qumran is found in Josephus (in *War* 2.147–49), who mentions that the Essenes were in the habit of purifying themselves in water after defecating. While the identification of the Qumran community with the Essenes remains a matter of debate, there is perhaps corroboration for Josephus's account in the archeological evidence from Qumran, in which a cesspit was found in proximity to a purification pool; see Jodi Magness, "A Reassessment of the Excavations of Qumran," in *The Dead Sea Scrolls Fifty Years after Their Discovery, 1947–1997*, ed. L. H. Schiffman, E. Tov, J. C. VanderKam, and G. Marquis (Jerusalem: Israel Exploration Society and the Shrine of the Book, 2000), 708–19, at 718.

44. See, for example, Joseph Baumgarten, "The Pharisaic-Sadducean Controversies about Purity and the Qumran Texts," *Journal of Jewish Studies* 31 (1980): 157–70; Sussman, "The Study of History of Halakhah," 27 and passim; Lawrence Schiffman, "The Dead Sea Scrolls and Rabbinic *Halakhah*," in *The Dead Sea Scrolls as Background to Postbiblical Judaism and Early Christianity*, ed. J. R. Davila (Leiden: Brill, 2003), 3–24, esp. 21; Harrington, *The Purity Texts*, 12 and passim.

45. See M. Niddah 2.6–7, and M. Niddah 4.1, which identifies those who do not distinguish between different kinds of genital bleeding as "Sadducees." On the different approaches toward genital bleeding in early Judaism, see Eyal Regev, "On Blood, Impurity, and Relation to the Body in the Jewish Schools of the Second Temple Period" [in Hebrew], *AJS Review* 27, no. 1 (2003): א-כב.

46. 11Q19 49–50; for an elaborate discussion of these rulings in comparison to rabbinic legislation, see Noam, *From Qumran to the Rabbinic Revolution*, 74–94, 124–37.

47. See Noam, *From Qumran to the Rabbinic Revolution*, 157–64, and my discussion in chapter 2.

48. Ibid., 324–30.

49. I am not referring here to the miasmatic-like effect of impurity on the entire camp as Milgrom explains it (see note 21 above), but rather to the ability of the source of impurity to make other persons or objects ritually impure through physical contact.

50. Both the Temple Scroll and the Damascus Document focus on the need to distance sources of impurity from the camp, the community, and the city of the Temple, and on the required procedures for purification designated for each source of impurity. The Community Rule emphasizes the restrictions placed upon new members in the community, for fear that they will render communal food and liquids impure, and various other purity-related texts emphasize the impure person's commitment to stay away from others, even from other impure persons (for example, 4Q274 1 i 1–8), and not to engage in activities that may lead to the conveyance of impurity to foods or liquids (for example, 4Q284 a 1–4); see Furstenberg, "Eating in a State of Purity," 123–58. For a helpful survey of the main themes of purity and impurity that appear in the different scrolls, see Harrington, *The Purity Texts*, 45–66.

51. As Esther Eshel showed, purification rituals in Qumran were accompanied by an elaborate liturgy of thanksgiving and repentance; see Eshel, "Ritual of Purification."

52. See also Neusner, *A History of the Mishnaic Law of Purities*, 22:92, who characterizes the notion of impurity a few times removed from the source as a rabbinic innovation. Conversely, Harrington strives to find biblical bases for this notion. Harrington, *The Impurity Systems*, 254–55.

53. The fact that impurity in rabbinic law "travels" in a very physical manner was overlooked by Jacob Milgrom, who contrasted the dynamic nature of impurity in the writings of Qumran with the rabbinic idea of impurity that he defined as "static," and asserted that "for the rabbis, impurity was solely an inert and powerless state." See Jacob Milgrom, "4QTohora," 66. As Birenboim showed, there is no basis for presenting the Qumranic and rabbinic concepts of impurity as opposed in this respect. Birenboim, "Observance of the Laws of Bodily Purity," 282–83.

54. See, for example, M. Kelim 19.4, 28.6; M. Tohorot 6.7; M. Zavim 5.2–10.

55. The only cases in which we find a "C" in the biblical paradigm, that is, items that are twice-removed from the source and are nonetheless impacted by it, are cases in which "B" functions like the source of impurity "A" itself, namely, when B is (1) a person or object who contracted impurity from a corpse, (2) the litter or seat of a person with genital discharge, or (3) a person who had intercourse with a menstruating woman.

56. See M. Hagigah 2.7; M. Tohorot 2.2–5. On the process through which these graded degrees of impurity were conceived and created, see Furstenberg, "Eating in a State of Purity," 303–49.

57. See, for instance, M. Kelim 8.4; M. Parah 8.2, 5–7; M. Tohorot 8.7; T. Parah 8.1–2.

58. The rabbis also make the point that when one impure liquid touches another liquid, the chain of impurity is infinite: "[An impure liquid] makes another [liquid] impure, and the other makes another impure, even if there are a hundred of them." T. Tevul Yom 1.3.

59. Baumgarten, "Liquids and Susceptibility to Defilement." See also Noam, "The Bounds of Non-Priestly Purity," 153–58.

60. 11Q19 49.8–11, and parallel in CD 12. 15–17; see Noam's elaborate discussion in *From Qumran to the Rabbinic Revolution*, 112–23.

61. 1QS 6.16–22. Further corroboration for the view of liquids as creating vulnerability to impurity among early Jewish communities can be found in Josephus's comment that the Essenes refrained from applying oil to their skin (*War* 2.123); and see Baumgarten, "The Essene Avoidance of Oil."

62. As Vered Noam noted, the concern with the "duplicating" power of liquids is mentioned in what is commonly thought to be the earliest legal tradition in the Mishnah, which conceivably dates back to the Hasmonean era: "Yose ben Yoezer of Tzereda testified . . . that liquids in the [Temple's] slaughterhouse are pure" (M. Eduyot 8.4). Noam, *From Qumran to the Rabbinic Revolution*, 118–19.

63. It is hard to determine how this principle, which has no biblical precedent, was established. As Noam noted, an expansive interpretive reading of the biblical rule that water makes plants susceptible to impurity (Leviticus 11:38) may have been at play here, as well as perhaps a more intuitive notion that liquids can establish contact in more pervasive ways than solids. Noam, *From Qumran to the Rabbinic Revolution*, 117–21.

64. There is a tannaitic controversy on the degree of impurity contracted by one who consumes foods that are "first of impurity" (that is, once-removed from the source): according to R. Eliezer, whoever eats food that is "first" also becomes "first," whereas according to R. Yehoshua, whoever eats food that is "first" becomes "second" of impurity (M. Tohorot 2.2; cf. M. Zavim 5.12). However, both agree that whoever eats food that is "second" becomes "second"; see also BT Hullin 34a.

65. Mark 7:15 (cf. Matthew 15:11). See Yair Furstenberg, "Defilement Penetrating the Body: A New Understanding of Contamination in Mark 7.15," *New Testament Studies* 54 (2008): 176–200; and see my discussion in chapter 2.

66. For example, 4Q284 a1–4; see Baumgarten, "Liquids and Susceptibility to Defilement," 93–95; and see also Furstenberg, "Eating in a State of Purity," 156–57.

67. 4Q274 3 i–ii; see Baumgarten, "Liquids and Susceptibility to Defilement," 96–99; and see also Furstenberg, "Eating in a State of Purity," 145–56.

68. This ruling is presented as based on a midrashic extrapolation of the verse "whoever touches a sword-slain *(halal herev)* in the open field . . . shall be impure for seven days" (Numbers 19:16). The rabbis derive from this verse that "the sword is like the slain *(herev ka-halal),*" that is, objects that touched a corpse convey the same kind of impurity as the corpse itself; see *Sifre* Numbers §127 on Numbers 19:16 (ed. Horovitz 164) and *Sifre* Numbers §158 on Numbers 31:22 (ed. Horovitz 214); BT Pesahim 14b; BT Hullin 2b.

69. See M. Oholot 1.1–4.

70. Numbers 19:15. In the rabbinic system, however, a person with scale disease also conveys impurity by overhang, and when entering a house he or she renders everything in it impure (M. Nega'im 13.11–12); see Harrington, *The Impurity Systems*, 186.

71. On the rabbinic transformation of the biblical "tent" into an abstract category, see Jeffrey Rubenstein, "On Some Abstract Concepts in Rabbinic Literature," *Jewish Studies Quarterly* 4 (1997): 33–73. See also Maccoby, *Ritual and Morality*, 17–29; Noam, "Between Qumran and Rabbinic Midrash," 88–94.

72. As noted in the Priestly Code, graves convey the same impurity as corpses; see Numbers 19:18.

73. The rabbis distinguish between "touch" *(maga),* in which the source of impurity is touched directly, and "carriage" *(masa),* in which the source of impurity is carried without direct contact (for example, if a carcass is placed on a gurney and one carries it), and maintain that the latter form of contact conveys impurity in somewhat different ways from the former. However, in the biblical setting it is quite clear that carriage and touch are essentially two forms of direct contact with identical consequences (for example, Leviticus 11:25; 15:10).

74. The rabbis distinguish between different sources of impurity in respect to their ability to convey impurity by shift: whereas persons with genital discharges (and the discharges themselves) can convey impurity both when causing the pure item to shift and when being shifted by the pure item, persons with scale disease and the litter and seat of persons with genital discharges can only convey impurity when they cause the pure item to shift, but not when they are being shifted by it. Corpses, conversely, do not convey impurity by shift at all.

75. M. Zavim 4.6.

76. As Furstenberg noted, this understanding also seems to underlie the conception of bodily impurity in the writings of Qumran. Furstenberg, "Eating in a State of Purity," 126–36.

77. See M. Makhshirin 6.6. The rabbis also include persons with scale disease in their list of those whose urine and saliva convey impurity.

78. Leviticus 15:8.

79. Robert Parker, *Miasma: Pollution and Purification in Early Greek Religion* (Oxford: Oxford University Press, 1983), 2.

80. By "the material world" I am referring only to the categories of things that can contract impurity (persons, artifacts, foodstuffs, and liquids), but not to natural elements (that is, water reservoirs, soil, trees, and so on) that are not susceptible to impurity.

81. As shown in detail by Furstenberg, "Eating in a State of Purity."

82. On this point, see also Jacob Neusner, "The Integrity of the Rabbinic Law of Purity (Mishnah-Tractate Tohorot)," *Review of Rabbinic Judaism* 9, no. 1 (2006): 167–80.

83. M. Tohorot 5.1–2.

84. M. Tohorot 8.3.

85. M. Tohorot 7.1.

86. M. Tohorot 7.3

87. Cf. BT Kettubot 24b.

88. For similar cases, guided by the same assumption, see M. Tohorot 7.4–6; cf. M. Hagigah 3.6.

89. M. Tohorot 5.7. "They follow the majority" *(holkhim 'ahar ha-rov)* is the version only in the printed editions of the Mishnah, as well as in MS Munich 95. In all the Mishnah's manuscripts as well as in Genizah fragments, the version is "they follow the spittle" *(holkhim 'ahar ha-roq)*. While I am reluctant to dismiss all the manuscripts in favor of the version in the printed edition, which is clearly the *lectio facilior* in this case, the manuscripts' version makes absolutely no sense. The case of treading and the case of spitting are presented in the Mishnah as two separate cases that warrant the application of two distinct halakhic principles, and they cannot be understood as somehow dependent on one another. The parallel Tosefta passage (T. Tohorot 6.11) clearly reads *holkhim ahar ha-rov* in all its versions.

90. The term *Kutim* in rabbinic literature is commonly understood to refer to Samaritans. On the attitude of the rabbis to this group, see Pieter van der Horst, "Anti-Samaritan Propaganda in Early Judaism," in *Persuasion and Dissuasion in Early Christianity, Ancient Judaism, and Hellenism*, ed. P. W. van der Horst, M. J. J. Menken, J. F. M. Smit, and G. V. Oyen (Leuven: Peeters, 2003), 25–44.

91. M. Tohorot 5.8. Cf. T. Tohorot 6.10.

92. See, most explicitly, T. Tohorot 6.2: "It is the manner of the daughters of Israel to wipe away their spittle while they are menstruating." The same premise is also implied in the subsequent part of our mishnaic passage (Tohorot 5.8): "If a woman trod on one's garments, or sat with one in a boat, if she knows him to be one who eats heave-offering (i.e., committed to a high standard of purity), his garments are pure." The assumption here is that if the woman is impure, she will be careful not to be in direct contact with people who are careful to maintain themselves in a state of purity.

93. According to M. Niddah 4.1, Kuthian women are considered to be incessantly impure, since their way of distinguishing between different bloods and thus their way of determining their own status of menstrual impurity are different from the rabbis' way; thus when Kuthian women believe they are pure they are not "really" pure. On this, see Fonrobert, "When Women Walk in the Way of Their Fathers." Gentile women, on the other hand,

were not seen as impure on account of menstruation but as a result of an intrinsic and unchanging quality.

94. See Norbert Elias, *The Civilizing Process*, trans. Edmund Jephcott (Oxford: Blackwell, 2000), 129–35.

95. Fonrobert, "Blood and Law."

96. My use of masculine pronouns when discussing the mishnaic intended subject throughout the book is deliberate. While there is no reason to assume that the various practices for discerning, avoiding, and managing impurity do not pertain to women as much as they do to men, there can be no doubt that the idealized subject which the rabbis imagine and to which they direct their discourse is male. On this, see my discussion in chapter 6.

97. See, for instance, Hyam Maccoby, who asserted that "the vast majority of Jews were not expected to be in a state of ritual purity except at festival times, when they entered the Temple area." Maccoby, *Ritual and Morality*, 149.

98. In this respect, there is a similarity between the rabbis' acknowledgment that not all members of the Jewish community observe the laws of purity with the same scrutiny (for example, M. Hagigah 2.7; T. Demai 2.2; T. Sukkah 2.3; T. Avodah Zarah 3.10), and the references we find in Qumranic literature to individuals who are "more pure" *(tahor yoter)* than others and adhere to more stringent rules (4Q274 3. ii 4; cf. 11Q19 49.8; and see Furstenberg, "Eating in a State of Purity," 138–48).

99. On the development of this notion and its origins, see John Poirier, "Purity beyond the Temple."

100. Mishneh Torah, *Hilkhot tum'at okhalim* 16.8–9.

101. For instance, consecrated meat that has had contact with a source of impurity cannot be eaten (Leviticus 7:19–21), and it is distinctly forbidden for impure priests to consume holy foodstuffs (Leviticus 22:4–9). In addition, a parturient is prohibited from entering the Temple and touching the sancta (Leviticus 12:4). Finally, only priests (Leviticus 21:1–3) and a Nazarite who takes a vow to separate him or herself unto God (Numbers 6:6–10) are explicitly prohibited from contracting impurity by touching a corpse; this implies, as Maimonides notes, that all others are not prohibited from such contact.

102. For a helpful overview of the Priestly texts that suggest that impurity must be avoided (to the extent that this is possible) regardless of the Temple, see Vered Noam, "The Bounds of Non-Priestly Purity," 1–3, and see her helpful references there. I disagree with Noam (who follows Alon on this) that there are two *conflicting* views of impurity in the Hebrew Bible. Noam unnecessarily maintains that if impurity is not forbidden it is seen as unproblematic, while I do not see any reason for this conflation of undesirability with prohibition. I completely agree with Noam, however, that two such conflicting views, namely, that impurity either is to be avoided at all times or is only relevant for the Temple, exist in rabbinic sources.

103. For example, Leviticus 11:24–40; 14:1–32; 15:1–15; Numbers 19:11–22.

104. Leviticus 5:2–4; 17:16.

105. See especially Leviticus 11:44–45. Nevertheless, it is unquestionable that at the center of the Priestly concepts of purity and impurity stands the Temple, not only because impurity is distinctly forbidden in its precincts, but also because several sources indicate that those who do not purify themselves actually defile the Temple (Leviticus 15:31; Numbers 19:20). According to Jacob Milgrom, this view is based on the notion that lingering

impurity anywhere in the camp of Israel affects the Temple even from afar. See Milgrom, *Leviticus 1–16*, 310–13; Milgrom, "Impurity Is Miasma: A Response to Hyam Maccoby," *Journal of Biblical Literature* 119, no. 4 (2000): 729–33.

106. For a helpful survey of the relevant evidence, see Birenboim, "Observance of the Laws of Bodily Purity," 23–68.

107. Alon, "The Bounds of the Laws of Levitical Cleanness."

108. Most of the literary evidence for the requirement of purification before prayer is from the Jewish Diaspora. For example, the Letter of Aristeas (306) mentions the Jewish custom of washing hands before prayer, and the Book of Judith (12:8) mentions that Judith performed a ritual immersion before praying. Alon also sees the abundant talmudic references to the custom of purification before prayer or Torah-reading as attesting to a custom that dates back to the Second Temple period. Alon, "The Bounds of the Laws of Levitical Cleanness," 149–57. In addition, scholars noted that the archeological evidence points to a custom of purification before entrance to synagogues; see Ronny Reich, "The Synagogue and the *Miqweh* in Eretz-Israel in the Second-Temple, Mishnaic, and Talmudic Periods," in *Ancient Synagogues: Historical Analysis and Archaeological Discovery*, ed. D. Urman and P. Flesher (Leiden: Brill, 1995), 1:289–97; Anders Runesson, "Water and Worship: Ostia and the Ritual Bath in the Diaspora Synagogue," in *The Synagogue of Ancient Ostia and the Jews of Rome: Interdisciplinary Studies*, ed. B. Olsson, D. Mitternacht, and O. Brandt (Stockholm: Paul Åströms, 2001), 115–29.

109. Leviticus 22:1–17; Numbers 18:8–24.

110. See Lawrence Schiffman, *Sectarian Law in the Dead Sea Scrolls: Courts, Testimony and the Penal Code* (Atlanta: Scholars Press, 1983), 191–210; Harrington, *The Purity Texts*, 23–25; Broshi, "Qumran and the Essenes."

111. Jacob Milgrom, "First Day Ablutions in Qumran," in *The Madrid Qumran Congress: Proceedings of the International Congress on the Dead Sea Scrolls*, ed. J T. Barrera and L. V. Montaner (Leiden: Brill, 1992), 2:561–70; see also Birenboim, "Observance of the Laws of Bodily Purity," 247–59.

112. See Roland Deines, *Jüdische Steingefäße und pharisäische Frömmigkeit* (Tübingen: Mohr Siebeck, 1993), 228–33; Regev, "Pure Individualism"; see also the helpful survey in Porier, "Purity beyond the Temple," 256–59.

113. This does not mean, of course, that those who approach the Temple or handle sacred foodstuffs are not required to take additional measures to be pure, and that the standard of purity in the Temple and its vicinity is not much higher than it is away from it; see M. Hagigah 2.6–7, M. Kelim 1.6–8.

114. However, as Vered Noam showed, the view of the observance of purity as part of everyday life and as not exclusively contingent upon the Temple is strikingly absent from the tannaitic halakhic Midrashim, which emphasize time and again that purity is only required when approaching the Temple; see Noam, "The Bounds of Non-Priestly Impurity."

115. M. Kelim 18.1–7.

116. M. Uqtsin 3.8.

117. The rabbinic evidence regarding the consumption of nonconsecrated food in a state of purity is multilayered. Rabbinic sources entail several references to particular individuals who were known for their habit of eating all their meals in a state of purity (for example, M. Hagigah 2.7; T. Sukkah 2.3; T. Hagigah 3.3; T. Demai 2.2). Based on these and similar sources,

Adolf Büchler reached the conclusion that eating in a state of purity was rarely practiced among nonpriests, and was only the custom of marginal and somewhat eccentric groups; see Büchler, *Der galiläische 'Am-ha 'Ares*, 115–26. For a similar position, see Maccoby, *Ritual and Morality*, 210–12. However, as Yair Furstenberg showed, the anecdotal references to the consumption of nonconsecrated food in a state of purity as an extraordinary practice in all likelihood date to the end of the tannaitic period, in which this custom was becoming increasingly rare, whereas in earlier sources this custom is taken for granted. See Yair Furstenberg, "The Purity of Hands and Eating of Ordinary Food in Purity: A Chapter in the History of Tannaitic Halakhah," [in Hebrew], MA thesis, Hebrew University, Jerusalem, 2005, 13–9, 139–55.

118. See Alon, "The Bounds of the Laws of Levitical Cleanness," 158.

119. Indeed, such position was forcefully expressed by E. P. Sanders, who argued that the mishnaic rules and regulations for purity observance are by and large inapplicable. Sanders, *Jewish Law from Jesus to the Mishnah*, 131–254.

120. M. Tohorot 3.7.

121. M. Tohorot 3.6.

122. M. Tohorot 4.5–11.

123. In T. Tohorot 6.17 Rabban Shimon b. Gamaliel explains this principle as follows: "One can ask a single person but one cannot ask the many."

124. As persuasively shown by Klawans, *Impurity and Sin*, 92–117.

125. This point was cogently made by Maccoby in his analysis of the Good Samaritan parable in Luke 10:30–37. Maccoby, *Ritual and Morality*, 150–51.

126. See Daniel Schwartz, "Law and Truth: On Qumran-Sadducean and Rabbinic Views of Law," in *The Dead Sea Scrolls: Forty Years of Research*, ed. D. Dimant and U. Rappaport (Jerusalem: Magnes Press and Yad Yitzhak Ben-Zvi, 1992), 229–40; Jeffrey Rubenstein, "Nominalism and Realism in Qumranic and Rabbinic Law: A Reassessment," *Dead Sea Discoveries* 6, no. 2 (1999): 157–83.

127. On the tension between "truth" and legal formalism in rabbinic literature, see Chaya Halberstam, *Law and Truth in Biblical and Rabbinic Literature* (Bloomington: Indiana University Press, 2010); specifically on the discernment of ritual impurity in this context, see pp. 17–41. See also Christine Hayes, "Legal Realism and the Fashioning of Sectarians in Jewish Antiquity," in *Sects and Sectarianism in Jewish History*, ed. S. Stern (Leiden: Brill, 2010), 119–46.

128. In a recent article, Vered Noam examined the rabbinic laws of corpse impurity to discern whether they present a "realistic" or a "nominalistic" concept of impurity, and concluded that the rabbinic purity system is dual in nature, since the rabbis' concept of impurity is "realistic" and "nominalistic" at the same time: on the one hand, impurity is clearly perceived in the tannaitic literature as an actual physical phenomenon, governed by natural laws, but on the other hand, this literature places great emphasis on the ways in which thoughts, intentions, and states of mind can govern impurity. According to Noam, both of these aspects are contemporaneous with each other, and more importantly, both aspects introduce independent rabbinic developments that go beyond the biblical text. See Vered Noam, "Is It True That 'a Corpse Does Not Defile'? On Ritual Contamination in Tannaitic Literature" [in Hebrew], *Tarbitz* 78, no. 2 (2009): 157–87. In a similar vein, Christine Hayes (in "Legal Realism") argued that the rabbinic approach can be described as an overall

realistic one, but that what distinguishes the rabbis from other sects is their willingness to incorporate nominalistic considerations into the equation, especially in cases of epistemological uncertainty. While I agree with Noam's and Hayes's analyses, I find the dichotomy of "nominalistic" and "realistic" to be somewhat problematic in the mishnaic context. This dichotomy is based on a Cartesian worldview, according to which things either are physical and natural and thus "real" or are mental constructs and thus "unreal." Such division is inappropriate for the ancient world, in which the physical and the mental were both considered constituents of the "real" world; see M. F. Burnyeat, "Idealism and Greek Philosophy: What Descartes Saw and Berkeley Missed," *Philosophical Review* 91, no. 1 (1982): 3–40; R. W. Sharples, *Stoics, Epicureans and Sceptics: An Introduction to Hellenistic Philosophy* (New York: Routledge, 1996), 32–35.

CHAPTER 2

1. See Klawans, *Impurity and Sin*, 92–117; See also Kazen, *Jesus and Purity Halakhah*, 200–62. Conversely, in the New Testament and in early Christian writings impurity gradually becomes an entirely spiritual phenomenon and is eventually robbed of its natural or physical characteristics altogether. See Klawans, *Impurity and Sin*, 136–57; Newton, *The Concept of Purity*, 52–114; Peter Tomson, "Jewish Purity Laws as Viewed by the Church Fathers and by the Early Followers of Jesus," in *Purity and Holiness: The Heritage of Leviticus*, ed. M. J. H. M. Poorthuis and J. Schwartz (Leiden: Brill, 2000), 73–91.

2. To clarify, the rabbis maintain that soil, insofar as it is a natural element, cannot contract impurity from an external source. However, they do maintain that soil in which bits and pieces of corpses are placed conveys impurity, not because the soil itself has become impure by the dead, but rather because contact with this soil entails contact with corpse parts contained in it.

3. As the Mishnah makes clear, a corpse can float inside a canal of water and still not render the water in this canal impure; see M. Miqva'ot 1.4.

4. In this, the rabbis' position differs from the approach presented in the writings of Qumran. On the Qumranic notion that houses require purification, see Vered Noam, "Between Qumran and Rabbinic Midrash," 84–94.

5. The words *guf* and *nefesh* or *neshama*, which are used to denote "body" and "soul," respectively, in rabbinic literature, have very restricted meanings in the Mishnah. *Guf* is usually used to contrast the greater bulk of one's body with more peripheral parts of the body, like the hands or head; occasionally, the possessive form *gufo* is used in a reflexive sense (*hu gufo*, "he himself"). *Nefesh* is used in the Mishnah to denote the life force, whether in humans or animals, and sometimes to denote a human living creature as such. *Neshama* is used quite rarely, roughly in the sense of "breath of life." Nowhere in the Mishnah do the rabbis contrast *guf* and *nefesh/neshama* with one another.

6. According to E. E. Urbach, the rabbis' view of human beings can be characterized as dualistic, insofar as they considered human beings to be composite entities, made of a combination of an earthly component with a heavenly (albeit probably not incorporeal) component. However, for the rabbis neither part has primacy over the other, and both the body and the soul are considered to be vital for human life and function, as well as equally responsible for one's actions and deeds. See Urbach, *The Sages*, 193–205. A similar view was

suggested by Alon Goshen-Gottstein, "The Body as Image of God in Rabbinic Literature," *Harvard Theological Review* 87, no. 2 (1994): 171–95; and by Daniel Boyarin, *Carnal Israel: Reading Sex in Talmudic Culture* (Berkeley: University of California Press, 1993), 33–35. For a recent concise summary of the topic, see Ishay Rosen-Zvi, *Body and Soul in Ancient Jewish Thought* [in Hebrew] (Ben-Shemen: Modan, 2012), 59–67.

7. See M. Shabbat 11.6; M. Betzah 2.4; M. Baba Metzi'a 9.12.

8. In my view of the capacity for self-reflection as the most quintessential component of subjectivity, I am influenced by the works of modern analytic philosophers such as Harry Frankfurt, "Freedom of the Will and the Concept of a Person," *Journal of Philosophy* 68 (1971): 5–20; and Thomas Nagel, *The View from Nowhere* (Oxford: Oxford University Press, 1986).

9. Here I am fully adopting Maurice Merleau-Ponty's critique of Cartesian and Kantian mind-body dualism with its pronounced view of the former as immaterial; see Maurice Merleau-Ponty, *Phenomenology of Perception*, trans. Colin Smith (1962; New York: Routledge, 2006), 429–75. For a helpful overview of Merleau-Ponty's theory of corporeality, see Grosz, *Volatile Bodies*, 86–111. For another critique of the mind-body dualism, and for an explanation of the ways in which this dichotomy is highly problematic, see Nancy Scheper-Hughes and Margaret Lock, "The Mindful Body: A Prolegomenon to Future Work in Medical Anthropology," *Medical Anthropology Quarterly* 1, no. 1 (1987): 6–41.

10. Bryan Turner, *The Body and Society* (London: Sage, 1996), 42.

11. The passive object-nature of the human body in the context of purity and impurity is especially evident upon examination of the occurrences of the word *adam* in the different orders of the Mishnah. Whereas in the first five orders only a minority of the total occurrences of the word *adam* appears in conjunction to artifacts or animals (six out of seventy occurrences in *Zerai'm*, four out of eighty-one in *Mo'ed*, two out of fifty-one in *Nashim*, twenty-two out of 109 in *Neziqin*, and seventeen out of fifty-two in *Qodashim*), in *Tohorot* over two-thirds of the occurrences of the word *adam* (sixty-six out of ninety-five) appear in conjunction with artifacts or animals.

12. It is of course one of the premises of the rabbinic impurity discourse that people knowingly and willingly choose to partake in activities that inevitably bring about impurity, such as intercourse or funerary rites, since they consider these activities worthwhile enough to bear their consequences in terms of impurity. Nonetheless, it is assumed that people are never interested in the impurity itself.

13. According to Howard Eilberg-Schwartz, the question of self-control is the key to understanding the biblical impurity system as a whole: the bodily phenomena that are classified as inducing impurity, he argues, are distinctly bodily phenomena that are utterly beyond one's control. Eilberg-Schwartz, *Savage in Judaism*, 177–94. For a critique and modification of this view, see Lawrence Hoffman, *Covenant of Blood: Circumcision and Gender in Rabbinic Judaism* (Chicago: University of Chicago Press, 1996), 148–57.

14. Douglas, *Purity and Danger*, 142.

15. Ibid., 150.

16. See, for example, Eilberg-Schwartz, *Savage in Judaism*, 177–94; Birenboim, "Observance of the Laws of Bodily Purity," 83–88; Simcha Fishbane, *Deviancy in Early Rabbinic Literature: A Collection of Socio-Anthropological Essays* (Leiden: Brill, 2007), 42–66; Fonrobert, "Blood and Law."

17. M. Zavim 5.6.

18. M. Zavim 5.7.

19. M. Zavim 5.10 mentions a few exceptions to this rule, that is, items that can only convey impurity in a once-removed degree to whatever touches them, even when the source and the toucher are still connected. These items include minor sources of impurity, which are specifically mentioned in the Bible as making whoever touches them impure only for one day (creeping-crawling creatures and seminal emission), a source of impurity that is itself secondary in nature (one made impure by the dead), persons or objects whose impurity is attenuated (purifying water of insufficient quantity and a person with scale disease who is already in the process of purification), and things that were specified in the Bible as conveying impurity only through carriage (animal carrion and a saddle of a person with genital discharge).

20. According to M. Zavim 5.1, one who touches a person with genital discharge renders only artifacts (except for clay artifacts), foods, and liquids impure, but not humans. In this sense, the impurity of the toucher, even while still "connected," is not entirely identical to that of the source of impurity, since he or she cannot make other persons impure. Nonetheless, it is identical to the source of impurity in terms of its impact on artifacts and foods.

21. M. Tohorot 1.8.

22. One could ask, of course, why this single "connected" body shares the impurity status of the source and not the purity status of the contractor, to which the simple answer is that in biblical and rabbinic thought, ritual purity is conceived more as a lack of impurity than as a positive quality, and under no circumstances does it have the force to overpower impurity.

23. This distinction is somewhat artificial in the context of the High Roman Empire, in which, as was noted by several scholars, medical knowledge became part of common *paideia* and every educated member of society was expected to be familiar with it. See Werner Jaeger, *Paideia: The Ideals of Greek Culture*, trans. G. Highet (New York: Oxford University Press, 1944), 3:3–45; Glen Bowersock, *Greek Sophists in the Roman Empire* (Oxford: Oxford University Press, 1969), 59–72; Katharina Luchner, *Philiatroi: Studien zum Thema der Krankenheit in der griechischen Literatur der Kaiserzeit* (Göttingen: Vandenhoeck & Ruprecht, 2004), 23–98. On the intricate relations between elitist medical discourse and "popular" medicine in the Roman world, see John Riddle, "High Medicine and Low Medicine in the Roman Empire," in *Aufstieg und Niedergang der römischen Welt* II.37.1: *Wissenschaften (Medizin und Biologie)*, ed. W. Haase (Berlin: Walter de Gruyter, 1993), 102–20.

24. Vivian Nutton, "Did the Greeks Have a Word for It? Contagion and Contagion Theory in Classical Antiquity," in *Contagion: Perspectives from Pre-Modern Societies*, ed. L. Conrad and D. Wujastyk (Aldershot: Ashgate, 2000), 136–62; see also Vivian Nutton, "To Kill or Not to Kill? Caelius Aurelianus on Contagion," in *Text and Tradition: Studies in Ancient Medicine and Its Transmission*, ed. K.-D. Fischer, D. Nickel, and P. Potter (Leiden: Brill, 1998), 233–42.

25. Nutton, "Did the Greeks Have a Word for It?," 151.

26. See *Galen on Diseases and Symptoms*, trans. Ian Johnston (Cambridge: Cambridge University Press, 2006), 164.

27. According to a talmudic account, the ruling that food which contracted impurity from something else renders whoever consumes it impure is one of the "eighteen decrees"

that were issued by the rabbis in the mid-first century (BT Shabbat 13b). On this tradition, see Menahem Kister, "Law, Morality and Rhetoric in Some Sayings of Jesus," in *Studies in Ancient Midrash*, ed. J. Kugel (Cambridge, MA: Harvard University Press, 2001), 145–54, at 152–53.

28. John Poirier, "Why Did the Pharisees Wash Their Hands?," *Journal of Jewish Studies* 47 (1996): 217–33.

29. Furstenberg, "Defilement Penetrating the Body."

30. Cf. Matthew 15:1–20. On this pericope, its different parts, and the history of its interpretation, see Jan Lambrecht, "Jesus and the Law: An Investigation of Mark 7:1–23," *Ephemerides Theologicae Lovanienses* 53 (1977): 24–82, esp. 28–39; Booth, *Jesus and the Laws of Purity*, 23–53.

31. On the many opinions regarding the relations between the rabbis of the Mishnah and the Pharisees of the Second Temple period, see Jacob Neusner, "Pharisaic-Rabbinic Judaism: A Clarification," *History of Religions* 12, no. 3 (1973): 250–70; Shaye Cohen, "The Significance of Yavneh: Pharisees, Rabbis, and the End of Jewish Sectarianism," *Hebrew Union College Annual* 55 (1984): 36–42; David Goodblatt, "The Place of the Pharisees in First Century Judaism: The State of the Debate," *Journal for the Study of Judaism* 20, no. 1 (1989): 12–30.

32. This analysis of Jesus' retort as fully commensurate with the cultural and halakhic context of first-century Palestine indicates that the interpretation of Jesus' words as permitting the consumption of all nonkosher foods (Mark 7:19) is a much later interpolation. See Booth, *Jesus and the Laws of Purity*, 74; William Loader, *Jesus' Attitude towards the Law: A Study of the Gospels* (Tübingen: Mohr Siebeck, 1997), 75; Kazen, *Jesus and Purity Halakhah*, 65. Most recently, see Daniel Boyarin, *The Jewish Gospels: The Story of Jesus Christ* (New York: New Press, 2012), 102–28.

33. See, for instance, *Galen on the Properties of Foodstuffs*, trans. Owen Powell (Cambridge: Cambridge University Press, 2003); and Mark Grant, *Dieting for an Emperor: A Translation of Books 1 and 4 of Oribasius' Medical Compilations, with an Introduction and Commentary* (Leiden: Brill, 1997), 34–47. See also Rebecca Flemming, "The Physicians at the Feast: The Place of Medical Knowledge at Athenaeus's Dinner-Table," in *Athenaeus and His World: Reading Greek Culture in the Roman Empire*, ed. D. Braund and J. Wilkins (Exeter: University of Exeter Press, 2000), 476–82.

34. The potentially detrimental effect of external substances on one's body is not restricted to the ingestion of food: as Galen makes clear in *De causis morborum* III.1 (= VII.11K) diseases are brought about even by mere proximity to things that drive the body out of its humoral balance.

35. It seems that the rabbis were familiar with basic ideas in Graeco-Roman medicine, as was shown already by Julius Preuss, *Biblisch-Talmudische Medizin* (Berlin: S. Karger Verlag, 1923). See also Samuel Kottek, "Medical Interest in Ancient Rabbinic Literature," in *The Literature of the Sages*, ed. S. Safrai, P. Tomson, and Z. Safrai (Assen: Uitgeverij Van Gorcum, 2006), 2:485–96.

36. However, as Furstenberg (in "Defilement Penetrating the Body") points out, it is not unlikely that the rabbis and their predecessors considered certain prevalent hygienic habits (such as hand-washing) to be promoting ritual purity, and thus partially conflated health with purity.

37. On the Greek (especially Hippocratic) view of the body as fluid and malleable, see Ruth Padel, *In and out of the Mind: Greek Images of the Tragic Self* (Princeton: Princeton University Press, 1994).

38. Dale Martin, *The Corinthian Body* (New Haven: Yale University Press, 2000), 25.
39. See, for example, M. Kelim 19.7, 20.3, 28.7.
40. M. Uqtsin 1.1–2.7.
41. M. Kelim 19.5.
42. M. Oholot 3.3; cf. *Sifre zutta* on Numbers 19:11 (ed. Horovitz 306).
43. M. Zavim 5.4.
44. T. Zavim 5.2; see also *Sifra* Zavim par. 2, per. 3:5 on Leviticus 15:18 (ed. Weiss 76b), which mentions only hair and nails, but not teeth.
45. See Furstenberg, "The Purity of Hands," 140–43.
46. M. Tohorot 7.8.
47. M. Kelim 8.10.
48. On this complex and much debated topic, see the comprehensive survey in Furstenberg, "The Purity of Hands," 25–54.
49. M. Miqva'ot 8.5.
50. The parity between artifacts and humans in the purification process is emphasized in the Mishnah both through the recurring phrase "they immerse [themselves] and dip [other things]" *(tovlim u-matbilin)*, and through many passages in which specific immersion procedures for humans are juxtaposed with identical procedures for artifacts. See M. Miqva'ot 7.6, 9.1–10.5.
51. Like impure substances ingested by humans, impure substances ingested by animals cannot convey impurity as long as the animal is alive. However, once the animal has died, if the impure substance is still contained in its body, it does convey impurity to its surroundings (T. Ahilot 12.3). It is therefore important to know when the animal swallowed the impure substance in order to know whether at the time of death it can be considered to have already passed through its system or not; see M. Oholot 11.7 and T. Ahilot 12.3; M. Parah 9.5 and T. Miqva'ot 7.11.
52. M. Miqva'ot 10.8.
53. M. Miqva'ot 10.8. There is one important exception to this rule: if one drank impure *water,* ritual immersion is considered to purify the water contained inside his body, in such a way that if he vomits the water it will be considered pure (M. Miqva'ot 10.8). It seems that as a unique substance that has the capacity both to become impure and to purify, water elicits a unique set of rules in the rabbinic impurity system.
54. For an elaborate discussion on these rules, see BT Hullin 71a–b.
55. M. Miqva'ot 10.8.
56. 11Q19 50.10–16; see Noam, *From Qumran to the Rabbinic Revolution,* 157–64.
57. *Sifre* Numbers §127 on Numbers 19:16 (ed. Horovitz 164); T. Ahilot 8.8. See Noam, *From Qumran to the Tannaitic Revolution,* 159–61.
58. M. Hullin 4.3; see also *Sifre zutta* on Numbers 19:16 (ed. Horovitz 311); BT Hullin 72a; and see Noam, *From Qumran to the Rabbinic Revolution,* 296–300.
59. Drew Leder, "Flesh and Blood: A Proposed Supplement to Merleau-Ponty," *Human Studies* 13 (1990): 209–219, at 212.
60. The rules regarding ingested impurity perhaps point toward another kind of distinction between different bodily areas. While the Mishnah states that if an impure substance is vomited its contact with the body on its way out (in this case through the throat) renders the body impure, it does not address the question of whether the same is the case if

the impure substance is excreted through the anus or the urethra. However, the Tosefta (T. Miqva'ot 7.8–9) explicitly states that in the latter cases the body remains *pure* after the impure substance has been excreted. Although we cannot go beyond conjecture here, it is possible that the lower bodily orifices were less identified with the subject than the upper orifices (perhaps because of their abject nature), and were thus seen as less consequential in terms of impurity.

61. M. Miqva'ot 10.8; T. Miqva'ot 7.9.
62. M. Nega'im 6.8.
63. M. Nega'im 7.1.
64. It should be noted that this list does not include the lower orifices of the body (the anus and the genitals), which could either mean that those places were considered to be consequential in terms of impurity, or—what I find more plausible—that they were considered to be so off-limits in the bodily map that it was not even necessary to mention them; and see note 51.
65. This is the interpretation suggested by R. Asher (HaRosh).
66. As suggested by R. Shimshon of Sens, Maimonides, and R. Obadia of Berteniro in their respective commentaries on the Mishnah.
67. On the skin as central to one's perception of self, see Didier Anzieu, *The Skin Ego*, trans. C. Turner (New Haven: Yale University Press, 1989); Jay Passer, "Skin Memories," in *Thinking through the Skin*, ed. S. Ahmed and J. Stacey (New York: Routledge, 2001), 52–68.
68. In M. Nega'im 2.4 it is ruled that when inspected for skin afflictions, men and women must assume certain bodily positions so that their armpits, their genitals, and the area under the breasts will be visible. While this seems contradictory to the ruling in M. Nega'im 6.8, the two passages can be reconciled by explaining that M. Nega'im 6.8 refers to areas that are never seen unless one makes an effort to see them, whereas M. Nega'im 2.4 refers only to the parts of these areas that are revealed in the course of common daily activities.
69. M. Miqva'ot 8.5; the same rule applies for hidden and wrinkled areas in inanimate objects (M. Miqva'ot 10.3–4).
70. See M. Miqva'ot 9.2; *Sifra* Nega'im par. 3, per. 4:3 on Leviticus 13:12 (ed. Weiss 63a-b); *Sifra* Zavim par. 3, per. 6:10 on Leviticus 15:18 (ed. Weiss 78a).
71. M. Niddah 5.1; see the detailed discussion in Fonrobert, *Menstrual Purity*, 43–67.
72. Since it is widely agreed by the rabbis that the sexual act in itself is not a source of impurity, they assume that it must be contact with semen that renders the couple impure after intercourse. However, this view is at odds with the notion that semen must be outside the body to convey impurity. Indeed, in the *Sifra* R. Shimon defines the ruling that a woman becomes impure after intercourse as incongruent with the notion that hidden places do not contract impurity, and defines it as "a ruling of the King" to indicate that he cannot fathom its logic; see *Sifra* Zavim par. 3, per. 6:10 on Leviticus 15:18 (ed. Weiss 78a).
73. M. Miqva'ot 8.4.
74. T. Miqva'ot 6.8.
75. See also BT Niddah 66b.
76. For another discussion of the same rabbinic theme, considered mainly through various ancient architectural paradigms, see Cynthia Baker, *Rebuilding the House of Israel: Architectures of Gender in Jewish Antiquity* (Stanford: Stanford University Press, 2002), 48–57.

77. Fonrobert, *Menstrual Purity,* 63–67.

78. On the objective principles that the rabbis put forth regarding subjective processes, see also Howard Eilberg-Schwartz, *The Human Will in Judaism: The Mishnah's Philosophy of Intention* (Atlanta: Scholars Press, 1986), 123–29.

79. The first items mentioned in this list, which I skipped here, are "strings of wool and strings of linen and the straps in the heads of girls." The consideration of these items as barriers is simple enough, and their inclusion in this list was probably meant to convey that the most negligible kinds of adornments are barriers, as well as to introduce R. Yehuda's contesting opinion that as long as these adornments are permeable to water they do not constitute a barrier. Cf. M. Shabbat 6.1.

80. I skipped a part of this passage in which the Mishnah digresses to define different kinds of mortar *(tit)* and their qualities.

81. M. Miqva'ot 9.1–2.

82. M. Miqva'ot 9.3–4. This passage concludes by referring to two "detachable" bodily elements not in terms of their function as barriers, but in terms of their ability to contract and convey impurity like the rest of the body: "The bodily hair of an infant is not impure (that is, cannot contract impurity) and cannot convey impurity, and a thin skin on a wound is impure (that is, can contract impurity) and can convey impurity." While these statements are not wholly irrelevant to my discussion here, they introduce so many textual and interpretive difficulties that I chose not to address them here.

83. The category of "clots of filth" *(milmulin)* could be ascribed to either the second or the third category, depending on whether we interpret it like Maimonides, as referring to dry dandruff-like sweat, or like R. Hayya Gaon, as referring to the residues of clay or dough. See Ya'akov Nahum Epstein, *The Gaonic Commentary on Order Taharot Attributed to Rav Hayya Gaon* [in Hebrew] (Jerusalem: Magnes Press, 1982), 123.

84. Sentence 3 of this passage can be read either as a continuation of the anonymous ruling in sentence 1 or as continuation of R. Eliezer's objection in sentence 2. Presumably, if one were to read sentence 3 as a continuation of R. Eliezer's objection, one could suggest that this principle was held by R. Eliezer alone and was not commonly held by the majority of rabbis; however, such a conclusion is quite implausible. The principle that "all that one is fastidious about constitutes a barrier" appears anonymously in M. Miqva'ot 9.7, which discusses barriers in artifacts, and is explicitly introduced there as a general rule (under the heading *ze ha-kelal*). This rule is also implied, again anonymously, in the Tosefta (T. Miqva'ot 7.10). In addition, it is mentioned anonymously in a completely different context in the Mishnah (M. Pesahim 3.2). Most commentators have therefore preferred to read sentence 3 as a continuation of sentence 1, that is, as a general rule prescribed by the anonymous Mishnah (see the commentaries of Maimonides, R. Obadiah of Berteniro, and Tosafot Yom Tov *ad locum*). Either way, even if sentence 3 is to be seen as a continuation of sentence 2, it is more likely that R. Eliezer is *using* a well-known principle to argue that the rule regarding tangled pubic hair as a barrier is identical for men and for women than that he is proposing a principle by which other rabbis do not abide at all.

85. On adornment and beautification as part of women's marital obligations, see Ishay Rosen-Zvi, "The One Vowing to Deny and the One Denied: Mishnah *Kettubot* Chapter 7 and the Tannaitic Perception of Marriage" [in Hebrew], *Dine Israel* 26 (2010): 91–119.

86. See MS Vienna for T. Miqva'ot 6.8. This version is also mentioned in several medieval works; see Lieberman, *Tosefet Rishonim*, 4:32–33.

87. The version in all the manuscripts of the Mishnah is *mor* (myrrh); however, the Gaonic commentary attests to the version *hemar* (clay), which is also mentioned in the *Arukh* (entry *mr*), in R. Isaiah diTrani's commentary on BT Rosh hashana 19a, and in Maimonides's *Mishneh Torah* (Hilkhot Miqva'ot 3:1).

88. M. Miqva'ot 9.5.

89. Some commentators suggested that R. Eliezer's opinion in the above passage (provided that the statement "all that one is fastidious about constitutes a barrier" is seen as part of his objection) be understood as introducing a conflicting notion of "fastidiousness" that is entirely individualistic, that is, that for R. Eliezer the question of whether one's tangled pubic hair constitutes a barrier or not depends not on one's gender but on each person's relation to his or her body. (This is the interpretation suggested by R. Menahem ha-Meiri and by R. Shlomo b. Aderet, as well as in Ephraim Yitzhak's commentary *Mishnah Aharona*.) It could be the case that different sages took the idea of fastidiousness to mean different things, or that the meaning of the term has evolved through time, but here we cannot go beyond conjecture.

## CHAPTER 3

1. I am using the word *artifacts* to translate the Hebrew term *kelim* (sgl. *keli*), which serves in rabbinic literature to denote usable objects of all kinds—furniture, clothes, utensils, and so on. I choose the word *artifacts* (rather than *articles* or *vessels*, which are sometimes proposed as translations for *kelim*) to emphasize both the inclusive nature of this category, and the most critical quality of a *keli* as the rabbis understood it, namely, that it is made by human beings for human beings.

2. See M. Miqva'ot 7.6, 9.1–10.5.

3. Just like artifacts, humans can be immersed by someone else, without any action or deliberation on their end (M. Miqva'ot 8.5). Moreover, like objects, humans can be purified simply by an inadvertent encounter with water in a sufficient amount (M. Miqva'ot 5.6). While later sources (most notably BT Hagigah 19a) insist that one must willfully intend to purify oneself for the immersion to be valid, Yair Furstenberg persuasively argued that this notion is nowhere to be found in the Mishnah, and that it was only introduced at a later stage, partially as a result of a misunderstanding of M. Hagigah 2.6. Furstenberg, "Eating in a State of Purity," 236–38.

4. M. Zavim 5.4.

5. M. Oholot 6.1.

6. M. Miqva'ot 5.5.

7. M. Oholot 11.3; cf. M. Eduyot 4.12.

8. The insusceptibility of animals to impurity contracted from *other things* must not be confused with the function of dead animals as primary *sources* of impurity, as mentioned in Leviticus 11:24–40.

9. A similar exclusion of nature and of unmanipulated natural objects from the halakhic sphere can be detected in the context of laws of idolatry, according to which natural elements do not fall under the category of "idols" and are not subject to the prohibitions

that pertain to idols, even when they are worshiped as such; see M. Avodah Zarah 3.5. I thank Ishay Rosen-Zvi for this comment.

10. Leviticus 11:31–38. JPS translation, with slight modifications.

11. The Hebrew phrase here is *zer'a zeru'a asher yizar'e'a*, "a seed of seed type which is to be sown." It is difficult to determine whether the term "seed" is to be taken literally here, as referring to loose seeds about to be planted or already planted, or as referring more generally to plants of all sorts (which is the way the rabbis interpret this phrase). It is not uncommon for the word *seed* to stand for plants in general in the Hebrew Bible, for example, Leviticus 27:30: "A tithe of everything from the land, whether grain from the soil *[mi-zer'a ha-aretz]* or fruit from the trees, belongs to the Lord," and Numbers 20:5: "It has no grain *[lo mekom zer'a]* or figs, grapevines or pomegranates."

12. While the biblical text is not explicit that plants need to be initially uprooted from the ground in order to contract impurity, it is difficult to assume that this is not taken to be the case. As various medieval and modern commentators noted, if the assumption in the biblical passage is that mere contact with water renders seeds susceptible to impurity even when they are still attached to the ground, then it is almost impossible to find any sort of plant that is not impure, considering how ubiquitous dead insects and rodents are in open fields. See also Milgrom, *Leviticus 1–16*, 680.

13. The Hebrew is *asher ye'ase melakhah bo*, literally, "with which labor can be done."

14. Milgrom maintains that the distinction between substances susceptible to impurity and substances insusceptible to impurity depends on whether the object at hand is connected to the ground or not. While this is not an unreasonable reading, it has several weaknesses. First, as Milgrom himself notes, ovens and stoves, which are connected to the ground but are mentioned as susceptible to impurity (Leviticus 11:35), are an exception to this rule. Second, there is no way to substantiate that the term "seed" mentioned in Leviticus 11:37 refers to seeds that are already or still planted in the ground, since *asher yizar'ea* is best translated as "may be sown" (that is, suitable for sowing). Finally, focusing only on the question of connection to the ground or lack thereof disregards the status of raw materials that are no longer connected to the ground but still cannot be considered "articles" (for example, logs of woods or lumps of raw clay). See Milgrom, *Leviticus 1–16*, 680–81.

15. Karl Marx, *Early Writings*, trans. R. Livingstone and G. Benton (London: Penguin, 1992), 329.

16. For a different perspective on the ways in which objects serve as extensions of persons, see Chris Fowler, *The Archeology of Personhood: An Anthropological Approach* (New York: Routledge, 2004), 53–78. Fowler emphasizes the role that objects play in social exchange, and argues that in certain societies, giving an object is considered, for all intents and purposes, like giving a part of oneself.

17. As Milgrom notes, similar distinctions between clay articles and other articles are made in various Ancient Near Eastern texts regarding impurity. Milgrom, *Leviticus 1–16*, 676–77.

18. M. Kelim 2.1; cf. *Sifra* Shemini par. 7 per. 8:4–7 on Leviticus 11:33 (ed. Weiss 53b), and see Milgrom, *Leviticus 1–16*, 675.

19. M. Kelim 15.1.

20. Milgrom maintains that by mentioning only certain substances, the Priestly author of Leviticus 11 did not mean to exclude other materials from the realm of impurity. Rather, he

went only through the trouble of mentioning substances that are commonly found in private households, but intended to include artifacts of any kind. Milgrom, *Leviticus 1–16*, 674.

21. The passage in Numbers 31:20–23 discusses the ordinance to purify all the loot from the Israelites' war with Midian: "You shall also cleanse every cloth, every article of skin, and all the work of goats (taken by the rabbis to include bones), and every object of wood.... Gold and silver, copper, iron, tin and lead—any article that can withstand fire—these you shall pass through fire, and they shall be clean."

22. As mentioned explicitly in T. Kelim Baba Batra 7.7.

23. According to Louis Ginzberg, the rabbis decreed that glassware is susceptible to impurity in order to discourage Palestinian Jews from purchasing glass products. Since Tyre and Sidon were major centers of glass production (whereas Palestine's glass industry was rather underdeveloped), the rabbis were concerned that the Jews in Palestine would prefer to acquire glass vessels from those cities, and thereby harm the local industry. See Louis Ginzberg, *Halakhah and Aggadah* [in Hebrew] (Tel-Aviv: Devir, 1960), 15. See also Azaria Ariel, "The Decree on the Impurity of Glassware" [in Hebrew], *Ma'alin ba-kodesh* 10 (2005): 125–58.

24. Artifacts made of these three substances are explicitly mentioned as insusceptible to impurity in *Sifre* Numbers §126 on Numbers 19:15 (ed. Horovitz 164) and *Sifre zutta* on Numbers 19:15 (ed. Horovitz 310), as well as in various passages in the Talmuds (BT Shabbat 58a; BT Shabbat 96a; BT Yoma 2b; BT Menahot 69b; PT Shabbat 8:7, 11c). In addition, multiple passages in the Mishnah and in the Tosefta mention these three substances in contexts that clearly pertain to their inability to contract impurity (for example, M. Oholot 5.5; M. Miqva'ot 4.1; T. Kelim Baba Metzi'a 5.1).

25. See also Noam, *From Qumran to the Rabbinic Revolution*, 88. In the halakhic writings of Qumran, however, stones and earth are explicitly mentioned to be susceptible to impurity and to require purification: see Yigael Yadin, *The Temple Scroll* [in Hebrew] (Jerusalem: Israel Expedition Society, 1977), 1:255; Hanan Eshel, "CD 12:15–17 and the Stone Vessels Found at Qumran," in *The Damascus Document: A Centennial of Discovery*, ed. J. M. Baumgarten, E. G. Chazon, and A. Pinnick (Leiden: Brill, 2000), 45–52; Noam, *From Qumran to the Rabbinic Revolution*, 124–27.

26. See Deines, *Jüdische Steingefäße und pharisäische Frömmigkeit*, 228–33; Regev, "Pure Individualism," 181–84.

27. M. Kelim 27.8.

28. M. Kelim 12.1.

29. M. Kelim 14.3.

30. M. Kelim 24.13.

31. M. Kelim 15.1. This passage presents a controversy between R. Meir and R. Yehuda on the susceptibility to impurity of receptacles that are able to hold more than forty *se'a* of liquids (or sixty *se'a* of dry ware): According to R. Meir, there are a few specific artifacts that are not susceptible to impurity because of their size and heft, but as a rule even receptacles that are able to hold more than forty *se'a* are susceptible to impurity. Conversely, R. Yehuda maintains that there are a few specific artifacts that *are* susceptible to impurity *despite* their size and heft, and these are distinctly objects that can be moved around even when full. Both R. Meir and R. Yehuda, however, assume that whatever receptacle is so large and heavy that it cannot be moved around when full is not susceptible to impurity; their disagreement

seems to be only on the question of which receptacles are movable despite their size and which are not.

32. Cf. *Sifra* Shemini par. 6 per. 7:4–5 on Leviticus 11:32 (ed. Weiss 52b).

33. M. Kelim 16.1-2.

34. *Sit*, according to the commentators, is the distance between the tips of the outstretched thumb and forefinger.

35. M. Kelim 13.4.

36. On the reluctance to throw away potentially usable articles in antiquity, see Kathryn Kamp, "From Village to Tell: Household Ethnoarchaeology in Syria," *Near Eastern Archeology* 63, no. 2 (2000): 84–93.

37. On this, see Joshua Schwartz, "Reduce, Reuse, and Recycle: Prolegomena on Breakage and Repair in Ancient Jewish Society," *Jewish Studies Internet Journal* 5 (2006): 147–80. Schwartz suggests that tractate *Kelim* reflects a prevalent practice of intentionally sabotaging household furniture in a way that makes them "officially" unusable (and thus insusceptible to impurity) but still allows them to be used in their compromised state.

38. M. Kelim 19.9.

39. M. Kelim 20.6.

40. See PT Pe'a 8:7, 21b.

41. The view that personal possessions are actually viewed, in certain social contexts, as part of their owner's body was influentially suggested by the anthropologist McKim Marriott in his studies of Indian society; see McKim Marriott, "Hindu Transactions: Diversity without Dualism," in *Transaction and Meaning: Directions in the Anthropology of Exchange and Symbolic Behavior*, ed. B. Kapferer (Philadelphia: Institute for the Study of Human Issues, 1976), 109–37. Several anthropologists have continued to develop this theme in their studies: see Cecilia Busby, "Permeable and Partible Persons: A Comparative Analysis of Gender and Body in South India and Melanesia," *Journal of the Royal Anthropological Institute* 3, no. 2 (1997): 261–78; Edward LiPuma, "Modernity and Forms of Personhood in Melanesia," in *Bodies and Persons: Comparative Views from Africa to Melanesia*, ed. M. Lambeck and A. Strathern (Cambridge: Cambridge University Press, 1998), 53–79. For a useful survey of this topic see Fowler, *The Archeology of Personhood*, 53–78.

42. M. Kelim 16.4.

43. M. Kelim 4.4.

44. M. Kelim 14.5.

45. Eilberg-Schwartz translates *mahshavah* as "plan" to stress that susceptibility to impurity depends on what the person plans to do with the object in question. While the kind of thought implied in the term *mahshavah* is clearly the thought of doing something, as can be inferred from the recurring expression "he thought about it to ... " *(hashav 'alav le ... )*, I find the modern connotations of the word "plan" to be misleading in this context. See Eilberg-Schwartz, *The Human Will*, 95–100.

46. It should be noted that only persons who are considered to be mentally competent, and thus fully empowered legal agents, can render things susceptible to impurity through the mental force of thought. Persons who have no such legal agency, namely, deaf-mutes, the mentally inept *(shotim)*, and minors, are considered to have no "thought," and thus they can only change the susceptibility of an object to impurity by actively doing something with this object; see M. Kelim 17.15; M. Tohorot 8.6; M. Makhshirin 3.8; M. Makhshirin 6.1.

47. M. Kelim 26.7. The Mishnah adds here "except for the *'utzba*," apparently referring to some sort of leather saddle cover, which is exceptionally deemed susceptible to impurity upon one's decision to use it, even before it is fully processed and prepared.

48. M.Kelim 22.2. In MS Kaufman A50 and MS Parma 2596 the version is "it is impure *until* he thinks about it" *(tame 'ad she-yahshov 'alav)*. However, "until" here probably means "by the time that," as is sometimes the case in Mishnaic Hebrew.

49. R. Yose expresses an opposing opinion here, and maintains that in this case the tabletop does not require "thought" to become susceptible to impurity again, presumably because it is not a new artifact but part of an artifact that has already been deemed susceptible to impurity.

50. M. Kelim 26.8; see also BT Baba Qamma 66b and 114a.

51. The concept of *ye'ush be'alim*, "despair of the owners," explicitly appears in the Mishnah twice (M. Baba Qamma 10.2 and M. Kelim 26.8), but is implied in dozens of other places (most notably and famously in the second chapter of tractate Baba Metzi'a).

52. M. Kelim 25.9.

53. In this I disagree with Milgrom, who takes the phrase "may be eaten" to refer to permitted foods. I would expect that if permissibility were the issue the author would have used the term "pure food," and in any case the question of permissibility pertains only to meat and is irrelevant for all other kinds of food, which are clearly included in this category. See Milgrom, *Leviticus 1–16*, 678.

54. M. Makhshirin 6.4; cf. *Sifra* Shemini par. 8 per. 9:4 on Leviticus 11:34 (ed. Weiss 54b).

55. While we do not often think of blood as a substance that "may be drunk"—in fact there is an explicit prohibition against consuming blood in Leviticus 17:10–13—the Mishnah (M. Makhshirin 6.5) indicates that sometimes blood is designated (or is at least used) for drinking, presumably for animals or for non-Jews.

56. *Sifra* Shemini par. 8 per. 9:4 on Leviticus 11:34 (ed. Weiss 54b); T. Tohorot 9.12.

57. M. Tohorot 8.6.

58. M. Uqtzin 3.2, 4–6.

59. M. Uqtzin 3.3. See also *Midrash Tanna'im* on Deuteronomy 14:7: "They are impure for you, but they are important [*hashuvin*, literally, "thought of"] for others" (ed. Hoffman 74).

60. M. Tohorot 8.6.

61. M. Uqtzin 3.1–2.

62. M. Uqtzin 3.2–3.

63. See M. Uqtzin 3.2, 3, 9.

64. Eilberg-Schwartz, *The Human Will*, 95–120.

65. Ibid., 106–15; see also Eilberg-Schwartz, *The Savage in Judaism*, 217–34.

66. For example, M. Kelim 3.3–4.

67. Harry Frankfurt, "The Importance of What We Care About," *Synthese* 53 (1982): 257–72. I am grateful to Nethanel Lipshitz for this invaluable reference.

68. Ibid., 259.

69. Ibid., 260 (emphasis in original).

70. Several anthropologists who studied societies in which personal boundaries are conceived as flexible and mutable emphasized the importance of the transmission of fluids in the making of familial and communal relations, and showed that the exchange of fluids is

seen as creating actual bodily connections, in a sense making different bodies into one body. See, for instance, Lawrence Babb, "The Physiology of Redemption," *History of Religions* 22, no. 4 (1983): 293–312; Busby, "Permeable and Partible Persons"; Sarah Lamb, *White Saris and Sweet Mangoes: Aging, Gender, and Body in North India* (Berkeley: University of California Press, 2000), 27–41; Beth Conklin, *Consuming Grief: Compassionate Cannibalism in an Amazonian Society* (Austin: University of Texas Press, 2001), 111–31. In many ways, the mishnaic system of impurity can be understood as manifesting a similar paradigm: fluids (not just bodily fluids) are perceived as particularly potent transmitters of impurity, because they are seen as capable of "connecting" separate entities and making them into one.

71. In MS Parma 2596 (De Rossi 497), however, the vocalization throughout the Mishnah is *ki yiten* (if one puts), presumably following the rabbinic reading according to which the placing of water on the plant must be voluntary; see BT Kiddushin 59b; BT Baba Metzi'a 22a.

72. M. Uqtzin 3.1.

73. M. Uqtzin 3.3.

74. M. Makhshirin 6.4–5.

75. M. Makhshirin 6.5.

76. These guidelines are especially notable in the mishnaic chapters that deal with procedures pertaining to the harvesting of grapes and olives and the production of wine and oil (M. Tohorot 9–10). For an elaborate analysis of these chapters, see Furstenberg, "Eating in a State of Purity," 173–89.

77. M. Makhshirin 1.1.

78. M. Makhshirin 1.6.

79. M. Makhshirin 3.5.

80. M. Makhshirin 6.1.

81. In MS Parma 3173 (De Rossi 138): R. Yose.

82. M. Makhshirin 1.3. Most commentators take it that R. Yehoshua is in disagreement with the anonymous view that liquids validate food for impurity even if the contact between the two took place incidentally (as long as the owner was content with this contact), and that he maintains that only when one *initiates* such contact liquids can generate susceptibility to impurity.

83. See also Furstenberg, "Eating in a State of Purity," 167n30.

84. M. Makhshirin 3.5.

85. M. Makhshirin 3.7.

86. According to Yitzhak Gilat, the emphasis on the importance of intention and thought in determining legal outcomes was put forth by the House of Hillel, whereas the House of Shammai rejected this idea. See Yitzhak Gilat, "Intention and Deed in the Teachings of the Tanna'im" [in Hebrew], in *Studies in the Development of Halakhah* (Ramat Gan: Bar Ilan University Press, 2001), 72–83. The same view was expressed by Joseph Baumgarten, "Liquids and Susceptibility to Defilement," 93; and Vered Noam, "The House of Shammai and Sectarian Halakhah" [in Hebrew], *Jewish Studies* 41 (2002): 45–67, at 55.

87. This is the argument made by Furstenberg, who submits that sectarian halakhah and early rabbinic halakhah show considerable similarity regarding the question of activation through liquids, and neither of those ascribed any importance to intention or will. Furstenberg, "Eating in a State of Purity," 164–84.

88. Eric Ottenheijm suggested that there is correspondence between the rabbinic emphasis on subjectivity in the determination of impurity and the early Christian notion that purity is a matter of the heart and not of physical reality; see Eric Ottenheijm, "Impurity between Intention and Deed: Purity Disputes in First Century Judaism and in the New Testament," in *Purity and Holiness: The Heritage of Leviticus*, ed. M. J. H. M. Poorthuis and J. Schwartz (Leiden: Brill, 2000), 129–47. In a similar vein, Eilberg-Schwartz presented the rabbinic notion of "thought" and the early Christian dismissal of physical impurity as parallel, reading Paul's statement that "nothing is unclean in itself, but if anyone regards something as unclean, then for that person it is unclean" (Romans 14:14) as resonating with the centrality of will and deliberation in rabbinic impurity legislation. Eilberg-Schwartz, *The Savage in Judaism*, 204–15. These studies do not properly distinguish between the question of *initial* susceptibility to impurity, which is determined by human consciousness, and the workings of impurity on susceptible objects, which have nothing to do with will and intention and certainly cannot be "spiritualized" in the way proposed in the New Testament.

89. Relying on Josephus's famous comment that compares the Pharisees to the Stoics (*Life of Josephus* 12), and taking for granted that the rabbis are directly descended from the Pharisees, scholars have attempted to show that certain aspects in the rabbinic "philosophy" are distinctly Stoic. See Flusser, *Judaism of the Second Temple*, 221–31; Steve Mason, *Flavius Josephus on the Pharisees* (Leiden: Brill, 1991), 138–56. While Josephus's statement cannot be taken at face value, and a straightforward identification of the rabbis with the Pharisees is quite problematic, there is some persuasive evidence of the rabbis' engagement with Greek philosophical ideas. See Henry Fischel, *Rabbinic Literature and Greco-Roman Philosophy: A Study of Epicurea and Rhetorica in Early Midrashic Writings* (Leiden: Brill, 1973).

90. See, for instance, Charles Kahn, "Discovering the Will: From Homer to Augustine," in *The Question of Eclecticism: Studies in Later Greek Philosophy*, ed. J. M. Dillon and A. A. Long (Berkeley: University of California Press, 1988), 234–58; Troels Engeberg-Pedersen, "Stoic Philosophy and the Concept of a Person," in *The Person and the Human Mind: Issues in Ancient and Modern Philosophy*, ed. C. Gill (Oxford: Oxford University Press, 1990), 109–35; Anthony Long, *Stoic Studies* (Cambridge: Cambridge University Press, 1996), esp. 264–85.

91. For a study of some of the critical divergences between rabbinic and Greek (as well as early Christian) notions of subjectivity, see Naiweld, "L'anti-sujet."

CHAPTER 4

1. The verb form in these cases is clearly passive-reflexive *(mitame/mitam'a/mitam'im)* and not active *(metame/metam'a/metam'in)*, as is confirmed by all the manuscripts, in which the initial *mem* is followed by a *yod;* in MS Parma 2596 and MS Kaufman A50 this vocalization is also confirmed by the *niqqud* marks.

2. M. Niddah 5.3. In the *Sifra*, however, the phrase "made impure by a menstruant" *(mitame be-niddah)* is used only to refer to a man who is made impure upon having intercourse with a menstruating woman, whereas the woman herself is said to be made impure by blood *(mitama be-damim)*. See *Sifra* Tazri'a par. 1 per. 1:10 on Leviticus 12:1 (ed. Weiss 58a) and *Sifra* Zavim par. 4 per. 7:6 on Leviticus 15:24 (ed. Weiss 77b).

3. M. Niddah 5.3; M. Zavim 2.3.

4. M. Nega'im 6.7–8.

5. M. Oholot 1.4.

6. While it is not mentioned explicitly in the biblical text, it is quite clear that menstrual blood and abnormal genital discharges were considered to be sources of impurity in and of themselves: this is implied in the ruling that the litter, seat, and saddle of impure persons, that is, objects that have direct contact with the genital area of persons with discharges, convey impurity like these persons themselves. As Furstenberg notes, this understanding seems to underlie the conception of bodily impurity in the writings of Qumran. The Mishnah, on its end, explicitly asserts that menstrual blood and abnormal genital emissions are sources of impurity in and of themselves (M. Makhshirin 6.5). It is quite plausible that for the rabbis, the body of a person with genital discharge was seen as parallel to the seat or litter of such a person: both were rendered impure in the same primary degree on account of the discharge itself. See Furstenberg, *Eating in a State of Purity*, 126–36.

7. It should be noted that Gentiles are also assumed to be able to convey impurity to others even though they did not contract impurity from anything or anyone themselves. However, as I discuss in chapter 5, the case of Gentiles is different and subject to a unique logic, since their impurity is considered to be only statutory.

8. *Sifre zutta* on Numbers 19:11 (ed. Horovitz 305). Cf. BT Niddah 70b; and see Saul Lieberman, *Sifre Zutta: The Midrash of Lod* [in Hebrew] (New York: Jewish Theological Seminary Press, 1968), 32; Noam, "Is It True," 20–23.

9. *De Specialibus Legibus* III, 207. Quoted from *The Works of Philo*, trans. Charles Yonge (Peabody: Hendrickson, 2006), 615.

10. Julia Kristeva, *The Powers of Horror: An Essay on Abjection*, trans. L. S. Roudiez (New York: Columbia University Press, 1982), 25.

11. Ibid., 109 (emphasis in original).

12. A very similar explanation for the impurity of corpses appears in the medieval compilation known as *The Book of Education (Sefer ha-hinukh)*: "And the dead human body—the Sages explained that this is the father of fathers of impurity, and its impurity is stronger than all other impurities. For when the good form of the mind is separated from it and it remains on its own . . . it is appropriate that it will defile all of its surroundings, for when it is stripped off of its glory, which is the soul, all that is left in it is bad matter" (§287). See Chaim Dov Shevel, ed., *The Book of Education* [in Hebrew] (Jerusalem: Mosad ha-Rav Kook, 1960), 370. It is quite implausible that the author of this book was directly familiar with Philo.

13. On the common view of death as the ultimate source of impurity, see Jonathan Klawans, *Purity, Sacrifice, and the Temple: Symbolism and Supersessionism in the Study of Ancient Judaism* (New York: Oxford University Press, 2006), 56–58, and notes on 265–66.

14. Numbers 19:14–16. However, in the rabbinic purity system the person with scale disease *(metzora)* is also taken to convey impurity to a space by entering it.

15. Numbers 19:11–15. In addition, corpse impurity is the only form of ritual impurity from which the priests are commanded to distance themselves (Leviticus 21:1), and which overthrows the vow of the Nazarite (Numbers 6:1–21).

16. See M. Kelim 1.4.

17. See M. Oholot 1.1–4.

18. On the difficulty of defining the corpse and clearly identifying it as either person or object in ancient legal discourse, see Hildegard Cancik-Lindemaier, "Corpus: Some Philological and Anthropological Remarks upon Roman Funerary Rites," in *Self, Soul and Body in Religious Experience*, ed. A. Baumgarten with J. Assmann and G. Stroumsa (Leiden: Brill, 1998), 417–29.

19. Numbers 19:14–16.

20. As Abraham Goldberg explains, while the common name for the tractate is *Oholot* (Tents), in most of the Mishnah's manuscripts as well as in other rabbinic compilations, such as the Tosefta and the two Talmuds, the tractate is titled *Ahelot* (or *Ahilot*), which is the plural form of the verbal noun *ahel*, meaning "to tent over." See Abraham Goldberg, *Tractate Oholot: Critical Edition* [in Hebrew] (Jerusalem: Magnes Press, 1956), 1–4.

21. M. Oholot 2.1–2.

22. In MS Parma 2596 the cantillation signs indicate that there should be a pause after the first occurrence of the word *dead*, thus suggesting that the sentence should be read in the following way: "The following convey impurity *by the overhang of the dead*: the volume of an olive-bulk from the dead," and so on. As Goldberg notes, according to this reading "the dead" is not mentioned in the list of impurity conveyors at all. Goldberg, *Tractate Oholot*, 13.

23. Indeed, both the Babylonian and the Palestinian Talmuds assume that the category of "the dead" is redundant unless it is explained as referring to a body that entirely lacks both flesh and bones. See PT Nazir 7:2, 56b and BT Nazir 50a.

24. On the notion that blood conveys corpse impurity, see Vered Noam, "Corpse-Blood Impurity: A Lost Biblical Reading?," *Journal of Biblical Literature* 128, no. 2 (2009): 243–51.

25. The category of "a limb from the living" is a perplexing one. If once a person was dismembered, the detached limb is considered to be corpse-matter, this raises the question of why other detached organs do not impart the same kind of impurity. While this topic is not developed in tractate *Oholot*, M. Eduyot 6.3 (cf. T. Ahilot 2.5-6) mentions some opinions according to which flesh that was detached from the living conveys corpse impurity as well.

26. In the two Talmuds we find the following definitions of *netzel*: "The flesh of the dead that congealed and the liquid (of the flesh) that coagulated" (PT Nazir 7:2, 56b and BT Nazir 50a).

27. Blood can convey impurity only if all or some of it came out of the body after one's death (in the latter case it is referred to as "mixed blood," *dam tevusah*). The blood of the living does not convey impurity, with the one notable exception of female uterine blood; see M. Makhshirin 6.4–7.

28. Cf. M. Eduyot 1.7; and see below.

29. M. Oholot 2.5.

30. Not so in the case of a limb from the living, which stops conveying impurity altogether when it is no longer intact; see M. Oholot 2.5.

31. M. Oholot 2.3.

32. Cf. M. Nazir 7.2–3.

33. As has been noted by several scholars and as can be observed in this passage, the "mishnah" that the *Sifre zutta* quotes is not identical with the Mishnah as we know it, although it is quite similar to it. On the relations between "our" Mishnah and the mishnah

of the *Sifre zutta*, see Lieberman, *Sifre Zutta*, 11–64; Epstein, *Introduction to Tannaitic Literature*, 741–46; Menahem Kahana, *Sifre Zutta Deuteronomy* [in Hebrew] (Jerusalem: Magnes Press, 2002), 85–88.

34. Cf. T. Ahilot 3.3. Lieberman (in *Tosefet Rishonim* 2:125) explains that the Tosefta, like the *Sifre zutta*, refers to three measures: the numerical majority *(rov minyan)*, the majority of the skeletal frame *(rov binyan)*, and the majority of one's height *(rov godel)*. However, in the Babylonian Talmud (BT Nazir 52b) the category of height is interpreted, in line with the Mishnah, as explanatory of the category of "skeletal frame" *(rov binyan)*.

35. *Sifre zutta* on Numbers 19:14 (ed. Horovitz 310). While most of the *Sifre zutta* did not survive and parts of it were only preserved in medieval midrashic compilations, this particular passage was found in the Cairo Genizah and was published by Ya'akov Nahum Epstein, "Sifre Zutta Parashat Parah" [in Hebrew], *Tarbitz* 1 (1930): 46–78. Here I used the edition prepared by Menahem Kahana, *Fragments of Halakhic Midrashim from the Genizah* [in Hebrew] (Jerusalem: Magnes Press, 2005), 1:219, lines 5–11.

36. The absence of these three items from the list could indicate that these items were seen as somewhat different in nature from the others, perhaps because of their small quantity or because of the fact that they cannot be easily identified as human. A similar view can be detected in a passage in the Tosefta (T. Sheqalim 1.5; see also BT Mo'ed Qatan 5b and PT Ma'aser Sheni 5:1, 55d), according to which if one buries an olive-volume of flesh he or she is not required to mark the grave so as to warn people of impurity, while one is required to do so when burying the skull, the spine, and the majority of bones. In addition, a baraita in the Babylonian Talmud suggests that while a priest is not allowed to have contact with fragments and limbs of the dead (but only with an entire dead body, in case it is a relative) he is allowed to have contact with an olive-volume of flesh, an olive-volume of congealed flesh, and a ladle-full of rot (BT Nazir 43b). However, the *Sifre zutta* does mention flesh, congealed flesh, and rot in another place, in regard to corpse impurity contracted by a Nazarite (*Sifre zutta* on Numbers 6:9, ed. Horovitz 242).

37. The *Sifre zutta*'s requirement of larger quantities both for blood and for bones corresponds with a tannaitic opinion that was eventually excluded from the Mishnah. The Tosefta mentions that the question regarding the minimal amount of blood and bones was the subject of an ongoing dispute between the early rabbis (T. Ahilot 4.7; T. Nazir 5.3), and that it was finally decided that while a quarter *log/qav* is enough to defile heave-offerings and the sancta, half a *log/qav* is required to undo the Nazarite's separation and to inculpate one who entered the Temple in a state of impurity. See also M. Nazir 7.2–4. On this controversy and its presumed ancient origins, see Epstein, *Introduction to Tannaitic Literature*, 507–8.

38. My use of the term *symbolic* here follows Roland Barthes's definition of a symbol as a kind of sign that invokes a mental representation of a particular object without being identical with this object. See Roland Barthes, *Elements of Semiology*, trans. A. Lavers and C. Smith (New York: Hill and Wang, 1973), 38.

39. Philippe Ariès, *The Hour of Our Death*, trans. H. Weaver (New York: Random House, 1982), 328.

40. See Peter Brown, *The Cult of the Saints* (Chicago: University of Chicago Press, 1981), 83–85; Caroline Walker Bynum, *The Resurrection of the Body in Western Christianity, 200–1336* (New York: Columbia University Press, 1995), 86–112; Robert Sharf, "On the Allure of Buddhist Relics," *Representations* 66 (1999): 75–99.

41. Emma-Jayne Graham, "Becoming Persons, Becoming Ancestors: Personhood, Memory and the Corpse in Roman Rituals of Social Remembrance," *Archeological Dialogues* 16, no. 1 (2009): 51–74. I thank Catherine Chin for this helpful reference.

42. *De lingua Latina* V, 23 (my translation). See Andreas Spengel, ed., *M. Terenti Varronis: De Lingua Latina Libri* (New York: Arno Press, 1979), 10.

43. As noted already by Maimonides in his commentary on M. Oholot 2.1: "It is apparent in each of those that it is a bone of a person." See also Noam, "Between Qumran and Rabbinic Midrash," 73–76.

44. See L. I. Rahmani, "Ancient Jerusalem's Funerary Customs and Tombs," *Biblical Archaeologist* 44, no. 3 (1981): 171–77; 44, no. 4 (1981): 229–35; 45, no. 1 (1982): 43–53; 45, no. 2 (1982): 109–119. See also David Kraemer, *The Meanings of Death in Rabbinic Judaism* (New York: Routledge, 1999), 35.

45. Vered Noam retraces a polemic between the Qumran Sect, as represented in the *Miqtsat Ma'ase ha-Torah* Scroll (4Q396 1–2 iv), and the rabbis, as represented in a passage from *Sifre zutta* on Numbers 19:11 (ed. Horovitz 306–7), regarding the status of broken or "lacking" bones. According to Noam, while the rabbis insisted that only whole bones convey impurity, the sect held that any kind of bone, whether whole or not, conveys impurity. Noam, "Between Qumran and Rabbinic Midrash," 67–78. Interestingly, the explanation that the *Sifre zutta* provides for its ruling is an analogy between a bone and a person: "In the same way that a person is whole the bone should be whole."

46. M. Oholot 3.6. See also T. Megillah 1.11: "There is no [difference] between an olive-volume of the dead and the dead, except that the aperture of an olive-volume of the dead is one handbreadth, and the aperture of the dead is four handbreadths." Cf. T. Kelim Baba Qamma 1.4.

47. T. Ahilot 5.2.

48. Commentators disagreed on whether R. Yose makes the point that *only* the spine and the skull are like the entire dead vis-à-vis the apertures in the house, or whether he simply points out that the spine and the skull are also like an entire dead, and not just an olive-bulk of flesh.

49. M. Eduyot 1.7.

50. M. Oholot 2.6. The controversy regarding blood appears also in M. Oholot 2.2, here with the Sages' opinion as the anonymous voice of the Mishnah: "A quarter [*log*] of blood and a quarter [*log*] of mixed-blood from one dead body [convey impurity by overhang]. R. Aqiva says: [Also] from two dead bodies." On the relation between the two renditions of this controversy, see Goldberg, *Tractate Oholot*, 20–21.

51. The Tosefta (T. Ahilot 4.2) presents a tradition in the name of R. Yehuda, according to which R. Aqiva eventually changed his opinion and declared that the skull and the spine from more than one person are pure. This tradition is followed by a disputing statement in the name of R. Shimon, according to which R. Aqiva never changed his position.

52. Echoes of the notion that corpse fragments in sufficient amount from more than one corpse convey impurity can also be found in the Tosefta, in an anonymous tradition according to which a ladle-full of rot and an olive-volume of flesh or congealed flesh from two dead bodies convey impurity by overhang (T. Ahilot 4.5).

53. In contrast, in the *Sifre zutta* on Numbers 19:11 (ed. Horovitz 307 = Kahana, *Fragments of Halakhic Midrashim*, 217, line 5) only R. Aqiva's position regarding blood is

presented, and it is presented anonymously (which is unsurprising considering the prominent role of R. Aqiva in this Midrash); see Lieberman, *Sifre Zutta*, 47. See also *Sifra Emor* par. 2 per. 1:4 on Leviticus 21:11 (ed. Weiss 94b), in which there is also no indication that the Sages disagree with R. Aqiva's ruling.

54. On the prominence of considerations of particularity and singularity in the Mishnah's concepts of personhood, see Mira Balberg, "Pricing Persons: Consecration, Compensation, and Individuality in the Mishnah," *Jewish Quarterly Review* 103, no. 2 (2013): 169–95.

55. This is most notable in cases of doubtful impurity, as I argued in the first chapter.

56. On the question of "hermeneutic" as opposed to "historical" considerations in rabbinic legal developments, see Christine Hayes, *Between the Babylonian and Palestinian Talmuds: Accounting for Halakhic Difference in Selected Sugyot from Tractate Avodah Zarah* (New York: Oxford University Press, 1997), 3–27.

57. M. Niddah 3.2. The Sages here dispute the opinion of R. Meir, according to which a woman who miscarried is rendered impure as a parturient regardless of the fetus' appearance.

58. M. Oholot 2.3.

59. "The plowed grave-field" *(bet ha-peras)* refers to a field that served as burial ground in the past but is now plowed and its ground overturned, and the "land of nations" refers to the soil of lands that are inhabited chiefly by non-Jews, which is considered to be impure since it presumably contains corpse parts. On the impurity of the land of the nations, see Hayes, *Gentile Impurities*, 199–204.

60. Cf. M. Nazir 7.2–3.

61. See also T. Ahilot 2.6.

62. M. Kelim 1.5.

63. T. Ahilot 3.2. See also BT Shabbat 32a.

64. *Sifre zutta* on Numbers 19:11 (ed. Horovitz 306 = Kahana, *Fragments of Halakhic Midrashim*, 216, line 26). See Lieberman, *Sifre Zutta*, 32.

65. The Palestinian Talmud replicates the same kind of explanation in regard to the category of rot, and suggests that a ladle-full of rot stands for the dust from which mankind was created: "R. Yuda ben Pazi said: One ladle-full of dust the Holy One, blessed be He, took from the place of the altar, and created Adam the First from it . . . after 120 years [in the grave], one returns to [the amount of] one ladle-full of rot" (PT Nazir 7:2, 56b).

66. *Sifre* Numbers §127 on Numbers 19:16 (ed. Horovitz 165).

67. T. Ahilot 16.2. See also PT Nazir 7:2, 56c; BT Nazir 51b and 65a.

68. This might correspond with the Jewish custom of burial, in which the corpse is treated like a living person: washed with warm water, anointed with oil, and so on. As Kraemer points out, this indicates that immediately after death, when still intact, the corpse is seen as sharing many attributes with the living, and these attributes gradually disappear with the physical deterioration of the corpse. Kraemer, *The Meanings of Death*, 26.

69. T. Ahilot 16.12.

70. See Noam, *From Qumran to the Rabbinic Revolution*, 300–304.

71. For discussions on the status of fetuses in Jewish law, see Jacob Bazak, "The Legal Status of the Fetus in Jewish Halacha and in Israeli Law," *Jewish Law Association Studies* 8 (2000): 1–5; Christiane Steuer, "Der Fetus ist ein Glied seiner Mutter ('ubar yerekh imo'): eine rabbinische Interpretation von Exodus 21:22–24," *Lectio difficilior* 2 (2008).

72. The possibility that a miscarriage will nonetheless result in the survival of the fetus is explicitly mentioned in M. Nazir 2.8.

73. In M. Baba Qamma 4.6 this ruling is mentioned in regard to a goring ox, which must not be put to death unless it killed a "viable" person; in M. Sanhedrin 9.2 the same rule is applied to a human killer. See also *Mekhilta deRabbi Ishmael*, Neziqin, par. Mishpatim 4 to Exodus 21:12 (ed. Horovitz-Rabin 261); *Mekhilta deRabbi Shimon ben Yohai* to Exodus 21:12 (ed. Epstein-Melamed 169); *Sifra* Emor par. 14 per. 20:1 on Leviticus 24:17 (ed. Weiss 104b).

74. While the root *qym* in Aramaic simply means "to exist" or "to be valid," an alternative understanding of the expression *bene qeyama* can be suggested based on the Syriac evidence, in which the term *qeyama* regularly denotes "covenant," and the combination *bene qeyama* is used to refer to the "sons of the covenant" (which in the Syriac context refers to members of the Church). As Murray notes, this term is equivalent to the common Hebrew expression *bene berit*; see Robert Murray, *Symbols of Church and Kingdom: A Study in Early Syriac Tradition* (New York: T & T Clark, 2005), 13–17. It could thus be suggested that aborted fetuses and premature born babies were considered to be excluded from the covenant of the people of Israel, presumably, again, because they were not considered as fully alive.

75. The Mishnah makes it clear that corpse impurity does not ensue until after one takes one's last breath, even if the body is already seriously corrupted before death; see M. Oholot 1.5.

76. Leviticus 17:15.

77. M. Hullin 3.1; see also BT Hullin 42a.

78. M. Kelim 1.5.

79. For a concise summary of this view, see Jacob Milgrom, *Leviticus: A Book of Ritual and Ethics* (Minneapolis: Augsburg Fortress, 2004), 12–13.

80. R. Eliezer's position stands in interesting contrast to the view that we find in the Temple Scroll from Qumran (11Q19 50.4–7), according to which only limbs from the dead convey impurity, but apparently not limbs from the living; see Yadin, *The Temple Scroll*, 258; Noam, *From Qumran to the Rabbinic Revolution*, 138–54.

81. M. Eduyot 6.3. According to Kahana, it is likely that the alternative explanation in this passage was added at a later stage, and should not be seen as a continuation of R. Eliezer's statement. See Menahem Kahana, "Studies in the Design and Purposes of Controversy in the Mishnah" [in Hebrew], *Tarbitz* 73 (2004): 51–81, at 64–67.

82. M. Kelim 1.4.

83. M. Oholot 2.2.

84. The Tosefta (T. Ahilot 2.2) explains the term "grave-dust" as referring to a mixture defined by one's inability to extricate rot from non-rot: "A mixture that was found in the grave, and it is not known what its nature is, this is grave-dust, a ladle-full and more . . . he removes what is certain [to be part of the corpse] and leaves what is uncertain, and this is grave-dust, a ladle-full and more."

85. T. Ahilot 2.2.

86. See also BT Niddah 27a-b.

87. See Kraemer, *The Meanings of Death*, 39, 65.

88. *Galgalin* (or *gilgalin*) is the version in all the manuscripts and printed editions of BT Nazir. In BT Niddah 27b, however, we find in the exact same context the version *gangalin*

(MS Vatican Ebr. 113), *ganglulin* (MS Vatican Ebr. 110–111), and *gangilon* (MS Munich 95 and the printed editions).

89. In PT Shabbat 6:4, 8b the term *galgalaya* appears as a translation of the biblical word *gilyonim* in Isaiah 3:23 (which is commonly translated into English as "gauze" or "bandages," following the LXX translation *bussina*); cf. Genesis Rabbah 19 (ed. Theodor-Albeck 1:176), in which the word *gulin* is used to denote a girdle or shawl. See also M. Nega'im 11.11, in which *galgalon* is mentioned among other types of artifacts that are made of fabric or hide, but are not clothing items per se.

90. PT Nazir 7:2, 56b.

91. PT Nazir 7:2, 56b; cf. BT Nazir 51a.

92. In the Babylonian Talmud (Nazir 51a–b) we find a series of discussions on the possibility that certain parts of one's actual body will function as *galgalin* to the rest of one's corpse. It starts with the suggestion that one's cut hair, if buried with him, will constitute *galgalin* for the rest of the body, followed by a suggestion that one's hair and nails will constitute *galgalin* even when still attached to the body. In what follows, the notion of *galgalin* is taken ad absurdum, with the rabbis considering the possibility that a fetus will constitute *galgalin* for its mother, that one's excrement or sputum will constitute *galgalin* for one's body (even when still contained within it), and even that one's skin will be considered as *galgalin* to the rest of the body. While these suggestions probably should not be taken as anything other than thought experiments, they do serve as a good indication of the way in which the category of rot serves the rabbis to define a pristine and unadulterated body.

93. T. Ahilot 16.2.

94. PT Nazir 7:2, 56c; BT Nazir 51b.

95. PT Nazir 7:2, 56c.

## CHAPTER 5

1. Douglas, *Purity and Danger*, 60–71.

2. Noam, *From Qumran to the Rabbinic Revolution*, 289. See also Fonrobert, "Blood and Law," 253.

3. On this, see Douglas, *Purity and Danger*, 141–59; James Aho, *The Orifice as a Sacrificial Site: Culture, Organization, and the Body* (New York: Walter de Gruyter, 2002).

4. Whether one determines (like Julia Kristeva in *The Powers of Horror*) that certain items are commonly identified as impure because they invoke disgust or maintains, like William Ian Miller, that these items invoke disgust because of the cultural taboo imposed on them, the connection between impurity and disgust is undeniable. See William Ian Miller, *The Anatomy of Disgust* (Cambridge, MA: Harvard University Press, 1997), 105–7.

5. Alexandra Cuffel, *Gendering Disgust in Medieval Religious Polemic* (Notre Dame: University of Notre Dame Press, 2007), 156–97.

6. See BT Shabbat 68b; BT Avodah Zarah 31b; BT Niddah 34b. An especially striking example for this can be found in the Palestinian Midrash Leviticus Rabbah 15:4 (ed. Margulies 327–28), in a homily on the biblical verse "when a person shall have in the skin of his flesh a rising, a scab, or a bright spot . . . he shall be brought unto Aaron the priest or unto one of his sons the priests" (Leviticus 13:2). According to this homily, since the verse does not say "a person from among you" *(adam mi-kem)* but rather only "a person," this is an

indication that only Gentiles are prone to suffering from skin afflictions, but the Israelites need not be concerned about them.

7. Indeed, this was the assumption of the German theologian Emil Schürer, who explained that for the Jews "the heathen, because he did not observe the laws of purity, was impure." See Emil Schürer, *Geschichte des Jüdischen Volkes im Zeitalter Jesu Christi* (Leipzig: Heinrich, 1886), 2:48. For a list of additional studies that present the same view, see Klawans, "Notions of Gentile Impurity," 285–86.

8. M. Nega'im 3.1.

9. M. Nega'im 11.1, 12.1.

10. M. Niddah 7.3. See also M. Niddah 4.3, in which there is a controversy between the House of Hillel and the House of Shammai on whether the menstrual blood of a Gentile woman is entirely pure or as impure as her other bodily fluids (as a result of the statutory impurity attributed to Gentiles).

11. M. Miqva'ot 8.4. See also Fonrobert, "Blood and Law," 261–65.

12. T. Ahilot 1.4, 14.6.

13. T. Parah 12.11.

14. T. Zavim 2.1. Cf. M. Zavim 2.1. See also *Sifra* Zavim par. 1 per. 1:1 on Leviticus 15:1 (ed. Weiss 72b); BT Niddah 34a.

15. See M. Sheqalim 8.1; M. Niddah 4.3, 10.4; M. Tohorot 5.8, 7.1, 7.6; M. Makhshirin 2.4; T. Yoma 4.20.

16. On this tendency in the books of Ezra and Nehemiah, see Saul Olyan, "Purity Ideology in Ezra-Nehemiah as a Tool to Reconstitute the Community," *Journal for the Study of Judaism* 35, no. 1 (2004): 1–16; on this ideology in the Letter of Aristeas, see Victor Tcherikover, "The Ideological Template of the Letter of Aristeas," in *The Jews in the Greek and Roman World* [in Hebrew] (Jerusalem: M. Newman Press, 1961), 316–38; on the Book of Jubilees, see Cana Werman, "Jubilees 30: Building a Paradigm for the Ban on Intermarriage," *Harvard Theological Review* 90, no. 1 (1997): 1–22. In particular, this ideology is central in the writings of Qumran; see Shemesh, "The Origins of the Laws of Separatism"; Harrington, *The Purity Texts*, 112–27.

17. Adolf Büchler, "The Levitical Impurity of the Gentile in Palestine before the Year 70," *Jewish Quarterly Review* 17, no. 1 (1926): 1–81

18. Büchler based this conclusion on a talmudic tradition (BT Shabbat 83a; BT Niddah 34a), according to which the ruling that Gentiles convey impurity like persons with abnormal genital discharges was issued in the mid-first century, at a time of increasing political tension.

19. Gedalyahu Alon, "Gentile Impurity," in *Studies in Jewish History in the Times of the Second Temple and the Talmud* [in Hebrew] (Tel-Aviv: Ha-Kibbutz ha-me'uhad, 1957), 1:121–47.

20. Klawans, "Notions of Gentile Impurity."

21. Hayes, *Gentile Impurities*, 107–45.

22. For example, M. Zavim 4.7.

23. For example, M. Kelim 24.8.

24. Hayes, *Gentile Impurities*, 113.

25. The understanding of the biblical term *ger* as referring to a convert (that is, a person who has actively and willfully become a Jew), rather than to a non-Israelite who lives among

the Israelites and is subject to some of their laws, is distinctly a rabbinic development; see Shaye Cohen, *The Beginnings of Jewishness: Boundaries, Varieties, Uncertainties* (Berkeley: University of California Press, 1999), 119–25.

26. Leviticus 17:15.

27. Numbers 19:10.

28. Numbers 31:19.

29. Hayes acknowledges that these cases present an exception to what she recognizes as the rule, but explains these three exceptions as reflecting the Priestly view that Gentiles are bound by the Noahide covenant (that is, the covenant of God with all of mankind, as opposed to His covenant exclusively with the people of Israel). The Noahide covenant prohibits murder and consumption of blood, explains Hayes, and thus the impurities that derive from the consumption of blood and from contact with corpses pertain to Gentiles as well as to Israelites. Hayes, *Gentile Impurities*, 37–40. However, Numbers 19:10 deals with corpses in general and not with murder victims (as opposed to Numbers 31:19), and Leviticus 17:15 deals with the consumption of carrion and not of blood. In general, it is not clear to me why the prohibition of certain actions entails the view that these actions also generate impurity.

30. Noam, *From Qumran to the Rabbinic Revolution*, 278–91.

31. Vered Noam similarly suggested that the insusceptibility of Gentiles to ritual impurity should be understood in concordance with the exclusion of certain artifacts and objects from the realm of impurity since they are based on the same principle. However, she identified this principle as the distinction between nature and culture: "The more [an artifact] belongs to the world of culture and the less it belongs to the world of nature, the more exposed to impurity it is." Noam, *From Qumran to the Rabbinic Revolution*, 288. I fully accept Noam's view that the insusceptibility of Gentiles to impurity is based on the same rabbinic principle that renders incomplete artifacts insusceptible to impurity; however, the distinction between nature and culture does not suffice to explain the categorization of artifacts as susceptible or insusceptible to impurity. Rather, as I argued, the classification of artifacts is based on the question whether the object at hand is *consequential* for human beings or not.

32. See also Birenboim, "Observance of the Laws of Bodily Purity," 69–158.

33. Klawans, *Impurity and Sin*, 21–42. Birenboim finds this distinction between two kinds of impurity unsatisfying, and prefers to distinguish between "impurity with practical implications" and "impurity without practical implications." Birenboim, "Observance of the Laws of Bodily Purity," 96.

34. See especially Leviticus 18 and 20; Klawans, *Impurity and Sin*, 25–35.

35. See, for instance, Deuteronomy 4:37; 7:6–7; 10:15; 12:2; 14:21; 26:19. On the prevalence of this notion in the book of Deuteronomy, see Ronald Clements, *God's Chosen People: A Theological Interpretation of the Book of Deuteronomy* (London: SCM Press, 1968). However, according to Milgrom, the notion of the unique standing of the people of Israel as holier than all the nations is traceable in the Priestly Code as well; see Milgrom, *Leviticus 1–16*, 718–42.

36. According to Moshe Weinfeld, whereas in the Priestly Code holiness is essentially a ritual matter, in Deuteronomy the holiness of the Israelites has strong implications of national separatism; see Moshe Weinfeld, "The Turn in the Perception of Divinity and Cult in the Book of Deuteronomy" [in Hebrew], *Tarbitz* 31 (1962): 1–17, at 7–9.

37. Most famously, Ezra contrasts the "holy seed" of the Israelites with the "peoples of the lands" (Ezra 9:2), and continues to define the land as "impure with the impurity of the peoples of the lands, with their abominations that have filled it from end to end with their uncleanness" (Ezra 9:10). A similar theme is highly prominent in the Book of Jubilees, most notably in 22:16–22; see Cana Werman, "The Relation to Gentiles in the Book of Jubilees" [in Hebrew], PhD diss., Hebrew University, Jerusalem, 1995, 210–16. Aharon Shemesh identified the same view in the writings of the Qumran Sect, which extends the notion of Gentile impurity as a result of unholiness to Jews who are not members of the sect; see Shemesh, "The Origins of Separatism."

38. See Klawans, *Impurity and Sin*, 92–117, 134–45.

39. Hayes, *Gentile Impurities*, 142–44. According to Hayes, since the rabbis of the Mishnah do not accept that Gentiles are barred from the Israelite community simply because of their genealogical descent (because the rabbis do consider conversion to be possible), there is no real sense in which Gentiles are inherently impure in the mishnaic system.

40. T. Niddah 9.14.

41. Hayes, *Gentile Impurities*, 143–44.

42. See also Hayes, *Gentile Impurities*, 161–63. The most famous tradition according to which Jews refrained from contact with Gentiles on account of their impurity appears in Acts 10:28, in which it is mentioned that Peter, during his visit to Cornelius's house, said, "You are well aware that it is against our law for a Jew to associate with a Gentile or visit him. But God has shown me that I should not call any man impure or unclean." While this passage should not necessarily be taken at face value, it might suggest that the notion of Gentile impurity played a part in an extreme isolationist ideology during the first century C.E. See Klawans, "Notions of Gentile Impurity," 301; Birenboim, "Observance of the Laws of Bodily Purity," 304–5. Another key text pertaining to Jews allegedly refraining from associating with Gentiles is Galatians 2:11–15; on this, see James Dunn, "The Incident at Antioch (Gal 2:11–18)," *Journal for the Study of the New Testament* 18 (1983): 3–57. See also Peter Tomson, *Paul and the Jewish Law: Halakha in the Letters of the Apostle to the Gentiles* (Assen: Uitgeverij Van Gorcum, 1990), 230–36.

43. Noam, *From Qumran to the Rabbinic Revolution*, 288, 295.

44. See especially T. Ahilot 14.6.

45. See Noam, *From Qumran to the Rabbinic Revolotion*, 291–94. In the Babylonian Talmud (BT Yebamot 61a), we find an explicit statement that the graves of Gentiles do not convey impurity by overhang since Gentiles are not considered to be "persons" *(en ha-goyim qruyin adam)*.

46. See Ishay Rosen-Zvi and Adi Ophir, "*Goy*: Toward a Genealogy," *Dine Israel* 29 (2011): 69–122. On the rabbinic view of Gentiles as nonpersons, see Yehezkel Cohen, "The Attitude to the Gentile in the Halacha and in Reality in the Tannaitic Period" [in Hebrew], PhD diss., Hebrew University, Jerusalem, 1975, 86–90.

47. On the motif of comparability of Gentiles to animals, see Sacha Stern, *Jewish Identity in Early Rabbinic Writings* (Leiden: Brill, 1994), 33–39.

48. M. Sanhedrin 9.2.

49. On the rabbinic approach toward conversion to Judaism, see Cohen, *Beginnings of Jewishness*, 198–236.

50. M. Tohorot 8.6.

51. See BT Nazir 61b; Noam, *From Qumran to the Rabbinic Revolution*, 289–91.
52. M. Nega'im 7.1.
53. In her recent work on the fetus in midrashic literature, Gwynn Kessler showed that fetuses were considered to be part of the Israelite community even when still in the uterus; see Gwynn Kessler, *Conceiving Israel: The Fetus in Rabbinic Narratives* (Philadelphia: University of Pennsylvania Press, 2009), 29–46. It is interesting to see that the halakhic sources do not suggest the same view.
54. For a discussion of this passage, see also Mira Balberg, "Rabbinic Authority, Medical Rhetoric, and Body Hermeneutics in Mishnah Nega'im," *AJS Review* 35, no. 2 (2011): 323–46. See also Moshe Lavee, "A Convert Is Like a Newborn Child: The Concept and Its Implications in Rabbinic Literature" [in Hebrew], PhD diss., Ben-Gurion University in the Negev, 2004, 151.
55. E. P. Sanders's explanation of Paul's idea of baptism nicely resonates with the rabbis' notion of an acquisition of a new body upon personal transformation, in which the physical body remains the same but is nonetheless conceived as other. See E. P. Sanders, *Paul: A Very Short Introduction* (Oxford: Oxford University Press, 1991), 83. I thank Ishay Rosen-Zvi for this reference.
56. M. Zavim 2.3.
57. For a similar discussion, see also BT Niddah 43a.
58. See M. Nega'im 11.1, 12.1.
59. Ron Naiweld, "Au commencement était la pratique: Les commandements comme exercices spirituels—la subjectivation pratique rabbinique," *Yod—Revue des études hébraïques et juives* 15 (2010): 13–41. For a similar claim on the rabbinic construction of selfhood vis-à-vis the Torah, see Schofer, *The Making of a Sage*, 71–83.
60. Joshua Levinson, "From Narrative Practice to Cultural Poetics: Literary Anthropology and the Rabbinic Sense of Self," in *Homer and the Bible in the Eyes of Ancient Interpreters*, ed. M. R. Niehoff (Leiden: Brill, 2012), 345–67.
61. Alon (in "Gentile Impurity," 122) argued that Gentile impurity was analogized to three different kinds of ritual impurity: that of creeping and crawling creatures, that of corpses, and that of persons with abnormal genital discharges; he thus implied that the question about which sort of impurity was attributed to Gentiles is marginal at best. However, Christine Hayes convincingly showed that the only form of impurity actually attributed to Gentiles is, unfailingly, the impurity of abnormal genital discharges. Hayes shows that the impurity of creeping and crawling creatures was attributed only to idols and not to Gentiles (Hayes, *Gentile Impurities*, 136–39), and that Alon's argument that the rabbis attributed corpse impurity to Gentiles is based on a misunderstanding of M. Pesahim 8.8 (ibid., 117–22).
62. In addition, the semen of Gentiles conveys impurity, not in the same way that the semen of Jews conveys impurity, but rather in the same way that all bodily fluids of Gentiles convey impurity (M. Makhshirin 6.6). As for the menstrual blood of a Gentile woman, there is a controversy between the House of Hillel and the House of Shammai on whether it is entirely pure, or as impure as her urine and saliva, as it would be in a woman with abnormal genital discharge (M. Niddah 4.3). Neither of the houses maintains that the menstrual blood of a Gentile woman is a source of impurity in and of itself, like the menstrual blood of a Jewish woman, as was suggested by Büchler, "The Levitical Impurity," 8–15; and Klawans, "Notions of Gentile Impurity," 303.

63. See also Fonrobert, "Blood and Law," 261–65.

64. As the Mishnah makes clear in several places, even when Gentiles are not physically present in the public space, they are present there though their spittle and through their urine. See, for instance M. Makhshirin 2.2.

65. On the structure of Leviticus 15 and its meaning, see Milgrom, *Leviticus 1–16*, 904; Fonrobert, *Menstrual Purity*, 43–46.

66. This difference has been practically abolished in later halakhah, since during talmudic times the custom has been established that women should count seven days without any bleeding after the last day of their menstruation (BT Berakhot 31a; BT Megillah 28b; BT Niddah 66a; PT Berakhot 5:1, 8d). Thereby, the only practical difference (which is of course no longer applicable in talmudic times) between a woman with normal bleeding and a woman with abnormal bleeding is that the latter must bring a sacrifice.

67. The term *seminal emission (qeri)* pertains in rabbinic literature to ejaculation in the course of sexual intercourse and to nocturnal emissions (as well as, presumably, to masturbation, although this is not explicitly mentioned). While nocturnal emissions cannot be seen as controllable to the same extent that sexual intercourse or masturbation are, the rabbis do maintain that such emissions are often results of sexual thoughts *(hirhur)* prior to one's sleep (for example, M. Miqva'ot 8.3, M. Zavim 2.2) and that nocturnal emissions can be prevented (for example, by staying awake at night; see M. Yoma 1.4–6). This is clearly not the case with female genital discharges and with male abnormal genital discharges.

68. As I mentioned, the purity legislation of Qumran presents a different picture, which homogenizes the impurity of seminal emissions with the impurity of other genital discharges, and minimizes the discrepancies between normal and abnormal male discharges. See Himmelfarb, *A Kingdom of Priests*, 98–112.

69. M. Hallah 4.8.

70. M. Kelim 1.8.

71. M. Pesahim 9.4.

72. See also M. Mo'ed Qatan 3.2; M. Niddah 10.4; M. Zavim 5.6; T. Berakhot 2.12; T. Pesahim 8.1, 8.9; T. Yoma 4.5; T. Kelim Baba Qamma 1.8, 1.14; T. Kelim Baba Metzi'a 11.1.

73. M. Niddah 1.7.

74. M. Niddah 2.1.

75. T. Niddah 2.8.

76. See also BT Niddah 13a; PT Niddah 2:1, 49d.

77. M. Niddah 10.3.

78. M. Zavim 1.1.

79. T. Zavim 2.4.

80. Aretaeus, *De causis et signis diuturnorum morborum*, bk. 2, chap. 5. The translation is quoted from John Moffat, *Aretæus on the Causes, Symptoms and Cure of Acute and Chronic Diseases* (London, 1875), 226. For a discussion of this passage, see Rebecca Flemming, *Medicine and the Making of Roman Women: Gender, Nature, and Authority from Celsus to Galen* (Oxford: Oxford University Press, 2000), 212–13.

81. See Thomas Laqueur, *Making Sex: Body and Gender from the Greeks to Freud* (Cambridge, MA: Harvard University Press, 1990), 25–62; Lesley Dean-Jones, *Women's Bodies in Classical Greek Science* (Oxford: Clarendon Press, 1996); Helen King, *Hippocrates' Women:*

*Reading the Female Body in Ancient Greece* (New York: Routledge, 1998), 21–40; Flemming, *Medicine and the Making of Roman Women*, 196–215.

82. Moffat, *Aretæus*, 226.

83. The same notion is discussed by Clement of Alexandria, who identifies the lack of hair as an indication of the lack of density of semen, which is brought about by insufficient heat; see Gleason, *Making Men*, 67–70.

84. As Maud Gleason showed, the prevalent notion that men can be feminine and women can be masculine led to the view that one's gender traits can change in the course of one's life, both as a result of various bodily conditions and as a result of rigorous training and lifestyle choices. See Gleason, *Making Men*, 55–81.

85. Aristotle, *Generation of Animals* 4:1, 765b. For a discussion of this theme, see Robert Con Davis, "Aristotle, Gynecology, and the Body Sick with Desire," in *Textual Bodies: Changing Bodies of Literary Representation*, ed. L. H. Lefkovitz (Albany: SUNY Press, 1997), 35–58, esp. 45.

86. See Levinson, "Cultural Androgyny in Rabbinic Literature," 119–40. For a contestation of Levinson's claim on the fluidity of gender in rabbinic literature, see Charlotte Fonrobert, "The Semiotics of the Sexed Body in Early Halakhic Discourse," in *Closed and Open: Readings of Rabbinic Texts*, ed. M. Kraus (Piscataway: Gorgias Press, 2006), 69–96. Fonrobert persuasively shows that in rabbinic legal texts sex is decided based solely on one's sexual organs, rather than on one's appearance or behavior. However, as Sarra Lev pointed out, even though the rabbis defined man and woman as halakhic categories strictly based on their genitalia, it is very clear that they were highly aware of the ambivalence and fluidity of gender as a cultural phenomenon. The very fact that the rabbis made a point of asserting multiple times that the *saris* (eunuch) is a man for every halakhic purpose indicates that there were also competing discourses in which men with feminine features were not seen as men. See Sarra Lev, "They Treat Him as a Man and See Him as a Woman: The Tannaitic Understanding of the Congenital Eunuch," *Jewish Studies Quarterly* 17, no. 3 (2010): 213–43. Following Lev, I contend that while the rabbis based their legal gender discourse on a cut-and-dry distinction between males and females, they were significantly influenced by cultural notions of "flawed" or "lacking" masculinity.

87. For the argument that only men were considered to be persons in the full sense of the word in the Mishnah, see Judith Romney Wegner, *Chattel or Person? The Status of Women in the Mishnah* (New York: Oxford University Press, 1992). For the argument that the unspecified person in rabbinic discourse is male, see Charlotte Fonrobert, "The Human Body in Rabbinic Legal Discourse," in *The Cambridge Companion to the Talmud and Rabbinic Literature*, ed. C. E. Fonrobert and M. S. Jaffee (New York: Cambridge University Press, 2007), 270–94, at 279.

88. See Benjamin Isaac, *The Invention of Racism in Classical Antiquity* (Princeton: Princeton University Press, 2004), 153–55.

89. M. Zavim 1.2–6.

90. M. Zavim 2.3.

91. M. Zavim 2.2. For a discussion of this passage in light of purity texts from Qumran, see Baumgarten, "Zab Impurity," 273–77.

92. In this respect, this passage resonates with other rabbinic "obliterations" of biblical laws, for example, T. Sanhedrin 11.6, 14.1; T. Nega'im 6.1.

93. On this theme in Greek literature, see Isaac, *The Invention of Racism*, 257–93, esp. 292; in Roman literature, see ibid., 324–51, esp. 340.

94. This observation might seem to be in tension with Daniel Boyarin's argument, according to which the rabbis identified themselves as effeminate as a form of resistance to the "masculine" Hellenistic culture; see Daniel Boyarin, "Homotopia: The Feminized Jewish Male and the Lives of Women in Late Antiquity," *Differences* 7 (1995): 41–81. However, as Boyarin acknowledges elsewhere, this theme is prevalent only in Babylonian texts, whereas rabbinic Palestinian texts largely endorsed Hellenistic notions of the ideal masculine body. See Daniel Boyarin, "Literary Fat Rabbis: On the Historical Origins of the Grotesque Body," *Journal for the History of Sexuality* 1, no. 4 (1991): 551–84, esp. 574–75.

95. Isaac, *The Invention of Racism*, 472, 481, 499.

96. As Craig Williams put it, "A common theme in the ancient sources is that true Roman men, who possess *virtus* by birthright, rightfully exercise their dominion or *imperium* not only over women but also over foreigners, themselves implicitly likened to women." See Craig Williams, *Roman Homosexuality* (New York: Oxford University Press, 1999), 135.

97. Joshua Levinson identified a similar tendency to the feminization of the other in later rabbinic narratives, and showed how Rome—through the figure of Esau—is depicted by the rabbis as a feminine and penetrated man. See Levinson, "Cultural Androgyny," 132.

98. Laqueur, *Making Sex*.

99. Anne Carson, "Putting Her in Her Place: Woman, Dirt and Desire," in *Before Sexuality: The Construction of Erotic Experience in the Ancient Greek World*, ed. D. Halperin, J. Winkler, and F. Zeitlin (Princeton: Princeton University Press, 1990), 135–70. See also Catharine Edwards, *The Politics of Immorality in Ancient Rome* (Cambridge: Cambridge University Press, 1993), 63–97.

100. Michael Satlow, "Try to Be a Man: The Rabbinic Construction of Masculinity," *Harvard Theological Review* 89, no. 1 (1996): 19–40. See also Levinson, "Cultural Androgyny."

101. As Stanley Stowers noted, the characterization of Jews as possessing greater sexual self-control than Gentiles is a prevalent theme already in Second Temple literature. See Stanley Stowers, *A Rereading of Romans: Justice, Jews, and Gentiles* (New Haven: Yale University Press, 1994), 58–65.

102. Satlow, "Try to Be a Man," 35–36.

CHAPTER 6

1. Levinson, "From Narrative Practice to Cultural Poetics," 346–47, and see his references there.

2. Ibid., 353.

3. See Hadot, *Philosophy as a Way of Life*, 206–13; Nussbaum, *The Therapy of Desire*; Vincent L. Wimbush and Richard Valantasis, eds., *Asceticism* (New York: Oxford University Press, 1998), xxix; Maria Antonaccio, "Contemporary Forms of *Askesis* and the Return of Spiritual Exercises," *Annual of the Society of Christian Ethics* 18 (1998): 69–92.

4. On this, see Paula Fredriksen, *Sin: The Early History of an Idea* (Princeton: Princeton University Press, 2012), 100–34.

5. See Schofer, *The Making of a Sage,* 9–11; Ron Naiweld, "Au commencement était la pratique"; Naiweld, "Lorsque la terre trembla: La muraille quie protège le Talmud de la philosophie" *Tzafon* 58 (2009–2010): 59–76.

6. See Levinson, "From Narrative Practice," 346: "My working assumption is that the [rabbinic] legal discourse constructs a specific type of subject which is interpellated not only as a subject-to-the-law, but is also called upon to assume a certain subject identity through-the-law."

7. Bartsch, *The Mirror of the Self,* 9.

8. M. Niddah 4.1–2.

9. For an attempt to retrace the different traditions and systems of knowledge of these groups, see Regev, "On Blood, Impurity, and Relation to the Body."

10. As Daniel Boyarin pointed out, this passage is of special importance in tracing the roots of rabbinic "heresiology." See Daniel Boyarin, *Borderlines: The Partition of Judeo-Christianity* (Philadelphia: University of Pennsylvania Press, 2004), 62–63. See also Fonrobert, "When Women Walk in the Ways of Their Fathers."

11. See, for example, M. Tohorot 5.8.

12. For different theories on the term *am ha-aretz* and on the group or groups it was used to denote, see Büchler, *Der galiläische Am ha-Ares*; Oppenheimer, *The Am ha-aretz*; David Rokeah, "Am ha-aretz, the First Pious Ones, Jesus and the Christians" [in Hebrew], in *Mekhqare Talmud* 3, ed. Y. Sussman and D. Rosenthal (Jerusalem: Magnes Press, 2005), 876–903. For an extensive survey of scholarship on the topic and for alternative suggestions, see Furstenberg, "Eating in a State of Purity," 209–62.

13. Indeed, according to Furstenberg, laxness in the observance of purity is the *only* defining characteristic of the People of the Land in the Mishnah. Furstenberg, "Eating in a State of Purity," 209–20.

14. See, for instance, M. Hagigah 3.4–7 and T. Hagigah 3.22–24; and see Furstenberg, "Eating in a State of Purity," 278–87. The notion that the People of the Land are particularly careful when the purity of priests and their possessions is concerned can also be discerned in M. Tohorot 5.8, 7.7, 8.2.

15. In the Tosefta, the People of the Land are distinctly mentioned as trustworthy in regard to corpse impurity (T. Tohorot 8.12, 9.4). However, several mishnaic sources suggest that when articles are deposited in the domain of the People of the Land they contract corpse impurity immediately (M. Eduyot 1.14; M. Tohorot 8.2). As Furstenberg persuasively suggested, the most probable explanation for this discrepancy is that the People of the Land were trusted in regard to the immersion and purification of their bodies from corpse impurity, but had different and more lenient standards regarding the corpse impurity of articles. Furstenberg, "Eating in a State of Purity," 265–73.

16. In this I differ from Furstenberg, who identifies the impurity of the People of the Land as intrinsic in nature, stemming from the fact that they are not members of the group of the "pure ones." Furstenberg, "Eating in a State of Purity," 221–45. I believe that Furstenberg's understanding is based on a misreading of M. Hagigah 3.7, according to which "if one immersed [for purity] but was not held [as pure]—it is as if he did not immerse" *(taval ve-lo huhzaq ke'ilu lo taval)*. Furstenberg assumes that one has to be considered pure *before* one's immersion, that is, one must be initially recognized as part of a particular social circle whose members are committed to purity, and that if he is not thus recognized he can never

become pure. The simpler reading, however, is that one has to be publicly recognized as pure *after* one immerses, that is, that "secret" immersion does not suffice to render one pure. If this reading is undertaken, there is no reason to assume that the People of the Land cannot purify themselves if they wish to do so, as long as their act of purification is accredited.

17. This is in opposition to later Babylonian traditions, which identify the People of the Land as hateful to the rabbis and contemptuous of the Torah; see Christine Hayes, "The 'Other' in Rabbinic Literature," in *The Cambridge Companion to the Talmud and Rabbinic Literature,* ed. C.E. Fonrobert and M.S. Jaffee (New York: Cambridge University Press, 2007), 243–69, at 260–62.

18. This is indeed one of the ways in which the People of the Land are defined in T. Avodah Zarah 3.10: "Which is [one of] the People of the Land? One who does not eat his ordinary food in a state of purity."

19. Consider, for example, M. Tohorot 1.10, in which it is suggested that the People of the Land fail to observe the laws of purity in full because they are not proficient in the intricate workings of shift impurity.

20. M. Tohorot 7.3.

21. On the category of *haverim,* "members," see Birenboim, "Observance of the Laws of Bodily Purity," 46–49.

22. M. Tohorot 7.4.

23. M. Tohorot 3.8.

24. The question of who the ones that the Mishnah contrasts with the People of the Land are, and what exactly the appropriate title for those who are characterized by their stringency in the observance of purity is, has received substantial scholarly attention. The three main suggestions are that the oppositional counterparts of the People of the Land are either Pharisees *(perushim),* "Members" *(haverim),* or Disciples of the Sages *(talmide hakhamim).* For a thorough survey of the existing scholarship on this question, and for helpful suggestions for reconstructing the meaning and context of each of these terms, see Birenboim, "Observance of the Laws of Bodily Purity," 23–68.

25. See M. Demai 2.2–3, 3.4, 6.9; M. Shevi'it 5.9; M. Tohorot 7.1–7.7, 8.1–5. There are numerous additional rulings regarding interaction with the People of the Land in the Tosefta, especially in chapters 2 and 3 of tractate *Demai.*

26. See M. Tohorot 3.6, 6.6; and see my discussion in the first chapter.

27. M. Tohorot 5.1–6.

28. Somewhat different is the case of skin afflictions, the discernment of which cannot exactly be described as a process of self-examination, since the biblical ordinance is that all inspections for skin afflictions be performed by a priest. Here too one could suggest that it is incumbent upon every individual to examine him- or herself regularly for suspicious skin afflictions and consequentially to seek the authorized opinion of a priest (or of a sage, according to the rabbis; see M. Nega'im 3.1). However, the Mishnah does not suggest any indication of self-examination on the part of the afflicted person. Presumably, the emphasis on self-examination in the context of genital discharges and not of skin afflictions stems not only from the different ways in which these conditions are addressed in the biblical text, but also from the assumption that skin afflictions are apparent to others whereas genital discharges are mostly known only to the one who experiences them; on this point see Halberstam, *Law and Truth,* 17–22.

29. M. Niddah 10.3.
30. See Fonrobert, *Menstrual Purity*, 43–55.
31. M. Niddah 1.7, 2.1.
32. M. Niddah 9.1.
33. M. Niddah 8.1–4, 9.3–5.
34. Leviticus 15:16.
35. M. Miqva'ot 8.2.
36. M. Miqva'ot 8.3.
37. For example, M. Tohorot 4.3.
38. M. Tohorot 5.9.
39. For example, M. Oholot 16.1; T. Ahilot 15.13.
40. For example, T. Kelim Baba Metzia 5.3; T. Kelim Baba Batra 1.2.
41. See, for example, M. Niddah 8.3; T. Niddah 1.9, 4.3–6, 5.3, 6.17, 7.3; BT Niddah 6b.
42. Fonrobert, *Menstrual Purity*, 107–10.
43. Halberstam, *Law and Truth*, 29.
44. See M. Niddah 2.6–7. As Fonrobert noted, there is absolutely no indication in the Bible that the discernment of menstrual impurity requires any set of skills or expertise: the idea that certain genital bloods are pure and others are impure is distinctly a rabbinic innovation. Fonrobert, *Menstrual Purity*, 104–8. See also Halberstam, *Law and Truth*, 26–32.
45. Fonrobert, "Blood and Law," 260.
46. See M. Niddah 3.2–7.
47. See, for instance, BT Berakhot 4a; BT Baba Metzi'a 84b; BT Niddah 20b.
48. Here I concur with Halberstam, *Law and Truth*, 29, pace Fonrobert, *Menstrual Purity*, 114.
49. Leviticus 18:19; 20:18.
50. See Fonrobert, *Menstrual Purity*, 20–22, 46–47.
51. As argued by Fonrobert, *Menstrual Purity*, 103–27.
52. See Leviticus 13:1–3; Deuteronomy 21.5; see also M. Nega'im 2.5.
53. Hadot, *Philosophy as a Way of Life*, 79–144; Hadot, *What Is Ancient Philosophy?* trans. Michael Chase (Cambridge, MA: Harvard University Press, 2002), 91–145. See also Nussbaum, *The Therapy of Desire*, 316–58; Antonaccio, "Contemporary Forms of *Askesis*."
54. Hadot, *Philosophy as a Way of Life*, 84.
55. Ibid., 134–35. See also Michael Trapp, *Philosophy in the Roman Empire: Ethics, Politics, and Society* (Aldershot, UK: Ashgate, 2007), 83–87.
56. Bartsch, *Mirror of the Self*, 193.
57. Ibid., 9.
58. Epistle 11.8–10, in L. D. Reynolds, ed., *L. Annaeius Seneca, Ad Lucilium Epistolae Morales*, vol. 1, I–XIII (New York: Oxford University Press, 1965), 25–26. See also Bartsch, *Mirror of the Self*, 211.
59. *De Ira* 3.36, in John W. Basore, ed., *L. Annaeius Seneca, Moral Essays* (Cambridge, MA: Harvard University Press, 1994), 1:340.
60. See Johan Thom, *The Pythagorean Golden Verses* (Leiden: Brill, 1995), 163, 167. Seneca himself attributes this practice to Sextius, his Pythagorean teacher.
61. James Ker, "Seneca on Self-Examination: On Anger 3.36," in *Seneca and the Self*, ed. S. Bartsch and D. Wray (New York: Cambridge University Press, 2009), 160–87.

62. See also Seneca, *Ad Lucilium Epistolae Morales,* epistle 83.1–2.//
63. See Bartsch, *Mirror of the Self,* 191–216, 236–44.
64. *De Ira* 2.36, in Seneca, *Moral Essays* 1:248. See also Bartsch, *Mirror of the Self,* 187–88.
65. See Foucault, *The Care of the Self,* 37–68, 97–144.
66. Andrew Crislip, *From Monastery to Hospital: Christian Monasticism and the Transformation of Healthcare in Late Antiquity* (Ann Arbor: University of Michigan Press, 2005), 39.
67. On Marcus Aurelius's letters to Fronto, see Foucault, *Technologies of the Self,* 28–30; Foucault, *The Hermeneutics of the Subject,* 157–64.
68. Perkins, *The Suffering Self,* 193–99.
69. Yair Furstenberg similarly identified the notion that mental distraction brings about impurity, and argued that this trend in mishnaic thought is particular to the Yavneh generation. However, Furstenberg suggested a very broad definition for distraction, which also includes leaving objects physically unattended, whereas I am focusing on cases in which the *mental* dedication to purity is specifically said to be flawed. Furstenberg, "Eating in a State of Purity," 290–95.
70. M. Tohorot 7.8.
71. Furstenberg, "Eating in a State of Purity," 291.
72. T. Kelim Baba Batra 1.2.
73. T. Kelim Baba Batra 1.3. Cf. BT Hagigah 20a; PT Hagigah 3:2, 79a. For a discussion of these passages in terms of the weaving technology described in them, see Peskowitz, *Spinning Fantasies,* 88–89.
74. I am indebted to Joshua Levinson for drawing my attention to these passages in Epictetus and to their relevance to rabbinic materials. Levinson himself discusses the relevance of "attention" to rabbinic themes of self-reflection in "From Narrative Practice to Cultural Poetics," 353–55.
75. Hadot, *Philosophy as a Way of Life,* 84.
76. See Ciarán Mc Mahon, "The Prehistory of the Concept of Attention," PhD diss., University College Dublin, 2007, 45–53.
77. Ibid., 66–77.
78. Epictetus, *Discourses* IV.12, 6. Quoted from George Long, *A Selection from the Discourses of Epictetus with the Encheiridion* (Teddington: Echo Library, 2009), 90.
79. Mc Mahon, *The Prehistory of the Concept of Attention,* 39.
80. Hadot, *Philosophy as a Way of Life,* 84–85.
81. Epictetus, *Discourses* II. 16, 15; Long, *Discourses of Epictetus,* 44.
82. For a survey of the history of the interpretation of the Delphic Oracle, see Eliza Gregory Wilkins, "'Know Thyself' in Greek and Latin Literature," PhD diss., University of Chicago, 1917; Hans Dieter Betz, "The Delphic Maxim ΓΝΩΘΙ ΣΑΥΤΟΝ in Hermetic Interpretation," *Harvard Theological Review* 63, no. 4 (1970): 465–84.
83. For extensive studies on the term and its meanings, see Helen North, *Sophrosyne: Self-Knowledge and Self-Restraint in Greek Literature* (Ithaca: Cornell University Press, 1966); Adriaan Rademaker, *Sophrosyne and the Rhetoric of Self-Restraint: Polysemy and Persuasive Use of an Ancient Greek Value Term* (Leiden: Brill, 2005).
84. North, *Sophrosyne;* See also Julia Annas, "Self-Knowledge in Plato," in *Platonic Investigations,* ed. D. J. O'Meara (Washington, DC: Catholic University of America Press,

1985), 111–38; Donald P. Verene, *Philosophy and the Return to Self-Knowledge* (New Haven: Yale University Press, 1997), 75–76; Joseph Roisman, *The Rhetoric of Manhood: Masculinity in the Attic Orators* (Berkeley: University of California Press, 2005), 163–203; Bartsch, *The Mirror of the Self*, 24–25.

85. Indeed, in Plato's *Charmides* (164d) we find the statement that self-knowledge *(to gignōskein heauton)*, self-control, and *sōphrosynē* are essentially one and the same; see North, *Sophrosyne*, 157.

86. See North, *Sophrosyne*, 258–311; Carlin Barton, "The Roman Blush: The Delicate Matter of Self-Control," in *Constructions of the Classical Body*, ed. J. Porter (Ann Arbor: University of Michigan Press, 2002), 212–34.

87. See Aline Rousselle, *Porneia: On Desire and the Body in Antiquity*, trans. F. Pheasant (Oxford: Basil Blackwell, 1993), 5–23.

88. See Roisman, *The Rhetoric of Manhood*, 162–85; Edwards, *The Politics of Immorality in Ancient Rome*, 78.

89. As scholars noted, the ideal of *sōphrosynē* in women is manifested primarily in sexual chastity. See Bruce Winter, *Roman Wives, Roman Widows: The Appearance of New Women and the Pauline Communities* (Grand Rapids: W. B. Eerdmans, 2003), 59–64; Roisman, *The Rhetoric of Manhood*, 176; Reydams-Schils, *The Roman Stoics*, 168. On the influence of this theme on early Christianity, see Peter Brown, *The Body and Society: Men, Women, and Sexual Renunciation in Early Christianity* (New York: Columbia University Press, 1988), 9–12; Rousselle, *Porneia*, 129–40.

90. For a similar claim about women in tannaitic sources, see Jordan Rosenblum, *Food and Identity in Early Rabbinic Judaism* (New York: Cambridge University Press, 2010), 104–24.

91. On such epithets, and especially on the expression *bat yisra'el*, "a daughter of Israel," see Cynthia Baker, "When Jews Were Women," *History of Religions* 45, no. 2 (2005): 114–34.

92. T. Demai 2.17.

93. For this reason, T. Avodah Zarah 3.9 mentions that one who is careful regarding the observance of purity is advised not to give his daughter in marriage to one of the People of the Land. On this passage in the Tosefta and its meanings, see Furstenberg, "Eating in a State of Purity," 216–18.

94. See Ishay Rosen-Zvi, "Do Women Have a *Yetzer*? Anthropology, Ethics, and Gender in Rabbinic Literature," in *Spiritual Authority: Struggles over Cultural Power in Jewish Thought*, ed. H. Kreisel, B. Huss, and U. Ehrlich [in Hebrew] (Be'er Sheva: Ben Gurion University Press, 2010), 21–34.

95. See Carson, "Putting Her in Her Place"; Flemming, *Medicine and the Making of Roman Women*, 215–28.

96. See M. Kelim 8.11; M. Niddah 1.2; M. Makhshirin 6.8; and see Fonrobert, *Menstrual Purity*, 57–65.

97. As Charlotte Fonrobert showed, the rabbinic science of menstrual impurity shared this premise with Graeco-Roman gynecology, which the rabbis were in many ways emulating. Fonrobert, *Menstrual Purity*, 130–47.

98. See also M. Arakhin 2.1.

99. M. Niddah 6.14.

100. In the Babylonian Talmud (BT Niddah 54a), the appellation "inept ones" *(shotot)* is interpreted as referring to women who get confused when keeping track of their cycle, and

thus do not know whether their bleeding is normal or abnormal *(to'ot)*. Consequentially, this was the interpretation that all the commentators of the Mishnah took on. This interpretation, however, makes little sense, and I chose to follow the reading of Albeck, *The Six Orders of the Mishnah*, 6:396.

101. Flemming, *Medicine and the Making of Roman Women*, 221.

102. The only other context in which the contrast between the mishnaic subject and the People of the Land is equally dominant is that of tithes-giving.

103. T. Tohorot 8.13. Cf. BT Hagigah 20a.

104. A similar notion appears also in T. Tohorot 8.14–15, in which it is implied that an object becomes impure as soon as it is left unattended, unless the owner is known not to have taken his or her mind off of the object. Particularly pertinent for our case is T. Tohorot 8.15, which mentions a case in which a woman was straining both pure and impure liquids in a barrel of heave-offering, and the Sages, as the story seems to suggest, did not render the entire barrel impure, because the woman did not take her mind off of it. Unfortunately, the text is quite corrupted here, and the crucial word "not" is missing before the words "take her mind off of it." In the text as it stands before us appears the somewhat confusing version "and the Sages did not render it impure because she took her mind off of it" *(ve-lo tim'uha mipne she-hesiha da'ata mimena)*. This version can be easily amended by adding the word *lo*, as several commentators have suggested; see Lieberman, *Tosefet Rishonim*, 4:88.

105. BT Hagigah 20b.

106. M. Tohorot 7.7.

107. I am following Maimonides's interpretation, which understands the appellation "Israel" in the second clause of the Mishnah as contrasted to "priest." R. Obadiah of Berteniro mentions an alternative version of the text, according to which the appellation "Israel" is contrasted to "Gentile" *(ba-goy kelav tehorin u-be-yisrael ad she-yomar haya be-libi leshomram)*.

108. M. Zevahim 2.2, 3.1, 3.3–6; see Levinson, "From Narrative Practice to Cultural Poetics," 351–52; Ishay Rosen-Zvi, "Realism and Nominalism in the Mishnah: The Case of Thoughts," paper delivered at New York University, April 2012.

EPILOGUE

1. M. Hagigah 1.8.

2. In the epistles of Paul we find a systematic utilization of the biblical language of purity and impurity to discuss matters of heart, mind, and social and sexual conduct rather than of ritual status: see Newton, *The Concept of Purity*, 52–116; L. William Countryman, *Dirt, Greed, and Sex: Sexual Ethics in the New Testament and Their Implications for Today* (Philadelphia: Fortress Press, 1988), 97–123. This rhetoric certainly did not dispense with the practical understanding of Levitical purity laws, at least not for Jews: see Paula Fredriksen, "Paul, Purity, and the 'Ekklesia' of the Gentiles," in *The Beginnings of Christianity*, ed. J. Pastor and M. Mor (Jerusalem: Yad Ben Zvi, 2005), 205–17; Fredriksen, "Judaizing the Nations: The Ritual Demands of Paul's Gospel," *New Testament Studies* 56, no. 2 (2010): 232–52. Nonetheless, this rhetoric did lay the foundations for a new and largely metaphorical way of understanding the requirements of purity.

BIBLIOGRAPHY

Aderet, Avraham. *From Destruction to Restoration: The Way of Yavneh in the Rehabilitation of the Nation.* [In Hebrew.] Jerusalem, Magnes Press, 1990.
Aho, James. *The Orifice as a Sacrifical Site: Culture, Organization, and the Body.* New York: Walter de Gruyter, 2002.
Albeck, Hanoch. *The Six Orders of the Mishnah with Commentary.* [In Hebrew.] Tel Aviv: Bialik Institute, 1959.
———. *Studies in Baraita and Tosefta.* [In Hebrew.] Jerusalem: Mosad ha-Rav Kook, 1954.
Alexander, Elizabeth Shanks. *Transmitting Mishnah: The Shaping Influence of Oral Tradition.* New York: Cambridge University Press, 2006.
Alon, Gedalyahu. *Studies in Jewish History in the Times of the Second Temple and the Talmud.* Vol.1. [In Hebrew.] Tel-Aviv: Ha-Kibbutz ha-me'uhad, 1957.
Annas, Julia. "Self-Knowledge in Plato." In *Platonic Investigations,* edited by D. J. O'Meara, 111–38. Washington, DC: Catholic University of America Press, 1985.
Antonaccio, Maria. "Contemporary Forms of *Askesis* and the Return of Spiritual Exercises." *Annual of the Society of Christian Ethics* 18 (1998): 69–92.
Anzieu, Didier. *The Skin Ego.* Translated by C. Turner. New Haven: Yale University Press, 1989.
*Aretæus on the Causes, Symptoms and Cure of Acute and Chronic Diseases.* Translated by John Moffat. London, 1875.
Ariel, Azaria. "The Decree on the Impurity of Glassware." [In Hebrew.] *Ma'alin ba-kodesh* 10 (2005): 125–58.
Ariès, Philippe. *The Hour of Our Death.* Translated by H. Weaver. New York: Random House, 1982.
Assmann, Jan, and Guy Stroumsa, eds. *Transformations of the Inner Self in Ancient Religions.* Leiden: Brill, 1999.
Atkins, Kim, ed. *Self and Subjectivity.* Oxford: Blackwell, 2005.

Babb, Lawrence. "The Physiology of Redemption." *History of Religions* 22, no. 4 (1983): 293–312.
Baker, Cynthia. *Rebuilding the House of Israel: Architectures of Gender in Jewish Antiquity.* Stanford: Stanford University Press, 2002.
———. "When Jews Were Women." *History of Religions* 45, no. 2 (2005): 114–34.
Balberg, Mira. "Pricing Persons: Consecration, Compensation, and Individuality in the Mishnah." *Jewish Quarterly Review* 103, no. 2 (2013): 169–95.
———. "Rabbinic Authority, Medical Rhetoric, and Body Hermeneutics in Mishnah Nega'im." *AJS Review* 35, no. 2 (2011): 323–46.
Barthes, Roland. *Elements of Semiology.* Translated by A. Lavers and C. Smith. New York: Hill and Wang, 1973.
Barton, Carlin. "The Roman Blush: The Delicate Matter of Self-Control." In *Constructions of the Classical Body,* edited by J. Porter, 212–34. Ann Arbor: University of Michigan Press, 2002.
Bartsch, Shadi. *The Mirror of the Self: Sexuality, Self-Knowledge, and the Gaze in the Early Roman Empire.* Chicago: University of Chicago Press, 2006.
Bartsch, Shadi, and David Wray, eds. *Seneca and the Self.* New York: Cambridge University Press, 2009.
Basore, John, ed. *L. Annaeus Seneca: Moral Essays.* Cambridge, MA: Harvard University Press, 1994.
Baumgarten, Albert. *The Flourishing of Jewish Sects in the Maccabean Era: An Interpretation.* Leiden: Brill, 1997.
Baumgarten, Joseph. "The Essene Avoidance of Oil and the Laws of Purity." *Revue de Qumran* 6, no. 2 (1967): 183–92.
———. "The Halakha in Miqsat Ma'ase ha-Torah (MMT)." *Journal of the American Oriental Society* 116, no. 3 (1996): 512–16.
———. "Liquids and Susceptibility to Defilement in New 4Q Texts." *Jewish Quarterly Review* 85, no. 1–2 (1995): 91–100.
———. "The Pharisaic-Sadducean Controversies about Purity and the Qumran Texts." *Journal of Jewish Studies* 31 (1980): 157–70.
———. "The Red Cow Purification Rites in Qumran Texts." *Journal of Jewish Studies* 46, no. 1–2 (1995): 112–19.
———. "Tohorot." In *Qumran Cave 4 XXV: Halakhic Texts,* Discoveries in the Judean Desert 35, edited by J. Baumgarten, T. Elgvin, E. Eshel, E. Larson, M. R. Lehmann, S. Pfann, and L. H. Schiffman, 79–122. Oxford: Clarendon Press, 1999.
———. "Zab Impurity in Qumran and Rabbinic Law." *Journal of Jewish Studies* 45, no. 2 (1994): 273–77.
Bazak, Jacob. "The Legal Status of the Fetus in Jewish Halacha and in Israeli Law." *Jewish Law Association Studies* 8 (2000): 1–5.
Berkowitz, Beth. *Execution and Invention: Death Penalty Discourse in Early Rabbinic and Christian Cultures.* New York: Oxford University Press, 2006.
Betz, Hans. "The Delphic Maxim ΓΝΩΘΙ ΣΑΥΤΟΝ in Hermetic Interpretation." *Harvard Theological Review* 63, no. 4 (1970): 465–84.
Birenboim, Hanan. "Observance of the Laws of Bodily Purity in Jewish Society in the Land of Israel during the Second Temple Period." [In Hebrew.] PhD diss., Hebrew University, Jerusalem, 2006.

Bockmuehl, Markus. *Jewish Law in Gentile Churches: Halakhah and the Beginning of Christian Public Ethics.* Edinburgh: T & T Clark, 2000.
Bokser, Ben Zion. *Pharisaic Judaism in Transition: R. Eliezer the Great and Jewish Reconstruction after the War with Rome.* New York: Bloch, 1935.
Booth, Roger. *Jesus and the Laws of Purity: Tradition and Legal History in Mark 7.* JSNT Supplement Series 13. Sheffield: JSOT Press, 1986.
Bowersock, Glen. *Greek Sophists in the Roman Empire.* Oxford: Oxford University Press, 1969.
Boyarin, Daniel. *Borderlines: The Partition of Judeo-Christianity.* Philadelphia: University of Pennsylvania Press, 2004.
———. *Carnal Israel: Reading Sex in Talmudic Culture.* Berkeley: University of California Press, 1993.
———. "Homotopia: The Feminized Jewish Male and the Lives of Women in Late Antiquity." *Differences* 7 (1995): 41–81.
———. "Literary Fat Rabbis: On the Historical Origins of the Grotesque Body." *Journal for the History of Sexuality* 1, no. 4 (1991): 551–84.
Brakke, David, *Demons and the Making of the Monk: Spiritual Combat in Early Christianity.* Cambridge, MA: Harvard University Press, 2006.
Brakke, David, Michael Satlow, and Steven Weitzman, eds. *Religion and the Self in Antiquity.* Bloomington: Indiana University Press, 2005.
Broshi, Magen. "Qumran and the Essenes: Six Realms of Purity." [In Hebrew.] *Megillot* 2 (2004): 9–20.
Brown, Peter. *The Body and Society: Men, Women, and Sexual Renunciation in Early Christianity.* New York: Columbia University Press, 1988.
———. *The Cult of the Saints.* Chicago: University of Chicago Press, 1981.
Büchler, Adolf. *Der galiläische 'Am-ha 'Ares des zweiten Jahrhunderts: Beiträge zur innern Geschichte des palästinischen Judentums in den ersten zwei Jahrhunderten.* Vienna: A. Hölder, 1906.
———. "The Levitical Impurity of the Gentile in Palestine before the Year 70." *Jewish Quarterly Review* 17, no. 1 (1926): 1–81.
Burnyeat, M. F. "Idealism and Greek Philosophy: What Descartes Saw and Berkeley Missed." *Philosophical Review* 91, no. 1 (1982): 3–40.
Busby, Cecilia. "Permeable and Partible Persons: A Comparative Analysis of Gender and Body in South India and Melanesia." *Journal of the Royal Anthropological Institute* 3, no. 2 (1997): 261–78.
Bynum, Caroline Walker. *The Resurrection of the Body in Western Christianity, 200–1336.* New York: Columbia University Press, 1995.
Cancik-Lindemaier, Hildegard. "Corpus: Some Philological and Anthropological Remarks upon Roman Funerary Rites." In *Self, Soul and Body in Religious Experience,* edited by A. Baumgarten with J. Assmann and G. Stroumsa, 417–29. Leiden: Brill, 1998.
Carson, Anne. "Putting Her in Her Place: Woman, Dirt and Desire." In *Before Sexuality: The Construction of Erotic Experience in the Ancient Greek World,* edited by D. Halperin, J. Winkler, and F. Zeitlin, 135–70. Princeton: Princeton University Press, 1990.
Cary, Phillip. *Augustine's Invention of the Inner Self: The Legacy of a Christian Platonist.* New York: Oxford University Press, 2000.

Clay, Diskin. "Missing Persons, or the Selfless Greeks." In *The Quest of the Individual: Roots of Western Civilization,* edited by W. Carroll, J. Furlong, and C. Mann, 13–22. New York: Peter Lang, 1990.

Clements, Ronald. *God's Chosen People: A Theological Interpretation of the Book of Deuteronomy.* London: SCM Press, 1968.

Cohen, Jeffrey, and Gail Weiss, eds. *Thinking the Limits of the Body.* Albany: SUNY Press, 2003.

Cohen, Shaye. *The Beginnings of Jewishness: Boundaries, Varieties, Uncertainties.* Berkeley: University of California Press, 1999.

———. "The Significance of Yavneh: Pharisees, Rabbis, and the End of Jewish Sectarianism." *Hebrew Union College Annual* 55 (1984): 27–52.

Cohen, Yehezkel. "The Attitude to the Gentile in the Halacha and in Reality in the Tannaitic Period." [In Hebrew.] PhD diss., Hebrew University, Jerusalem, 1975.

Conklin, Beth. *Consuming Grief: Compassionate Cannibalism in an Amazonian Society.* Austin: University of Texas Press, 2001.

Conway, Colleen. "Toward a Well-Formed Subject: The Function of Purity Language in the Serek ha-Yahad." *Journal for the Study of the Pseudepigrapha* 21 (2000): 103–20.

Countryman, L. William. *Dirt, Greed, and Sex: Sexual Ethics in the New Testament and Their Implications for Today.* Philadelphia: Fortress Press, 1988.

Crislip, Andrew. *From Monastery to Hospital: Christian Monasticism and the Transformation of Healthcare in Late Antiquity.* Ann Arbor: University of Michigan Press, 2005.

Cuffel, Alexandra. *Gendering Disgust in Medieval Religious Polemic.* Notre Dame: University of Notre Dame Press, 2007.

Davies, Phillip. "Food, Drink, and Sects: The Question of Ingestion in the Qumran Sect." *Semeia* 86 (1999): 151–63.

Davis, Robert Con. "Aristotle, Gynecology, and the Body Sick with Desire." In *Textual Bodies: Changing Bodies of Literary Representation,* edited by L. H. Lefkovitz, 35–58. Albany: SUNY Press, 1997.

Dean-Jones, Lesley. *Women's Bodies in Classical Greek Science.* Oxford: Clarendon Press, 1996.

Deines, Roland. *Jüdische Steingefäße und pharisäische Frömmigkeit.* Tübingen: Mohr Siebeck, 1993.

Deines, Roland, and Martin Hengel, "E. P. Sanders' 'Common Judaism,' Jesus, and the Pharisees." *Journal of Theological Studies* 46, no. 1 (1995): 1–70.

Douglas, Mary. *Purity and Danger: An Analysis of the Concepts of Pollution and Taboo.* 1966; New York: Routledge, 2002.

DuBois, Page. "The Subject in Antiquity after Foucault." In *Rethinking Sexuality: Foucault and Classical Antiquity,* edited by D. Larmour, P. A. Miller, and C. Platte, 85–103. Princeton: Princeton University Press, 1998.

Dugan, John. *Making a New Man: Ciceronian Self-Fashioning in the Rhetorical Works.* New York: Cambridge University Press, 2005.

Dunn, James. "The Incident at Antioch (Gal 2:11–18)." *Journal for the Study of the New Testament* 18 (1983): 3–57.

Edelstein, Ludwig. *Ancient Medicine: Selected Papers.* Edited by O. Temkin and C. L. Temkin. Translated by C. L. Temkin. Baltimore: Johns Hopkins University Press, 1967.

Edwards, Catharine. *The Politics of Immorality in Ancient Rome*. Cambridge: Cambridge University Press, 1993.
Eilberg-Schwartz, Howard. *The Human Will in Judaism: The Mishnah's Philosophy of Intention*. Atlanta: Scholars Press, 1986.
———. *The Savage in Judaism: An Anthropology of Israelite Religion and Ancient Judaism*. Bloomington: Indiana University Press, 1990.
Elias, Norbert. *The Civilizing Process*. Translated by E. Jephcott. 1969; Oxford: Blackwell, 2000.
Engberg-Pedersen, Troels. "Philosophy of the Self in the Apostle Paul." In *Ancient Philosophy of the Self*, edited by P. Remes and J. Sihvola, 179–94. Springer.com, 2008.
———. "Stoic Philosophy and the Concept of a Person." In *The Person and the Human Mind: Issues in Ancient and Modern Philosophy*, edited by C. Gill, 109–35. Oxford: Oxford University Press, 1990.
Epictetus. *A Selection from the Discourses of Epictetus with the Encheiridion*. Translated by George Long. Teddington: Echo Library, 2009.
Epstein, Ya'akov Nahum. *The Gaonic Commentary on Order Tohorot Attributed to Rav Hayya Gaon*. [In Hebrew.] Jerusalem: Magnes Press, 1982.
———. *Introduction to Tannaitic Literature: Mishnah, Tosefta, and Halakhic Midrashim*. [In Hebrew.] Jerusalem: Magnes Press, 1959.
———. "Sifre Zutta Parashat Parah." [In Hebrew.] *Tarbitz* 1 (1930): 46–78.
Epstein, Ya'akov Nahum, and Ezra Zion Melamed, eds. *Mekhilta d'Rabbi Shimon ben Yokahi*. Jerusalem: Sha'are Rahamim, 1955.
Eshel, Esther. "Ritual of Purification." In *Qumran Cave 4 XXV: Halakhic Texts*, Discoveries in the Judean Desert 35, edited by J. Baumgarten, T. Elgvin, E. Eshel, E. Larson, M. R. Lehmann, S. Pfann, and L. H. Schiffman, 135–54. Oxford: Clarendon Press, 1999.
Eshel, Hanan. "CD 12:15–17 and the Stone Vessels Found at Qumran." In *The Damascus Document: A Centennial of Discovery*, edited by J. Baumgarten, E. G. Chazon, and A. Pinnick, 45–52. Leiden: Brill, 2000.
Fischel, Henry. *Rabbinic Literature and Greco-Roman Philosophy: A Study of Epicurea and Rhetorica in Early Midrashic Writings*. Leiden: Brill, 1973.
Fishbane, Simcha. *Deviancy in Early Rabbinic Literature: A Collection of Socio-Anthropological Essays*. Leiden: Brill, 2007.
Flemming, Rebecca. *Medicine and the Making of Roman Women: Gender, Nature, and Authority from Celsus to Galen*. Oxford: Oxford University Press, 2000.
———. "The Physicians at the Feast: The Place of Medical Knowledge at Athenaeus's Dinner-Table." In *Athenaeus and His World: Reading Greek Culture in the Roman Empire*, edited by D. Braund and J. Wilkins, 476–82. Exeter: University of Exeter Press, 2000.
Flusser, David. "The Dead Sea Sect and Pre-Pauline Christianity." *Scripta Hierosolymitana* 4 (1958): 215–66.
———. *Judaism and the Origins of Christianity*. [In Hebrew.] Tel Aviv: Sifriyat Poalim, 1979.
———. *Judaism of the Second Temple: The Jewish Sages and Their Literature*. Translated by A. Yadin. Grand Rapids: W. B. Eerdmans, 2009.
Fonrobert, Charlotte Elisheva. "Blood and Law: Uterine Fluids and Rabbinic Maps of Identity." In *Blood and the Boundaries of Jewish and Christian Identities in Late Antiquity*, edited by R. Boustan and A. Yoshiko Reed. Special issue, *Henoch* 30, no. 2 (2008): 243–66.

———. "The Human Body in Rabbinic Legal Discourse." In *The Cambridge Companion to the Talmud and Rabbinic Literature*, edited by C. E. Fonrobert and M. S. Jaffee, 270–94. New York: Cambridge University Press, 2007.

———. *Menstrual Purity: Rabbinic and Christian Reconstructions of Biblical Gender*. Stanford: Stanford University Press, 2000.

———. "On *Carnal Israel* and the Consequences: Talmudic Studies since Foucault." *Jewish Quarterly Review* 95, no. 3 (2005): 462–69.

———. "The Semiotics of the Sexed Body in Early Halakhic Discourse." In *Closed and Open: Readings of Rabbinic Texts*, edited by M. Kraus, 69–96. Piscataway: Gorgias Press, 2006.

———. "When Women Walk in the Way of Their Fathers: On Gendering the Rabbinic Claim for Authority." *Journal of the History of Sexuality* 10, no. 3–4 (2001): 398–415.

Forth, Christopher, and Ivan Crozier, eds. *Body Parts: Critical Explorations in Corporeality*. Lanham, MD: Lexington Books, 2005.

Foucault, Michel. *The Care of the Self*. Volume 3 of *The History of Sexuality*. Translated by R. Hurley. New York: Random House, 1986.

———. *The Hermeneutics of the Subject: Lectures at the College de France, 1981–1982*. Translated by G. Burchell. New York: Picador, 2001.

———. "On the Genealogy of Ethics: An Overview of Work in Progress." In *The Foucault Reader*, edited by P. Rabinow, 340–72. New York: Pantheon Books, 1984.

———. "Technologies of the Self." In *Technologies of the Self: A Seminar with Michel Foucault*, edited by L. Martin, H. Gutman, and P. Hutton, 16–49. Amherst: University of Massachusetts Press, 1988.

Fowler, Chris. *The Archeology of Personhood: An Anthropological Approach*. New York: Routledge, 2004.

Frankfurt, Harry. "Freedom of the Will and the Concept of a Person." *Journal of Philosophy* 68 (1971): 5–20.

———. "The Importance of What We Care About." *Synthese* 53 (1982): 257–72.

Frede, Michael. "A Notion of a Person in Epictetus." In *The Philosophy of Epictetus*, edited by T. Scaltsas and A. Mason, 153–82. New York: Oxford University Press, 2007.

Fredriksen, Paula. "Judaizing the Nations: The Ritual Demands of Paul's Gospel." *New Testament Studies* 56, no. 2 (2010): 232–52.

———. "Paul, Purity, and the 'Ekklesia' of the Gentiles." In *The Beginnings of Christianity*, edited by J. Pastor and M. Mor, 205–17. Jerusalem: Yad Ben Zvi, 2005.

———. *Sin: The Early History of an Idea*. Princeton: Princeton University Press, 2012.

Friedman, Shamma. "Mishnah-Tosefta Parallels." [In Hebrew.] *Proceedings of the 11th World Congress of Jewish Studies* C.1 (1994): 15–22.

———. "The Primacy of Tosefta to Mishnah in Synoptic Parallels." In *Introducing Tosefta: Textual, Intratextual, and Intertextual Studies*, edited by H. Fox, T. Meacham, and D. Kriger, 99–121. Hoboken: Ktav, 1999.

Furstenberg, Yair. "Defilement Penetrating the Body: A New Understanding of Contamination in Mark 7.15." *New Testament Studies* 54 (2008): 176–200.

———. "Eating in a State of Purity during the Tannitic Period: Tractate Teharot and Its Historical and Cultural Contexts." [In Hebrew.] PhD diss., Hebrew University, Jerusalem, 2010.

———. "The Purity of Hands and Eating of Ordinary Food in Purity: A Chapter in the History of Tannaitic Halakhah." [In Hebrew.] MA thesis, Hebrew University, Jerusalem, 2005.
*Galen on Diseases and Symptoms*. Translated by Ian Johnston. Cambridge: Cambridge University Press, 2006.
*Galen on the Properties of Foodstuffs*. Translated by Owen Powell. Cambridge: Cambridge University Press, 2003.
Gilat, Yitzhak. "Intention and Deed in the Teachings of the Tanna'im." [In Hebrew.] In *Studies in the Development of Halakhah*, 72–83. Ramat Gan: Bar Ilan University Press, 2001.
Gill, Christopher. *Personality in Greek Epic, Tragedy, and Philosophy: The Self in Dialogue*. Oxford: Clarendon Press, 1998.
———. *The Structured Self in Hellenistic and Roman Thought*. New York: Oxford University Press, 2006.
Ginzberg, Louis. *Halakhah and Aggadah*. [In Hebrew.] Tel-Aviv: Devir, 1960.
Ginzberg, Louis, and Burton Visotzky. *Genizah Studies in Memory of Doctor Solomon Shechter: Midrash and Haggadah*. 1928; Piscataway: Gorgias Press, 2003.
Gleason, Maud. *Making Men: Sophists and Self-Presentation in Ancient Rome*. Princeton: Princeton University Press, 1995.
Goldberg, Abraham. "The Tosefta—Companion to the Mishnah." In *The Literature of the Sages*, volume 1, edited by S. Safrai, 283–302. Assen: Van Gorcum, 1987.
———. *Tractate Oholot: Critical Edition*. [In Hebrew.] Jerusalem: Magnes Press, 1956.
Goodblatt, David. "The Place of the Pharisees in First Century Judaism: The State of the Debate." *Journal for the Study of Judaism* 20, no. 1 (1989): 12–30.
Goshen-Gottstein, Alon. "The Body as Image of God in Rabbinic Literature." *Harvard Theological Review* 87, no. 2 (1994): 171–95.
Graham, Emma-Jayne. "Becoming Persons, Becoming Ancestors: Personhood, Memory and the Corpse in Roman Rituals of Social Remembrance." *Archeological Dialogues* 16, no. 1 (2009): 51–74.
Grant, Mark. *Dieting for an Emperor: A Translation of Books 1 and 4 of Oribasius' Medical Compilations with an Introduction and Commentary*. Leiden: Brill, 1997.
Grosz, Elizabeth. *Volatile Bodies: Towards a Corporeal Feminism*. Bloomington: Indiana University Press, 1994.
Hadot, Pierre. *Philosophy as a Way of Life*. Edited by A. Davidson. Translated by M. Chase. Oxford: Blackwell, 1995.
———. *What Is Ancient Philosophy?* Translated M. Chase. Cambridge, MA: Harvard University Press, 2002.
Halberstam, Chaya. *Law and Truth in Biblical and Rabbinic Literature*. Bloomington: Indiana University Press, 2010.
Harrington, Hannah. "Did the Pharisees Eat Ordinary Food in a State of Ritual *Purity*?" *Journal for the Study of Judaism* 26 (1995): 42–54.
———. *The Impurity Systems of Qumran and the Rabbis*. Atlanta: Scholars Press, 1993.
———. "Purity and the Dead Sea Scrolls—Current Issues." *Currents in Biblical Research* 4, no. 3 (2006): 397–428.
———. *The Purity Texts: Companion to the Qumran Scrolls 5*. New York: T & T Clark, 2004.

Hauptman, Judith. *Rereading the Mishnah: A New Approach to Ancient Jewish Texts*. Tübingen: Mohr Siebeck, 2005.

Hayes, Christine. *Between the Babylonian and Palestinian Talmuds: Accounting for Halakhic Difference in Selected Sugyot from Tractate Avodah Zarah*. New York: Oxford University Press, 1997.

———. *Gentile Impurities and Jewish Identities: Intermarriage and Conversion from the Bible to the Talmud*. New York: Oxford University Press, 2002.

———. "Legal Realism and the Fashioning of Sectarians in Jewish Antiquity." In *Sects and Sectarianism in Jewish History*, edited by S. Stern, 119–46. Leiden: Brill, 2010.

———. "The 'Other' in Rabbinic Literature." In *The Cambridge Companion to the Talmud and Rabbinic Literature*, edited by C. E. Fonrobert and M. S. Jaffee, 243–69. New York: Cambridge University Press, 2007.

———. "What Is (the) Mishnah? Concluding Observations." *AJS Review* 32, no. 2 (2008): 291–97.

Himmelfarb, Martha. "Impurity and Sin in 4QD, 1QS, and 4Q512." *Dead Sea Discoveries* 8, no. 1 (2001): 9–37.

———. *A Kingdom of Priests: Ancestry and Merit in Ancient Judaism*. Philadelphia: University of Pennsylvania Press, 2006.

Hoffman, David Zvi, ed. *Midrash Tannaim on Deuteronomy*. Berlin: Itzkowski, 1908.

Hoffman, Lawrence. *Covenant of Blood: Circumcision and Gender in Rabbinic Judaism*. Chicago: University of Chicago Press, 1996.

Horovitz, Hayim Saul, ed. *Sifre on the Book of Numbers and Sifre Zutta*. 1917; Jerusalem: Shalem, 1992.

Horovitz, Hayim Saul, and Israel Avraham Rabin, eds. *Mekhilta d'Rabbi Ishmael*. 1930; Jerusalem: Shalem, 1998.

Isaac, Benjamin. *The Invention of Racism in Classical Antiquity*. Princeton: Princeton University Press, 2004.

Jaeger, Werner. *Paideia: The Ideals of Greek Culture*. Volume 3. Translated by G. Highet. New York: Oxford University Press, 1944.

Jaffee, Martin. *Torah in the Mouth: Writing and Oral Tradition in Palestinian Judaism, 200 B.C.E.–400 C.E.* New York: Oxford University Press, 2001.

Kahana, Menahem. *Fragments of Halakhic Midrashim from the Genizah*. Volume 1. [In Hebrew.] Jerusalem: Magnes Press, 2005.

———. *Sifre Zutta Deuteronomy*. [In Hebrew.] Jerusalem: Magnes Press, 2002.

———. "Studies in the Design and Purposes of Controversy in the Mishnah." [In Hebrew.] *Tarbitz* 73 (2004): 51–81.

Kahn, Charles. "Discovering the Will: From Homer to Augustine." In *The Question of Eclecticism: Studies in Later Greek Philosophy*, edited by J. M. Dillon and A. A. Long, 234–58. Berkeley: University of California Press, 1988.

Kamp, Kathryn. "From Village to Tell: Household Ethnoarchaeology in Syria." *Near Eastern Archeology* 63, no. 2 (2000): 84–93.

Kazen, Thomas. *Jesus and Purity Halakhah: Was Jesus Indifferent to Impurity?* Winona Lake: Eisenbrauns, 2010.

Ker, James. "Seneca on Self-Examination: On Anger 3.36." In *Seneca and the Self*, edited by S. Bartsch and D. Wray, 160–87. New York: Cambridge University Press, 2009.

Kessler, Gwynn. *Conceiving Israel: The Fetus in Rabbinic Narratives*. Philadelphia: University of Pennsylvania Press, 2009.
King, Helen. *Hippocrates' Women: Reading the Female Body in Ancient Greece*. New York: Routledge, 1998.
Kister, Menahem. "Law, Morality and Rhetoric in Some Sayings of Jesus." In *Studies in Ancient Midrash*, edited by J. Kugel, 145-54. Cambridge, MA: Harvard University Press, 2001.
Klawans, Jonathan. *Impurity and Sin in Ancient Judaism*. New York: Oxford University Press, 1999.
———. "The Impurity of Immorality in Ancient Judaism." *Journal of Jewish Studies* 48, no. 1 (1997): 1-16.
———. "Notions of Gentile Impurity in Ancient Judaism." *AJS Review* 20, no. 2 (1995): 285-312.
———. *Purity, Sacrifice, and the Temple: Symbolism and Supersessionism in the Study of Ancient Judaism*. New York: Oxford University Press, 2006.
Kottek, Samuel. "Medical Interest in Ancient Rabbinic Literature." In *The Literature of the Sages*, volume 2, edited by S. Safrai, P. Tomson, and Zeev Safrai, 485-96. Assen: Van Gorcum, 2006.
Kraemer, David. *The Meanings of Death in Rabbinic Judaism*. New York: Routledge, 1999.
Kristeva, Julia. *The Powers of Horror: An Essay on Abjection*. Translated by L. S. Roudiez. New York: Columbia University Press, 1982.
Lamb, Sarah. *White Saris and Sweet Mangoes: Aging, Gender, and Body in North India*. Berkeley: University of California Press, 2000.
Lambrecht, Jan. "Jesus and the Law: An Investigation of Mark 7:1-23." *Ephemerides Theologicae Lovanienses* 53 (1977): 24-82.
Laqueur, Thomas. *Making Sex: Body and Gender from the Greeks to Freud*. Cambridge, MA: Harvard University Press, 1990.
Lavee, Moshe. "A Convert Is Like a Newborn Child: The Concept and Its Implications in Rabbinic Literature." [In Hebrew.] PhD diss., Ben Gurion University in the Negev, 2004.
Lawrence, Jonathan. *Washing in Water: Trajectories of Ritual Bathing in the Hebrew Bible and Second Temple Literature*. Atlanta: Society of Biblical Literature, 2006.
Leder, Drew. "Flesh and Blood: A Proposed Supplement to Merleau-Ponty." *Human Studies* 13 (1990): 209-19.
Lev, Sarra. "They Treat Him as a Man and See Him as a Woman: The Tannaitic Understanding of the Congenital Eunuch." *Jewish Studies Quarterly* 17, no. 3 (2010): 213-43.
Levin, Benjamin. *Otzar ha-Geonim*. Haifa and Jerusalem, 1928-1953.
Levine, Baruch. *Numbers 1-20: A New Translation with Introduction and Commentary*. Anchor Bible 4A. New York: Doubleday, 1993.
Levinson, Joshua. "Bodies and Bo(a)rders: Emerging Fictions of Identity in Late Antiquity." *Harvard Theological Review* 93, no. 4 (2000): 343-72.
———. "Cultural Androgyny in Rabbinic Literature." In *From Athens to Jerusalem: Medicine in Hellenized Jewish Lore and in Early Christian Literature*, edited by S. Kottek, M. Horstmanhoff, G. Baader, and G. Ferngren, 119-40. Rotterdam: Erasmus Publishing, 2000.
———. "From Narrative Practice to Cultural Poetics: Literary Anthropology and the Rabbinic Sense of Self." In *Homer and the Bible in the Eyes of Ancient Interpreters*, edited by M. R. Niehoff, 345-67. Leiden: Brill, 2012.

Lieberman, Saul. *Sifre Zutta: The Midrash of Lod.* [In Hebrew.] New York: Jewish Theological Seminary Press, 1968.
———. *Tosefet Rishonim: Tohorot.* Volumes 1–4. [In Hebrew.] Jerusalem: Bamberger & Wahrman, 1937–1939.
———. *Tosefta kipshuta.* [In Hebrew.] New York: Jewish Theological Seminary Press, 1962.
LiPuma, Edward. "Modernity and Forms of Personhood in Melanesia." In *Bodies and Persons: Comparative Views from Africa to Melanesia,* edited by M. Lambeck and A. Strathern, 53–79. Cambridge: Cambridge University Press, 1998.
Loader, William. *Jesus' Attitude towards the Law: A Study of the Gospels.* Tübingen: Mohr Siebeck, 1997.
Lock, Margaret, and Judith Farquhar, eds. *Beyond the Body Proper: Reading the Anthropology of Material Life.* Durham: Duke University Press, 2007.
Long, Anthony. *Epictetus: A Stoic and Socratic Guide to Life.* New York: Oxford University Press, 2002.
———. *Stoic Studies.* Cambridge: Cambridge University Press, 1996.
Luchner, Katharina. *Philiatroi: Studien zum Thema der Krankenheit in der griechischen Literatur der Kaiserzeit.* Göttingen: Vandenhoeck & Ruprecht, 2004.
Maccoby, Hyam. *Ritual and Morality: The Ritual Purity System and Its Place in Judaism.* Cambridge: Cambridge University Press, 1999.
Magness, Jodi. "A Reassessment of the Excavations of Qumran." In *The Dead Sea Scrolls Fifty Years after Their Discovery, 1947–1997,* edited by L. H. Schiffman, E. Tov, J. C. VanderKam, and G. Marquis, 708–19. Jerusalem: Israel Exploration Society and the Shrine of the Book, 2000.
Mandelbaum, Bernard, ed. *Pesiqta dRav Kahana.* New York: Jewish Theological Seminary Press, 1962.
Mansfield, Nick. *Subjectivity: Theories of the Self from Freud to Haraway.* New York: NYU Press, 2000.
Margulies, Mordecai, ed. *Midrash Leviticus Rabbah.* 1953; New York: Jewish Theological Seminary Press, 1993.
Marriot, McKim. "Hindu Transactions: Diversity without Dualism." In *Transaction and Meaning: Directions in the Anthropology of Exchange and Symbolic Behavior,* edited by B. Kapferer, 109–37. Philadelphia: Institute for the Study of Human Issues, 1976.
Martin, Dale. *The Corinthian Body.* New Haven: Yale University Press, 2000.
Marx, Karl. *Early Writings.* Translated by R. Livingstone and G. Benton. London: Penguin, 1992.
Mason, Steve. *Flavius Josephus on the Pharisees.* Leiden: Brill, 1991.
Mauss, Marcel. "A Category of the Human Mind: The Notion of Person; The Notion of Self." Translated by W. D. Walls. In *The Category of the Person: Anthropology, Philosophy, History,* edited by M. Carrithers, S. Collins, and S. Lukes, 1–25. New York: Cambridge University Press, 1985.
Mc Mahon, Ciarán. "The Prehistory of the Concept of Attention." PhD diss., University College Dublin, 2007.
Merleau-Ponty, Maurice. *Phenomenology of Perception.* Translated by C. Smith. 1962; New York: Routledge, 2006.

Milgrom, Jacob. "4QTohora: An Unpublished Qumran Text on Purities." In *Time to Prepare the Way in the Wilderness: Papers on the Qumran Scrolls by Fellows of the Institute for Advanced Studies of the Hebrew University, Jerusalem 1989-1990*, edited by D. Dimant and L. Schiffman, 59-68. Leiden: Brill, 1995.

———. "First Day Ablutions in Qumran." In T*he Madrid Qumran Congress: Proceedings of the International Congress on the Dead Sea Scrolls*, volume 2, edited by J. T. Barrera and L. V. Montaner, 561-70. Leiden: Brill, 1992.

———. "Impurity Is Miasma: A Response to Hyam Maccoby." *Journal of Biblical Literature* 119, no. 4 (2000): 729-33.

———. "Israel's Sanctuary: The Priestly Picture of Dorian Gray." *Revue Biblique* 83 (1976): 390-99.

———. *Leviticus 1-16: A New Translation with Introduction and Commentary*. Anchor Bible 3. New York: Doubleday, 1991.

———. *Leviticus: A Book of Ritual and Ethics*. Minneapolis: Augsburg Fortress, 2004.

———. "The Qumran Cult: Its Exegetical Principles." In *Temple Scroll Studies*, edited by G. J. Brooke, 165-80. Sheffield: JSOT Press, 1989.

Miller, Paul Allen. "Catullan Consciousness, the 'Care of the Self,' and the Force of the Negative in History." In *Rethinking Sexuality: Foucault and Classical Antiquity*, edited by D. Larmour, P. A. Miller, and C. Platte, 171-203. Princeton: Princeton University Press, 1998.

Miller, William Ian. *The Anatomy of Disgust*. Cambridge, MA: Harvard University Press, 1997.

Murray, Robert. *Symbols of Church and Kingdom: A Study in Early Syriac Tradition*. New York: T & T Clark, 2005.

Nagel, Thomas. *The View from Nowhere*. Oxford: Oxford University Press, 1986.

Naiweld, Ron. "L'anti-sujet: Le rapport entre l'individu et la loi dans la littérature rabbinique classique." PhD diss., l'École des hautes études en sciences sociales, 2009.

———. "Au commencement était la pratique: Les commandements comme exercices spirituels—la subjectivation pratique rabbinique." *Yod—Revue des études hébraïques et juives* 15 (2010): 13-41.

———. "Lorsque la terre trembla: La muraille quie protège le Talmud de la philosophie." *Tzafon* 58 (2009-2010): 59-76.

Neusner, Jacob. *Ancient Israel after Catastrophe: The Religious Worldview of the Mishnah*. Charlottesville: University of Virginia Press, 1982.

———. *A History of the Mishnic Law of Purities*. Leiden: Brill, 1974-1977.

———. *The Idea of Purity in Ancient Judaism*. Leiden: Brill, 1973.

———. "The Integrity of the Rabbinic Law of Purity (Mishnah-Tractate Tohorot)." *Review of Rabbinic Judaism* 9, no. 1 (2006): 167-80.

———. "Pharisaic-Rabbinic Judaism: A Clarification." *History of Religions* 12, no. 3 (1973): 250-70.

———. *The Rabbinic Traditions about the Pharisees before 70*. Leiden: Brill, 1971.

Newsom, Carol. *The Self as Symbolic Space: Constructing Identity and Community in Qumran*. Leiden: Brill, 2004.

Newton, Michael. *The Concept of Purity at Qumran and in the Letters of Paul*. Cambridge: Cambridge University Press, 1985.

Noam, Vered. "Beit Shammai and Sectarian Halakhah." [In Hebrew.] *Jewish Studies* 41 (2002): 45–67.
———. "Between Qumran and Rabbinic Midrash: Common Exegesis and Implied Polemics." [In Hebrew.] *Megillot* 7 (2009): 71–98.
———. "The Bounds of Non-Priestly Purity: A Reassessment." [In Hebrew.] *Zion* 72 (2007): 127–60.
———. "Corpse-Blood Impurity: A Lost Biblical Reading?" *Journal of Biblical Literature* 128, no. 2 (2009): 243–51.
———. *From Qumran to the Rabbinic Revolution: Conceptions of Impurity.* [In Hebrew.] Jerusalem: Yad Ben Zvi Press, 2010.
———. "Is It True That 'a Corpse Does Not Defile?' On Ritual Contamination in Tannaitic Literature." [In Hebrew.] *Tarbitz* 78, no. 2 (2009): 157–87.
North, Helen. *Sophrosyne: Self-Knowledge and Self-Restraint in Greek Literature.* Ithaca: Cornell University Press, 1966.
Nussbaum, Martha. *The Therapy of Desire: Theory and Practice in Hellenistic Ethics.* Princeton: Princeton University Press, 1994.
Nutton, Vivian. "Did the Greeks Have a Word for It? Contagion and Contagion Theory in Classical Antiquity." In *Contagion: Perspectives from Pre-Modern Societies,* edited by L. Conrad and D. Wujastyk, 136–62. Aldershot, UK: Ashgate, 2000.
———. "To Kill or Not to Kill? Caelius Aurelianus on Contagion." In *Text and Tradition: Studies in Ancient Medicine and Its Transmission,* edited by K.-D. Fischer, D. Nickel, and P. Potter, 233–42. Leiden: Brill, 1998.
Olyan, Saul. "Purity Ideology in Ezra-Nehemiah as a Tool to Reconstitute the Community." *Journal for the Study of Judaism* 35, no. 1 (2004): 1–16.
Oppenheimer, Ahron. *The Am ha-aretz: A Study in the Social History of the Jewish People in the Hellenistic-Roman Period.* Translated by I. H. Levine. Leiden: Brill, 1977.
Ottenheijm, Eric. "Impurity between Intention and Deed: Purity Disputes in First Century Judaism and in the New Testament." In *Purity and Holiness: The Heritage of Leviticus,* edited by M. J. H. M. Poorthuis and J. Schwartz, 129–47. Leiden: Brill, 2000.
Padel, Ruth. *In and out of the Mind: Greek Images of the Tragic Self.* Princeton: Princeton University Press, 1994.
Parker, Robert. *Miasma: Pollution and Purification in Early Greek Religion.* Oxford: Oxford University Press, 1983.
Passer, Jay. "Skin Memories." In *Thinking Through the Skin,* edited by S. Ahmed and J. Stacey, 52–68. New York: Routledge, 2001.
Perkins, Judith. *The Suffering Self: Pain and Narrative Representation in the Early Christian Era.* New York: Routledge, 1995.
Peskowitz, Miriam. *Spinning Fantasies: Rabbis, Gender and History.* Berkeley: University of California Press, 1998.
Philo. *The Works of Philo.* Translated by Charles Yonge. Peabody: Hendrickson, 2006.
Poirier, John. "Purity beyond the Temple in the Second Temple Era." *Journal of Biblical Literature* 122, no. 2 (2003): 247–65.
———. "Why Did the Pharisees Wash Their Hands?" *Journal of Jewish Studies* 47 (1996): 217–33.
Porter, James. "Foucault's Ascetic Ancients." *Phoenix* 59, no. 2 (2005): 121–31.

Preuss, Julius. *Biblisch-Talmudische Medizin.* Berlin: S. Karger Verlag, 1923.
Rademaker, Adriaan. *Sophrosyne and the Rhetoric of Self-Restraint: Polysemy and Persuasive Use of an Ancient Greek Value Term.* Leiden: Brill, 2005.
Rahmani, Levy Yitzhak. "Ancient Jerusalem's Funerary Customs and Tombs: Part One." *Biblical Archaeologist* 44, no. 3 (1981): 171–77.
———. "Ancient Jerusalem's Funerary Customs and Tombs: Part Two." *Biblical Archaeologist* 44, no. 4 (1981): 229–35.
———. "Ancient Jerusalem's Funerary Customs and Tombs: Part Three." *Biblical Archaeologist* 45, no. 1 (1982): 43–53.
———. "Ancient Jerusalem's Funerary Customs and Tombs: Part Four." *Biblical Archaeologist* 45, no. 2 (1982): 109–119.
Regev, Eyal. "Non-Priestly Purity and Its Religious Aspects according to Historical Sources and Archeological Findings." In *Purity and Holiness: The Heritage of Leviticus,* edited by M. J. H. M. Poorthuis and Joshua Schwartz, 223–44. Leiden: Brill, 2000.
———. "On Blood, Impurity, and Relation to the Body in the Jewish Schools of the Second Temple Period." [In Hebrew.] *AJS Review* 27, no. 1 (2003): א-כב.
———. "Pure Individualism: The Idea of Non-Priestly Purity in Ancient Judaism." *Journal for the Study of Judaism* 31, no. 2 (2000): 176–202.
———. "The Sadducees, the Pharisees, and the Sacred: Meaning and Ideology in the Halakhic Controversies between the Sadducees and the Pharisees." *Review of Rabbinic Judaism* 9 (2006): 126–40.
Reich, Ronny. "Miqwa'ot (Jewish Ritual Immersion Baths) in Eretz-Israel in the Second Temple and the Mishnah and Talmud periods." [In Hebrew.] PhD diss., Hebrew University, Jerusalem, 1990.
———. "The Synagogue and the *Miqweh* in Eretz-Israel in the Second-Temple, Mishnaic, and Talmudic periods." In *Ancient Synagogues: Historical Analysis and Archaeological Discovery,* volume 1, edited by D. Urman and P. Flesher, 289–97. Leiden: Brill, 1995.
Reydams-Schils, Gretchen. *The Roman Stoics: Self, Representation and Affection.* Chicago: University of Chicago Press, 2005.
Reynolds, L. D., ed. *L. Annaeius Seneca: Ad Lucilium Epistolae Morales.* New York: Oxford University Press, 1965.
Riddle, John. "High Medicine and Low Medicine in the Roman Empire." In *Aufstieg und Niedergang der römischen Welt* II.37.1: *Wissenschaften (Medizin und Biologie),* edited by W. Haase, 102–20. Berlin: Walter de Gruyter, 1993.
Robertson Smith, William. *The Religion of the Semites.* New York: Meridian Books, 1956.
Rokeah, David. "Am ha-aretz, the First Pious Ones, Jesus, and the Christians." [In Hebrew.] In *Mekhkare Talmud* 3.2, edited by Y. Sussman and D. Rosenthal, 876–903. Jerusalem: Magnes Press, 2005.
Roisman, Joseph. *The Rhetoric of Manhood: Masculinity in the Attic Orators.* Berkeley: University of California Press, 2005.
Rosenblum, Jordan. *Food and Identity in Early Rabbinic Judaism.* New York: Cambridge University Press, 2010.
Rosen-Zvi, Ishay. *Body and Soul in Ancient Jewish Thought.* [In Hebrew.] Ben-Shemen: Modan, 2012.

———. "The Body and the Temple: The List of Priestly Blemishes in the Mishnah and the Place of the Temple in the Tannaitic Study House." [In Hebrew.] *Jewish Studies* 43 (2006): 49–87.

———. *Demonic Desires: Yetzer hara and the Problem of Evil in Late Antiquity*. Philadelphia: University of Pennsylvania Press, 2011.

———. "Do Women Have a *Yetzer*? Anthropology, Ethics, and Gender in Rabbinic Literature." [In Hebrew.] In *Spiritual Authority: Struggles over Cultural Power in Jewish Thought*, edited by H. Kreisel, B. Huss, and U. Ehrlich, 21–34. Be'er Sheva: Ben Gurion University Press, 2010.

———. "The One Vowing to Deny and the One Denied: Mishnah Kettubot Chapter 7 and the Tannaitic Perception of Marriage." [In Hebrew.] *Dine Israel* 26 (2010): 91–119.

———. *The Rite That Was Not: Temple, Midrash and Gender in Tractate Sotah*. [In Hebrew.] Jerusalem: Magnes Press, 2008.

Rosen-Zvi, Ishay, and Adi Ophir. "*Goy*: Toward a Genealogy." *Dine Israel* 29 (2011): 69–122.

Rousselle, Aline. *Porneia: On Desire and the Body in Antiquity*. Translated by F. Pheasant. Oxford: Basil Blackwell, 1993.

Rubenstein, Jeffrey. "Nominalism and Realism in Qumranic and Rabbinic Law: A Reassessment." *Dead Sea Discoveries* 6, no. 2 (1999): 157–83.

———. "On Some Abstract Concepts in Rabbinic Literature." *Jewish Studies Quarterly* 4 (1997): 33–73.

Runesson, Anders. "Water and Worship: Ostia and the Ritual Bath in the Diaspora Synagogue." In *The Synagogue of Ancient Ostia and the Jews of Rome: Interdisciplinary Studies*, edited by B. Olsson, D. Mitternacht, and O. Brandt, 115–29. Stockholm: Paul Åströms, 2001.

Sanders, E. P. *Jesus and Judaism*. Philadelphia: Fortress Press, 1985.

———. *Jewish Law from Jesus to the Mishnah: Five Studies*. London: SCM Press, 1990.

———. *Paul: A Very Short Introduction*. Oxford: Oxford University Press, 1991.

Satlow, Michael. *Tasting the Dish: Rabbinic Rhetorics of Sexuality*. Atlanta: Scholars Press, 1994.

———. "Try to Be a Man: The Rabbinic Construction of Masculinity." *Harvard Theological Review* 89, no. 1 (1996): 19–40.

Scheper-Hughes, Nancy, and Margaret Lock. "The Mindful Body: A Prolegomenon to Future Work in Medical Anthropology." *Medical Anthropology Quarterly*, new series, 1, no. 1 (1987): 6–41.

Schiffman, Lawrence. "The Dead Sea Scrolls and Rabbinic *Halakhah*." In *The Dead Sea Scrolls as Background to Postbiblical Judaism and Early Christianity*, edited by J. R. Davila, 3–24. Leiden: Brill, 2003.

———. "The Pharisees and Their Legal Traditions according to the Dead Sea Scrolls." *Dead Sea Discoveries* 8, no. 3 (2001): 262–77.

———. *Sectarian Law in the Dead Sea Scrolls: Courts, Testimony, and the Penal Code*. Atlanta: Scholars Press, 1983.

Schofer, Jonathan. *Confronting Vulnerability: The Body and the Divine in Rabbinic Ethics*. Chicago: University of Chicago Press, 2010.

———. *The Making of a Sage: A Study in Rabbinic Ethics*. Madison: University of Wisconsin Press, 2005.

Schürer, Emil. *Geschichte des Jüdischen Volkes im zeitalter Jesu Christi.* Leipzig: Heinrich, 1886.
Schwartz, Daniel. "Law and Truth: On Qumran-Sadducean and Rabbinic Views of Law." In *The Dead Sea Scrolls: Forty Years of Research,* edited by D. Dimant and U. Rappaport, 229–40. Jerusalem: Magnes Press and Yad Izhak Ben-Zvi, 1992.
Schwartz, Daniel, and Zeev Weiss, eds. *Was 70 C.E. a Watershed in Jewish History? On Jews and Judaism before and after the Destruction of the Second Temple.* Leiden: Brill, 2012.
Schwartz, Joshua. "Reduce, Reuse, and Recycle: Prolegomena on Breakage and Repair in Ancient Jewish Society." *Jewish Studies Internet Journal* 5 (2006): 147–80.
Schwartz, Seth. *Imperialism and Jewish Society, 200 B.C.E. to 640 C.E.* Princeton: Princeton University Press, 2001.
Sharf, Robert. "On the Allure of Buddhist Relics." *Representations* 66 (1999): 75–99.
Sharples, R. W. *Stoics, Epicureans and Sceptics: An Introduction to Hellenistic Philosophy.* New York: Routledge, 1996.
Shemesh, Aharon. "The Origins of the Laws of Separatism: Qumran Literature and Rabbinic Halacha." *Revue de Qumran* 18, no. 2 (1997): 223–41.
Shevel, Chaim Dov, ed. *The Book of Education.* [In Hebrew.] Jerusalem: Mosad ha-rav Kook, 1960.
Sorabji, Richard. *Self: Ancient and Modern Insights about Individuality, Life, and Death.* Chicago: University of Chicago Press, 2006.
Spengel, Andreas, ed. *M. Terenti Varronis: De Lingua Latina libri.* New York: Arno Press, 1979.
Stern, Sacha. *Jewish Identity in Early Rabbinic Writings.* Leiden: Brill, 1994.
Steuer, Christiane. "Der Fetus ist ein Glied seiner Mutter ('ubar yerekh imo'): Eine rabbinische Interpretation von Exodus 21:22–24." *Lectio difficilior* 2 (2008).
Stiegman, Emero. "Rabbinic Anthropology." In *Aufstieg und Niedergang der römischen Welt* II.19.2: *Religion (Judentum),* edited by W. Haase, 487–579. Berlin: Walter de Gruyter, 1979.
Stowers, Stanley. *A Rereading of Romans: Justice, Jews, and Gentiles.* New Haven: Yale University Press, 1994.
Sussman, Ya'akov. "Babylonian Sugyot for Zerai'm and Tohorot." [In Hebrew.] PhD diss., Hebrew University, Jerusalem, 1969.
———. "The Study of the History of Halakhah and the Dead Sea Scrolls: First Talmudic Contemplations in light of the *Miqsat Ma'ase ha-Torah* Scroll." [In Hebrew.] *Tarbitz* 59 (1990): 11–76.
Syed, Yasmin. *Vergil's Aeneid and the Roman Self: Subject and Nation in Literary Discourse.* Ann Arbor: University of Michigan Press, 2005.
Taylor, Charles. *Sources of the Self: The Making of Modern Identity.* Cambridge: Cambridge University Press, 1989.
Tcherikover, Victor. *The Jews in the Greek and Roman World.* [In Hebrew.] Jerusalem: M. Newman Press, 1961.
Theodor, Julius, and Chanoch Albeck, eds. *Midrash Rabbah Genesis.* 1929; Jerusalem: Shalem, 1996.
Thom, Johan. *The Pythagorean Golden Verses.* Leiden: Brill, 1995.

Tomson, Peter. "Jewish Purity Laws as Viewed by the Church Fathers and by the Early Followers of Jesus." In *Purity and Holiness: The Heritage of Leviticus,* edited by M. J. H. M. Poorthuis and Joshua Schwartz, 73–91. Leiden: Brill, 2000.

———. *Paul and the Jewish Law: Halakha in the Letters of the Apostle to the Gentiles.* Assen: Uitgeverij Van Gorcum, 1990.

Trapp, Michael. *Philosophy in the Roman Empire: Ethics, Politics, and Society.* Aldershot, UK: Ashgate, 2007.

Tsukermandel, Moshe Samuel, ed. *Tosefta nach den Erfurter und Wiener Handschriften.* Trier: Fr. Lintzschen Buchhandlung, 1892.

Turner, Bryan. *The Body and Society.* London: Sage Press, 1996.

Urbach, Ephaim Elimelech. *The Sages: Their Concepts and Beliefs.* [In Hebrew.] Jerusalem: Magnes Press, 1976.

Van der Horst, Pieter. "Anti-Samaritan Propaganda in Early Judaism." In *Persuasion and Dissuasion in Early Christianity, Ancient Judaism, and Hellenism,* edited by P. W. van der Horst, M. J. J. Menken, J. F. M. Smit, and G. V. Oyen, 25–44. Leuven: Peeters, 2003.

Verene, Donald. *Philosophy and the Return to Self-Knowledge.* New Haven: Yale University Press, 1997.

Wegner, Judith Romney. *Chattle or Person? The Status of Women in the Mishnah.* New York: Oxford University Press, 1992.

Weinfeld, Moshe. "The Turn in the Perception of Divinity and Cult in the Book of Deuteronomy." *Tarbitz* 31 (1962): 1–17.

Weiss, Isaac, ed. *Sifra de-bei rav.* 1862; New York: Om, 1946.

Werman, Cana. "The Attitude towards Gentiles in the Book of Jubilees and Qumran Literature Compared with Early Tanaaic Halakha and Contemporary Pseudepigrapha." [In Hebrew.] PhD diss., Hebrew University, Jerusalem, 1995.

———. "Jubilees 30: Building a Paradigm for the Ban on Intermarriage." *Harvard Theological Review* 90, no. 1 (1997): 1–22.

Wheeler Robinson, Henry. *Corporate Personality in Ancient Israel.* Philadelphia: Fortress Press, 1981.

Wilkins, Eliza Gregory. "'Know Thyself' in Greek and Latin Literature." PhD diss., University of Chicago, 1917.

Williams, Craig. *Roman Homosexuality.* New York: Oxford University Press, 1999.

Wimbush, Vincent, and Richard Valantasis, eds. *Asceticism.* New York: Oxford University Press, 1998.

Winter, Bruce. *Roman Wives, Roman Widows: The Appearance of New Women and the Pauline Communities.* Grand Rapids: W. B. Eerdmans, 2003.

Yadin, Yigael. *The Temple Scroll.* [In Hebrew.] Jerusalem: Israel Expedition Society, 1977.

## SUBJECT INDEX

Alon, Gedalyahu, 41, 126
*am ha-aretz. See* People of the Land
Aretaeus of Cappadocia, 143
Ariès, Philippe, 105
artifacts (*kelim*), im/purity of, 49–50, 64, 69; as extensions of the body, 9, 15, 75–78, 80–82, 84 (*see also* body); usability, role of in purity system, 75–76, 79–84, 88, 123, 127
Aristotle, 143
*askesis*, 150, 162–64, 169, 176. See also *meditatio*
attention, 15–16, 151, 154, 165–71, 173, 175–79

Bar Kokhva revolt, 5
barriers (*hatzitzah*) in immersion, 66, 69–73, 208n79, 208n82, 208n84, 209n89. *See also* immersion
Bartsch, Shadi, 150, 162
Baumgarten, Joseph, 31
biblical purity laws, 1, 5–6, 17–23, 28–29, 32–35, 40–41, 45, 52, 76, 100, 116, 128, 181–82; derivation of rabbinic purity system from, 1–6, 15, 18–19, 24–30, 32–35, 44–45, 53–54, 56–57, 78–79, 83–84, 86–87, 95, 99–100, 104, 106, 113, 116, 126–29, 139, 180–84. *See also* Priestly Code
birth, 20, 22, 27, 159
blood, 26, 86, 91, 99, 102–6, 108–9, 112, 114, 217n27, 218n37. *See also* genital discharge, blood (non-menstrual); genital discharge, blood (menstrual)

body, 2, 5–6, 8–9, 11–12, 15–16, 35, 39, 50–53, 55–63, 68–75, 77–78, 85, 94, 98–99, 133–37, 163, 173–74, 183; fluidity of boundaries and modularity of, 52, 55–66, 69, 73, 146, 173. *See also* artifacts (*kelim*), as extensions of the body; corpse impurity
bones, 99–114, 218nn36–37. *See also* corpse impurity
Boyarin, Daniel, 8
Büchler, Adolf, 126–27

carcasses: of dead animals, 20–21, 25, 53, 76–78, 97, 132; of dead creeping and crawling creatures, 20–21, 37, 97
"carriage." *See* transmission and contraction of impurity
Carson, Anne, 146
categorical purity (insusceptibility to impurity), 49, 67, 76–80, 86–87, 122. *See also* Gentiles, insusceptibility to impurity; stone, function in purity system; visibility, implications of for im/purity
Cicero, 169
Christianity, 138, 148–49, 183, 186n16, 202n1, 215n88, 226n55, 235n2
Community Rule, 194n37, 195n50. *See also* Qumran and Qumranic texts
contraction of impurity. *See* transmission and contraction of impurity

253

conversion to Judaism, 123–24, 132–37, 152
corpse impurity, 6, 15–16, 20–22, 24–26, 31–33, 53, 59, 64–65, 78, 96–121, 127–28, 132, 153, 184, 202n2. *See also* blood; bones; flesh (from a corpse); rot (*raqav*) impurity
Crislip, Andrew, 163
Cuffel, Alexandra, 125

Damascus Document, 194n37, 195n50. *See also* Qumran and Qumranic texts
Dead Sea Scrolls. *See* Qumran and Qumranic texts
doubtful impurity (*safeq tum'a*), 36–40, 42–44, 46, 158
Douglas, Mary, 52, 122
duplication of impurity. *See* liquids, transmission and duplication of impurity by; transmission and contraction of impurity

Eilberg-Schwartz, Howard, 88–89
Epictetus, 168–69
ethics, 16, 149–51, 164–66, 178–79
excrement, 71, 194–5n43, 222n92

fastidiousness (*haqpada*), 70–73, 209n89
fetuses, 26, 65, 110, 114–5, 135, 160
Flemming, Rebecca, 174
flesh (from a corpse), 101–6, 112. *See also* corpse impurity
Fonrobert, Charlotte, 39, 69, 159
food, im/purity of, 1–2, 7, 31–32, 40–42, 45, 49–50, 53, 56–57, 59–60, 63–64, 76–78, 86–88, 90–95, 125, 153, 171–72, 182, 184, 200–1n117; usability, role of in purity system, 86–88
Foucault, Michel, 8, 11
Frankfurt, Harry, 89
Friedman, Shamma, 14
Furstenberg, Yair, 57, 167, 230–31n16

Galen, 204n26, 205n34,
garments and clothing, im/purity of, 21–22, 25, 34, 38, 119, 125
gender, 69, 71–72, 124–25, 139–47, 160, 170–75, 199n96, 228n86
genital discharge, 24–25, 34–35, 53–54, 59, 68, 78, 97, 141, 145, 157, 160, 193n31; abnormal, 16, 20, 22, 27, 34, 125, 136–37, 140–45, 157; blood (menstrual), 36, 54, 68, 125, 157, 159, 174, 226n61; blood (non-menstrual), 20, 26, 140–41, 152, 159, 174. *See also* Gentiles, as sources of impurity; menstrual impurity and menstruating women; semen; seminal emissions

Gentiles, 16, 38, 122–47, 139–40, 145–46, 152–54, 165, 226n61; as sources of impurity, 16, 25, 124–31, 139, 147, 152–54, 194n37; insusceptibility to impurity, 16, 122–31, 133–35, 137–39, 146, 224n31. *See also* person/hood; subject/ivity
graded system of impurity, 28–30, 35, 53–56, 98, 100–104, 106, 109–10. *See also* transmission and contraction of impurity
Graham, Emma-Jayne, 105
graves and graveyards, 33, 100, 110–11, 113–14, 118–21, 202n2, 225n45. *See also* corpse impurity
Graeco-Roman medical discourse, 52–53, 56–57, 146, 173–74

Hadot, Pierre, 11, 162, 169
Halberstam, Chaya, 159
hands, impurity of, 31, 59–60, 62, 166–67; washing of, 31, 57, 156, 166, 171, 182, 200n108
*hatzitzah*. *See* barriers in immersion
*haqpada*. *See* fastidiousness
Hayes, Christine, 127–28, 130–31
heave-offering (*terumah*), 29–30, 38, 40–41, 54, 59, 64, 173
*heset*. *See* transmission and contraction of impurity, through "shift"
hidden place (*bet ha-starim*). *See* visibility, implications of for im/purity
Himmelfarb, Martha, 26
holy articles (*qodesh*), 29, 40, 52, 97, 153, 175
houses, im/purity of, 21–22, 24–26, 31, 49, 107, 125, 154–55

immersion, 20–22, 24, 36, 52, 60–61, 63–64, 66, 68–74, 76, 78, 156, 166, 200n108, 230n15. *See also* barriers
intention (*kavanah*), role of in purity system, 15, 76, 88–93, 95, 148, 183
intercourse. *See* transmission and contraction of impurity, through sexual intercourse
Isaac, Benjamin, 145–46

Jesus, 31, 57, 186n16
Josephus, 23, 194n37, 195n43, 196n61, 215n89

*kashrut*, 1, 21, 31, 87, 115–16
Ker, James, 163
Klawans, Jonathan, 48, 127, 129
Kristeva, Julia, 17, 98
Kuthians. *See* Samaritans

Laqueur, Thomas, 146
Leder, Drew, 66

## SUBJECT INDEX

Levinson, Joshua, 138, 148–50
liquids: activation of impurity though, 90–94; im/purity of, 21, 49–50, 64, 76–77, 86, 91; transmission and duplication of impurity by, 30–32, 53, 59–60, 76–77, 91, 182, 196n58. *See also* blood, saliva, semen, urine

Maimonides, Moses, 40
Marcus Aurelius, 163–64
Martin, Dale, 57
Marx, Karl, 77–78
Mc Mahon, Ciarán, 169
*meditatio*, 150, 162. See also *askesis*
*mei hattat. See* purifying water
menstrual impurity and menstruating women, 6, 20, 22, 27, 34–35, 39, 53, 60, 97, 125, 140–41, 152–53, 157, 159–60, 171, 174, 185n2. *See also* genital discharge, blood (menstrual)
mentally inept person (*shoteh/-ah*), 38, 43, 174, 212n46, 234–35n100
*midras. See* transmission and contraction of impurity, through "treading"
mildew, 21–22, 125. *See also* houses, im/purity of
Milgrom, Jacob, 24, 41, 116, 196n53
*miqveh. See* immersion
moral impurity, 25–26, 129–30

Naiweld, Ron, 138, 150
Neusner, Jacob, 7
New Testament, 23
Noam, Vered, 26, 65, 123, 128, 132–34, 199n102
North, Helen, 170
Nutton, Vivian, 56

Ophir, Adi, 132
"overhang." *See* transmission and contraction of impurity, through "overhang"

Parker, Robert, 36
parturient women. *See* birth
People of the Land, 153–56, 161–62, 165, 172–73, 176, 178, 230n15, 231n24
Perkins, Judith, 164
person/hood, 9–10, 12, 50–51, 74; of corpses (symbolic personhood), 98–99, 104–21; of Gentiles, 117, 123, 132–34. *See also* corpse impurity
Pharisees, 31, 57
Philo of Alexandria, 23, 98, 169
Plato, 234n85
Plutarch, 169
Poirer, John, 56–57

Priestly Code, 3–4, 20–25, 27–28, 31, 34–35, 49, 51, 77, 84, 96–97, 99, 103, 106, 116, 125, 128–29, 139–41, 151, 157, 180. *See also* Biblical purity laws
priests, 7, 29, 40–41, 177–78, 194n37
public domain, impurity in, 35–36, 38–39, 43–44, 140, 152, 184, 227n64
purification. *See* hands, washing of; immersion; purifying water (*mei hattat*); red cow ashes; sacrifice; sprinkling (for purification)
purifying water (*mei hattat*), 25, 29

*qodesh. See* holy articles
Qumran and Qumranic texts, 19, 23–27, 30–31, 35, 41, 45, 65, 186n16, 194n37, 195n43. *See also* Community Rule; Damascus Document; Temple Scroll

red cow ashes, 20–21
Robertson Smith, William, 17
Rosen-Zvi, Ishay, 132, 172
rot (*raqav*) impurity, 99, 101–5, 115, 117–21, 218n36, 219n52, 220n65, 221n84, 222n92. *See also* corpse impurity

sacrifice, 5, 7, 20, 141–42, 178, 227n66
Sadducees, 152, 195n45
*safeq tum'a. See* doubtful impurity
saliva, 34–35, 38–39, 54, 60–62, 91, 126, 139–40
Samaritans, 38, 152, 198n93
sanctuary. *See* Temple
Satlow, Michael, 147
scale disease, 20–22, 24–25, 27, 53, 67, 116, 140, 192n20, 193n31, 197n70, 197n74, 198n77, 204n19, 216n14. *See also* skin discolorations/afflictions
Schofer, Jonathan, 150
self, 2, 5–6, 9–12, 15, 51, 66, 75, 138, 148–49, 162, 175, 180, 182–84, 189n30; bodily, 2, 15, 61–62, 69, 73; control, 12, 16, 146–47, 162–65, 167, 169–75, 184 (*see also* Stoicism); examination and scrutiny, 16, 142, 151–169, 171, 175–76, 231n28; formation/making of, 2–3, 11–12, 138, 150, 161–165, 172, 176, 183; knowledge, 16, 165, 169–71, 174–75; mishnaic, 46–47, 137–39, 146–47, 149, 165, 170–71, 176 (*see also* subject/ivity, [idealized] mishnaic subject); reflection, 16, 51, 138, 148, 151, 164, 183; sense of, 20.
semen, 20–21, 54, 68, 143, 157, 207n72, 226n62
seminal emissions, 25, 27, 68, 125, 136–37, 140–44, 157, 227nn67–68

Seneca, Lucius Annaeus, 162–63, 165. See also *meditatio,* Stoicism
"shift." *See* transmission and contraction of impurity, through "shift"
*shoteh/-ah. See* mentally inept person
sin, 25–26, 149, 151, 179
skin discolorations/afflictions, 67, 97, 125, 134–36, 231n28. *See also* scale disease
spittle. *See* saliva
sprinkling (for purification), 21, 64
Stoicism, 148–49, 162–65, 168–69. *See also askesis;* Epictetus; Marcus Aurelius, *meditatio;* Seneca
stone, function in purity system, 26, 41, 79, 119, 187n21, 211n25
subjective investment, 49–50, 62, 65, 68–73, 75, 82, 84–85, 87–90, 92, 94, 109, 128–29, 137, 149, 180. *See also* artifacts, usability, role of in purity system; food, usability, role of in purity system; transmission and contraction of impurity
subject/ivity, 2, 4–5, 9–12, 15–16, 61–62, 75, 95, 98, 137–39, 148–51, 180, 182–84; (idealized) mishnaic subject, 3, 8, 16, 20, 39–40, 42–47, 49–52, 58, 62, 123–25, 131, 152–56, 161, 164–66, 170–72, 175–79, 199n96 (*see also* self, mishnaic); legal, 8–9, 16, 50–51, 61, 124, 132–39, 149, 151, 172, 175, 179, 184; of Gentiles, 16, 124–25, 129, 133, 137–39; role of in purity system (*see* subjective investment). *See also* person/hood; self

Tabernacle. *See* Temple
Temple, 5, 21–22, 40–41, 151, 154, 186n14, 195n50, 199n105; destruction of, 1, 5–7, 23
Temple Scroll, 31, 65, 181, 194n37, 195n50, 221n80. *See also* Qumran and Qumranic texts
tent impurity. *See* transmission and contraction of impurity, through "overhang,"
*terumah. See* heave-offering
thought (*mahshava*), role of in purity system, 15, 76, 82–91, 95, 148–49, 183, 212nn45–46
transmission and contraction of impurity, 18–19, 26–36, 52–56, 63; through "carriage", 33, 54, 56, 59, 100–101, 103, 105, 110–12, 132, 197n73; through "touch", 22, 28–29, 32–35, 52–56, 58–59, 99–101, 103, 105, 110–12, 132, 140, 197n73; through "overhang," 21, 24, 32–33, 53, 74, 99–105, 107–12, 114, 118, 132; through sexual intercourse, 22, 53, 68, 125, 152, 160, 207n72; through "shift" (*heset*), 33–34, 53–54, 56, 140, 197n74; through "treading" (*midras*) 22, 32, 34, 140. *See also* graded system of impurity

urine, 34–35, 39, 54, 91, 126, 139–40, 157

Varro, Marcus Terentius, 107
visibility, implications of for im/purity, 66–69, 72–73, 134–35, 207nn68–69

will (*ratzon*), role of in purity system, 15, 89, 92–95. *See also* thought; intention
Wisdom of Solomon, 169

# SOURCE INDEX

### HEBREW BIBLE

#### Genesis
| | |
|---|---|
| 2:19–20 | 88 |

#### Leviticus
| | |
|---|---|
| 5:2–4 | 199n104 |
| 7:19–21 | 199n101 |
| 11:1–23 | 192n19 |
| 11:24–28 | 192n9 |
| 11:24–40 | 199n103, 209n8 |
| 11:29–38 | 192n10 |
| 11:31–38 | 76–77 (210n10) |
| 11:32 | 79 |
| 11:32–33 | 78, 86 |
| 11:32–35 | 78 |
| 11:32–38 | 78 |
| 11:34 | 86, 90 |
| 11:35 | 210n11 |
| 11:37 | 210n11 |
| 11:38 | 90–91, 196n63 |
| 11:39–40 | 192n9 |
| 11:44–45 | 199n105 |
| 12:1–8 | 192n14 |
| 12:4 | 199n101 |
| 13:1–3 | 232n52 |
| 13:1–46 | 192n15 |
| 13:2 | 222n6 |
| 13:47–59 | 192n18 |
| 14:1–32 | 199n103 |
| 14:33–57 | 192n18 |
| 15:1–15 | 140, 192n16, 199n103 |
| 15:4–11 | 192n22 |
| 15:8 | 198n78 |
| 15:16 | 232n34 |
| 15:16–18 | 140, 192n12 |
| 15:19 | 185n2 |
| 15:19–24 | 140 |
| 15:19–31 | 192n17 |
| 15:20–23 | 192n22 |
| 15:24 | 192n23 |
| 15:25–31 | 140 |
| 15:26–27 | 192n22 |
| 15:31 | 199n105 |
| 17:10 | 213n55 |
| 17:15 | 221n76, 224n26, 224n29 |
| 17:16 | 199n104 |
| 18:19 | 185n2, 232n49 |
| 20:18 | 232n49 |
| 21:1 | 216n15 |
| 21:1–3 | 199n101 |
| 22:1–17 | 200n109 |
| 22:4–9 | 199n101 |
| 27:30 | 210n11 |

#### Numbers
| | |
|---|---|
| 5:1–3 | 192n20 |
| 6:1–21 | 216n15 |

## Numbers (continued)

| | |
|---|---|
| 6:6–10 | 199n101 |
| 15:13–15 | 192n7 |
| 18:8–23 | 200n109 |
| 19:9–10 | 192n13 |
| 19:10 | 224n27, 224n29 |
| 19:11–15 | 216n15 |
| 19:11–22 | 192n11, 199n103 |
| 19:14 | 104 |
| 19:14–16 | 100 (217n19), 216n14 |
| 19:15 | 197n70 |
| 19:16 | 113, 197n68 |
| 19:18 | 197n72 |
| 19:20 | 199n105 |
| 19:21 | 192n13 |
| 19:22 | 193n24 |
| 20:5 | 210n11 |
| 31:19 | 224nn28–29 |
| 31:20–23 | 79, 211n21 |

## Deuteronomy

| | |
|---|---|
| 4:37 | 224n35 |
| 7:6–7 | 224n35 |
| 10:15 | 224n35 |
| 12:2 | 224n35 |
| 14:21 | 224n35 |
| 21:5 | 232n52 |
| 23:13–15 | 195n43 |
| 26:19 | 224n35 |

## Isaiah

| | |
|---|---|
| 3:23 | 222n89 |

## Ezra

| | |
|---|---|
| 9:2 | 225n37 |
| 9:10 | 225n37 |

## NEW TESTAMENT

### Matthew

| | |
|---|---|
| 15:1–20 | 205n30 |
| 15:11 | 197n65 |

### Mark

| | |
|---|---|
| 7:1–23 | 31, 57 |
| 7:15 | 31 (197n65), 57 |
| 7:19 | 205n32 |

### Acts

| | |
|---|---|
| 10:28 | 225n42 |

### Romans

| | |
|---|---|
| 14:14 | 215n88 |

### Galatians

| | |
|---|---|
| 2:11–15 | 225n42 |

## SECOND TEMPLE PERIOD SOURCES

### Dead Sea Scrolls

#### 4Q Harvesting

| | |
|---|---|
| 4Q284 a 1–4 | 195n50, 197n66 |

#### 4Q Tohorot A

| | |
|---|---|
| 4Q274 1 i 1–3 | 193n31 |
| 4Q274 1 i 1–8 | 195n50 |
| 4Q274 2 i 8 | 194n34 |
| 4Q274 3 i-ii | 197n67 |
| 4Q274 3 ii 4 | 199n98 |

#### Community Rule (Serekh ha-Yahad)

| | |
|---|---|
| 1QS 6.16–22 | 194n37, 196n61 |
| 1QS 7.20 | 194n37 |

#### Damascus Document

| | |
|---|---|
| 4Q265 6.2 | 195n43 |
| 4Q265 7 i 3 | 195n43 |
| 4Q266 5 ii 5–7 | 194n37 |
| 4Q266 6 i 14–16 | 194n34 |

#### Damascus Document (Cairo Genizah version)

| | |
|---|---|
| CD12 8–11 | 194n37 |
| CD12 15–17 | 196n60 |

#### Some Precepts of the Law (Miqsat Ma'ase ha-Torah)

| | |
|---|---|
| 4QMMT B 72–74 | 219n45 |
| 4QMMT C 49 | 194n37 |

#### The Temple Scroll

| | |
|---|---|
| 11Q19 39.5–7 | 194n37 |
| 11Q19 45.11–12 | 194n34 |
| 11Q19 45.15 | 195n43 |
| 11Q19 49–50 | 195n45 |
| 11Q19 48.8–11 | 31 (196n60) |
| 11Q19 49.8 | 199n98 |
| 11Q19 50.4–7 | 221n80 |

| | | | |
|---|---|---|---|
| 11Q19 50.10–16 | 65 (206n56) | *Sheqalim* | |
| 11Q19 63.15 | 194n37 | 8.1 | 223n15 |

**Flavius Josephus**

*Yoma*
1.4–6 — 227n67

*The Jewish War*
| | |
|---|---|
| 2.123 | 196n61 |
| 2.147–49 | 195n43 |
| 2.150 | 194n37 |

*Betzah*
2.4 — 51 (203n7)

*Life of Josephus*
12 — 215n89

*Mo'ed Qatan*
3.2 — 227n72

**Jubilees**
22:16–22 — 225n37

*Hagigah*
| | |
|---|---|
| 1.8 | 182 (235n1) |
| 2.6 | 209n3 |
| 2.6–7 | 200n113 |
| 2.7 | 196n56, 199n98, 200n117 |
| 3.4–7 | 230n14 |
| 3.6 | 198n88 |
| 3.7 | 230n16 |

**Judith**
12:8 — 200n108

**Letter of Aristeas**
306 — 200n108

**Philo**

*On the Special Laws*
III. 207 — 98 (216n9)

*Yebamot*
16.4 — 115

*Kettubot*
2.5 — 192n7

## RABBINIC LITERATURE

*Nedarim*
11.12 — 192n7

**Mishnah**

*Nazir*
| | |
|---|---|
| 2.8 | 221n72 |
| 7.2–3 | 217n32, 220n60 |
| 7.2–4 | 218n37 |

*Demai*
| | |
|---|---|
| 2.2–3 | 231n25 |
| 3.4 | 231n25 |
| 6.9 | 231n25 |

*Sotah*
| | |
|---|---|
| 1.5 | 192n7 |
| 3.3 | 192n7 |
| 3.6 | 192n7 |
| 4.2 | 192n7 |

*Shevi'it*
5.9 — 231n25

*Hallah*
4.8 — 227n69

*Baba Qamma*
| | |
|---|---|
| 4.6 | 221n73 |
| 10.2 | 213n51 |

*Shabbat*
| | |
|---|---|
| 6.1 | 208n79 |
| 11.6 | 50–51 (203n7) |

*Baba Metzi'a*
9.12 — 51 (203n7)

*Pesahim*
| | |
|---|---|
| 3.2 | 208n84 |
| 9.4 | 227n71 |

### Sanhedrin
| | |
|---|---|
| 9.2 | 221n73, 225n48 |

### Eduyot
| | |
|---|---|
| 1.7 | 108 (219n49), 217n28 |
| 1.14 | 230n15 |
| 4.12 | 209n7 |
| 6.3 | 117, 217n25, 221n81 |
| 8.4 | 196n62 |

### Avodah Zarah
| | |
|---|---|
| 3.5 | 210n9 |

### Zevahim
| | |
|---|---|
| 2.2 | 235n108 |
| 3.1 | 235n108 |
| 3.3–6 | 235n108 |

### Hullin
| | |
|---|---|
| 3.1 | 221n77 |
| 4.3 | 65 (206n58) |
| 4.6 | 115 |

### Arakhin
| | |
|---|---|
| 2.1 | 234n98 |

### Kelim
| | |
|---|---|
| 1.4 | 216n16, 221n82 |
| 1.5 | 112 (220n62), 116 (221n78) |
| 1.6–8 | 200n113 |
| 1.8 | 227n70 |
| 2.1 | 210n18 |
| 3.3–4 | 213n66 |
| 4.4 | 212n43 |
| 8.4 | 30 (196n57) |
| 8.10 | 60 (206n47) |
| 8.11 | 234n96 |
| 12.1 | 211n28 |
| 13.4 | 81 (212n35) |
| 14.3 | 211n29 |
| 14.5 | 212n44 |
| 15.1 | 210n19, 211n31 |
| 16.1–2 | 81 (212n33) |
| 16.4 | 212n42 |
| 17.15 | 212n46 |
| 18.1–7 | 200n115 |
| 19.4 | 196n54 |
| 19.5 | 58 (206n41) |
| 19.7 | 206n39 |
| 19.9 | 212n38 |
| 20.3 | 206n39 |
| 20.6 | 212n39 |
| 22.2 | 81 (212n48) |
| 24.8 | 223n23 |
| 24.13 | 211n30 |
| 25.9 | 84–85 (213n52) |
| 26.7 | 83 (213n47) |
| 26.8 | 213nn50–51 |
| 27.8 | 211n27 |
| 28.6 | 196n54 |
| 28.7 | 206n39 |

### Oholot
| | |
|---|---|
| 1.1–4 | 32 (197n69), 216n17 |
| 1.4 | 216n5 |
| 1.5 | 221n75 |
| 1.8 | 102 |
| 2.1 | 108–9, 111 |
| 2.1–5 | 103 |
| 2.1–2 | 101 (217n21) |
| 2.2 | 109, 118 (221n83), 219n50 |
| 2.3 | 110–11 (220n58), 217n31 |
| 2.5 | 217nn29–30 |
| 2.6 | 108 (219n50), 109 |
| 3.3 | 206n42 |
| 3.6 | 107 (219n46) |
| 5.5 | 211n24 |
| 6.1 | 209n5 |
| 11.3 | 209n7 |
| 11.7 | 206n51 |
| 16.1 | 232n39 |

### Nega'im
| | |
|---|---|
| 2.4 | 207n68 |
| 2.5 | 232n52 |
| 3.1 | 223n8 |
| 6.7–8 | 216n4 |
| 6.8 | 67 (207n62), 207n68 |
| 7.1 | 134–35 (226n52), 207n63 |
| 11.1 | 223n9, 226n58 |
| 11.11 | 222n89 |
| 12.1 | 223n9, 226n58 |
| 13.7 | 194n33 |
| 13.11–12 | 194n33, 197n70 |

### Parah
| | |
|---|---|
| 8.2, 5–7 | 30 (196n57) |
| 9.5 | 206n51 |

## Tohorot

| | |
|---|---|
| 1.8 | 55 (204n21) |
| 2.2 | 197n64 |
| 2.2–5 | 196n56 |
| 3.5–4.13 | 42 |
| 3.6 | 43 (201n121), 231n26 |
| 3.7 | 201n120 |
| 3.8 | 231n23 |
| 4.3 | 232n37 |
| 4.5–11 | 201n122 |
| 5.1 | 38 (198n89) |
| 5.1–2 | 198n83 |
| 5.1–6 | 231n27 |
| 5.8 | 38 (198n91), 223n15, 230n11, 230n14 |
| 5.9 | 232n38 |
| 6.6 | 231n26 |
| 6.7 | 196n54 |
| 7.1 | 37 (198n85) |
| 7.1–7 | 231n25 |
| 7.3 | 37 (195n86), 154 (231n20) |
| 7.4 | 154 (231n22), 172 |
| 7.4–6 | 198n88 |
| 7.6 | 223n15 |
| 7.7 | 177–78 (235n106), 230n14 |
| 7.8 | 166 (233n70), 206n46 |
| 7.9 | 173 |
| 8.1–5 | 231n25 |
| 8.2 | 230n14, 230n15 |
| 8.3 | 198n84 |
| 8.6 | 86 (213n57), 212n46, 213n60, 225n50 |
| 8.7 | 30 (196n57) |
| 10.3 | 232n29 |

## Miqva'ot

| | |
|---|---|
| 1.4 | 202n3 |
| 4.1 | 211n24 |
| 5.5 | 209n6 |
| 5.6 | 209n3 |
| 7.6 | 206n50, 209n2 |
| 8.2 | 232n35 |
| 8.3 | 227n67, 232n36 |
| 8.4 | 207n73, 223n11 |
| 8.5 | 60 (206n49), 207n69, 209n3 |
| 9.1–10.5 | 206n50, 209n2 |
| 9.1–2 | 71 (208n81) |
| 9.2 | 207n70 |
| 9.3 | 71 |
| 9.3–4 | 70–71 (208n82) |
| 9.5 | 72 (209n88) |
| 9.7 | 208n84 |
| 10.3–4 | 207n69 |
| 10.8 | 63 (206n52), 64 (206n55), 206n53, 207n61 |

## Niddah

| | |
|---|---|
| 1.2 | 234n96 |
| 1.7 | 227n73, 232n31 |
| 2.1 | 142 (227n74), 174, 232n31 |
| 2.6–7 | 195n45, 232n44 |
| 3.2 | 220n57 |
| 3.2–7 | 232n46 |
| 4.1 | 195n45, 198n93 |
| 4.1–2 | 230n8 |
| 4.3 | 223n10, 223n15, 226n62 |
| 5.1 | 207n71 |
| 5.3 | 215nn2–3 |
| 6.14 | 174 (234n99) |
| 7.3 | 223n10 |
| 8.1–4 | 232n33 |
| 8.3 | 232n41 |
| 9.1 | 232n32 |
| 9.3–5 | 232n33 |
| 10.3 | 227n77 |
| 10.4 | 193n31, 223n15, 227n72 |

## Makhshirin

| | |
|---|---|
| 1.1 | 92 (214n77) |
| 1.3 | 214n82 |
| 1.6 | 214n78 |
| 2.2 | 227n64 |
| 2.4 | 223n15 |
| 3.5 | 93 (214n84) |
| 3.7 | 93 (215n85) |
| 3.8 | 212n46 |
| 3.9 | 93 (214n79) |
| 6.1 | 93 (214n80), 212n46 |
| 6.4 | 213n54 |
| 6.4–5 | 214n74 |
| 6.4–7 | 217n27 |
| 6.5 | 213n55, 214n75, 216n6 |
| 6.6 | 198n77, 226n62 |
| 6.8 | 234n96 |

## Zavim

| | |
|---|---|
| 1.1 | 227n78 |
| 1.2–6 | 228n89 |

### Zavim (continued)

| | |
|---|---|
| 2.1 | 223n14 |
| 2.2 | 144–45 (228n91), 160, 227n67 |
| 2.3 | 136 (226n56), 215n3, 228n90 |
| 3.1 | 34 |
| 4.1 | 34 |
| 4.6 | 197n75 |
| 4.7 | 223n22 |
| 5.2–10 | 196n54 |
| 5.4 | 59 (206n43), 209n4 |
| 5.6 | 53–54 (204n17), 193n31, 227n72 |
| 5.7 | 54 (204n18) |
| 5.10 | 204n19 |
| 5.12 | 197n64 |

### Uqtsin

| | |
|---|---|
| 1.1–2.7 | 206n40 |
| 3.1 | 214n72 |
| 3.1–2 | 213n61 |
| 3.2 | 213n58, 213n63 |
| 3.2–3 | 213n62 |
| 3.3 | 213n59, 213n63, 214n73 |
| 3.4–6 | 213n58 |
| 3.8 | 200n116 |
| 3.9 | 213n63 |

## Tosefta

### Berakhot

| | |
|---|---|
| 2.12 | 227n72 |

### Demai

| | |
|---|---|
| 2.2 | 199n98, 200n117 |
| 2.17 | 172 (234n92) |

### Pisha

| | |
|---|---|
| 8.1 | 227n72 |
| 8.9 | 227n72 |

### Sheqalim

| | |
|---|---|
| 1.5 | 218n36 |

### Yoma

| | |
|---|---|
| 4.5 | 227n72 |
| 4.20 | 223n15 |

### Sukkah

| | |
|---|---|
| 2.3 | 199n98, 200n117 |

### Megillah

| | |
|---|---|
| 1.11 | 219n46 |

### Hagigah

| | |
|---|---|
| 3.3 | 200n117 |
| 3.22–24 | 230n14 |

### Nazir

| | |
|---|---|
| 5.3 | 218n37 |

### Sanhedrin

| | |
|---|---|
| 11.6 | 228n92 |

### Avodah Zarah

| | |
|---|---|
| 3.9 | 172 (234n93) |
| 3.10 | 199n98, 231n18 |

### Kelim Baba Qamma

| | |
|---|---|
| 1.4 | 219n46 |
| 1.8 | 227n72 |
| 1.14 | 227n72 |

### Kelim Baba Metzi'a

| | |
|---|---|
| 5.1 | 211n24 |
| 5.3 | 232n40 |
| 11.1 | 227n72 |

### Kelim Baba Batra

| | |
|---|---|
| 1.2 | 167 (233n72), 232n40 |
| 1.3 | 167 (233n73) |
| 7.7 | 211n22 |

### Ahilot

| | |
|---|---|
| 1.4 | 223n12 |
| 2.2 | 119 (221n85), 221n84 |
| 2.5–6 | 217n25 |
| 2.6 | 220n61 |
| 3.2 | 220n63 |
| 3.3 | 218n34 |
| 4.2 | 219n51 |
| 4.5 | 219n52 |
| 4.7 | 218n37 |
| 5.2 | 107 (219n47) |
| 8.8 | 206n57 |
| 12.3 | 206n51 |
| 14.6 | 223n12, 225n44 |
| 15.13 | 232n39 |
| 16.2 | 113 (220n67), 120 (222n93) |
| 16.12 | 220n69 |

## SOURCE INDEX

### Nega'im
| | |
|---|---|
| 6.1 | 228n92 |

### Parah
| | |
|---|---|
| 8.1–2 | 30 (196n57) |
| 12.11 | 223n13 |

### Tohorot
| | |
|---|---|
| 1.10 | 231n19 |
| 5.8 | 198n92 |
| 6.2 | 198n92 |
| 6.10 | 198n91 |
| 6.11 | 198n89 |
| 6.17 | 201n123 |
| 8.12 | 230n15 |
| 8.13 | 177 (235n103) |
| 8.14–15 | 235n235 |
| 8.15 | 235n235 |
| 9.4 | 230n15 |
| 9.12 | 213n56 |

### Miqva'ot
| | |
|---|---|
| 6.8 | 72, 207n74, 209n86 |
| 7.8–9 | 207n60 |
| 7.9 | 207n61 |
| 7.10 | 208n84 |
| 7.11 | 206n51 |

### Niddah
| | |
|---|---|
| 1.9 | 232n41 |
| 2.8 | 227n75 |
| 4.3–6 | 232n41 |
| 5.3 | 232n41 |
| 6.17 | 232n41 |
| 7.3 | 232n41 |
| 9.14 | 225n40 |

### Zavim
| | |
|---|---|
| 2.1 | 126 (223n14), 194n39 |
| 2.4 | 143 (227n79) |
| 5.2 | 206n44 |

### Tevul Yom
| | |
|---|---|
| 1.3 | 196n58 |

## Tannaitic Midrashim

### Mekhilta deRabbi Ishmael
| | |
|---|---|
| Mishpatim 4 | 221n73 |

### Mekhilta deRabbi Shimon ben Yohai
| | |
|---|---|
| 21:12 | 221n73 |

### Sifra
| | |
|---|---|
| Shemini par. 6, 7:4 | 212n32 |
| Shemini par. 7, 8:4–7 | 210n18 |
| Shemini par. 8, 9:4 | 213n54, 213n56 |
| Nega'im par. 3, 4:3 | 207n70 |
| Zavim par. 1, 1:1 | 223n14 |
| Zavim par. 2, 3:5 | 206n40 |
| Zavim par. 3, 6:10 | 207n70, 207n72 |
| Zavim par. 4, 7:6 | 215n2 |
| Ahare mot par. 9, 13:10 | 192n4 |
| Emor par. 2, 1:4 | 220n53 |
| Emor par. 14, 20:1 | 221n73 |

### Sifre Numbers
| | |
|---|---|
| 126 | 211n24 |
| 127 | 113 (220n66), 197n68, 206n57 |
| 158 | 197n68 |

### Sifre Zutta Numbers
| | |
|---|---|
| 6:9 | 218n36 |
| 19:11 | 97 (216n8), 112 (220n64), 206n42, 219n45, 219n53 |
| 19:14 | 105 (218n35) |
| 19:15 | 211n24 |
| 19:16 | 206n58 |

### Midrash Tanna'im on Deuteronomy
| | |
|---|---|
| 14:7 | 213n59 |

## Palestinian Talmud

### Berakhot
| | |
|---|---|
| 5:1 (8d) | 227n66 |

### Pe'a
| | |
|---|---|
| 8:7 (21b) | 212n40 |

### Ma'aser Sheni
| | |
|---|---|
| 5:1 (55d) | 218n36 |

### Shabbat
| | |
|---|---|
| 6:4 (8b) | 222n89 |
| 8:7 (11c) | 211n24 |

### Hagigah
3:2 (79a)      233n73

### Nazir
7:2 (56b)      120 (222nn90–91),
                   217n23, 217n26,
                   220n65
7:2 (56c)      121 (222nn94–95),
                   220n67

### Niddah
2:1 (49d)      227n76

## Babylonian Talmud

### Berakhot
4a      232n47
22b-26a      195n43
31a      227n66

### Shabbat
13a      3 (185n6)
13b      205n27
32a      220n63
58a      211n24
68b      222n6
83a      223n18
96a      211n24

### Pesahim
14b      197n68

### Yoma
2b      211n24
67b      192n4

### Megillah
28b      227n66

### Mo'ed Qatan
5b      218n36

### Hagigah
19a      209n3
20a      233n73, 235n103
20b      177 (235n105)

### Yebamot
61a      225n45

### Kettubot
24b      198n87

### Nazir
43b      218n36
50a      217n23, 217n26
51a      222n91
51a-b      222n92
51b      222n94, 220n67
52b      218n34
61b      226n51
65a      220n67

### Qiddushin
59b      214n71

### Baba Qamma
66b      213n50
114a      213n50

### Baba Metzi'a
22a      214n71
84b      232n47

### Avodah Zarah
31b      222n6

### Menahot
69b      211n24

### Hullin
2b      197n68
34a      197n64
42a      221n77
71a-b      206n54
72a      206n58

### Niddah
6b      232n41
13a      227n76
20b      232n47
27a-b      221n86
27b      221n88
34a      223n14, 223n18
34b      222n6
43a      226n57
54a      234n100
66a      227n66

| | |
|---|---|
| 66b | 207n75 |
| 70b | 216n8 |

## Aggadic Midrashim

*Genesis Rabbah*

| | |
|---|---|
| 19:6 | 222n89 |

*Leviticus Rabbah*

| | |
|---|---|
| 15:4 | 222n6 |

*Pesiqta deRav Kahana*

| | |
|---|---|
| Parah 1 | 192n5 |
| Parah 6 | 192n4 |
| Parah 7 | 192n5 |